Edward Dmytryk

Edward Dmytryk

Reassessing His Films and Life

FINTAN MCDONAGH

McFarland & Company, Inc., Publishers
Jefferson, North Carolina

All photographs courtesy the Estate of Edward Dmytryk.

ISBN (print) 978-1-4766-8092-7
ISBN (ebook) 978-1-4766-4314-4

LIBRARY OF CONGRESS AND BRITISH LIBRARY
CATALOGUING DATA ARE AVAILABLE

Library of Congress Control Number 2021026544

Front cover: Film director Edward Dmytryk, November 8, 1979

Printed in the United States of America

*McFarland & Company, Inc., Publishers
Box 611, Jefferson, North Carolina 28640
www.mcfarlandpub.com*

Acknowledgments

Foremost among those I must thank for enabling this book are Rebecca and Vicky Dmytryk, who trusted me to tell their father's story. My sincere gratitude to Rebecca for permitting access to and use of her family's photo archive and for inviting me into her home and enthusiastically encouraging the progress of the book. Equally sincere gratitude to Vicky, a brightly burning film starlet thanks to her father, for access to her archive of memories. Without their eager collaboration, this current book would be much paler.

Thanks to all those at the Margaret Herrick Library in Los Angeles, who observed this book grow from a tight focus on one single film to encompassing more than fifty films in the life of a director. The librarians of the Special Collections, in particular, were extremely helpful, invariably friendly and helped make my visits to Los Angeles a pleasure. With apologies for those whose names I didn't discover, thanks to Marisa, Jeffrey, Andrea, Wanisha, Kevin, Amber, Christina and Mona. Thanks also to Brendan and those involved with the Oral Histories.

At UCLA, I consulted the RKO Archives, as well as viewed several extremely difficult to locate films. Thanks to all there who were unfailingly courteous in assisting me.

Thanks to the staff at the British Library in London, and at the Reuben Library of the British Film Institute, who attempted to locate the Denham Studio Archives for me. Those archives unfortunately appear to be lost to the mists of time.

For their support and practical assistance on my research trips to California, thanks to Harvey and Louis Jason, Pamela Franklin and Duane Titus.

Thanks to Neil Sinyard for his invaluable advice and encouragement.

Cheers to Justin, who was there at the outset of this film criticism escapade and who has always prodded me gently in the right direction, whether regarding my writing or broadening my taste in film.

And naturally, thanks to Steve, for far too many reasons to list. I genuinely can't see me having finished this book if it weren't for him. I'll gloss over the fact that he's dashed off a couple of his own books in the time it's taken me to prepare and write this one.

Table of Contents

Introduction

A clear indication of the antipathy that the name of Edward Dmytryk continues to attract, decades after his testimony before the House Un-American Activities Committee (HUAC), was found when I was researching this book in the British Library in London. In his autobiography, Dmytryk had written the sentence, "Compromise is the single most difficult problem facing any creator."[1] Some researcher or student in the Reading Room, for which a registered card is necessary, had taken it upon themselves to scrawl in pencil alongside this statement, "You should know." On another occasion, I brought up the subject of this book with a well-known film historian, for whom I have the greatest respect, and his focus was on what Edward Dmytryk did, rather than what he created. When Dmytryk appeared before HUAC on 25 April 1951, he was well aware that his testimony would rupture relationships with erstwhile comrades and colleagues. What he is unlikely to have foreseen was just how long the repercussions of his decision would endure.

Those without a political axe to grind who worked with Dmytryk were full of praise for his skills. Dore Schary, among other positions Head of Production at both RKO and MGM: "An excellent director."[2] Edward Anhalt, Oscar winner for the screenplays of both *Panic in the Streets* and *Becket*: "Dmytryk is a very, *very* underestimated director."[3] C. Pennington-Richards, British cinematographer for Humphrey Jennings, among others, who worked on three films for Dmytryk: "Eddie was a marvellous director.... Technically for me he was the top."[4] Actors at the top of their profession chose to work with Dmytryk more than once: Spencer Tracy, Humphrey Bogart, Montgomery Clift, Maximilian Schell, Robert Mitchum. He directed six performers to Academy Award nominations—Robert Ryan and Gloria Grahame for *Crossfire*, Bogart and Tom Tully for *The Caine Mutiny*, Katy Jurado for *Broken Lance*, Elizabeth Taylor for *Raintree County*—and Deborah Kerr, Spencer Tracy, Marlon Brando and José Ferrer to BAFTA nominations for *The End of the Affair*, *The Mountain*, *The Young Lions* and *The Caine Mutiny*, respectively. The Directors Guild of America nominated him twice—for *The Caine Mutiny* and *The Young Lions*. At Cannes, he was in competition for the Palme d'Or with *The End of the Affair*, nominated for the Grand Prix with *Obsession* and won Best Social Film with *Crossfire*. At Venice, he was in competition for the Golden Lion with *The Caine Mutiny* and won the Pasinetti Award with *Give Us This Day*.

By contrast, those who felt betrayed by his testimony, were inevitably dismissive of his filmmaking abilities. Walter Bernstein, writer of *Fail-Safe* and *Yanks*: "Dmytryk was at best merely a competent director."[5] John Berry, director of *Claudine*: "A typical hack."[6] Bruce Cook, in his biography of Dalton Trumbo, discusses the *cause celèbre* of *Tender Comrade*, which Trumbo scripted, without a single mention of its director Dmytryk. Norma Barzman asserts that her husband Ben and screenwriter John Paxton judged Dmytryk to be "'a good technician,' which meant he wasn't creative."[7] When not related through the mouthpiece of Barzman, Paxton's own opinion is much more complimentary. Referring to *Hitler's Children*, he wrote: "[Dmytryk] did a fine job and was thereafter very hot, known as a very bright fellow, very fast, very economical, efficient, technically superb."[8]

The purpose of this book is to rescue Edward Dmytryk from the critical black hole to which he was consigned, with no sign of re-emergence twenty years after his death. My aim is not to whitewash his actions but to shine a more compassionate light on them. He was at a career zenith when HUAC began its repellent creep into American lives, but his future was sabotaged as soon as he and the other Nine of the Hollywood Ten made their disastrous appearances before the Committee. Despite no longer being in the Communist Party, he stuck by his former comrades to the extent of going to prison in support of what he then believed was a common cause of free speech. After he had served his time for Contempt of Congress, he was unable to find employment, his formerly proven ability and bankability null and void. He was heavily in debt, with a new wife and young family to support. As a film director, unlike the writers who comprised the other Nine, he was unable to operate under a pseudonym, and an attempt to placate the Committee by delivering anti–Communist statements proved insufficient. They wanted blood. They wanted names. How easy to say that one would not succumb to a malign body and would remain pure of heart under extreme financial pressure. How impossible to know what one would actually do.

Dmytryk publicly displayed a firm lack of regret about his testimony in the succeeding decades, asserting that it was the right thing to do, given the devious methods of the Communist Party. He often maintained that he had only testified to the Committee about those who had already been named, but later in life, made aware that Bernard Vorhaus was named for the first time by him, he modified his statements: "All but one of them had been named before—many times. I didn't give them any new stuff."[9] This public display of bravado contrasts with the man in private. His daughter Vicky told me: "According to mom, he was really stressed out because mom was brown listed and couldn't work, and my brother had been born, so he named names…. He said they already knew who was there at the meetings, so at the time it didn't seem like such a big deal. But he regretted it later and said he would have done things differently if he had it to do over again."[10]

Most unfair about Dmytryk's treatment was that he was doubly damned—the Left wouldn't forgive him, and the Right wouldn't trust him. There were double standards at play with his treatment from the Left, the fact that he had actually served time in prison considered irrelevant to these opponents. Walter Bernstein concedes that Dmytryk served prison time but compared his attitude unfavorably to that of Elia Kazan, who displayed no qualms about testifying: "I hate to quantify, although Dmytryk would definitely be among the lowest of the low for me…. Dmytryk has been vociferous over the years in defending himself, and he continues to attack the same people he attacked in his testimony, often gratuitously. Kazan has at least kept his mouth shut, except in his autobiography, where he remains defiant." Dmytryk's crime is clearly perceived as greater.

The treatment he received could smack of sadism: "'We bumped into Dmytryk one night in a restaurant sometime in 1956 or 1957,' says Mrs. Adrian Scott. 'We were seated in a booth adjoining Dmytryk, his wife and a guest. Dmytryk pretended not to see Adrian. Adrian said in an aside to me, 'Dmytryk is sitting there with his wife.' So I said, 'Do you want to move?' Adrian said, 'Hell, no. I want to look.' And he sat and stared and Dmytryk refused to look back. He just drank. Dmytryk was miserable.'"[11] This treatment endured through the decades and reached its nadir at the Barcelona Film Festival in 1988 when an opportunity to understand the past and build bridges was squandered during an ill-tempered confrontation between Dmytryk and some of his most vociferous critics.

In Hollywood, success trumps all, and once Dmytryk proved to be a money-maker in the mid–1950s, he was ostensibly welcomed back into the fold. There was evidence, however, of persistent distrust from the Right. Hedda Hopper waged a small campaign against him in print, harking back to her viewing of *So Well Remembered* in October 1947, while HUAC was in session in Washington, D.C.: "While there is not a single mention of Communism in the film, not one suggestion of the hammer and sickle, capitalism is represented as decaying, corrupt, perverted, unfeeling."[12] Dmytryk eventually convinced her not to mention him again but his persistent liberal sensibility would have prevented her from even considering retraction. In the 1960s, Vicky Dmytryk was denied entry to an exclusive school due to perceptions about her father's politics.

On a personal level, Edward Dmytryk did not adhere to the cliché of brash, autocratic director. In researching this book, it was notable that almost none of his collaborators had a negative thing to say about him, the marked exception being Kirk Douglas. Dmytryk said, "I was known as a very, very quiet director. I wouldn't let my assistant director shout ever. Then I'd go home and I'd be nasty to my wife and kids. You know, somewhere that had to come out."[13] Vicky Dmytryk told me about her father: "I have a great admiration for my father and his intelligence and talent … he had mellowed out a lot by the time that he had [Rebecca]. He never wanted kids, and was honest with my mom about it, but she had us anyway. He was a good provider. He was an impatient man, but while my brother [Rick] and I were still young and cute, like a kitten or a puppy, he could be supportive. He was gone a lot of course, but when he was home, he would sometimes help me with my homework. I'll never forget how when I would ask how to spell a word, he would always tell me, 'Look in the dictionary!,' which can be a daunting activity when you don't know how to spell the word. The dictionary was one of those huge six-inch, maybe more, thick books on a beautiful wood stand. I still have that dictionary. He was of course happiest when he was working. When at home, he enjoyed working out in the yard. I remember *Bonanza* being one of his favourite shows. And *Ed Sullivan*…. Also, my father was an atheist—a total materialist. If it couldn't be measured and quantified, he wouldn't take it seriously. I used to try and discuss Helena Blavatsky with him. That was a riot!"[14]

Rebecca Dmytryk remembers him as doing "the best he could…. He tried. He tried to be a better father."[15] Dmytryk had experienced real violence from his own father, but he did his utmost not to take his frustrations out on the children and he improved at fathering with each child he had. Rebecca says, "He never struck me. I don't think he struck Vicky. I know a time my mother demanded Vicky be spanked so Dad pulled her into the downstairs bathroom and said, 'Just scream when I hit my hands together.'"[16] The sweet memories Rebecca has of her father, alongside the location trips to Europe, are of horseback-riding, playing with hand puppets called Oscar and Felix and of going to the dump: "We would fill up the back of the pick-up truck and we would get the 7–Eleven cherry slurpy afterwards."[17]

I am not making the claim that Edward Dmytryk is some undiscovered auteur but there are some interesting strands that run through his career. In writings on *film noir*, he has been given credit for being instrumental in the development of the genre. *Murder, My Sweet* is a core text in *noir* studies, alongside *Cornered* and *Crossfire*, with the strong case often made for the inclusion of *The Sniper*. Low-key, atmospheric photography is a frequent characteristic of his films whatever the genre, stretching from *The Devil Commands*, through *Hitler's Children*, *Obsession* and *Give Us This Day*, all the way up to *Mirage*. Collaborators such as Pennington-Richards spoke of his ability to bring out the best in their photographic skills. Dmytryk made four films that directly attacked anti–Semitic prejudice—*Crossfire*, *The Juggler*, *The Young Lions*, *Bluebeard*—though that would become a quintet if the more veiled references in *Hitler's Children* were to be included. Assertions have been made that there is a sustained focus on physical dismemberment in his films, reflecting some psychological characteristic of the director, with *Till the End of Time*, *The End of the Affair* and *Warlock* being quoted as examples. Not only would Dmytryk have dismissed these tenuous links out of hand but the case for their relevance is unconvincing. Edward Dmytryk was not an auteur. He was a highly talented film-maker, excellent when the material suited him, with an undeniable skill for cutting, decided knack for action sequences and noted ability to draw effective performances from his actors. A few of his films are acknowledged as classics, another half dozen deserve to be, and the vast majority of his filmography is worthy of reappraisal.

In an interview given a few years before his death, Edward Dmytryk expressed his sense of being side-lined: "'My greatest pleasure would be recognition from Hollywood,' Dmytryk says, choking back tears. 'They pretty much have buried me. I'm not asked to the important events. I taught at the American Film Institute. They've given awards to people with far less background, far less record of achievement, than I have.'"[18] His commercial success had been considerable. He had delivered one of the biggest hits of the 1950s—*The Caine Mutiny*—and one of the biggest hits of the 1960s—*The Carpetbaggers*—and directed a succession of Hollywood's greatest stars in a string of effective vehicles. Yet full acceptance from his community and constructive critical attention eluded him. The aim of this book is to right at least a portion of that wrong.

I

Rising Through the Ranks
(1923–1942)

On 23 March 1923, 14-year-old Edward Dmytryk reported for his first day's work at Famous Players-Lasky, the studio which had Paramount as its distributing company, and which would ultimately become known as Paramount Pictures. Eddie's job was as messenger and handy boy in the studio's sample-copy room, for which he was paid $6 a week. The studio was located on one square block in Hollywood, hemmed in by Sunset and Vine, Selma and Argyle. It had four stages, three of which had no floors or ceilings with the fourth boasting walls and a roof of clear glass, and the studio had a back lot across Argyle to the east, where it was building a new laboratory. Paramount was

pre-eminent: "Paramount became the leader of the business by 1917 or so. It was not only the most successful studio, but the most intently competitive one, ceaselessly attempting to force its advantage. Much of the early history of the movies may be seen in Paramount instigating and the rest of the industry resisting or imitating. Paramount's advantages were many, but two above all: Paramount had the stars and Paramount had the theatres.... Of particular note in the matter of studio stylistics is the edge this gave Paramount in experimentation, in deviating from the confines of genre and cliché."[1] Dmytryk's start in the film business may have been inauspicious but chance could not have picked a better location for it. He later called Paramount "the 'country club' of the studios ... an easy-going lot [with a] reputation for making the most finished pictures."[2]

Edward with his mother Frances.

Edward (far left) with his father Mike and his brothers.

Eddie Dmytryk was a Canadian-born Ukrainian, whose parents had left their homeland to escape persecution due to their ethnicity (Slavic) rather than religion (Catholic). They settled in Grand Forks, British Columbia, just north of the American border, where Eddie was born on 4 September 1908. His father Mike farmed and worked in a copper smelter, while his mother Frances worked at all manner of jobs, saving money with the intention of returning to the Ukraine. When World War I broke out, the Canadian government began interning citizens of the Austro-Hungarian Empire, including Ruthinian Ukrainians. The Dmytryks, with four sons in tow, fled across the border to the United States and settled in Northport, Washington State, where his mother died of a ruptured appendix in 1917 at the age of 33. That same year the five remaining males moved again, this time to California, initially San Francisco. In 1919 Mike Dmytryk remarried a woman of Pennsylvania Dutch extraction and the new family unit headed further southward to a suburb of Los Angeles called Sherman, later to be known as West Hollywood. Mike was a martinet of a father and to escape the beatings Eddie ran away from home at 14. After initially heading for Chicago, Eddie realized he liked the warmth of California too much and doubled back to Los Angeles, where a friend at a boys' organization called the Woodcraft Rangers was able to arrange the opening for him at Famous Players-Lasky.

Young Eddie's first brush with stardom came when the messenger boy got a summons from the main entrance, across the lot on Vine Street. Lillian Gish required help transporting a large box of flowers to her car which was parked at a distance: "She was perceptive enough not to offer me a tip."[3] The sample-copy room where he was also employed was where rushes were assembled from the previous day's shooting. On a balcony circling the room, editors would combine scenes and titles to fill a reel, and then drop it down to the floor below where it would be hand-spliced together by mostly female staff. Eddie found his niche by being a proficient catcher on the splicing floor, at the same time as learning how to operate the projectors in the machine booths. The knack was keeping the carbon crater properly centered in the lamp-house, which required close attention to seven knobs. He acquired the skill so effectively that, after a few months, he received his first promotion to projectionist. He observed how films would progress through various cuts to the completed "answer print" and remembered running camera tests for neophyte actors like Richard Arlen and a certain Gary Cooper. Eddie enjoyed watching movies being shot on the lot, one of which was Cecil B. DeMille's *The Ten Commandments*. For this, he watched Theodore Roberts as Moses parting an imaginary Red Sea on set, and then Roy Pomeroy creating the special effect on a workbench in a little workshop. To Eddie's eyes, the hugely more expensive Red Sea moment in DeMille's 1956 remake did not look more effective than this primitive budget version.

Ensconced in such a stellar environment, Eddie was able to observe the megastars of the day, if not quite rub shoulders with them. He was shocked to hear Pola Negi say "damn" a few times while watching rushes, never having heard a woman swear before. He was the projectionist for the first cut of Erich von Stroheim's *The Wedding March*, which was between 50 and 100 reels, depending on the source. It took them several days to screen it all. Von Stroheim hacked it down over a period of months to 25 reels before the studio took it away from him and Paul Weatherwax, under the supervision of Josef von Sternberg, produced a cut of two feature films, the first of which failed disastrously and the second of which never received a U.S. release. Part of the reason for this was the sudden change in fashion that made stylish silents much less sellable than static talkies. Gone were the days of Eddie running a film for music arrangers so that they could assemble a score that would be sent out with the studio's more prestige silent productions.

Eddie's career in the film industry appeared to wither along with the silents. A supervisor at the studio, Hector Turnbull, who was also brother-in-law to company founder Jesse Lasky, took a shine to the young high school student who was a part-time worker at the studio. He gave Eddie a check for $1,000, an enormous sum in 1926, so the young man with a bent for mathematics could attend the California Institute of Technology. Eddie's academic career was short-lived, however. He hankered after the fast pace of the life he had left behind, doubted whether he wanted to spend his life as a mathematics teacher and by summer of 1927 had latched upon a football injury as a reason for abandoning his studies. Hector Turnbull was sanguine about wasting his $1,000 but pulled no strings to re-employ the prodigal son. After some months of increasingly desperate unemployment, Eddie bumped into a projectionist friend who informed him of a vacancy at Paramount's newly built studio at Bronson and Marathon, and his life in movies continued after its academic blip. His only problem was inbuilt: "I had very little ambition. I had a great deal of competitiveness (I'm a lousy loser), a strong desire to excel, a fair amount of drive—but no goal at all. So I just let the swelling tide carry me along."[4]

The transition to sound required huge changes in working practice and utter time commitment from the workforce. Since much of the work now took place at night, to minimize the noise from traffic, Eddie once spent three days and three nights on the set without going home, operating the portable projector in order to match close-up dialogue scenes to already shot silent scenes. Films were often assigned co-directors, one to take charge of the actors and dialogue, another to manage staging and camera placement. In the editing department, the introduction of recorded sound considerably complicated the process, and through voluntary retirement and sexual bias, many of the female cutters left or were made to leave. Due to a much greater quantity of film to process and the need to synchronize picture and soundtrack, Eddie Dmytryk was one of those elevated to the role of assistant cutter, his first (uncredited) film being *The Dance of Life*, co-directed by John Cromwell and Edward Sutherland in 1929.

Dmytryk had been quietly picking up knowhow for years by viewing daily rushes and editing choices from his projection booth and would eavesdrop if a director called into the editing department to supervise a particular sequence. On one occasion, he observed Josef von Sternberg and Marlene Dietrich intently examining a scene being played on the Moviola: "'Why that particular cut?' she asked. 'It looks like a bad jump.' (She was as smart as she was beautiful.) 'I want it to jump,' said von Sternberg. 'I want people to know there was a cutter on the film—me.'"[5] Dmytryk's decades of experience in the editing suite would confirm his suspicion at the time that he did not agree with the great von Sternberg and that cuts should be invisible. Since there were no sound Moviolas at Paramount, the cutters would learn to read lips and accustomed themselves to identifying the varying patterns of sound modulation on the soundtrack, and Dmytryk relished the challenge of overcoming obstacles that a brand-new technology was bound to generate. He remembered that "the thrill of solving even small problems creatively stayed with me and helped shape my career in the ensuing years."[6] Since he could speak Spanish, he was assigned to cut a few Spanish-language films which in the early days of sound would be constructed simultaneously to the same film for the Anglophone market, a task that could be performed by an assistant cutter. Through this process he met Cyril Gardner, who gave Dmytryk his first assignment—and his first credit—as full editor on a film Gardner was co-directing, *Only Saps Work*. When Gardner was given the co-directing job alongside George Cukor of a prestigious play adaptation, to be shot at Paramount's Astoria studio on Long Island, Dmytryk joined the eastbound exodus from Hollywood as the production's editor.

The Royal Family of Broadway starred Ina Claire and Fredric March and was filmed in 1930. On the first day of production, Dmytryk was introduced to Claire: "'So you're the cutter,' she smiled. 'I suppose I'll have to be particularly nice to you.' And that was about the last thing she said to me during the entire production.'"[7] George Cukor did not warm to the neophyte editor who conformed to his profession's stereotype by being unenthusiastic about the day's rushes and overlooking "clever staging or effective acting to nitpick at some bit of mismatched action."[8] When Cukor and Dmytryk were assigned to *Girls About Town* in 1931, the fastidious director was initially unenthusiastic about working again with the critical editor but by the end of that production, they had a strong working relationship that led to successful collaboration later. Dmytryk did not enjoy his six months in New York and when he was suffering from the flu on New Year's Day 1931, the pull of sunny Californian skies was too great to bear and he was back in Los Angeles four days later, to find himself out of a job. For not the first or the last time, a change of administration at Paramount had swept through and Dmytryk was one of the casualties. He would be out of regular employment for seven months, at the height of the Depression.

For those on the edge of the film industry, times were extremely tough. Dmytryk remembered John Carradine walking along Hollywood Boulevard trying to look as dapper as zero budget would allow and paying bellboys to page him in industry hangouts in order to make some sort of impression on clientele with clout. In better times, Carradine would appear in Dmytryk's *Captive Wild Woman*. Dmytryk himself worked as a janitor at an apartment block close to Columbia Pictures but left when he realized that he would be seen by some tenants who were in the industry and would consider him washed up at 22 years old. In some degree of desperation, Dmytryk eventually mustered the courage to ask a cutting colleague at Paramount, Eddie Knopf, for $300, which Knopf provided. Not long after that, Knopf invited Dmytryk on a private cruise to Ensenada in Mexico along with William Wyler and their wives. Wyler and Knopf hit the gambling spots and quickly lost all of their spending money, requiring them to wire Hollywood to send a few thousand more, which was also gambled away. Dmytryk later wrote: "The effect on me was considerable. A few days before I had had to nearly get down on my knees to borrow $300, and here was my benefactor, throwing thousands away. It was enough to drive a man to socialism."[9]

Eventually, Dmytryk did get a call from Paramount and the offer of a position at his old salary, but it was effectively a demotion. He was taken on as an assistant cutter,[10] under a new system whereby the main cutter would stay on set with the director while his assistant prepared a rough cut under his supervision. Years later, Dmytryk would appreciate that this seeming set-back in his career actually helped prolong it, since it enabled him to develop a much stronger bedrock of understanding about the film medium. He was working under supervision of Leroy Stone, future Oscar nominee for *Going My Way*, but was allowed to perform the physical process of cutting, enabling him to experiment and to make his contribution without pressure. In collaboration with Stone, he edited *Duck Soup*, *If I Had a Million* and *Six of a Kind*. On *The Phantom President* in 1932, he experimented on musical numbers performed by the film's star George M. Cohan and remembered the tradition of Cohan giving a silver dollar to every beggar he encountered. Two years later, on *Belle of the Nineties*, Mae West bristled at her leading man getting the picture's loudest laugh at a preview, and the next day insisted to director Leo McCarey and the editing team that it be deleted. The case was made that deleting a funny line from a comedy was no laughing matter, but West won the day, as her contract enabled her to.

In 1932, Dmytryk married Madeleine Robinson, described by Norma Barzman as "tall, thin, angular. Her short-short platinum hair crowned a cold, expressionless face."[11] Dmytryk said that he "married out of sheer loneliness. Not an unusual reason for marriage, but not a very good one. It lasted for sixteen years—the first twelve of them spent together—with not one truly happy moment to remember."[12] Consequently, Dmytryk avoids any personal recollections about his first wife in the several memoirs he wrote, and she only returns to reasonable focus in the mid–1940s when the marriage was petering to a conclusion. In the meantime, he was focusing on his job and carefully observing the big-name directors to whose pictures he was assigned: "Cukor was … a perfectionist with dialogue. McCarey, in my opinion, was the best comedy-drama director in Hollywood. [Henry] Hathaway … a master of action … [Norman] Taurog knew his way around the set and around people."[13] It was for a Hathaway B-western—probably *The Thundering Herd* with Randolph Scott in 1933—that Dmytryk was finally elevated back to the position that he had once occupied: editor.

Having survived the rigors of Henry Hathaway, a notoriously demanding director,[14] and a stint in tumbleweed-strewn B-movies with their rapid turnaround, Dmytryk was soon getting A-assignments among the programmers. He found the B-universe a more fertile learning ground: "There is less to work with—less time, less film, and less artistry—so more ingenuity is needed to arrive at something passable."[15] His most high-profile A-picture of this period was *Ruggles of Red Gap*, directed by Leo McCarey in 1935. Dmytryk developed a strong working relationship with McCarey, starting with *Duck Soup* in 1933, and was able to ease some of the director's insecurities, despite McCarey's long apprenticeship shooting comedy shorts. The Paramount routine of having the cutter on set helped Dmytryk keep McCarey focused on the script, in the funniness of which he tended to lose faith, and coax him back to his original instincts. Those instincts were pure: "Leo had tremendous comic inventiveness coupled with superior recall. He remembered every funny thing that had ever been said or done in his presence."[16]

Ruggles of Red Gap was a huge hit, one of the main reasons being the performance of Charles Laughton, which his biographer writes "served to establish him as a kind of folk hero."[17] The film might not have been quite so successful if it hadn't been for some necessary editing choices. A core scene has the butler, played by Laughton, delivering Abraham Lincoln's Gettysburg Address to a bar full of rapt listeners. It was a very difficult scene to shoot, since Laughton was extremely nervous and highly strung, and he flubbed take after take. To capture his shots took a day and a half, and Dmytryk judged there to be forty or fifty attempts at the speech: "rarely did he get a complete take, and never a perfect one. Finally Laughton was literally on his knees, begging for mercy."[18] In the editing suite, Dmytryk cobbled together an audio track of the complete speech using pieces of eighteen or twenty takes, and because so many differing takes of Laughton were used, was obliged to use reaction shots of onlookers as the visual track. Ernst Lubitsch was production manager at Paramount in 1935, and when he viewed the scene, he insisted that more shots of Laughton delivering the Address be inserted despite McCarey and Dmytryk feeling that the actor's facial expressions were grossly overplayed. At the preview, the speech went down very well until the inserts of Laughton's face came on the screen, at which point the cinema erupted into laughter which only increased with each additional appearance. The scene was not written to provoke hilarity, so the cuts to Laughton were deleted again and the scene gained a certain iconic status. Judicious editing salvaged the impact of a performance that Laughton's biographer admits was "comedically constricted and uncertain in character."[19]

In 1939, Dmytryk was informed by his Paramount bosses that McCarey needed his help with editing *Love Affair*, which he was making at RKO. The film, starring Irene Dunne and Charles Boyer, had gone into production without a script and McCarey encouraged improvisation from his actors. Paramount released Dmytryk for this assignment and when he examined the cut of the picture, he found it to be "a shambles."[20] He characterized the editor up to that point, George Hively, as being a working alcoholic who had created a cut that made little sense. He ordered a complete set of rushes from day one and discovered that one sequence had been entirely deleted. McCarey told him that he was so dissatisfied with how the scene turned out that he had scrapped it entirely. With McCarey's consent, Dmytryk reconstructed the sequence, almost certainly a lovely set of silent reaction shots between Dunne and Boyer as their cruise ship reaches New York and they spot their hitherto partners awaiting them on the dock. The scene was restored to the edit and "it turned out to be one of the funniest routines in the film. It was no big deal—any sober cutter could have done it."[21] McCarey was so nervous at the first preview in San Bernardino that he dragged Dmytryk away from the cinema and consumed a considerable amount of alcohol. He needn't have worried. Apart from some griping about Charles Boyer's accent, the previews were excellent for what RKO historian Richard B. Jewell calls "one of the most carefully constructed and skilfully executed love stories in the history of the cinema."[22] It made a profit of $221,000 and picked up six Academy Award nominations, losing out to *Gone with the Wind* in almost every case.

The year before, Dmytryk had edited *Bulldog Drummond's Peril* starring John Barrymore, whom he remembered as having an astonishing working vocabulary when they would play Scrabble together and of possessing challenging body odor. He also cut *Zaza*, a remake by George Cukor of a Gloria Swanson vehicle, this time starring Claudette Colbert and Herbert Marshall. The story told of a French music-hall performer who enters a relationship with a suave benefactor, unaware that he is married with a child. It was a lavishly mounted production, championed by the top executives at Paramount, very well performed by Colbert and received with enthusiasm by Louella Parsons and other journalists. The public expressed a different opinion. At the first preview in Oakland, the film played extremely well until the scene three-quarters of the way through where Marshall returns to the home in which he has set up Colbert, unaware that she now knows the whole deception. At this point, Dmytryk recalled that the audience started to hiss loudly: "Though one of the film's best scenes now unrolled on the screen, no one heard it. The audience's angry reaction continued right through to the bitter end."[23] Panicking slightly, the makers made a few cuts the next day before that night's preview in San Francisco, but the outraged reaction from the audience was the same. In 1938, filmgoers could not accept this degree of deception without expressing their disapproval. Cukor reshot parts of the ending and, in the cut that exists today, the scene that initiated the furor is truncated to diminish its impact. This doctored version, running less than 90 minutes, was released early in 1939 and flopped.

In the mid–1930s, Dmytryk had become involved in the Screen Editors Guild, an attempt by the studios to pre-empt union activity. As the Paramount representative, he became the Guild's first Secretary and holder of card number four, but throughout this time his technical knowledge expanded beyond the sphere of editing. He had grasped the opportunity to direct an independent western, *The Hawk*, in 1935, and enthusiastically accepted additional tasks that directors threw his way. Kurt Neuman directed *Hold 'Em Navy* in 1937 and allowed his editor to shoot the climactic football sequence, a sport of which he knew nothing. B-movie director Louis King, brother of A-movie director Henry King, let Dmytryk stage and shoot certain scenes on *Prison Farm*, and at the next day's rushes, subtly pointed out errors that he had made. While shooting *Zaza*, George Cukor would rehearse and stage a scene and encourage Dmytryk to work out its camera setups. By the end of the decade, the experience he had gathered did not go unnoticed by the studio and, while he was considering taking up a new role as script editor, he was asked to help out Nick Grindé with directorial duties on **Million Dollar Legs**. His contribution went uncredited but led to him being offered a $250 a week director's contract.

In June 1939, Edward Dmytryk signed and became a Paramount contracted director, in the same month that he became a U.S. citizen. In quick succession, he made four B-movies—**Television Spy**, **Emergency Squad**, **Golden Gloves** and **Mystery Sea Raider**—but just before the end of his contract, he became victim of one of Paramount's sporadic reorganizations. The new boss of the B-movie division was Sol Siegel who got rid of all of his predecessor's creative team and Dmytryk was out of a job. Since he was no longer moving in prestigious circles, he changed from the elite Berg-Allenberg Agency to the rather more modest Hallam Cooley, "a second-line agent. But he dogged the second-line producers, and that was where my immediate future lay."[24] In 1940 he made **Her First Romance** for independent producer I.E. Chadwick and right at the end of the year was employed by Columbia for **The Devil Commands**. In January 1941, Madeleine gave birth to a son, Michael. For the next eighteen months, he labored in the B-movie department of Columbia, a

The young director.

studio which he regarded as the lowest of the lot, and, against the odds of indifferent scripts, reduced schedules and meager budgets, made something out of *Sweetheart of the Campus*, *The Blonde from Singapore*, *Secrets of the Lone Wolf*, *Confessions of Boston Blackie* and *Counter-Espionage*. By the time Cooley got him an interview at RKO, Edward Dmytryk was more than content to leave behind Columbia, "the Black Hole of Calcutta."[25] America's War had just started and would prove core to the launching of Dmytryk as an A-movie director at RKO.

The Hawk (1935)
(a.k.a. The Trail of the Hawk)

Several years before Paramount gave him the chance to get behind the camera, the 26-year-old Edward Dmytryk was given a directorial dry run with an independent film initially titled *Pride of Triple X*. It was no coincidence that the western was the most popular genre for B-movies of the era—movies with men in Stetsons on horses were very cheap to make. Dmytryk received the proposal from a friend who had been entrusted with $5,000 to produce what would become *The Hawk*, with the proviso that wannabe film star Betty Jordan be given the leading female role. Dmytryk felt he had nothing to lose in accepting the challenge and took leave of absence from Paramount, having just completed editing duties on Leo McCarey's *Ruggles of Red Gap*.

The Hawk was shot over five days in May 1935, four on location and one on a Monogram sound stage. It is the type of film where several of the characters bear the same name as the actor playing them, and where leading man Yancey Lane wears a white Stetson and kerchief while cattle-rustling villain Rollo Dix is garbed in black and stops just short of twirling his moustache. Lane had appeared as a male beauty contestant alongside similarly uncredited Miss Texas Ann Sheridan in Paramount's racy pre–Code comedy *Search for Beauty*, which culminates in a celebration of the physique that combines Busby Berkeley with Leni Riefenstahl. Yancey kicks off his career with a few lines as Mr. Alabama, breaking up a party at which Ida Lupino, in her first Hollywood film, is performing a rhumba. In *The Hawk* he displays a certain unaffected charm in the role of a cowhand attempting to reunite with his long-lost father, but his delivery is moribund.

The most accomplished and professionally most experienced member of the cast is eight-year-old Dickie Jones. Dickie would achieve a certain immortality as the voice of Disney's *Pinocchio* and here provides intermittent comic relief, performs his own horseback stunts, rescues the hero in the climax and even squeezes in a cutesy tap-dance routine. Historical veracity is not a priority for the film: not only does frontierswoman Betty wear a Marcel Wave in her hair, but when Dickie beats our hero at target practice, managing a more effective bullseye with his slingshot than Yancey with his revolver, his pay-off line is "If you ever want some lessons, come up and see me sometime." The Mae West drawl from the boy actor rings bizarre to modern ears.

Inexperience and the tight shooting schedule meant that Dmytryk restricts himself mostly to uncomplicated camera setups, though he dollies into the action on occasion and his editing ability is evident in the rather visceral climactic fistfight between hero and villain. The budgetary limitations are also apparent in the total lack of non-diegetic music outside of the credits. Cameraman Roland Price brought along his own camera and asked merely $90 for the five days work. While editing the film, Dmytryk's personal funds ran out: "We lived on milk-bottle returns and the tag-end receipts of a 25-cent chain-letter scheme."[26]

The film was quickly sold for $10,000, delivering instantly on its investment, and was released in July as *The Hawk*. The following year it was re-released as *Trail of the Hawk*, and years later was sold on for $20,000. Dmytryk may not have had a slice of the profits and suffered the indignity of having his name spelled "Dymtryk" in the credits, but the experience had at least given him the taste for directing. Betty Jordan did not have the glittering career she dreamt of. This is her sole film credit.

Million Dollar Legs (1939)

Edward Dmytryk's big break came early in 1939 at the expense of Nick Grindé, a director who never made it out of Division "B." Grindé, who had been active as a director for a decade, had just delivered two films for Paramount—*King of Chinatown* and *Sudden Money*—that were considered disappointing to studio executives, who were uncertain about his ability. They decided to appoint Dmytryk as co-director on his next picture, provisionally titled *Campus Dormitory*. Whether or not this decision was designed to deliberately destabilize Grindé, that was the end result. Grindé was nominally in charge but with an editor looking over his shoulder, and he let Dmytryk know that he was most unhappy with the arrangement. After a week or so of this uncomfortable set-up, the studio decided Grindé's work was not up to scratch and sacked him, announcing to the press that he had dropped out due to a "serious throat infection."[27] For another director to take on the project would require a few days' break in production, which was considered not cost-effective for a B-picture. Dmytryk was asked if he "felt competent to take over. Who ever heard of a thirty-year-old who felt incompetent?"[28] Thus April 1939 saw the beginning of Edward Dmytryk's directing career proper.

The nominal star is Betty Grable, which may begin to explain the picture's retitling as *Million Dollar Legs*. However, Grable's role is strictly subsidiary and the only legs which feature to any degree are the beefy thighs of the college rowing team, which remain unpriced. The plot concerns the efforts of a student (Peter Lind Hayes) to convince his girlfriend (Dorothea Kent) of his sporting credentials by resurrecting the college rowing team, contrary to the wishes of the university's sponsor. The plot may be perfunctory and the script less than scintillating but the cast list is full of interest. Betty Grable was acting alongside her husband Jackie Coogan, although the marriage was in trouble due to his philandering. Grable began divorce proceedings after the picture had wrapped, on 30 July 1939. She was making $500 a week at Paramount but not making sufficient headway with the audience. As with Grindé, *Million Dollar Legs* saw the dropping of her contract, although at least the studio regime permitted her to finish the film. After one film for RKO, she was signed to 20th Century–Fox. When she replaced Alice Faye in *Down Argentine Way* in June 1940, a star was truly born. Also reaching the end of his Paramount contract with *Million Dollar Legs* was Larry Crabbe. He had made two *Flash Gordon* serials (*Flash Gordon* in 1936 and *Flash Gordon's Trip to Mars* in 1938) for Universal, as well as *Red Barry* in 1938. He was able to regain the billing he preferred, Larry "Buster" Crabbe, with his next venture: back at Universal for *Buck Rogers*.

Million Dollar Legs is brisk but unexceptional. The script by Lewis R. Foster, who also wrote *Golden Gloves* for Dmytryk, mines the college sports milieu for amusing scenarios without striking gold but the good-naturedness never flags. The actor who makes the most impact is the college chiseller Freddie "Ten-per-cent" Fry, played with finger-clicking verve and adept timing by Peter Lind Hayes. Freddie earns his nickname by constantly finding renumeration opportunities where no-one else sees them. This capitalist bravado finds tacit approval in the college's financial benefactor Gregory Melton (Thurston Hall). When the college coach (Larry Crabbe) asserts that the rowing team has no need for sponsorship, Melton protests, "Do you realise you're talking Communism, Sir? Our money has always been needed." Betty Grable and Dorothea Kent are mere foils to fraternity male exploits involving basketball, rowing, horse-racing and hazing of inferiors. A regular refrain is to "Assume the Angle," whereupon the poor student has to bend over to be paddled on the rear. The jocks count among their number Richard Denning, who made almost 50 pictures at Paramount in the five-year period from 1936, and an uncredited William Holden, making an inauspicious start to his career in a blink-and-miss bit part. More prominent is the thirteen-year-old Donald O'Connor as a horse-racing jockey, displaying technique and confidence beyond his years.

Shooting wrapped on 6 May: "I finished on schedule. The film was probably no worse—and certainly no better—than if the original director had finished it."[29] Dmytryk was initially uncertain whether the studio intended him to return to the cutting department, until he was offered a director's contract at $250 a week. By early June, the publicity department was trumpeting his promotion: "Edward Dmytryk, former Paramount film editor who directed *Million Dollar Legs*, was awarded his second directorial assignment, *The World on Parade*, in which William Henry and Janet Waldo will be featured. Dmytryk has been in the cutting department for the past ten years."[30] By the time *Million Dollar Legs* was released in July, Paramount had decided to credit Nick Grindé and Dmytryk's contribution was concealed. Grindé had moved on to Columbia where he would again cross paths with Dmytryk. By the time of its release in October, the William Henry film had lost both Janet Waldo as its female lead and its working title, but credit was given where due: *Television Spy* was "Directed by Edward Dmytryk."

Television Spy (1939)

After the false start of *The Hawk* and the uncredited studio debut on *Million Dollar Legs*, Edward Dmytryk's first directorial credit for Paramount did not receive an auspicious welcome. The *Motion Picture Herald* of 14 October 1939 called *Television Spy* an "unimpressively fabricated melodrama…. After imagining that [invention of long-distance television] has been achieved, however, imaginations of the four writers credited with the script seem to have gone dead, for nothing exciting to children over ten follows." Dmytryk himself escapes individual censure.

Having been assigned the project, Dmytryk was "nervous as a child bride"[31] to ensure that he didn't squander the opportunity. On location at a ranch in the San Fernando Valley on 13 June, the second day of shooting, he found himself being chaperoned by Lou King, B-movie director and younger brother of Henry King. This was similar to the ordeal that Nick Grindé had to endure on *Million Dollar Legs* but the scrutiny nevertheless dented Dmytryk's ego and frayed his nerves. He knew that the executives would be checking the first day's rushes before lunchtime back at the studio. At 11:30 a phone call came through for King at a nearby farmhouse; when he returned, he told Dmytryk that Harold Hurley, the top B-movie executive at Paramount, wanted to speak to him. Fearing the worst, Dmytryk trudged to the farmhouse to take the call. "Congratulations," said Hurley. "The dailies looked great. I just told Lou to come home."[32]

The storyline, accurately judged as below-par by the *Motion Picture Herald*, is overly complicated and insufficiently shaded. These are cut-out characters, rather too many of them for a slight running time, with dialogue that attempts to blind with pseudo-science but is tone deaf to reality. Doug Cameron (William Henry), an engineer for the Llewellyn Radio Corporation owned by irascible tycoon James Llewellyn (William Collier, Sr.), successfully develops a technique of transmitting television signals over long distances, 50 miles being cited as the erstwhile limit. Llewellyn puts the prototype into development, unaware that the blueprints have been copied for a society lady-cum-black market profiteer Reni Vonich (Dorothy Tree), and handed to Burt Lawson (Minor Watson), a rival of Llewellyn's, who is unwittingly developing the invention for sale to a foreign power.

The shadow of war in Europe, imminent when the film was being shot, reality when it was released, seeps into the production. When the stolen plans are offered to Lawson, he is informed by Vonich that the inventor is a prisoner in a "European concentration camp." The working system, once developed, will be sold for $1 million to "European" clients, who will pay handsomely for "a wartime advantage." Payment will be made in "European bonds." The omnipresent euphemism of "European" to indicate "Nazi" is understandable given the paranoid reluctance of the Hollywood studios to upset lucrative "European" markets. This reticence is rather undercut by the fact that each of the bad guys in the film has either a Germanic or Slavic name (Reni Vonich, Carl Venner, Boris) or a foreign accent (the butler Frome is the source of the leaked blueprints and is played by Wolfgang Zilzer). The good guys all possess Anglo-Saxon or Celtic surnames (Cameron, Lawson, Llewellyn, Randolph). The subtext will have been missed only by the least engaged patrons of the American public.

It is fascinating to see how television is treated by Hollywood in the early days of the technology and before it would become an existential threat to the studios. *Television Spy* was shot under the working title of *The World on Parade* but between June and October it was decided that the word "television" would be instrumental in selling the film. Early in the film Llewellyn declares, "Television is a headache and there's no use spending money on it." He dismisses the project that Cameron has been developing for years as "an inter-office communication set." "But with pictures" is Cameron's weak response. It is only when Cameron proves that he has managed to make the transmission waves "follow the curvature of the earth" and enable two-way communication over long distances that Llewellyn agrees to fund further research. He patriotically declares that he will sell the results to the U.S. military for $1, though the benefits on the battlefield that are attributed to these huge television sets have certainly been enhanced by creative marketing.

When *Television Spy* was produced, broadcast technology was just as experimental as depicted in the film and would only become commercialized in 1941. For such a minor movie conceived at the birth of broadcast, the scriptwriters show remarkable foresight for the potential of the medium, though notably without Hedy Lamarr's eye for technical detail. Outside broadcasts of sporting events, trans-continental television transmission, spyware and wall-sized screens are all envisaged in the course of the film. The invention of this last-mentioned also handily solves the cinematic problem of how to have actors in two locations communicate with each other via two-way television—simply construct a set on the other side of the huge "screen" and the actors in the "remote location" can interact through this proscenium arch.

Anthony Quinn appears in the first of his movies for Dmytryk in the not wholly unexpected role of heavy, although oddly, given the slant of the film's characterizations and his habitual racial stereotyping, one with the Anglo-Saxon name Forbes. After the plot has been revealed, the film rather whimpers to a conclusion with an explosion taking place just off-screen and a bathetic chat-up via television link providing the final lines: "You don't look like a scientist"—"I used to wonder what a dream looked like. Now I know." The technology that produced Tinder is a long way off.

In his autobiography, Quinn related a peculiar story: "Once, while a cutter was working on an Edward Dmytryk gangster picture called *Television Spy*, he absent-mindedly grabbed a length of film from the discard barrel of a 'B' jungle picture, which was being cut in the adjacent room, and spliced it into his working spool. For the longest time, the mistake went unnoticed. Somehow, when the gangster picture was finally screened, it contained about forty seconds of jungle footage. There I was, shooting it up on screen, when out of nowhere there came a parade of elephants, and tigers, and giraffes. It was the most incongruous thing. The next day, the trade newspapers checked in with their approval. What an act of genius, they hailed, for Dmytryk to break with convention to show the jungle that is New York. With reviews like that, no one bothered to recut the picture."[33] Dmytryk makes no mention of this mix-up in his own autobiography, and the version that is available today doesn't contain the jungle footage. Someone clearly did bother to recut it.

Emergency Squad (1940)

In the second of his four films with Dmytryk, Anthony Quinn played, in resolutely typecast fashion, a shady character on the wrong side of the law. At this stage in his career, the Mexican-American could only foresee an Oscar-winning career in his wildest dreams. "People were afraid to work with me because I was Cecil B. DeMille's son-in-law.... Casting directors would only put me to work as a gangster, or a bandit, or a thug. (No one wanted to be the first to give the son-in-law a decent part!)"[34] Talent will however occasionally out, and Quinn's expansive personality would eventually force its way out of the multi-ethnic heavy supporting bracket and into emotionally volatile leading man status.

Dmytryk was fond of Quinn ("one of the best around"[35]) but found him prone to upstaging, which is not altogether surprising when one considers the scene-stealing that took place throughout the remainder of his career. In *Emergency Squad*, Dmytryk was attempting, for efficiency reasons, to capture a scene in a "two-shot," wherein both actors appear in the frame. Quinn, despite attempts to direct him otherwise, kept moving away from the camera, forcing the other actor to turn his back. The solution hatched by Dmytryk was to stand Quinn in an upturned apple box to keep his wandering actorly instincts in check. All is fair game if out of camera shot.

The Emergency Squad are a crack team of police officers with the necessary training to enter burning buildings, attend construction accidents and rescue cats from trees. The city of Newford is of sufficient metropolitan scale to have its own streetcar network and a construction project tunneling under its river. The local newspaper has a female cub reporter Betty Bryant (Louise Campbell) trying to make a name for herself, while the tunnel construction boss Wiley (John Miljan) is trying to make a killing for himself by lowering the stock price of the construction company through staging controlled "accidents" at the site and buying up stock when the price hits rock bottom. Nick Buller (Quinn) is his co-conspirator and Betty is their unwitting stooge by providing publicity.

Betty is also the source of a love rivalry between squad members Dan Barton (Richard Denning) and "Chesty" Miller (Robert Paige), though the course of real romance never runs smooth when we have the slick presence of an Anthony Quinn gangster loitering in the wings. The climax has Wiley and Buller attempting to deflect suspicion from themselves by orchestrating an explosion mere minutes after they have left the tunneling site with Betty. A tunnel collapse traps the bomb with the villains, and it takes the rapid reflexes of Dan and Chesty to apprehend the conspirators and rescue Betty, who had been abandoned to perish below.

Emergency Squad rattles through plenty of plot in its tight 58-minute running time and endeavors to provide something for everyone in order to stave off boredom before the Bing Crosby or Dorothy Lamour feature begins. The dialogue sequences, in particular the jocular rivalry between Dan and Chesty, fail to rise above the mundane, but a few action sequences make their mark. The setup of a fire at a chemical works could have come straight from an early silent feature, with its damsel to be rescued from the upper-story window of a burning building, but it is staged efficiently. Even more effective are the explosions and cave-ins at the tunneling construction site, though it is unclear whether this is due to stock footage from another film or an upper B-level budget.

The climactic sequence with the ticking bomb successfully conveys tension but provided Dmytryk's first brush with an actor using a "method." A construction worker has been hired by the conspirators to plant the device but when he realizes he is trapped, with it about to explode, he reveals the plot to Betty: "They paid me to do it. But they didn't pay me to die!" Dmytryk recalled: "The actor asked me to give him a couple of minutes before we started the scene. In those days, that kind of request was an eyebrow raiser, and I wondered a bit, but agreed…. He circled a couple of times; then, grabbing a six-by-six upright which supported the tunnel's ceiling, he banged his skull against it two or three times just as hard as he could. I thought he'd split his head like an overripe watermelon, but he merely staggered a little and nodded his head in my general direction. I started the camera, and we shot the scene. Thank God we were able to print the first take."[36] Eduardo Thomajan, by taking his craft seriously, does indeed make an impact in the film, but was alas unable to channel this intensity into an enduring screen career.

The type of rave that Dmytryk had received in the *Daily News* for *Television Spy* was not repeated—*Harrison's Reports* dismissed it thus: "The direction is amateurish, and the acting worse, while the characters talk themselves to death."[37] It did however provide him with an insight into the publicity mechanisms at play in the industry. His producer Stuart Walker encouraged Dmytryk to write his own review for the film, which he was reluctant to do, so Walker produced one himself. Walker's writing was "Artfully done, not overboard,"[38] according to Dmytryk. This review was run in its entirety in *Variety*.

Golden Gloves (1940)

The first film of quality in Edward Dmytryk's career and his best at Paramount for another 15 years was *Golden Gloves*, a punchy melodrama about boxers and grift. It was also the first credited role for Robert Ryan ("I started Robert Ryan"[39]) with whom Dmytryk would make another four films, including the one for which he gained his only Oscar nomination. The two men had a strong rapport. "I always considered Bob Ryan the most honest actor that I ever worked with in my life," recalled Dmytryk in 1979, as well as him being "a very liberal man personally and politically."[40] His role in *Golden Gloves* is small but pivotal, that of a professional who infiltrates an amateur tournament to discredit it. He had been tested for the lead role but "we decided he wasn't quite ready for us. (Later I wondered if we had been ready for him.)"[41] The boxing match between Ryan and Richard Denning that climaxes the picture breathes authenticity because Ryan had been Intercollegiate Heavyweight Champion while at Dartmouth College, and was able to pull Denning up to his level—though not painlessly. "He tapped Denning in the ribs during their fight, and Dick made three trips to the hospital for X rays. To this day he insists his ribs were broken, though the pictures showed nary a crack."[42]

The strength of a B-movie lies in its attention to subsidiary characters and minor incident outside of the main arc of its plot. This screenplay by Maxwell Shane and

Lewis R. Foster is rich in both. Byron Foulger, a regular character actor for Dmytryk during the 1940s, has a single short scene and is uncredited, but he makes an impact as Hemingway, a character that Vito Russo in his book *The Celluloid Closet* would have termed "the sissy." When his department store boss asks what he thinks of the new employee gymnasium, Hemingway responds enthusiastically, "Lovely, simply lovely! So manly." Jenny (Lorraine Krueger), the perfume counter colleague of heroine Mary (Jeanne Cagney), could as easily be termed "the sassy": "So he makes a pass at me and I knock his ears down, just to show him I'm a lady. That's what I always say, make 'em think you're a lady."

Villainous boxing promoter Joe Taggerty is played by J. Carrol Naish, an Irish-American from New York City. Naish was often cast as the heavy and in a wide variety of ethnicities, except his own: "When the part of an Irishman comes along, nobody ever thinks of me."[43] Despite the seemingly Irish name, Taggerty is Italian, complete with comically thick mispronunciation. The circuit he runs for amateur boxers is corrupt and exploitative of its competitors. Mary's brother Joey (George Ernest) is unwillingly pitted against Gumdrop (David Durand), a much more proficient "slugger," with padding removed from his gloves, and the length of the round is surreptitiously increased from two minutes to three. When Joey dies from a blow to the heart, crusading journalist Wally Matson (Robert Paige) accuses Taggerty: "You killed that kid. Just as if you'd stuck a gun in his belly and pulled the trigger." Matson resolves to set up a rival amateur tournament and destroy Taggerty's racket.

Dmytryk parries the script's ducking and weaving through melodrama, comedy and action, maintaining momentum and delivering flashes of brio. When Mary's boyfriend Bill (Denning) arrives at Joey's 16th birthday party to inform Mary that her young brother has just died, the birthday cake looms inescapably in the foreground of the shot. Bill approaches and blows the candles out. Later, in a scene played with conviction by Naish and Durand, Taggerty's machinations are discovered by Gumdrop. The young boxer threatens to uncover the corruption ("You made me kill Joey Parker! I'm gonna make up for it!") and is killed by a blow to the head. Gumdrop's boxing comrades suspect Taggerty and lure him away to beat a confession out of him. The retribution scene is well-staged, with the camera pulling back to reveal the size of the kangaroo court, and ominous angles of the bereaved boxers indicating just how seriously Taggerty should take this confrontation. Dmytryk cross-cuts between the justice being meted out to Taggerty at the hands of the gang and the pulverizing Bill is receiving in the ring from the fists of the professional Pete Wells (Ryan). The sequence is delivered with adrenaline and builds to the inevitable, but inevitably satisfactory, conclusion of Taggerty confessing and Bill knocking out Wells, after a feisty pep-talk from Mary—"If you think I'm going to marry a second-rate also-ran, you're crazy." Challenging a boxer's manhood will clearly work wonders.

Dmytryk worked hard to make the fight scenes as authentic as possible and to improve on earlier boxing films such as *Kid Galahad* which had employed figures painted on backdrops behind three rows of live extras. He had hoped to get a stadium with a few thousand extras but even Paramount wasn't so profligate, and he was supplied with a sound stage and 300 extras. He observed that at real fights "the house lights were turned on only between rounds; while the fighters were at work the ring was brightly lit and the house lights were dimmed."[44] He decided to only have long shots of the stadium when fighting was in progress and placed his extras judiciously within each camera setup to give the impression of a huge crowd. A hazy atmosphere supplied by bee-smokers helped aid the illusion. He hung black drapes across the entire length and height of the stage walls, with a small group of extras strategically placed on rostra at various heights in front. "During the scene they would from time to time, at random, light their flare matches. The effect on the screen was of a couple of thousand fight fans, invisible in the darkness behind the ring, except when occasional smokers lit their cigarettes."[45]

The effort that went into imitating authenticity of the boxing sequences provoked a congratulatory note from the production head at Paramount about the "'most realistic fight scenes' he had ever seen in a film."[46] Dmytryk was very proud of what he had achieved on a B-movie budget, and justifiably so. The prowess of sportsmen such as Ryan and the ingenuity of the production design gifts the tang of reality to those scenes focused on the ring, and the film features an effective example of the training montage, that standard cliché of the sporting movie since its inception.

The character of Mary deviates from the stock girlfriend role. We observe her strength of character in her home and work environment, and not simply with reference to her boxing boyfriend. Naturally the plot puts obstacles in the path of their relationship that would in reality be easily surmountable, but the script uses a narrative sleight of hand to make it appear that she is wavering in her dedication to Bill by going on multiple dates with Wally. These romantic interludes echo each other nicely as the couples consider the night sky. While staring at the stars from Central Park, Bill asks Mary, "How's that for a load of diamonds, baby?" When Wally takes her to a nightclub on top of a skyscraper, the perspective is reversed: "See that string of lights down there? Tenth Avenue." Mary is nonetheless dazzled: "So close to heaven up here." The wooing by Wally is ultimately revealed to be for Bill's benefit, and by fadeout it is clear that Bill's pugilistic instincts are to be curbed by domesticity. Mary's final line ("For now on, the only fighting you'll ever do is with me") indicates that a fighter is featherweight when confronted with a determined sister of James Cagney.

Mystery Sea Raider (1940)

The American screen entered the Second World War in 1940, long before Pearl Harbor. Notwithstanding the potential alienation of lucrative European markets, it would have been derelict of the studios to avoid this rich new source of material. Most of the films made in the opening months of the war dealt with what was taking place in Germany (*Beasts of Berlin*, *The Mortal Storm*, *Four Sons*) or with what might happen to hapless Americans in Germany (*The Man I Married*). Only a handful brought the threat onto home soil. Jack Warner had angered Hitler with his pre-war production of *Confessions of a Nazi Spy*, and the spring of 1940 saw *Hidden Enemy*

Behind the camera for *Mystery Sea Raider* (1940).

and *Enemy Agent* released by Monogram and Universal, respectively. Ripping sto-
ries from the headlines was clearly easier for a quick-turnaround B-unit, and thus in
August 1940 Edward Dmytryk became the first director at Paramount to depict the
Nazi peril, beating Mitchell Leisen's prestige A-picture *Arise, My Love* by two months.

The headlines that *Mystery Sea Raider* were torn from are the U-boat sinking of
the British liner *Athenia* and the German seizure of the American ship *City of Flint*
in October 1939. The plot that was strung between these facts was of minimal credibility but moderate entertainment value. Showgirl June McCarthy (Carole Landis)
is sailing back to the U.S. from England when war is declared. Fellow passenger Carl
Cutler (Onslow Stevens) breaks off from wooing her to telegraph the liner's coor-
dinates in code, whereupon the ship is torpedoed by a German submarine. Back in
New York, June attempts to repair her fractious relationship with on-off boyfriend
Jimmy Madden (Henry Wilcoxon) by offering Carl the charter of Jimmy's docked
boat SS *Apache*, a deal that cash-strapped Jimmy gratefully accepts. This is a particularly poor peace offering from June, since the *Apache* is seized at sea by a U-boat crew
and Jimmy suspects June of having conspired with Carl in the capture.

At this point the film changes gear from character-driven intrigue to naval
action. The *Apache* fakes its own sinking and, by posing as a Danish vessel in distress, lures a succession of ships to their fate by submarine torpedo. Eventually the
raider ship is overloaded with 300 survivors from various wrecks and Jimmy hatches

a plan involving timed sea flares and bottled messages to signal their predicament. The plan succeeds and a British cruiser arrives to save the day. The climax involves mutiny—prefiguring *Mutiny* (1952) and *The Caine Mutiny* (1954)—by the prisoners onboard, the sinking of both a submarine and the raider, and the obligatory fade-out kiss between the reconciled June and Jimmy.

Dmytryk saw *Mystery Sea Raider* as "a step up—a B-plus"[47] but the budgetary limitations are still obvious. Stock and newsreel footage is used throughout. This is perfectly acceptable when submarine visuals are necessary; indeed, there are well-integrated and rather exciting shots of a submerging U-boat, as well as the unusual sight of a plane taking off from within a U-boat. However, the sinking of the sea liner SS *Aleria* on which June and Carl are travelling, an effectively staged sequence, is somewhat diminished by the insertion of dramatic footage of another ship being sunk—those lifesavers emblazoned with SS *Paradise* are a bit of a giveaway.

Since the film lacks a music credit, it can only be assumed that this element was also stock in the Paramount library. In a sequence towards the end of the film where German and British naval officers stand on their respective bridges and face off against each other via binocular and semaphore, Dmytryk refrains from using music to underscore the dialogue, before cranking the accompaniment up again for the action-packed climax. The result is that the sequence smacks more of documentary than anything else in the film, though somewhat at odds with an already disjointed piece of work. The character development at the start of the film is jettisoned overboard once Carl dons his Nazi naval uniform and the interpersonal relationships instantly matter much less than seafaring machinations.

The character of June has the familiar Hollywood trajectory of good-time showgirl ("I like to play—as long as it's just play") turned spirited resister. Her centrality to the rescue scheme is implausible, though credibility was not the stock in trade of wartime B-movies. Carole Landis, on loan to Paramount, was under contract to Hal Roach. At his studio she had just made *One Million BC* and had shared a dressing-room with 14-year-old Jean Porter, the future Mrs. Dmytryk, regularly giving the juvenile a lift to the studio. Porter recalled Landis as declaring, "I really shouldn't get old!"[48]—a tragically prescient remark, given that she committed suicide at the age of 29. Landis is a capable presence for Dmytryk, though her side-lining in the second half is par for the course of her disappointing career. Her biographer calls *Mystery Sea Raider* "one of Carole's most tightly directed films."[49]

The direction is indeed tight, and even at this early stage of his directorial career, Dmytryk marshals his material effectively, his apprenticeship as an editor apparent. Fluid camerawork enlivens the atmospheric credit sequence and later gives a succinct impression of life below deck in a long crane shot past the massed prisoners-of-war. The script is also above par, with some interesting subsidiary characters like Maggie the innkeeper, played with vim by Kathleen Howard. Carl's espionage techniques and his plot to commandeer the *Apache* demonstrate clearly that the Germans are a malign force to be reckoned with.

It is nonetheless interesting that Carl Cutler should be one of the first examples of the Noble Nazi. Even though devious tricks are part of his repertoire and he does order the execution of June, by the film's conclusion he is content to have Jimmy and

June survive ("Jump, you fools!") and to go down with his ship. Dmytryk regrettably found Onslow Stevens "a bit pompous, as older actors who are still playing little theatre are sometimes inclined to be,"[50] and his habit of suggesting corrections to the day's scene prior to shooting proved an irritating test of strength. He managed to tame the over-zealous actor by calling his bluff, pre-empting Stevens' own modifications—"When I put the responsibility onto his shoulders, he backed away. I never had a moment's trouble with him again, not even when I had some real changes to suggest."[51]

Dmytryk relished the luxury of a 24-day shooting schedule, which straddled May and June 1940, and of having his leading lady dressed by Edith Head. However, changes at the top at Paramount meant that he and the whole B-unit were disposed of upon expiry of their contracts. The film itself came under criticism from the *Motion Picture Herald* for not addressing the new wartime realities—"there is no denouncing of Hitler or Nazism or Germany in the manner of other war films of contemporary distribution and no atrocities are depicted."[52] Within a few years, this accusation could no longer be leveled at Dmytryk, director of the mold-breaking *Hitler's Children*.

Her First Romance (1940)

Deanna Durbin, the sweet-voiced savior of Universal Pictures, turned 17 in December 1938. She had only been active in films since 1936 but her sprightly personality and soaring soprano effervesced the five films in which she had appeared, making them hugely successful at the box-office. Now was the moment to swerve that tricky corner into adult roles. The 1939 vehicle for her first screen kiss was titled *First Love* and the recipient of that kiss was Robert Stack, in his screen debut.

Edith Fellows was by no stretch as successful as Deanna Durbin and didn't save any studio, but she also possessed a sweet singing voice and had been acting in films since being five years old in 1929. She had been signed to a seven-year contract with Columbia Pictures on the back of her appearance as Melvyn Douglas' daughter in *She Married Her Boss* (the "She" being Claudette Colbert) and Bing Crosby soothingly crooned "Pennies from Heaven" to her in the film of the same name. Much as Durbin had starred in *Three Smart Girls* and its sequel, Fellows was cast as the leading sibling of the *Five Little Peppers* in a series of four films. She turned 17 in 1940 and independent producer I.E. Chadwick felt that now was the moment to launch her as a mature performer. He engaged Edward Dmytryk to direct Fellows in *Her Father's Daughter*, which filmed for two weeks in early November. By the time it was released on Christmas Day, it had been retitled *Her First Romance* in a presumably intentional nod to the Durbin template, since she would receive her first kiss in the film from baritone Wilbur Evans. When acting in *First Love*, Robert Stack was 20 years old. Wilbur Evans, the apple of little Edith's eye in *Her First Romance*, was 35 years old.

From a modern perspective, the film is a rather queasy experience. The opening scene, shot at UCLA just as the opening scene of *The Caine Mutiny* would be 14 years later, introduces us to Linda (Fellows), a studious girl who is disdained by both sexes at her college. The mean girls chide her for her "V.P." (visible petticoat) and are painfully abusive to her: "Gosh, where's your vanity? You're subnormal!" The boys fail to see past her spectacles and force one student to invite her to the upcoming dance, merely as a cruel dare for him to gain entry to a fraternity. The echoes of Cinderella resound louder with each plot development. She is an orphan, forbidden by her guardian and wicked half-sister Eileen (Jacqueline Wells) from attending the dance, but her fairy housekeeper springs to her rescue with a ballgown. She had already encountered her Prince Charming Philip (Evans) on a fishing trip, and after he unexpectedly turns up to whisk her off to the dance, her lack of spectacles and spruced up appearance make her the Belle of the Ball.

The film proceeds like *The Bachelor and the Bobby-Soxer* with light operatic interludes from the two leads. In that film Shirley Temple pursues Cary Grant, with the audience secure in the knowledge that it is Myrna Loy he will end up with. Here, Edith Fellows initially pursues the considerably older Wilbur Evans as a beau for her cousin and then, stirring into a particularly complicated romantic bouillabaisse, sets out to snare him for herself. She is defensive about her tender age ("When Juliet was my age, she'd been dead four years") and employs a book titled "How to Get Your Man" with its timeless, presumably unironic advice: "Praise him whenever possible. Laugh at his humour. Tell him he's wonderful." When instructed by the book to "Get him off alone" and "Be provocative, display your charms," she lures him to a secluded cabin, unzips her dress to reveal a swimsuit and forces a kiss on him. Pointedly, the cabin where she attempts to seduce this father figure was a joint building/design effort by her and her late father.

The squirm quotient, which has been gradually building throughout this sequence, hits its peak in the final minutes of the film. One moment Philip is telling Linda, "You're a crazy kid and you ought to be spanked" and we are convinced he is interested in Eileen, and the next he is asking Eileen to consent to his marriage to Linda: "I realise she's terribly young in many ways, but quite mature in others." When Eileen refuses consent, Philip and Linda resolve to wait until October when she will be eighteen and they can get married without guardian consent. The film ends with a fade-out of them embracing on a bench. It's a most peculiar turn of events, intended to be a twist in the tail for contemporary audiences, but succeeding merely to unease modern audiences. Reviews at the time took the "story of adolescent love"[53] at face value: "Told with feeling, the picture … has charm, freshness and poignancy."[54]

Edith Fellows does indeed exhibit charm and there is sparkiness about her that is appealing. Perhaps benefiting from the sheen of hindsight, the second male lead also acquits himself well. Alan Ladd was busily churning through a succession of bit parts and unpromising supporting roles in the pursuit of stardom. He recalled, "I tried for better roles, over and over again, but directors or producers just kept saying I was too young or too old, too slight or too blond. Or else my name lacked prestige for the part. It was always something."[55] Sue Carol, his tenacious agent, plugged him relentlessly and Dmytryk recalled her coming to his office next to Columbia and pushing for her client: "He looked good, sounded very masculine, his price was right, but did he have a tuxedo?"[56] Carol lied that he did and hired one for him the next day. The break Dmytryk gave him was just one of dozens of moments in the spotlight before his big break of *This Gun for Hire* in 1942, by which stage Ladd and Carol had left their respective spouses and married each other. Chadwick re-released *Her First Romance* on the back of Ladd's sudden fame and Dmytryk belatedly received more from his small percentage on the film than his initial fee: "Particularly notable was the fact that Chadwick was the only producer in my experience to pay me my share without pressure or threat of suit."[57]

The Devil Commands (1941)

Anne Revere was a descendant of the revolutionary Paul Revere and of signatory of the American Constitution John Adams—and was a victim of the Committee whose opponents were branded Un-American. A highly respected character actress, she was nominated for the Academy Award for Best Actress in a Supporting Role for *The Song of Bernadette* and *Gentleman's Agreement*, and won the same award for *National Velvet*. Her onscreen image was of sincerity and integrity, often playing a maternal figure with a serious demeanor and a warm heart. She was listed in the publication *Red Channels* for her espousal of progressive causes in 1950 and was twice named as a Communist Party member, by Larry Parks in March 1951 and by Lee J. Cobb in June 1953. HUAC summoned her to appear on 17 April 1951, and her blacklisting was effectively immediate. Paramount persuaded George Stevens to cut her best scenes from the about-to-be-released *A Place in the Sun*[58] and for her face to be removed from the final scene. Over a tight close-up of Montgomery Clift, her disembodied voice is heard to say, "God bless you, my boy; God forgive me if I've failed you." She would not act in another film until Otto Preminger's *Tell Me That You Love Me, Junie Moon*, in 1970.

Her appearance before HUAC was one of the shortest on record, a mere ten minutes. Revere was asked whether she was affiliated with the Actors' Laboratory, a non-profit theatrical school. She declined to answer, "on the basis of the fifth amendment, possible self-incrimination, and also the first amendment."[59] During the hearing, she was handed a Communist Party membership card which she returned without comment. Resigning from the Board of the Screen Actors Guild, she wrote, "I should have preferred to testify that I had never held a party card, which they alleged to be mine and which had been so carelessly concocted as to carry an incorrect address."[60] Revere's screen career shriveled up completely and she moved to New York in 1957, eventually enjoying a triumphant return to critical recognition by winning a Tony for Lillian Hellman's *Toys in the Attic* in 1960. But the spirit of HUAC continued to haunt her and in order to get a role in a daytime television soap in 1965, she felt obliged to make a sworn affidavit regarding her political history. Her statement, "I considered myself a liberal reformer who had joined the Communist Party in order to bring about desirable social ends that would make this the best of all possible worlds"[61] chimes exactly with Edward Dmytryk's rationale for joining the Party, though neither of them had taken that step at the time they worked together.[62]

Anne Revere's appearance in *The Devil Commands*, her only horror film, is striking. Dmytryk recalled, "Oh, she was [good], and I was very lucky to get her."[63] The film was the last of a "mad doctor" cycle that Boris Karloff made at Columbia, the other entries being *The Man They Could Not Hang*, *The Man with Nine Lives* and *Before I Hang*. Karloff is reliably good in all of them, and *The Man They Could Not Hang* in particular has an interesting plot, but the other three suffer from a lack of visual panache, and were all directed by Nick Grindé, the man whom Dmytryk had replaced on Paramount's *Million Dollar Legs*. Grindé never escaped the B-movie ranks, and this second chance crossing of paths reinforced the fact that as his cinema career was grinding to a halt, Dmytryk's was very much on the ascent. Karloff for his part was tiring of the formula in which he was becoming typecast, but the studio was resistant to tweaking it: "I must confess that I didn't accept this constant and continual madness quite placidly myself. Once, during the crazed-scientist cycle, I said wearily to the producer: 'These things are all right but don't you think we should perhaps spend a little more in the writing, or change the format?' He was in an expansive mood. He opened his desk drawer and pulled out a great chart. 'Here,' he said, 'here's your record. We know exactly how much these pictures are going to make. They cost *so* much. They earn *so* much. Even if we spent more on them, they wouldn't make a cent more. So why change them?'"[64]

Karloff ("an extremely thoughtful and unselfish person who made the whole effort worthwhile,"[65] according to the director) plays Dr. Julian Blair who has discovered that the human brain emits a recordable impulse, "a carrier wave on which the true thoughts are transmitted." After losing his beloved wife in a car accident, he detects her wavelength lingering after her death and pursues his research using corpses in order to re-connect with her spirit. The film is introduced by a fatalistic voiceover from Blair's daughter Anne (Amanda Duff), which, combined with notably inky photography, makes *The Devil Commands* an intriguing precursor to the *noir* style that Dmytryk helped establish later in the decade. He provided a rationale for the structure: "I'm not a lover of flashback, but I must say that as a 'frame' for a picture, it very often is a good idea. You set up a situation, and then you say, 'Now, what *led* to this situation, we'll tell you about….' I don't particularly care for flashbacks within a film itself."[66]

Using his wife Helen (Shirley Warde) as a subject during his experimentation, Blair has discovered that "the wave impulse of *woman*, the so-called weaker sex, is much stronger and is much more regular than man's. Evidently there's a greater natural power in the brain of woman." The affectionate bond between the Blairs is palpable and his grief after her death is keenly portrayed by Karloff. The appearance of Anne Revere's character reinforces this key feminist theme of the film and shifts proceedings into a darker gear. Mrs. Walters, with the ironic first name Blanche, is a charlatan exponent of the Dark Arts, feigning contact with the dead at phony séances for self-enrichment. Blair confronts Walters with her fakery but is intrigued by the electricity he sensed during the séance. Requesting her assistance with his experiments, she coolly comments, "I'm not in this business for my health, Dr. Blair." When he responds that she will be well paid, Revere pauses briefly before saying, "I'll get my coat."

Once it is discovered that the incredibly high current emitted by Walters would make her an ideal conduit for receiving brainwaves, the title of the film comes into focus. This schemstress, hair tightly wound into practically horn-like formation, habitually dressed in long flowing black gowns and possessed of a manic glint in her eyes as her body withstands 10,000 volts, now vocalizes the hubristic thought that is every mad scientist's downfall: "If you can do what you're trying to do, you'll own the world." From now on, it is Walters who calls the shots, as when the brain of an assistant is accidentally fried in an experiment ("The world can get along without him") and she moves the trio to a clifftop house on the wild Maine coast. Any horror film in which a scientist plays God implicitly invokes His diabolical other, and here the superior power of the female has its evil incarnation in black widow Mrs. Blanche Walters. The devil is a woman, indeed.

The look of *The Devil Commands* is striking, and since the filmography of cinematographer Allen G. Siegler is undistinguished, credit for this likely lies with Dmytryk. Throughout the film, a single light source (candle, oil lamp, console desk) provides harsh illumination for the immediately proximate characters while casting the remainder of the set in sharply shadowed gloom. It is in this blackness that Blair is casting around, endeavoring to make connections with the unseen. It is his stated intention to "wipe out the horror that superstition conjures up out of fear of darkness" but his attempts only deepen the darkness. The light from his console desk provides illumination for him alone and conjures shady demons around the others. There is also a clear visual echo of Mrs. Walters' fake séances in the configuration of Blair's final experiments. The corpses that are stolen to provide a brainwave circuit are arranged in a circle with Walters as the central figure, the same strong controlling presence in trying to contact the dead through scientific methods as through those of the occult. The science in the sci-fi/horror hybrid may be as silly as any propounded in a B-movie but the visual panache drowns out any deficiencies in credibility. Dmytryk's composition within the frame displays a fun flair, such as when Blair's joy at contacting his wife's spirit in the background is somewhat undercut by the out-of-focus image of his assistant being electrocuted in the foreground.

The style that Dmytryk has wrought from his low budget and his two-week schedule is impressive but, as with so many programmers of the era, the wind comes out of the narrative sails in the final minutes. A standard angry mob has been whipped up and, as it descends on the Blair experimental residence, the doctor is upstairs in the laboratory attempting to contact his dead wife while recklessly endangering his living daughter. The powerful vortex summoned up by contacting the spirits has already claimed the life of Mrs. Walters, and now also wrests the doctor to the other side, but, frustratingly, offscreen. The special effects at the climax involve collapsing walls and ceilings but don't stretch to demonstrating what actually happens to Blair when the vortex rips him from his buckled-in position, having just clearly heard the voice of Helen. The audience is left with the voice of his daughter Anne, warning against the folly of playing God while simultaneously rather relishing the concept: "When he seemed to be so close to what he sought, something reached for him—a warning that human beings must not try to reach beyond death ... and yet perhaps the time will come when the door to infinity will open ... perhaps ... perhaps...."

Dmytryk recalled previewing *The Devil Commands*, its title changed from the original choice *Edge of Running Water*, in a suburb of Los Angeles. The cinema chosen was termed a "cinch house," because "if you just wanted to make sure that a picture would play well, you took it to Inglewood, the El Capitan, because *anything* went there."[67] The preview had been advertised and after the main feature the title card appeared, "COLUMBIA PICTURES PRESENTS BORIS KARLOFF." "And half the people got up and walked out! I thought, 'My God, how do they know that it's lousy this early?' I was really *so* let down!"[68] He hadn't realized that certain elements of the audience simply wouldn't stomach a film starring Boris Karloff and that the audience for horror was limited from the outset. The producer who had shown Karloff the box-office projections knew his business.

Decades later, Anne Revere had a similar perspective on the blacklist years as Dalton Trumbo, who rather infamously declared that "it will do no good to search for villains or heroes or saints or devils because there were none; there were only victims."[69] Revere said, "Nobody went to jail because they were Communists. They went to jail for contempt. But the awful thing about the whole bloody era was that whether you answered or didn't, cooperated or not, you were dead in the business."[70] The screen was immeasurably poorer without the vibrant presences of Anne Revere and Gale Sondergaard and Lee Grant and so many others, for the joy in many a film is to be found in its supporting performances. With an equanimity appropriate to the aura of calm sense that she projected on screen, Revere didn't appear to look back in rancor: "I don't know what my life would've been like without the blacklist.... Maybe, if I had stayed on in Hollywood, I would have fit into the new studioless structure, but it wouldn't have been the same as the golden years of Hollywood."[71]

Under Age (1940)

As was the inclination of exploitation films of earlier eras, *Under Age* begins with onscreen text explaining its crusading mission in revealing unsavory realities about motel networks: "Most of these highway homes are honestly operated by respectable citizens. But some are nothing but tourist traps, operated by racketeers whose secret criminal activities menace every traveler.... The producers of this picture are glad to join with [the] forces of decency in frankly exposing hidden plague spots that lurk behind glittering signs on certain highways." Armed with this purple prose, the viewer can indulge in salaciousness with their integrity intact and the censor can look the other way in the knowledge that public morality is being upheld. And a film with a tease of a title, as irrelevant as it might be to the actual content, can justify its existence.

Intriguingly, Edward Dmytryk doesn't even mention *Under Age* by name in his autobiography, merely grouping it in with his *Lone Wolfs* and his *Boston Blackie*. It is in fact one of the most interesting of his early B-movies, and certainly, along with *The Devil Commands*, his best work of his six Columbia releases in 1941. The story is credited to Stanley Roberts, who later wrote *The Caine Mutiny*, and the screenplay to Robert Hardy Andrews, writer of Dmytryk's first three pictures for Columbia, the other two being *The Devil Commands* and *Sweetheart of the Campus*. It concerns a racket whereby homeless and desperate girls are offered positions as "hostesses" at a nationwide chain of motels, luring men to the roadhouses by posing as hitchhikers and parting them from their cash by both legitimate and criminal means. The motel chain is called House by the Side of the Road, an ironic reference to the Sam Walter Foss poem: "I would not sit in the scorner's seat, or hurl the cynic's ban; Let me live in a house by the side of the road and be a friend to man."

The only time the age of the girls is referred to is when a batch including our heroine sisters Jane and Edie Baird (Nan Grey and Mary Anderson) are recruited upon release from a County Detention Home for Minor Girls. The unspoken and unspeakable undercurrent of the plot is that this is a prostitution ring, with the girls regularly moved around the nationwide network to prevent law enforcement from catching a whiff of the racket.

Under Age is an unexpectedly dark and gritty piece of work. Until the final three minutes, the Law is totally absent and is maligned as force for ill that will lock girls up merely for being jobless and sleeping on park benches. It falls upon the girls themselves to bring about the demise of the racketeers with the assistance of one of the gang's male victims, travelling jewelry salesman Rocky Stone (Tom Neal). We are spared few details of the crooked enterprise, how the girls are paid a basic wage and commission but are overcharged for expenses such as clothing, leaving them in permanent debt to their pimps. The owner of the motel chain is known as The Widow, using her girls as assets and discarding them when their profitability declines, and she is played with icy insouciance by Leona Maricle. One of her henchmen is Tap Manson (Alan Baxter), sizing up suckers when they are brought to the roadhouse, classing them as "lone wolves" or "stiffolas" and beefing up their bill or engaging in blackmail for a bigger payday. This seamy world of scam is trenchantly realized by scriptwriter and prowled watchfully by director. It is an environment all the more claustrophobic for seeming inescapable. Jane refuses Rocky's assistance on several occasions because Edie has lodged herself too deeply with the gangsters and has compromised her own safety.

Nan Grey, in her final film role, is very effective as the protective elder sister despairing of Edie's taste for the good life, whatever the cost. Grey had been one of the *Three Smart Girls*, with a rather more amenable younger sister in Deanna Durbin, and had been a Universal contract player until this single film with Columbia had her quitting the screen for good. She would later be married to the singer Frankie Laine for 43 years until her death. Tom Neal labored under Oriental eye make-up in *Behind the Rising Sun* for Dmytryk a few years later, before his most famous role in Edgar G. Ulmer's blistering *Detour*.

As in *The Devil Commands*, Dmytryk's deployment of shadow is dramatic. His director of photography this time was John Stumar, born in Hungary and active in the American film industry since 1917. The cinematography turns particularly atmospheric as events hurtle to a conclusion. When Jane is caught after a clandestine meeting with Rocky, she is interrogated by The Widow and Manson, while two heavies lurk in the background, their faces lit from below. It is a sinister, disquieting scene, made all the more unpleasant by Manson's words to his henchmen as he leaves the room: "Oh boys, don't mess up that pretty face." The camera exits with him and beyond the door we hear Jane's anguished screams. Edie discovers that her sister has been badly beaten up and resolves to bring Manson to justice, but before she can act on her promise she is run over and killed by him.

The final quickfire three minutes of the film see the police round up the criminal gang, the ringleaders convicted in court and the obligatory romantic payoff, but not before another startlingly *noir* sequence. When the group of girls inform Jane of Edie's murder, two of them hover in the background, like shadowy Lady Justices encouraging the oppressed to rise up. The expressionistically shot scene where the girls lure Manson to a room to exert justice heavily echoes a similar sequence in *Golden Gloves* that Dmytryk had made for Paramount the year before. The girls literally rise up to confront their pimp: "This is a murder trial. We're all on the jury and we're all witnesses." Jane, blonde and dressed in white like an avenging angel, walks towards him, with calculated menace: "And she's the prosecutor." Jane observes the panic on his face as he realizes he is utterly outnumbered: "No, you can't get out. Not till we're through with you. And we don't care what happens to your face." True to their word, he is slapped across the face, leaving a mark. Fade to meaningful black. The imagination is the most exploitative element of all.

Sweetheart of the Campus (1941)

Ruby Keeler's style prioritized energy over élan. Keeler had been hoofing and high-kicking with gusto onscreen for a decade, most successfully at Warner Bros, but by the time she made *Sweetheart of the Campus* at Columbia, her thighs were tired and her zest had waned. It was, barring a cameo in *The Phynx* thirty years later, her swan song. "It was so bad, I had no regrets about quitting," was her assessment. "I wasn't disillusioned with show business. I just thought there was more to life. I was right."[72]

Edward Dmytryk was equally unimpressed with the material. Feeling he had served his apprenticeship ("with sufficient practice one can easily learn to be a hack"[73]), he had been expecting a boost up the pecking order at Columbia but the Ruby Keeler musical was foisted on him by Columbia's top B-executive Irving Briskin. The following year, he was so dissatisfied with the quality of what he was being offered that he refused assignments on B-pictures for six months, but the state of his bank balance obliged him to accept one more *Lone Wolf* crime caper.

The resignation in having to knuckle down to this project is almost discernible on screen, since *Sweetheart of the Campus* is one of the most lackluster entries in Dmytryk's filmography. The feeble script from Robert Hardy Andrews and Edmund L. Hartmann concerns the attempts to attract new students to a failing university through enrolling showgirl Betty Blake (Keeler) as the sole female student. Alongside the simultaneously enrolled members of a swing band, the college radio and experimental television station broadcasts musical numbers to advertise how fun it is to study at Lambert Tech College, with the 300 males to one female student ratio being used as a somewhat oblique selling point.

The swing bandleader Ozzie Norton is played by Ozzie Nelson. The university staffer turned crooner Harriet Hale is played by Harriet Hilliard. Already at this stage, in their debut film and before they became fictionalized versions of themselves on radio and television, the real-life married couple Ozzie and Harriet are being branded with some prescience as a joint product. The shift to Los Angeles to make this film was to be a decisive moment in the life of the Nelsons: "what we didn't know was that California was to be our home from then on."[74] At this point in his career Ozzie is considerably more successful at wielding a baton than delivering dialogue but it is interesting to observe such a long-running media fixture at the germination stage. His assessment of the film is less damning than Keeler's: "It wasn't good and it wasn't bad."[75]

For the most part, Dmytryk neglects to inject much visual interest into the musical numbers, apart from a split screen effect for Keeler dancing alongside piano keys. He reserves the most interesting camera setups and editing for a number from the African American quartet The Four Spirits of Rhythm, although these efforts are somewhat undone by their unmemorable song and the stereotype of them being as interested in gambling dice as in performing their music. Outside of the musical numbers, camera fluidity is kept to a minimum. The cinematographer Franz Planer had worked with F.W. Murnau and Max Ophüls in Germany before moving to Hollywood, and would go on to work with Dmytryk another three times, as well as photographing *Letter from an Unknown Woman*, *Roman Holiday* and *The Nun's Story*. His work here is as uninspired as Dmytryk's.

Aside from her enthusiastic tapping, Ruby Keeler is an uncomfortable fit as a sassy showgirl, a role that Ginger Rogers or Barbara Stanwyck would have slipped into with ease. Her unsisterly treatment of Harriet is mean-spirited and initially focused on her rival's prim, bespectacled appearance. A star image that had never encompassed sexiness is required to make sexiness her defining characteristic, in the midst of a remarkably sex-obsessed student body. It's a casting against type that is abrasive against Keeler's persona, producing an awkward performance.

For the second time in as many years, television features in a Dmytryk film—not as centrally as in *Television Spy*, but the television station in *Sweetheart of the Campus* is nonetheless an important element of the plot. Television had appeared as a plot device since the early 1930s in films such as *International House*, and in 1936 Mary Astor had battled the baddies in a tepid invention-stealing yarn, *Trapped by Television* from the same Columbia B-division as *Sweetheart of the Campus*. At this stage, television had yet to become the *bête noire* of the cinema industry that would lead to

Jack Warner banning a single television set from appearing in any Warner Bros. film. Columbia was instead concentrating on the promotional potential of *Sweetheart of the Campus*. Though the songs in the movie are rather banal, someone at the studio decided to insert an unusual coda, a snappy reprise of the main numbers during the feature, the intention clearly being to have the audience leave the theater humming the tunes and rush to stores to purchase some Columbia records.

The Blonde from Singapore (1941)

Edward Dmytryk had six films released by Columbia in 1941, running from *The Devil Commands* in February to *Confessions of Boston Blackie* in December. Considering that he was also editing his films, this displays a laudable work ethic, though the rate of working was no doubt a contributory factor to Dmytryk's distaste for the studio. He called Columbia "the Black Hole of Calcutta. It was the worst one, you know, the studio itself was a rat maze, and they made cheap pictures."[76] His judgment of studio president Harry Cohn and head of the B-movie division Irving Briskin was equally scathing: "all of them were crude, vulgar, uncouth men."[77] The material and shooting schedule were not equivalent to what he was used to at Paramount—18 days were typical for a B-movie at Paramount; 14 days were standard at Columbia—but it enabled him to develop his ability at capturing the essence of the scene in as efficient a manner as possible. In the realm of rapid-fire B-movies, no skill was as precious.

By the end of 1942, Dmytryk would have shifted studios to RKO, where his first film *Seven Miles from Alcatraz* made the necessity of bolstering the war effort central to its plot. When *The Blonde from Singapore* was released on 16 October 1941, Pearl Harbor had yet to be attacked and the Hollywood studios were still teetering on the tightrope between appeasement and engagement. For the film's heroes, the clarion call of the European war is not one of moral duty but an appeal to the American spirit of adventure. Leif Erickson and Gordon Jones play Terry and Waffles, pilot and mechanic respectively, whose goal overriding all is to enlist in the Royal Air Force in Singapore and defend the new frontier: "There's a job to be done and we want to help do it." Their libido can prove their undoing however—on one occasion they permitted a female companion to fly their plane, only for her to crash it. An RAF commodore is not impressed with their flighty attitude, assuring them that this is "no time for any tomfoolery."

The tone of the film is much more that of tomfoolery than of heroic endeavor and the buddies in this movie display an endearing homosociality. After Waffles forgets to pump air to Terry while deep-sea diving for pearls, Terry fixes him with a look when he comes to the surface, and simply says, "Well?" Waffles turns around, presents his rear to be kicked and says, "Thank you, Terry." Later, when Terry is duped by the titular blonde, the same ritual is performed in reverse. Their relationship is so sweetly unconditional that someone tells Waffles to "take care of your boyfriend." The female in this escapade proves an inconvenient obstacle between them. Florence Rice plays Mary Brooks, a stranded showgirl who masquerades as the orphaned daughter of missionaries in order to swindle her way into the affections of Prince Sali (Alexander D'Arcy).

The Blonde from Singapore is a light confection in which no misbehavior has serious consequences. Mary's deviousness doesn't prevent her from being wooed by the Prince, and, though Terry ends up in prison for inadvertently poaching pearls, he is swiftly released by the Prince's mother to perform a fake kidnapping. More entertaining than the meandering plot are the amusing moments studded throughout. Realizing that the seat of Terry's pants has split, he and Waffles perform a comedy walk out of the scene. Terry masquerades as Mary's abandoned husband in a crowded casino. When asked by a policeman whether Mary has any distinguishing marks on her body, Terry responds with mock outrage: "Constable!"

It is the wide-faced openness of Leif Erickson's performance that is the film's chief asset. His affable breeziness carries the scenes with less-skilled actors, though Rice and Jones prove able sparring partners. Dmytryk's contribution is unshowy, save for a few shots such as a high-diving plunge into the ocean, and his editing keeps matters brisk. *The Blonde from Singapore* lands the man she was after, only to discover that marrying the Prince means joining his harem. She bristles and rejects sharing her man ("I wouldn't share a toothbrush with any other woman!") and at fade-out is married to second choice suitor Terry. Though Terry's first choice buddy Waffles is clearly not going anywhere.

Secrets of the Lone Wolf (1941) and *Counter-Espionage* (1942)

The period 1932–1934 was peak Warren William. He appeared in 21 feature films including *Cleopatra* and *Imitation of Life*, and was commended in the first volume of *The Picturegoer's Who's Who and Encyclopaedia* for his 1932 performance in *The Mouthpiece*: "A piece of acting that runs the gamut of emotion with sincerity."[78] By October 1938 his white-hot status had cooled somewhat and he signed a non-exclusive contract with Columbia for two Lone Wolf films per year. This B-movie series featured the latest incarnation of the gentleman thief Michael Lanyard, created by the novelist Louis Joseph Vance in 1914 and who had appeared in films since 1917, the most recent being *The Lone Wolf Returns* with Melvyn Douglas in 1935. The Lone Wolf was the inspiration for a slew of other smooth characters who shifted from the wrong side of the law to the right, such as the Saint and the Falcon.

William's debut was *The Lone Wolf Spy Hunt*, appearing alongside Ida Lupino and Rita Hayworth, but it wasn't until the following film *The Lone Wolf Strikes* that Michael Lanyard's valet Jamison was introduced, and the casting of Eric Blore alongside William initiated a memorable comic pairing. Blore would make eight appearances in the role opposite William, and another three opposite Gerald Mohr after William had departed from the series in 1943.

The casting was perfect. Warren William possessed a suavity of which the pencil moustache was merely the physical manifestation, but a smoothness edged with dark disdain, hinting at a lack of sincerity that cast doubt on his status as a law-abiding citizen. Eric Blore was an Englishman from Finchley who had been a consummate character actor in Hollywood films since the early 1930s. His diction and bearing led to him being frequently typecast as a butler or manservant, which irked him: "Personally, I am no worshipper at the shrine of butlers. If anything, my feelings are tinged with resentment. Butlers invariably wear high-stiff collars and my neck rebels at such confinement."[79] Though the distinction would be slight to most observers, he expressed preference for valets and waiters, who displayed "more dash" and "a superior zip."[80]

The two Lone Wolf films that Edward Dmytryk directed, though consecutive in the series, were distinct in being released either side of America's entry into the war, which colored the content of their scripts. *Counter-Espionage* also indicated an attempt to refresh the franchise by removing the Lone Wolf imprimatur from the titles and by setting the films in distant locales, though naturally these very modestly budgeted vehicles never set foot outside the Columbia lot. The script of neither of the films exhibited a superior zip, both having plots in which Lanyard is suspected of a crime and keeps evading the cack-handed arm of the law in order to clear his name, and both deploying tired moments of comedy and crime movie clichés. Such clichés ("Follow that cab/car!" crops up in both) provoke their own pleasures.

Secrets of the Lone Wolf concerns the theft of the Napoleon Jewels, the national treasure of an unnamed country that wants to sell them in order to finance the wartime resistance against an unnamed foe back home. Despite the lack of identifying accents, the assumption is that the country is France, and such squeamishness about addressing global realities was par for the course for the nervously neutral American studios. Dmytryk manages to inject a few interesting set-ups into the rapid-fire shooting schedule, such as an unconscious body falling down towards the floor-level camera. When being questioned by the hapless cops, Lanyard wonders whether they are about to give him a "third degree session" and angles a lamp for the interrogation to begin. The next shot wittily has Lanyard, composure cool, standing looking down at a sweaty and flustered Inspector Crane (Thurston Hall) in the interrogating chair.

The relationship between master and servant is subject to some cheeky scrutiny. Lanyard masquerades as his own valet at one point, much to Jamison's pleasure. While a trouserless Lanyard practices a speech with "You cannot outsmart the police" as the ironic theme, his reminiscence of "the wild escapes with every man's hand against you" elicits a dreamy sigh from Jamison. The censors must have been sleeping to let that innuendo pass. Lanyard is also perplexingly chaste in this pair of films. Of the two female characters in *Secrets of the Lone Wolf*, one has a boyfriend and the other, played by Marlo Dwyer, flirtatiously kisses him, to negligible response. In *Counter-Espionage*, Pamela (Hillary Brooke) is engaged to be married and therefore off-limits.

In the earlier of the Dmytryk duo, Eric Blore is given fifth billing, a demotion from his usual third or fourth placing. In *Counter-Espionage* he is second in the credits, a belated sign of how important he was to the success of the series. This time our heroes are temporarily decamped to London, and the script has the courage to call a Nazi a Nazi. The chief villain Gustav Soessel (Kurt Katch) is bald of head, wide of eye and possesses a sledgehammer Teutonic accent. When Lanyard steals plans from the British for a "beam detector" to sell to the Nazis, he is operating as a double agent. Unfortunately, the only person who knows his undercover status is killed, and neither Scotland Yard nor his regular American cop adversaries Crane and Detective Dickens (Fred Kelsey) believe his story.

London is predictably shrouded in fog and all of its citizens take leave by saying, "Thumbs up!"—an expression which American pilots and GIs would soon disseminate through several continents. The Londoners are portrayed as more stoic than Americans—when an air raid is underway, they want to stay in their nightclub and party on regardless. Scotland Yard is also depicted as more efficient than the NYPD—when a call is successfully traced (in the U.S. "that never works"), Dickens is ecstatic: "It works! What a wonderful country!" The film features a very early fax machine, or "radio photo sending station," although this German technology is used against its operators to defeat the spies. An uncredited Lloyd Bridges appears in the final sequence as a Nazi waiter, able to outfox the American cops but no match for the wiles of the Lone Wolf.

The production and script values of *Counter-Espionage* are marginally better this time round, though still flimsy, and the running-time is bolstered by much stock footage and explosion shots from films with higher budgets. However, a film which features the insouciant presence of Warren William and the precise delivery by Eric Blore of lines such as "This is no time for persiflage" and "I'm positively bathed in perspiration, if you'll pardon my vulgarity" will reward the patient viewer.

Confessions of Boston Blackie (1941)

Chester Morris tends to feature as a peripheral in histories of Hollywood, but he certainly had his moment in the sun. He notched up an Oscar nomination in 1929 for the crime movie *Alibi* and, as a reliably sturdy pair of shoulders for leading ladies such as Norma Shearer, Jean Harlow and Carole Lombard, he satisfied critics throughout the 1930s as much as he boosted audiences. In 1939 Graham Greene wrote of "the superb acting of Mr. Chester Morris, sweating, badgered, disintegrating"[81] in his film *Blind Alley*. The character he played in *Public Hero Number 1* in 1935 was indicative of his range—initially a ruthless convict, then revealed to be an upright law-enforcement officer, finding time to charmingly woo Jean Arthur along the way. His features were street-tough and frequently menacing but would crack into a winning smile when a pretty dame required romancing. His star had fallen somewhat by 1941 when Columbia began to produce the Boston Blackie series, but his gutsy presence remained undimmed.

The silent era had seen a succession of films featuring Boston Blackie, a character created by Jack Boyle in 1914, while the Columbia run of B-movies lasted between 1941 and 1949, introducing Chester Morris in the role in *Meet Boston Blackie*. Blackie was that suave staple, the gentleman jewel thief, or, as the character himself insists in *Confessions of Boston Blackie*, an "ex-confidence man and ex-jewel thief." The plot of the Dmytryk entry in the series follows the template that would extend through Chester Morris's tenure of the role—Blackie is suspected of a crime and must prove the police wrong by apprehending the true culprit.

It is remarkable just how inept the NYPD are shown to be in this film. The forces of law and order, normally a bulwark for a stable society under the Production Code, are consistently undermined ("Listen my boy, if you insist on wearing long trousers, you'd better begin acting like an adult") and even shown to be corrupt when they steal ice-cream from a delivery boy. An Irish cop has the ultimate slur cast on him: "You've got a little Gestapo in you!" Inspector Farraday (Richard Lane), Blackie's would-be nemesis, rarely makes a correct call, permits himself to be handcuffed to a chair and when he is shown to be capable enough to check a room for possible escape routes, he somewhat undermines this nous by declaring, "It's a little precaution I learnt from the movies."

The criminal gang that Blackie is up against are art forgers, specifically of a Roman statue that Diane Parrish (Harriet Hilliard) is selling to fund medical treatment for her brother. This setup gives rise to a notable poster tagline comparing the statue with Hilliard: "A fabulous treasure … 2000 years old! A luscious treasure … old enough to kiss!" When Diane raises the alarm at the auction that a fake is being sold in place of her heirloom, a shot aimed at her kills the chief forger of the gang and the wrongly accused Blackie must go on the run. The convolutions of the plot provoke another post-modern line from Farraday: "Too much plot. Dime novel stuff."

Before the script runs out of steam, *Confessions of Boston Blackie* is a fun, pacey affair, bolstered by nimble dialogue and punchy direction. By now Dmytryk was clearly a man exhibiting confidence in where to place his camera and how long to hold a shot. Some of his camerawork transcends the expectations of a minor crime series episode, such as the sweeping crane work and perspective shots that embrace a huge, multi-level warehouse space in several sequences of the film. The concluding gunfight in this location is peppered with overhead shots and creative angles, propelling the film to its climax. It's an object lesson on what can be achieved on a tight budget and provided an effective calling card for Dmytryk's imminent move to RKO.

Chester Morris invests Boston Blackie with a pugnacious, spiky charm, George E. Stone operates effectively as Blackie's sidekick the Runt ("I wouldn't give her the sweat off a cold bottle!") but the picture is stolen by a lovely comic performance from Lloyd Corrigan as millionaire and Blackie confidante Arthur Manleder. He bumbles and dithers with expert timing, managing to make handcuffing himself to a candelabra look plausible, and provides a counterpoint to Morris's more contained delivery of the witty script. The longevity of a series like Boston Blackie depends as much on the quality of support as the talent of the lead and the contribution of Lloyd Corrigan to six of the films undoubtedly helped prolong the series to fourteen installments.

II

The RKO Years
(1942–1947)

In 1942, RKO was facing a renewed financial slump akin to the one that had nearly capsized the studio in the 1930s. The musicals with Ginger Rogers and Fred Astaire that proved so profitable earlier in the decade had begun to lose money by decade end, though from that point Rogers solo became the studio's top box-office attraction in films such as *Bachelor Mother* and *Kitty Foyle*. In June 1942, new production chief Charles Koerner was instructed by the corporate president George Schaefer "to make 'no further commitments on the pictures that are to be produced later in the year for 1942–43.' This message was issued because it appeared that fiscally challenged RKO might close its studio or fall back into receivership."[1] Under Schaefer's presidency, Orson Welles had been hired and had produced two masterworks of cinema, both of which regrettably lost a lot of money. Under the presidency of the same man, Edward Dmytryk was employed and in 1943 directed two sensational B-movies that performed sensationally. Dmytryk joined the 1942 roster of contract directors that included Leo McCarey, William Dieterle, Robert Stevenson and Jacques Tourneur, in charge of contract stars such as Charles Laughton, Maureen O'Hara, Agnes Moorehead and Dana Andrews. His arrival at the studio coincided with the beginning of the most successful period in RKO's history, which can be attributed to the wartime attendance boom and to Koerner's leadership from 1943 to 1946. It was a remarkable turnaround in which Dmytryk played a small but key part, the Koerner regime leading him later to designate RKO as "at the time, the best-run studio in the business."[2]

Dmytryk's first film for RKO was **Seven Miles from Alcatraz**, a stylish B-movie that was shot in August and which did not go unnoticed by Koerner, who wrote in September: "The place is gradually whipping into shape and I feel exceptionally optimistic. We have completed eight pictures under my so-called regime, namely, *Once Upon a Honeymoon*, which looks terrific.... *Cat People, Seven Miles from Alcatraz* ... there really isn't a bad picture in the bunch."[3] Koerner terminated the contracts with Orson Welles[4] and documentarian Pare Lorentz, both of whose projects had been hemorrhaging money for the studio. Dmytryk tried unsuccessfully to revive their abandoned projects. His praise for Koerner was effusive: "He was the best executive I have ever known. He made decisions quickly and firmly, he could be convinced, and he had the one truly great executive talent—once he delegated authority, he never interfered."[5] This admiration would certainly have been mutual in 1943 when

On set with his son Michael (1945).

Dmytryk delivered two huge successes, **Hitler's Children** and **Behind the Rising Sun**, in what was an extraordinary year for RKO. John Paxton, soon be a regular collaborator, remarked of *Hitler's Children*, "[Dmytryk] did a fine job and was thereafter very hot, known as a very bright fellow, very fast, very economical, efficient, technically superb."[6] Dmytryk was aware of his reputation: "I was always considered one of the most efficient set-up men in Hollywood, even in those days."[7]

Hitler's Children had been filmed in October 1942 and, before they realized what an asset they had upon its release in January 1943, RKO loaned Dmytryk to Universal to make **Captive Wild Woman** in December. The following year saw a flurry of activity around the newly in-demand director. He filmed **The Falcon Strikes Back** in January/February and *The Mad Brood of Japan*, which would eventually become *Behind the Rising Sun*, was announced in April. That same month, he was attached to a propaganda short for foreign release to be made by the Office of War Information (OWI) and to be titled *America's Children*, as a positive riposte to *Hitler's Children*. *China Sky* was announced in May with him at the helm but that film starring Randolph Scott was not made until 1945 and was directed by Ray Enright. In July, the project about America's youth had morphed into *Are These Our Children?*—a despairing examination of juvenile delinquency. This picture also did not proceed with Dmytryk, for in August he was assigned his first A-picture, the Ginger Rogers vehicle **Tender Comrade**. The film was scripted by Dalton Trumbo, whom Dmytryk met casually at this point, neither realizing how they would ultimately enjoy the fame/infamy of being members of the Hollywood Ten.

October 1943 witnessed a rather ironic juxtaposition of speakers at the United Nations Writers' Congress at UCLA. At a seminar on feature films, the representative of the Soviet Union, the ally of the United States, spoke of placing the common man and woman in heroic prominence in films. In his speech, Edward Dmytryk declared that it was "possible to give a propaganda picture conviction and make it acceptable to the public, if it can show a native of the enemy country reacting against his government because of its effect on himself."[8] Just a few years later, the Soviet Union would be the enemy country and Dmytryk would be accused of disseminating unacceptable propaganda. In November he was assigned to direct *Elizabeth Kenny*, a biopic about a pioneering Australian nurse, and met its proposed star Rosalind Russell and Kenny herself in New York, as well as visiting the Kenny institution in Minneapolis. RKO would eventually make the film as *Sister Kenny* in 1946 with Russell starring and Dudley Nichols directing. To confirm his new status, Dmytryk changed agency when Hal Cooley sold his contract to Famous Artists. He had wanted to stay loyal to his "little" agent, but Cooley convinced him that representation with a higher profile agency was a necessity as his career took off.

Since Dmytryk expected to be called up for service in the war, he sold his home in Sherman Oaks in the San Fernando Valley to the actor Richard Arlen and bought an apartment house in Beverly Hills, with a view to settling Madeleine and Michael there. He volunteered his services as an editor to the new Signal Corps film unit being set up by Colonel Frank Capra, and was surprised when his offer, enthusiastically received, was never accepted: "It was some ten years later that I learned the Signal Corps had turned me down as a security risk; I had been a premature antifascist."[9] The phrase "premature antifascist" was one of the more absurd linguistic formulations of the witch-hunting era.

Before the war, Dmytryk was against fascism on humanitarian rather than political grounds but gradually his perspective changed as an influx of intellectuals from Europe and the New York theatrical world settled in Hollywood: "They seemed to live much closer to reality, and whatever their political affiliations, their dramatic theories were based on Marxist philosophy. Their ideas flooded our arid community, and some of us began to realize how unsophisticated we really were."[10] Dmytryk started attending events and supporting organizations that were concerned with social causes and instigating action in the community: the Actors' Lab, the People's Educational Center, the Writers Mobilization ("the only group in town that concerned itself with the causes and the purposes of the war against fascism").[11] At a school building on Vine Street, he chaired an orientation course in filmmaking with guest lectures from Lewis Milestone, George Cukor, William Cameron Menzies and James Wong Howe. Dmytryk was informed that most of these organizations were funded either by communist members of the Hollywood community or by the Communist Party of America. He observed that "neither the Democrats nor the Republicans were taking any organized action to mobilize American youth. It suddenly seemed quite clear that only the communists cared."[12]

In May 1944 he was invited to a meeting of around twenty people at the home of Frank Tuttle, director of *The Glass Key* and *This Gun for Hire*. Among the attendees was Alvah Bessie, later one of the Hollywood Ten, who spoke with fervor of his time in the Lincoln Brigade in the Spanish Civil War, a clear badge of honor as a "premature antifascist." The passion of the evening and its air of seductive secrecy encouraged many to sign up to the Communist Party at the end of the evening. For 50 cents, Dmytryk received his membership book dated 6 May 1944 in the name of Michael Edwards, containing the preamble of the constitution of the Party including such stirring phrases as "upholds and defends the United States Constitution"[13] and "striving toward a world without oppression and war, a world of brotherhood of man."[14] He paid $2.00 in dues in June and $2.50 in July ("my only financial contribution to Communism")[15] before the Communist Party changed its name to the Political Association and he was issued with a new card. The $5 he spent were to alter the course of his life.

With the success of *Tender Comrade* upon its release in June 1944, Dmytryk was firmly on the A-track, making **Murder, My Sweet** with Dick Powell early that summer and **Back to Bataan** with John Wayne in spring 1945. In April 1945, Dmytryk made a research trip to Buenos Aires, the journey taking about eight days, flying only in daytime with the DC-3 stopping every few hundred miles to refuel. **Cornered**, the Argentina-set film being prepared by him and his producer on *Murder, My Sweet*, Adrian Scott, had its first script written by John Wexley, all three men being Communist Party members. The fallout from that unacceptable script and Wexley's replacement by John Paxton led to Dmytryk leaving the Communist Party. Professionally, however, Dmytryk was on a roll, all of his films earning sizeable profits, especially the Dick Powell vehicles that were keystones in the edifice of *film noir*: *Murder, My Sweet*—$597,000; *Cornered*—$413,000.

On 2 February 1946, Charles Koerner died of leukemia, after sudden hospitalization at the start of the year. According to RKO historian Richard Jewell, he was "without question, one of the best studio heads of the 1940s. He repaired RKO's broken production machinery in astoundingly short order; contributed to film art through the Val Lewton productions and important early examples of *film noir* such as *Murder, My Sweet*; developed relationships that would continue to pay tangible dividends for years to come; and boosted RKO's reputation to a level not seen since the heyday of the Astaire-Rogers pictures, if then."[16] Peter Rathvon, who took charge of production at RKO, oversaw a slate of productions that had been greenlit by Koerner and that made 1946 the best and most profitable release year in the history of the studio, its corporate profit being more than double that of the previous year. Of the top seven box-office earners that RKO released that year, two were directed by Edward Dmytryk: ***Till the End of Time*** and *Cornered*. Four of the others are perennially revived favorites—*Notorious*, *It's a Wonderful Life*, *The Best Years of Our Lives* and *The Spiral Staircase*—with the seventh being *Badman's Territory*, a western starring Randolph Scott and directed by Tim Whelan.

The two years between October of 1945, when Dmytryk started shooting *Till the End of Time* having just left the Communist Party, and October of 1947, with the catastrophe of HUAC, were "the most carefree and happy years of my life."[17] Not only was he one of RKO's top directors but on the set of *Till the End of Time* he met his future wife and the woman with whom he would spend the rest of his life, Jean Porter. While his wife Madeleine, who was in New York with their son Michael, was discussing a property settlement in anticipation of a divorce, Jean "was bringing me out of myself for the first time in my life."[18] Irving Reis, the director who had inadvertently kickstarted Dmytryk's golden streak by developing what Charles Koerner characterized as "an extreme case of jitters"[19] on the set of *Hitler's Children*, decided that he didn't want to fly to England to film ***So Well Remembered***. Adrian Scott asked Dmytryk to take his place and the co-production between RKO and the Rank Corporation got a new director.

Dmytryk's first trip to England proved something of a culture shock to the naturalized Californian. The post-war scrum for space and dingy boarding quarters in London gave way to rather more comfortable lodgings in a manor house near Denham Studios that had once belonged to the Mosley family. He found the English very hospitable, apart from one cycling trip to Oxford when he and his assistant Bill Watts got drenched by the rain and received a hostile reception from every hotel where they requested to dry off. Faith was restored in British good nature when a policeman (from Scotland) invited them to his family home, fed them, let them dry their clothes, and refused to take payment. "Before we left, we managed to stuff a £10 note into a chair where it would be easily found. Then we pedaled our way out of the most inhospitable town in all of Great Britain."[20]

The trip to Europe to make the film was to be combined with a location scouting trip in June to the French Alps for *The White Tower*, which Paul Jarrico was writing, Scott was to produce and Dmytryk was to direct. With sympathy for the painful post-war recovery Britain was suffering, he found Paris unscathed physically and possessing ebullient morale, and recalled the nightclub in which he drank green champagne and was mesmerized by an unknown singer named Edith Piaf. Thereafter Dmytryk, Jarrico and Watts travelled to Chamonix, where he was astounded by the beauty of the landscape, relished the twenty-mile hike from the top of the Aiguille du Midi to the Mer de Glace glacier and enjoyed "the finest non–Chinese meal I have ever had in my life."[21]

Rank were enthusiastic about the collaboration with Dmytryk and Scott on *So Well Remembered* and expressed an interest in co-producing *The White Tower*. In response to a letter from Rathvon making this proposal, Dmytryk wrote that "the prospect of spending a year in this slow-moving obstinate country would make it very difficult to persuade me to make the picture here…. The only positive benefit [of working in England] has been to make me a 110% rather than a 100% American."[22] The main reason for his dissatisfaction at the time was a yearning to be reunited with Jean and he was relieved to be on board the *Queen Elizabeth* sailing back to New York, in the company of the Duke of Windsor who "like Erich von Stroheim, never avoided a gaze but looked you squarely in the eye as he passed by."[23] *So Well Remembered*, with its rawly ironic title, was the first of Dmytryk's films at RKO not to make money, losing $378,000. In later years Hedda Hopper used this film as her main ideological weapon in a print campaign against Dmytryk. He eventually arranged a meeting with her and pointed out that J. Arthur Rank was a capitalist and staunch churchgoer and therefore unlikely to be supporting a Communist tract. They reached an agreement that she would never mention his name again.

In December 1945, it was announced that "Edward Dmytryk, having signed a new contract with RKO, has been assigned as director of *Build My Gallows High*, which will be a John Garfield starrer under the actor's new RKO deal."[24] The following August, the trade press noted that he had been taken off the picture "since his chore in England on *So Well Remembered* will not be completed in time for him to get back here for the starting date."[25] The same item announced that John Garfield was not going to be available after all. The whiff remains of a tantalizing might-have-been. *Build My Gallows High* was released as *Out of the Past*, directed by Jacques Tourneur and starring Robert Mitchum, Jane Greer and Kirk Douglas. It is universally recognized as one of the finest specimens in the *film noir* universe, the genre of which Edward Dmytryk is one of the godfathers.

Dore Schary, who had produced *Till the End of Time*, was made head of production at RKO in January 1947, with Peter Rathvon becoming chief executive. Schary was instrumental in pushing the adaptation of the novel *The Brick Foxhole* from exploitation B-status to taboo-busting A-status. Anti–Semitism, and explicit Jewishness in general, had been assiduously avoided by Hollywood studio bosses, worried of what demons they might stir up. In Britain, *Loyalties*, starring Basil Rathbone as the victim of anti–Jewish prejudice, had been made in 1933. That same year, *Counsellor at Law* from Universal Pictures was extremely careful not to specify the ethnic background of John Barrymore's character, with only his mother's strong accent and reference to his coming from Second Avenue providing clues. In the Oscar-winning *The Life of Emile Zola*, released in 1937, Jack Warner ordered all mention of the Jewishness of central figure Alfred Dreyfus to be removed. RKO's **Crossfire** was brave and controversial and highly successful—and the pinnacle of Edward Dmytryk's soon-to-be-ruptured ascent.

Seven Miles from Alcatraz (1942)

Dmytryk's first film for RKO, negotiated while completing his last film at Columbia, was a reasonably budgeted B-movie scripted by Joseph Krumgold that had originally been assigned to Al Rogell. In RKO's roster of films in the 1942–43 schedule, the A-musical *Seven Days Leave*, starring Lucille Ball and Victor Mature, was budgeted at $561,325 while B-thriller *The Falcon's Brother* had a budget of $134,361. Though *Seven Miles from Alcatraz* was assigned slightly less (budgeted at $127,597, finally costing $134,539), its cost just exceeded the total expenditure on three Tim Holt westerns during the same season ($37–38,000 each). Even within B-movies there was a hierarchy, and men on horses galloped along the bottom.

The vast majority of the film takes place in a single, multi-level location—the lighthouse where escaped convicts Champ Larkin (James Craig) and Jimbo (Frank Jenks) take refuge after escaping from Alcatraz prison. The set is of impressive scale for a film of this rank, featuring five different lighthouse floors as well as the jetty at choppy sea level. The scenes where the convicts swim to freedom with the flotation

Directing *Seven Miles from Alcatraz* (standing in boat) (1942).

assistance of a handy wooden crate were shot at the Pathé Tank, with enough concern for the safety of the actors that the call sheet for Monday 10 August 1942 instructs "Have Nurse on Duty while Company Shooting."

Seven Miles from Alcatraz starts out like a regular prison drama, which happens to be playing out post–Pearl Harbor. By the conclusion of the craftily plotted and niftily directed thriller however, the message has been sledgehammered home—We're all in this war together. How Champ and Jimbo escape from the impregnable rock is cutely glossed over: "And we're not gonna tell you how we did it, on account of that's a professional secret." Having evaded the pursuing guards with Jimbo nearly drowning in the process, their salvation comes in the form of a second rock, and the lighthouse manned by Captain "Cap" Porter (George Cleveland), his assistant Brenner (Erford Gage) and his daughter Anne (Bonita Granville).

With this first film at his new studio, Dmytryk felt obliged to impress the front office from the outset. "Few executives can look at rushes and really see just how well it will all add up. So they look for technique—and you give them technique—armpit shots, crotch shots, shots through odd foreground pieces, low setups, high setups…. Among ourselves we called these angles 'gruesomes.' But they did the trick. When you have no substance, you accentuate the form. It pays to have a few 'gruesomes' in your arsenal."[26] As dismissively as Dmytryk describes these setups, it cannot be denied that they provide pleasure and novelty for the viewer. A shot that calls attention to itself for no good reason can be gauche but, properly integrated, it adds immeasurably to the texture of the scene. The introduction of the lighthouse is a good "gruesome" example that shifts focus most effectively—a pan from our anti-heroes at sea-level up the rocks, cutting to lighthouse level and a slow pull into the window where we can see the three occupants listening attentively to the radio.

The radio broadcast is announcing the prison escape, Champ Larkin being a sufficiently notorious gangster that his name requires no elaboration. The ensuing conversation sets out the film's theme of how fundamentally life has changed with the outbreak of war.

> ANNE: Think of that! Gangsters. Seems a bit old-fashioned now.
> BRENNER: Sounds like the good old days. Remember when all we had to worry about were racketeers and gun molls?
> CAP: We've grown up, Brenner. If you keep playing at cops and robbers, it stops being a game after a while.

The gangsters are men out of time, remnants of a more selfish age. Cap reinforces the point later to Champ: "You've no place here on the outside. We've got an important job to do and you're no part of it. You're simply a bad mistake and what we're doing is erasing you and everyone like you and starting all over again." It takes Champ the full course of the film to be won over by this argument, even after the more heavy-handed Jimbo has been convinced:

> CHAMP: This isn't my war.
> CAP: This is your war, whether you like it or not. It's being fought all over the world by every store-keeper, preacher, ditch-digger—and even gangster.
> JUMBO: He's right, Champ. We're hoodlums but we're American hoodlums.

The casting of James Craig in the lead role of Champ is a handicap to the film. He has leading man stature and looks but his line readings are rather wooden, especially given that his voiceover is dominant in the opening five minutes. Bonita Granville is much more successful as his romantic foil. Anne's character arc regarding Champ is not fleshed out much beyond attraction-revulsion-capitulation but she manages to invest meaningful looks with a surfeit of meaning. Champ initially kisses her when she attempts to scream for help: "There must be a better way to keep that mouth of yours shut." The resulting slap chastens him. It doesn't take long from her declaring, "It's what's between those ears that makes a monster out of you" to teaching him the new rhumba dance that has sprung up since he's been in prison. This gently seductive sequence provides respite from the hostage tension but nicely ratchets up the romantic tension.

The film is adept at misinformation, the most effective twist being when it is revealed to the audience that Brenner is a Nazi spy. A seemingly nonsensical message has been received by radio. When left alone for a moment, Brenner is able to decode with the aid of a codebook: SUB ARRIVES POINT A AT ONE AM. His radio response to the German submarine and listening German agents is in the form of a word puzzle (or charade) to headquarters, the decoded message indicating that he will convey three Nazi agents to the submarine. While in the real world, teams of intellectuals were employed by the Allies to break such codes, the film merely requires puzzle-lover Jimbo, a man so non-intellectual that he can't spell the word "deceiving," to chew his pencil for a while before cracking the "double reverse acrostic." The Superior Race is no match for the Common American Man.

Nazi tics are ripe for ridicule once the three German agents arrive at the lighthouse, though Nazi ideology is treated as incomprehensibly alien. The most ruthless of the three agents, an icy-eyed fanatic whom Champ dubs Duchess (Tala Birell), stares into middle distance as she expounds her credo: "As individuals, we don't exist. Only one thing lives: the superior race. And to think that you can deal with it is a dirty presumption." When Champ mocks Hitler, she slaps him, to which he responds, "That was a mistake, lady. I'll take one of those when I ask for it." He shoots a meaningful look at Anne who understands the reference. Nazi ladies are to be treated differently than American ladies. In one very amusing moment, Champ and Jimbo search the spies for concealed weapons. The camera sidles across to Jimbo frisking the men, while the same procedure happens just offscreen between Champ and the Duchess:

DUCHESS: Mr. Larkin!
CHAMP: Look lady, I don't like this any more than you do. It's strictly routine.
DUCHESS: I can assure you that there's nothing.
CHAMP: I know, I know, but I gotta look for myself.

Such cheeky intimacy would most likely have been vetoed by the censors but all is fair with the nasty Nazis.

Much fun is had at the expense of the Nazi salute ("Hello Hitler!") and "that lightweight with the hairpiece on his lip." Jimbo comments, "I've been trying to tell you these are hotheads—been waving their arms in the air so long, they're dizzy."

However, eight months into America's war, the fearsomeness of the enemy is not downplayed. The three agents are attempting to escape with a map of the entire San Francisco region, detailing factories, hospitals, airfields: "They could blow half a million people right into the ocean." From cutaway shots of those listening to the coded radio transmission, the film makes clear that enemy agents are working covertly in industrial locations throughout the region. If this sense of paranoia is not sufficient to convince the wavering filmgoer of the threat, then the cruelty of the Nazis surely will. The Duchess urges the Aryan heavy Max to "bleed it out of him," before herself brutally beating Anne with an electricity cable.

The film builds up to an effectively rousing climax, with fistfights being carried out on various levels of the lighthouse and on the spiral staircases between them, the editing hand of Dmytryk pulsing the film towards its conclusion. Anne, who had been prepared to sacrifice herself to prevent the plans from reaching the submarine, manages to turn the turn the tables on the Duchess and knocks her out with the line "I'll show you a young lady!" The ending of the film is more universally happy than expected. The foiling of the Nazi plot is a given, but both of the hoodlums at the beginning of the picture survive to the end, with the promise of a shorter sentence in reward for their patriotism, and with the promise of Anne for Champ: "He's an ape all right but I'm going to wait until he gets out and make a man of him." This is a brave new world indeed, where patriotism and duty will outweigh self-interest. It may have taken the entire length of the film for Champ to shrug off the gangster, but he got there in the end.

The sixteen-day shoot of *Seven Miles from Alcatraz* took place between 4 and 21 August 1942, and the negative was ready on 23 October. At a showing for the Sales and Publicity departments, preview sheets were distributed with the instruction to "Give your personal candid opinion." The comments were unanimously positive. "Fine action picture, loaded with suspense. With a box office name this would be definitely an 'A' picture." "Damn fine picture of its type." "Head and shoulders above several pictures of this class." "Way above average in story, suspense, performances and timeliness." Edward Dmytryk and his "gruesomes" hadn't flunked the opportunity and his career at RKO breezed off the starting blocks.

Hitler's Children (1943)

Hitler's Children is Round Two of Bonita Granville versus the Nazis. Where *Seven Miles from Alcatraz* initially disguised its intentions in the folds of an escaped convict hostage drama, *Hitler's Children* bears its polemic on its sleeve, and indeed in its title. That title would become the source of some contention but, despite initially troubled production circumstances, the film went on to become "the champion sleeper in RKO history."[27]

Gregor Ziemer was an American who lived in Germany from 1928 until 1939, spending time as headmaster of the American Colony School in Berlin. He witnessed the inexorable rise of National Socialism during that period and was permitted by the Minister of Education to observe and study the practices of the Nazi educational system. His eyewitness account formed the basis for the book he published in America in 1941, *Education for Death*. Doubt was cast at the Nuremberg trials after the war as to how much of his account was factually objective and how much propagandistic. The content was certainly lurid:

> "Here's my young patient," Schroeder whispered. "Age nine, pneumonia."
> On a cot lay the restless form of a boy with an emaciated face. The doctor touched the boy's wrist to take his pulse. The boy tore his hand away, shot it high and shouted in a delirious unnatural voice, "Heil Hitler." … His lips kept forming the words his burning soul prompted him to utter: "I must die for Hitler."
> "His father says if he dies, then he dies for Hitler," the mother said tonelessly.
> "Now do you see what I mean?" asked Doctor Schroeder when we were again in the car. "He wants to die. What is this strange ideology that can even pervert instincts?"[28]

The book formed the basis for both the Walt Disney animated short *Education for Death*, which traces the making of a Nazi from young boy to goose-stepping soldier, and for RKO Production No. 392. The feature film was instigated by producer Edward Golden who set up a tentative releasing agreement with RKO before writing to Geoffrey Shurlock of the Production Code Administration in May 1942 to seek advice in finding a scriptwriter. Emmet Lavery, whose only previous credit was the ungarlanded World War I melodrama *Army Surgeon*, was employed to write the script, and the new title *Hitler's Children* was registered in July. The production received the explicit blessing of the Production Code—Joseph Breen wrote to Golden on 21 August with an appreciation of the "splendid way in which you have handled this difficult story, and to wish you all success in the production of an outstanding picture."[29]

The film was initially assigned to Irving Reis, who began directing on 5 October 1942. According to Dmytryk, "Irving was rather headstrong and somewhat touchy—a bad combination in Hollywood."[30] The production report indicates that his rate of work was not what would have been expected. On his second day of shooting, he managed 15 scenes with seven set-ups, recording one minute 15 seconds of footage. On the seventh day, he filmed seven scenes with six set-ups and one minute 20 seconds of footage. On 16 October, the eleventh day of production, it was a paltry one minute 55 seconds in the can.

Whether it was his slow rate of working that caused disagreement with producer Golden or vice versa is unclear, but a clash occurred. Dmytryk wrote, "Getting his back up, he quit the film, expecting, so he told me later, to win a quick apology and a free hand. Instead, the studio said, 'As you wish,' and asked me to take over direction. Following guild procedure, I talked it over with Irving before making my decision. He gave me his blessing, asking only that his name be completely removed from the film's credits."[31] Dmytryk had been trying to revive two still-born projects at RKO: *Name, Age and Occupation*, a film starring Robert Ryan that had been on course to vastly exceed its budget and which, according to Dmytryk, documentarian Pare Lorentz had spent 90 days shooting, ending up 87 days behind schedule; and *It's All*

True, the ill-fated Orson Welles project designed to foster Pan-American solidarity. It transpired, however, that both Lorentz and Welles were suing RKO, tying their footage up in litigation.

The offer to take over *Hitler's Children* from Reis arrived at this opportune moment, with no work scheduled. Obviously, with the film in production and behind schedule, the discussions were not prolonged. Reis finished work on the picture on 16 October, and Dmytryk started the following day. Throughout his career, Edward Dmytryk held the reputation as a safe and efficient pair of hands. The case of *Hitler's Children* was contributory to this reputation. On his first day, he shot 23 scenes with 27 set-ups, and recorded three minutes 35 seconds of footage. The film had been scheduled to wrap on 27 October. Despite the problems at the beginning of the shoot, work at the studio wrapped just one day late, on 28 October, with some exterior work, chiefly a chase through woods, performed on the final day of production, 30 October.

With this sensationalist material, RKO initiated a beefy publicity campaign. The 1 February 1943 issue of *Life* magazine selected *Hitler's Children* as "Picture of the Week" and, in addition to a three-page story filled with publicity photos, ran a double-page advertisement from RKO proclaiming, "The Greatest Mass Selling Campaign in the History of the Industry!" It boasted of "the amazing promotion that helped skyrocket grosses in every one of the theatres anywhere from 150% to 300% of the average for TOP GROSSING pictures of the past … paving the way for a perfect record of HOLDOVERS, and setting the stage for unheard-of business for every theatre in the territory!—Now it's headed YOUR way on a tidal-wave of box-office publicity that's sweeping everything before it!"[32]

As hyperbolic as this sounds, it was reflecting reality. The film was doing sensational business. The studio production file for *Hitler's Children* doesn't record a budget, so there is discrepancy between historical records—Dmytryk claimed it cost "a little over $100,000"[33] while RKO historian Richard B Jewell asserted it was "a slender $205,000."[34] Jewell writes that "the picture attracted $3,355,000 in film rentals—more than *Top Hat*, *King Kong*, *Little Women* and other famous blockbusters from the studio's past."[35] According to Dmytryk, "running only in England and the Western Hemisphere (exclusive of pro–Axis Argentina) [it] grossed, by some accounts $7,500,000."[36] Whichever numbers for box-office are taken, the return to the studio was phenomenal.

The *Life* article ramped up the sensation: "*Hitler's Children* is a powerful and dramatic motion picture. It is not a pretty one. Parts of it will make audiences want to throw things at the movie screen. A modern-day horror story of how German children are scientifically molded into goose-stepping and freedom-hating Nazis…. RKO has made a motion picture which is almost documentary in form. For a plot the love story of a German-born American girl and a young Nazi soldier has been added, but Hollywood has been careful to keep this secondary to the picture's main theme."[37] To designate the film as documentary with a subsidiary love story is a misrepresentation, but "modern-day horror story" is a valid claim. Indeed, the pre-credits image is of a bonfire of books, upon which the Ziemer book is superimposed, with blood dripping onto its cover.

The love story which motors the film and upon which the elements of exposé have been hung is between Anna Miller (Bonita Granville) and Karl Bruner (Tim Holt). They first meet in 1933 Berlin as students of the American Colony School and Horst Wessel Schule, respectively, the schools situated next door to each other and the student bodies regularly engaging in fights, or "popular demonstrations" as teacher Dr. Schmidt (Erford Gage) names them. The transatlantic differences are sharply etched in these opening scenes. The American kids are wholesome and care-free, enjoying a questioning, relaxed relationship with their teacher Professor Nichols (Kent Smith). The German boys are educated militaristically, parroting the perceived wisdoms of the Nazi state. Both classes are simultaneously taught about the concept of *Lebensraum*—the Americans debate the issue, while the other class is taught that Germany was robbed by the Treaty of Versailles of "holy German soil"—"It is our birth right to rule." Towards the end of the film, another German character tries to explain the difference: "You Americans will never understand us. Maybe it is the will to obey that is in us Germans. How easy to march in step once you are started."

It is the richness of German culture that bridges the chasm, at least between Anna and Karl. Karl's savage breast is soothed by Anna's skill at the piano—her playing of Beethoven lures him from one school to the other, beguiled almost against his will. Nichols teaches Anna and Karl about Goethe, and two translated quotations from his work resurface as beacons of enlightenment throughout the film: "And those who live for their faith shall behold it living" and

> "If the whole world I once could see
> On free soil stand with the people free
> Then to the moment might I say,
> Linger a while, so fair thou art."

That these quotations are from *Faust* is briefly alluded to. The subtext that Germany is in the process of selling its soul to the Devil is made explicit in a scene late in the film. H.B. Warner, Jesus Christ himself in DeMille's *King of Kings*, gives a beautiful, quietly impassioned performance as a Bishop defending Anna after she has sought sanctuary in his church, where his sermon demands that sides be taken: "The time has come, my friends, when you must choose once and for all, between the Gospel of Christ and the Gospel of Hitler." With contained disdain he denounces a Nazi Major, a portrait of the Führer looming over him: "No wonder you take away the breath of life so readily. The breath of death is already upon you." The lack of histrionics in Warner's performance contrasts with the eye-widening fervor of the Nazis and positions the Church, alongside the icons of Teutonic culture, as the potential savior of a noble Germanic spirit.

The course of Anna and Karl's love is ruptured by their different reactions to the discovery of a boy, in a scene straight from *Education for Death*: "I almost stumbled across a youngster of nine or ten, lying on the ground, scientifically staked out. He was gagged.… He had been acting as spy and had been caught. Being staked out was part of his punishment. He knew he deserved it."[38] Such sequences, though melodramatically portrayed, fulfill the film's exposé brief. An unmarried mother speaks with glassy-eyed pride of her hope that her labor will be painful: "I shall have a child for the state and for the Führer." Another mother is informed that her debt to the state will be cancelled after she has had her fifth child. Anna's horror at Karl's suggestion that they should have a child out of wedlock for the regime is intended to mirror the domestic audience's reaction to this regimented breeding of the next Aryan generation.

The most shocking scene of the film, strikingly shot by Dmytryk, also concerns reproduction rights. Nichols, Karl and Colonel Henkel (a controlled Otto Kruger) watch from an observation booth as women considered unfit for motherhood are forcibly sterilized. It is the moment that Karl recognizes the depravity of the regime. When the other two withdraw, he is left alone in the glass booth. Shot from below, we see the ongoing operations reflected in front of him and sense his resolve stiffen. Even the suggestion of such a surgical procedure would ordinarily have been unacceptable to the censor but wartime ruptured convention. The punishment whipping that Anna receives late in the film was instructed to feature no "unacceptable exposure."[39] Nevertheless the ripping of her blouse and her reaction shots during the lashing are strong meat for a Hollywood film of 1943. The British censor instructed the whipping to be minimized, and the sterilization scene was cut altogether.

The climax of the film tips into melodramatic excess when the trial of Karl is broadcast on national radio for him to recant his criticism of the regime in order to demonstrate to the youth of Germany the error his ways. Instead he manages to denounce the state ("[Freedom] is like a breath of fresh air that lasts to eternity. Long live the enemies of Nazi Germany!") before being shot dead on air, as is Anna when she rushes to him. Listening to the broadcast are Nichols and German journalist Franz Erhart (Lloyd Corrigan downplaying his comic skills), the fogbound airfield providing a coincidental echo of the final scene in the exactly contemporaneous *Casablanca*. Nichols flies out to inform the world of the dangers of Nazism, Erhart prepares for internal resistance, while the voiceover of Nichols directly challenges the audience leaving the cinema: "Can we stop Hitler's children before it's too late?"

Hitler's Children displays less of a directorial imprint than *Seven Miles from Alcatraz*, undoubtedly due to the change of director and the fact that Dmytryk worked quickly in order not to run too far over schedule. There is however a noticeable contrast between the scenes filmed by Irving Reis and those by Dmytryk. Before he was replaced, Reis "shot about a quarter of the film…. Basically the early stuff."[40] Thus the sequences involving the feuding schools have an entirely different visual quality and more mundane texture than those that foreshadow Dmytryk's development of a *noir* aesthetic and sensibility. Cinematographer Russell Metty, in the first of his three RKO films with Dmytryk, was instrumental in forging atmospherically shot sequences such as the shadow-shrouded Hitler Youth rally that opens the film and the scenes in the church and sterilization clinic. A dark visual distinction is also given to an abnormal love scene between Anna and Karl at a Nazi party event where "they've gotten together for inter-breeding."[41]

By its very subject matter, the film cannot escape the accusations of being lurid, but it manages to avoid the dangers of exploitation. Using the word "Hitler" in the title was considered by exhibitors a genuine turn-off for audiences and they appealed to RKO to change the title. Golden stood firm and the title was maintained, his decision vindicated by the scale of its success. Dmytryk, who had been paid $500 to take over from Reis, received a bonus of $5000 and a contract with RKO. Propaganda pays.

The Falcon Strikes Back (1942)

The beauty of B-movie crime franchises, at least to the studios that produced them, was their resilience to the impermanence of casting. At RKO, George Sanders had taken over from Louis Hayward as The Saint in 1939, a choice that maintained the success of the series. By 1941, however, a disagreement with Leslie Charteris, creator of the character, led to The Saint being dropped by RKO, and a series about the elegant sleuth Gay Lawrence being initiated. The Falcon proved to be even more profitable than The Saint.

Sanders was unenthusiastic about swapping one modestly budgeted crime fighter for another but continued to fend off the bad guys in increasingly sardonic style through a handful of films: *The Gay Falcon* and *A Date with the Falcon*, both in 1941, and *The Falcon Takes Over* in 1942. This last-mentioned was the first film to be based on Raymond Chandler's *Farewell, My Lovely*, from which Edward Dmytryk would create the classic adaptation *Murder, My Sweet* just two years later.[42] Promising source material or not, George Sanders had had enough of playing The Falcon and insisted he be released from "these lousy pictures."[43]

The solution was a neat one. Sanders agreed to one more picture, provided his character die in it. *The Falcon's Brother* introduces Tom Conway, Sanders' elder brother, as Tom Lawrence who takes over investigating a Nazi espionage plot when Gay Lawrence is incapacitated by a car accident. By the conclusion of the film, Gay has sacrificed himself by taking a bullet in order to foil an assassination, and Tom has assumed the mantle of The Falcon. *The Falcon Strikes Back* was Conway's first solo outing. Tom Conway may not have possessed his brother's thespian range, but he looked at least as dashing, spoke with the same languorous English tones and was able to create just as rakish a character as Sanders could with such ease throughout his career.

The opening scene introduces the new Falcon with a slyly humorous summation of his character. Waking up to a grandiose hangover, it gradually becomes apparent that the disturbing noise of construction hammering is in reality his alarm clock ticking. He casually tosses the offending device into a bedside drawer. Within a few minutes his bedroom has been invaded by a damsel in distress (Rita Corday) and his sometime girlfriend Marcia (Jane Randolph). During the course of the film, Lawrence cannot walk past a pretty lady without craning his neck or wolf-whistling, and the pretty ladies have much the same reaction to him. He can silence Marcia's complaints ("I don't know one good reason why I should trust you") with a lingering kiss ("*I do.*") At the conclusion of the film, having wooed one of the crime suspects Gwynne Gregory (Harriet Hilliard) while Marcia has toiled as assistant sleuth, it's unclear which of the leading ladies he will end up with. The wicked solution is to have a brand-new damsel in distress enter stage left and for Lawrence to depart arm-in-arm with her: "Vamos señorita."

The Falcon Strikes Back is a snappy, zesty addition to the series. It rattles through a complicated plot involving the theft and mis-selling of war bonds, the framing of The Falcon for the theft and a succession of murders at a luxury health resort, with good subsidiary characterization and a constant undertow of knowing humor. The comic sidekick of Goldie Locke may be broadly portrayed this time round by Cliff Edwards, but there is subtler delivery from Conway, Randolph and Hilliard, this last-mentioned being directed by Dmytryk for the third and last time. The murderous villain of the piece, an additional baddie to the war bond scammers, is the ironically named Smiley Dugan, a puppeteer played by a menacing Edgar Kennedy.

The puppet theater permits some macabre content to brush past the Production Code office. Goldie overhears Dugan talking about disposing of a puppet: "I gouged her eyes out. I just couldn't stand her staring at me all the time." And of another: "I got tired of her. Her legs didn't look right so I sawed them off." Goldie comically misconstrues Dugan to be a serial killer, especially after seeing the gruesome silhouette of a puppet hung by the neck. The last laugh is his, however, since Dugan actually is dispatching those who had cheated him. The marionette content did not completely escape Production Code censure—in a letter of 11 January 1943, alongside the standard demands to reduce the number of gunshots and sexual references ("We assume that there will be no vulgar emphasis by Goldy [*sic*] on the words 'false bottom'"[44]), specific attention was drawn to the "puppet's grind routine."[45]

The photography by Jack MacKenzie displays bubblings of *noir*. When Lawrence is questioned by the police, the room is shrouded in black, save for the interrogation lamp. The image of Goldie's head entering the light halo of the lamp only to then be swallowed up again by the black is a striking example of the potential of sharply contrasted lighting in a crime context. Dmytryk would become a master in marshaling such murky cinematography. The visual tone of the film gets darker and more atmospheric as the plot lurches towards its conclusion, the normally genial face of Edgar Kennedy revealing unsuspected sinister edges.

The backdrop of the war is constantly evoked—Volunteer Knitters for America is a cover organization for the fraudsters; the misuse of War Bonds is denounced as unpatriotic; the wheelchair-confined refugee is implicitly German-Jewish—though The Falcon's conspicuous inattention to the war effort is not addressed. The Chinese valet Jerry (Richard Loo) is initially introduced as a typically subservient "houseboy" but is later permitted to masquerade as the Chinese Trade Commissioner. For this ethnic actor to be able to portray a figure of authority, albeit briefly, and explicitly without recourse to pidgin English, is refreshing and attributable to the fact that the Chinese and the Americans were facing a common enemy.

The Falcon Strikes Back was the last film in a B sleuthing series that Edward Dmytryk would make. There would be no more Falcons or Boston Blackies or Lone Wolves. The film was shot over 18 days in January and February 1943, running exactly to schedule, and Dmytryk managed to deliver it more than $10,000 under budget.[46] The director earned $2,500 for the picture, less than the supporting actors Edgar Kennedy and Harriet Hilliard. By the time *The Falcon Strikes Back* was released in May 1943, *Hitler's Children* had been on release for four months and had become a sensation. He was now bankable behind-the-camera talent and had proved himself to be efficient with time and resources. The RKO top brass shifted his career up a gear.

Captive Wild Woman (1943)

Captive Wild Woman is a problematic watch from a modern perspective. There is much promise in the premise of a mad scientist grafting human glands into a gorilla to produce a mutated creature, but this horrific scenario is itself grafted into a rather more mundane and unpalatable tale of a circus animal trainer, resulting in a curious hybrid with racially insensitive undertones.

By the early 1940s Universal's monstrously successful horror cycle had been devouring properties for over a decade. Dmytryk began shooting *Captive Wild Woman* in December 1942 just after *Frankenstein Meets the Wolf Man* had wrapped, and just before *Son of Dracula* and *Phantom of the Opera* were due to commence. Two months earlier *Dr. Renault's Secret* from 20th Century–Fox had transformed a gorilla into apeman J. Carrol Naish, while at Paramount the year before, Phillip Terry had his brain implanted into a gorilla in *The Monster and The Girl*. With the permutation churning practiced by horror movies, it was only a matter of time before the monster and the girl would become the same creature.

Beating Yvonne de Carlo to the debatably coveted role of Paula the Gorilla Girl was Acquanetta. When she had been a fashion model in New York, the publicity machine labeled her the "Venezuelan Volcano" and, despite her inability to speak Spanish, the Hispanic ethnicity stuck to her biography for decades. She was in fact Native American, part Arapaho, part Cherokee, and had been brought up in Pennsylvania. She was unfazed by playing a simian woman ("I thought it was great to play a gorilla. That doesn't bother me"[47]) but the fact that she is non–Caucasian is uncomfortable to modern eyes, particularly when she reverts from human back to gorilla, passing through a phase of black skin. This aspect was perhaps contributory to the *New York Times* reviewer declaring that "[t]he picture as a whole is in decidedly bad taste."[48]

The opening credits of *Captive Wild Woman* include the dedication, "We hereby make grateful acknowledgement to Mr. Clyde Beatty for his cooperation and inimitable talent in staging the thrilling animal sequences in this picture." What this wording carefully disguises is that these animal training and performing sequences are lifted wholesale from Universal's 1933 film *The Big Cage*. In fact, the romantic lead of the film, Milburn Stone, was a character actor bumped up to leading man because of his resemblance to Beatty. The circus sequences display careful editing of this footage into fresh material, successful when one compares the physiques of Beatty and Stone, effectively his body double. However, the older footage is of markedly inferior quality, often scratched, and in audience shots the female headgear betrays its source as coming from a decade earlier.

Captive Wild Woman was the first of only two Dmytryk films for Universal, the next one being *Mirage* over 20 years later. He was not impressed with the studio: "one of the most unpleasant setups … same level of cheapness as Columbia…. I found producers on the make for actresses…. Universal was the first place where I saw that."[49] Dmytryk grants the film only a couple of lines in his autobiography and saw it merely as a paycheck assignment while serving his apprenticeship. His editing know-how must have been helpful when shooting and assembling the shots that would be inserted into the *Big Cage* footage—one could conjecture that this is why he was offered the job at Universal for this single film.

His leading simian had fond memories of him. Acquanetta recalled, "What a nice man. I think he was single at the time, and he tried to date me. I was dating Barry Nelson."[50] Her appreciation of him extended beyond personal rapport: "What a career he should have had—what a talent! He was my favorite director…. Eddie and I used to talk. Oh God, we could sit and talk for hours! I thought he was tremendous…. Eddie gave me more freedom than other directors."[51]

Regardless of nifty editing, the scenes at the circus drag the film into mediocrity and unpleasantness. They display training techniques of the big cats that are uncomfortable to view today, and at one point a lion and tiger engage in a prolonged vicious fight in the ring. It smacks of bear baiting or dog fighting.

Much more successful are the scenes at the Crestview Sanatorium where Dr. Sigmund Walters is experimenting with transfusing glandular extractions from humans into animals. Heroine Evelyn Ankers is impressed rather than concerned when reading in a scientific journal that he "has furthered not one but three attempts at racial improvement," despite the raging thunderstorm outside and the manic glint in John Carradine's eye. Carradine, here in his first starring horror role, gives an impressively measured mad scientist performance, watching the gorilla kill a man with chilling calm and coolly delivering lines like "Why should a single life be considered so important?" His assistant Miss Strand (Fay Helm) eventually develops a conscience, having "watched a brain that once was fine and brilliant begin to warp, and tamper with things no man or woman should ever touch." One of those things being her own cerebrum which Dr. Walters soon removes from her skull for transplantation.

The atmospheric lighting and angles during the transfusion scenes, allied to Carradine's presence, make these sequences the most arresting in the picture. The mood is not as creepy as in *The Devil Commands* two years earlier, but Dmytryk is making the best of a clearly minimal budget. He would not make another horror film for the rest of his career, unless the blood-letting in the rather individual *Bluebeard* makes it bleed into the horror genre. Even though her character is seemingly shot dead at the end of *Captive Wild Woman*, Acquanetta reprised her role the following year in *Jungle Woman*. Despite the discomfort of the process ("I sat sometimes for two and a half hours being made up"[52]), decades later her memories of having her beauty obscured by Jack Pierce's make-up were celebratory: "Every day was Halloween!"[53]

Behind the Rising Sun (1943)

All is fair in war and propaganda, as far as the Production Code was concerned. *Behind the Rising Sun* features brutal details that would have been considered

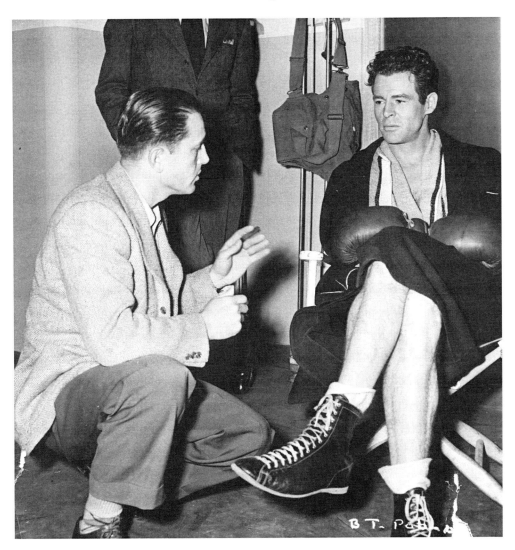

Pep-talking champion boxer Robert Ryan for *Behind the Rising Sun* (1943).

unconscionable under normal circumstances, but which were fair game in depicting the viciousness of a wartime enemy. Intriguingly, this is the only film of those that Edward Dmytryk made for RKO for which a Production Code file was not available for research. Thus, it was not possible to discover what correspondence between studio and MPAA resulted in the sanctioning of scenes of enforced prostitution, fingernail torture and bayoneting of babies.

The Office of War Information (OWI) was created in June 1942 and its Bureau of Motion Pictures oversaw the production of government propaganda shorts. The OWI wanted the film industry to avoid resorting solely to depictions of the enemy through atrocity stories and hate triggers, as had happened in the First World War. It wanted a concerted effort to "enlighten the people in concrete terms"[54] about the issues of the war, the motives of the enemy and the causes behind fascism, which it summarized as "many people infected with a poisonous doctrine of hate, or might making right."[55] According to a study of wartime cooperation between government and Hollywood, "OWI found the studios more receptive to a nuanced treatment of the German enemy than of the Japanese; despite all the agency's lobbying, the Japanese were shown primarily as the beast in the jungle."[56]

In early 1943, in the face of the overwhelming success of *Hitler's Children*, RKO's announcement to rush into production a film examining the Asian enemy appeared to be addressing these concerns of the OWI. It would ultimately be "the only major wartime picture set in Japan that attempted to portray the growth of Japanese militarism in the 1930s."[57] Confident of a winning formula, production chief Charles Koerner assigned the team behind *Hitler's Children*, Dmytryk and screenwriter Emmet Lavery, to a book that had been bought for its title, *Behind the Rising Sun*, with the brief to construct a fictional plot around documented events in Japan since the mid–1930s. At a writers' conference that October, Dmytryk explained that he had wanted "to prove that the Japanese government was bad because it was in the hands of the military,"[58] not due to it being Japanese. Dmytryk felt that war took otherwise good men and "hardened them to the point where there was no longer room in their minds for liberalism, consideration of the people, or any of the ideas which make possible a free government of the people."[59] This was precisely the type of nuanced viewpoint that OWI was encouraging.

Running somewhat against this intention, the film was initially retitled *The Mad Brood of Japan* or, as the Screen Actors Guild erroneously listed it, *The Mad Brute of Japan*. As was Hollywood's custom in those days, against a background of authentically Oriental bit players, the roles of the Japanese leading characters were cast with Occidental actors augmented by prosthetic eye makeup. That multi-ethnic everyman J. Carrol Naish played Reo Seki, a Japanese industrialist; his son Taro Seki, newly returned to Asia after an American college education, was played by Tom Neal; Margo was cast as his secretary Tama Shimamura. Just prior to commencing shooting on 29 April, it was decided to stick with the rather less inflammatory title of *Behind the Rising Sun*. Despite the expectations of box-office success, the film was still conceived as a B-movie, with a 24-day shooting schedule and a budget of $227,000. Dmytryk overran on both only slightly. In comparison, RKO A-pictures of that same slate, *Government Girl* and *Around the World*—vehicles for Olivia de Havilland and Kay Kyser respectively—were budgeted just short of $700,000 each. The film was generously ballasted with stock footage from the OWI production *The World at War* and the Japanese film *Flaming Skies*, among others.

As a propaganda piece, *Behind the Rising Sun* is undeniably effective. If the intention of the film was to enlighten the audience about the Japanese psyche, the message becomes rather muddled in having two of the central trio of Japanese characters switch political sides during the course of the film and effectively change their personalities. In 1936, during a purge of liberals, the Americanized Taro returns to his homeland, having forgotten its native customs to the extent that his father Reo feels the need to deliver an imperialistic boost to his son's nationalism in front of a map of Asia: "Japan is the very centre of the universe.... Who holds the heartland holds the world. For here is one fourth of the earth's surface and one half of its population." Taro resists and clings to western ideals, such as the ability to marry Tama, the woman he loves, despite her unsuitability according to Japanese cultural norms. Stressing the fact that Japan is "still a feudal society," Reo tells his son that "you can either live at the top or die at the bottom" and that "we may use the tools of the twentieth century but believe me, our minds are of another day."

Just after this exchange, Taro is conscripted to the Japanese conflict with China and the hardening of which Dmytryk spoke begins to change his personality. The film pulls few punches in depicting the brutal treatment meted out to the Chinese. They are referred to as "animals" by an occupying Japanese officer who oversees the distribution of opium to ensure a docile population. A baby is shown tossed into the air with an edit quickly curtailing the shot before the child is impaled on a bayonet. Taro's resistance to such events is worn down to acceptance—"Sometimes it is better to ignore that which is unpleasant"—until finally we see a proclamation signed by him that "all women will welcome Japanese soldiers." His transformation is not far removed from the beast in the jungle that OWI was keen to avoid. His father follows the opposite trajectory. He laments that Taro "is nothing more than a savage.... He wants to kill now for the sheer joy of killing," and once Reo realizes that war with America is imminent, he fears that "we are not fit to rule the world. We have come of age too quickly." Such personality switches make for interesting drama but compromise the depiction of an alien culture. Which is the *real* Japan that is being fought?

The film doesn't stint in representations of Japan as the exotic other. The camera observes the delicacies of geisha ceremony while having the characters debate the role of women in this society, from the "privilege" of the geisha's role to "the forgotten women of Japan—the wives and mothers who are the real drudges in this slave society." As with a samurai sword dance demonstrating the war-mongering attitude towards the Chinese, the film doesn't so much attempt to understand as become an appalled, uncomprehending onlooker. One scene deliberately echoes the brainwashed Hitler Youth boy in *Hitler's Children*. Taro and Tama encounter a schoolboy who is diligently learning the constructional details of the Panama Canal. The voice-over from Reo informs us that "his study of the world is a study of the world he one day must master. After all, it is a duty that he owes his ancestors, or so he is taught."

Nuanced performances fail to emerge from beneath the Orientalized eyes of Naish, Neal and Margo, such is the deadening effect of the make-up. The best performance comes from Gloria Holden as newspaperwoman Sara Braden. Sara's encounters with Taro over the months chart his moral descent and provide the initial critical voice against him, and as such she is the main audience surrogate. Holden projects a touching vulnerability beneath the traditional journalistic carapace of wisecrack, a performance utterly distinct from her most famous role of *Dracula's Daughter*. She is one of a trio of foreign nationals (Robert Ryan and Donald Douglas playing the other two) who are tortured in an attempt to prove that they are spies. The shadowy sequences that characterized Dmytryk's contribution to *Hitler's Children* re-emerge prominently in these torture scenes. We have an extreme close-up of Sara's face as pliers are applied to her fingernails and Ryan's character Lefty is strung up, blood coursing from his wrists, before being killed. These shots are shocking for their content and for being permitted in a film from 1943, but they are rendered extremely well for Dmytryk by his cameraman from *Hitler's Children*, Russell Metty. Even at this stage in his career, before he had made a single A-picture, it was clear that Dmytryk had a refined sense of shade and shadow.

One of the most memorable sequences in *Behind the Rising Sun* is a prolonged fight scene between Lefty and a Japanese wrestler embodied by Mike Mazurki. Mazurki was a professional wrestler at the time, soon to get his big break in *Murder, My Sweet*, and Ryan was a champion boxer, as had already been demonstrated in Dmytryk's *Golden Gloves*. The bout between these two 6'4" sportsmen is almost certainly Hollywood's first portrayal of mixed martial arts and was based on an actual incident in pre-war Japan. Normal rules of combat are suspended as Ryan boxes and Mazurki wrestles with some jiu-jitsu moves. It is an impressively athletic scene, the actors clearly working without body doubles, their exertions palpable from the sheen of sweat. Some Hollywood magic has undoubtedly been deployed but for the most part the bout has the whiff of genuine effort. As had happened in real life, the boxer is the victor. Dmytryk recalled, "Even the pro–Axis Argentines cut the fight out of the film and ran it as a special short. Both *Hitler's Children* and *Behind the Rising Sun* had long runs across the bay in Montevideo. The Argentines organized overnight boat excursions to Uruguay, which included a ticket to the film. They did a land-office business."[60]

James R. Young, the author of the book which provided factual detail for the

Getting a kick out of rehearsing Robert Ryan (right) for his mixed martial arts bout in *Behind the Rising Sun* (1943).

film, was an experienced foreign correspondent in Japan. The novelization to tie in with the film's release has the foresight to accurately envisage the post-war period as being 1946, and in it Young is stark in his judgment of the desired outcome to the war: "The Emperor of Japan must not be spared in the final cleaning up of the war situation in the Far East. The quicker he is killed (and the sooner Tokio [*sic*] and the nation's paper-built towns are bombed and burned) the faster we will bring panic and pandemonium and defeat to the Japanese nation, and peace to the world."[61] The conclusion of the film has two of the expatriates escaping Tokyo during an American air raid with the assistance of Reo, Tama refusing the offer of exile with a determination to help rebuild Japanese society after the war and Taro being shot down in his fighter plane. Most tellingly and at the time controversially, the final scene is given to Reo Seki whose last words before he commits hara-kiri are "To whatever gods there are left in the world—destroy us as we have destroyed others. Destroy us before it is too late." Screenwriter Lavery asserted that this conclusion was "a dramatic statement on the necessity for better understanding between the people of Japan and the people of America in a post-war world."[62] Other elements earlier in the same speech by Reo do indicate this intention but, as with much in the film, messages are mixed and the conclusions drawn are firmly in the hands of the individual viewer.

Behind the Rising Sun opened in August 1943 to solid reviews and very strong business. James R. Young had been a writer for Hearst newspapers, an organization that had been warning of the Yellow Peril for many a year. The consequent huge push by the newspaper chain was instrumental in the film attaining a domestic profit of $1,480,000. RKO historian Richard B. Jewell calls it and *Hitler's Children* "the most spectacular successes in a year that would have been extraordinary without them."[63] It was certainly an extraordinarily good one for Edward Dmytryk, who was about to leave the B-movie treadmill behind him for good.

Tender Comrade (1943)

In her 1991 autobiography, Ginger Rogers wrote: "As the summer of 1943 was winding down, I was cast in a picture at RKO entitled *Tender Comrade....* To my great surprise, some of Dalton Trumbo's dialogue had a Communistic turn, which upset me deeply. I complained to the front office and sent notices to those in authority, including director Edward Dmytryk, that they would have to make a finer sifting of this script if they wanted me to continue with the film. In order to satisfy me, David Hempstead, the producer, gave the other actors the dialogue, 'Share and share alike!' that I was unhappy about. I still hold strong feelings about communism because it is atheistic and anti–God."[64] There are several issues with this account, the main one being that it is demonstrably inaccurate.

Ginger Rogers had taken the mantle of RKO's top box-office attraction from Katharine Hepburn in the late 1930s. Her run of successes had culminated in 1941 with

Celebrating his 35th birthday with Robert Ryan and Ginger Rogers (second and third from left, flanked by two unidentified personnel) on the set of *Tender Comrade* (4 September 1943).

an Oscar for *Kitty Foyle*, which had also earned its screenwriter Dalton Trumbo an Oscar nomination. Right at the start of 1942, in the very early days of America's war, Trumbo approached RKO with an original script about the home front, with Rogers firmly in mind for the lead role—initially Pepper Jones, ultimately Jo Jones. *Tender Comrade*, alongside its romance between Jo and her serviceman husband Chris (Robert Ryan), involves Jo moving into accommodation with three female colleagues from the aircraft factory and a co-operative spirit developing between them. When the idea of living together is first mooted, Jo is its main enthusiastic proponent: "We could run the joint like a democracy. And if anything comes up, we'll just call a meeting…. We could sell one car and use the other on a share and share alike basis."

The idea that Ginger Rogers, with her unique box-office clout at the studio, would accept a script about which she had moral misgivings is scarcely credible. All the indications are that she was most enthusiastic about working again with the screenwriter whose words had helped win her an Oscar. A review in *Motion Picture Daily* of the finished film begins "When the story was submitted to Ginger Rogers she immediately grasped the possibilities in *Tender Comrade* and accepted it with alacrity as her next vehicle for RKO. This proves Miss Rogers knows her dramatic oats. It also demonstrates she is a keen business woman"[65] This last point was proved by the fact that *Tender Comrade* became RKO's biggest hit of its 1943–44 slate and earned a domestic profit of $843,000. On top of her salary of $150,000, Rogers' contract for the film entitled her to 10 percent of the gross receipts in excess of $1.5 million, and by 1953 this percentage had netted her just short of $105,000.

And yet, this tear-jerking flag-waver which promoted a wartime collaborative effort was perceived entirely differently through the prism of anti–Communist paranoia just a few years later. During the initial HUAC hearings in Los Angeles in spring 1947, Lela Rogers, Ginger's mother, claimed that her daughter had objected to the "share and share alike" line during shooting of the picture. It was pointed out to her that the line was not a demonstration of subversive content and she dropped the story when she testified in Washington, D.C., that autumn. Many decades later, Ginger Rogers was misremembering the incident and defending the distortion of this effective little film into a weapon against its left-wing creators.

In April 1943 Dmytryk was initially assigned to a different film addressing the home front. Called *America's Children*, it was to be produced by Val Lewton and scripted by Emmet Lavery, and was intended to be a two-reel reverse of the theme of *Hitler's Children*, for distribution in foreign countries: "Working with the OWI [Office of War Information], they will depict the contrast between American and Nazi educational methods and objectives."[66] By July the film had mutated into a rather less flag-waving piece and had been retitled *Are These Our Children?*, which the studio described as an "exploitation feature ... which will deal with the teen-aged of the country, their misguided, undirected activities, the threat they constitute to the nation's moral fiber ... based on the problems that face parents and their children caught in the backwash of the war."[67] When the announcement was made in August that Edward Dmytryk had been assigned to *Tender Comrade*, RKO were displaying considerable confidence in their director by removing him from another brash exposé[68] and entrusting him with the latest production featuring their biggest star.

Having collaborated successfully with him on his Axis exploitation features, Dmytryk hauled cameraman Russell Metty up from the "B"s alongside him. Metty's inexperience in capturing the glamor of A-list stars revealed itself on his first day of shooting Rogers. According to Dmytryk, she possessed a facial fuzz which her Christian Scientist beliefs wouldn't allow her to remove. Metty initially failed to disguise this, resulting in a tense conference between director, cameraman and star. The studio records logged two lost days due to unsatisfactory photography but Dmytryk recalled that Rogers was "very kind, decided to give Metty another chance."[69] The experience stood the future cinematographer of *Spartacus* and *Touch of Evil* in good stead. Dmytryk was in awe of the power of stardom for the first few days of the shoot and found Ginger Rogers to be "a ball breaker.... She's a tough baby, I like her but she's tough, tough, tough. Strangely enough, the top women stars are all tough, and the men stars are usually soft. Not homosexual, a couple of them are, but soft, just soft. The women are ten times, twenty times as tough."[70]

The three women with whom Jo sets up house were played by Ruth Hussey, Patricia Collinge and Kim Hunter. Hunter would go on to incarnate Stella Kowalski on Broadway and on screen in *A Streetcar Named Desire*. She would also fall victim to a particularly nasty racket from an organization called Aware Inc. They would study old photographs and newspaper articles to discover liberal-minded individuals in the arts, or "Red sympathizers" as they termed them. Their inquisitor-in-chief Vincent Hartnett would send a letter demanding to know if they had changed their views. If they said they had, he would offer to clear them for a fee. If they hadn't, or wouldn't comply, their name was published in the organization's magazine, and blacklisting would generally follow. Hunter had never been a Communist but had supported progressive causes, including raising money for the defense of the Hollywood Ten. Refusing to pay up to this professional blacklister, Hunter soon discovered that employment had dried up. In 1955 and in some desperation, she felt compelled to issue a statement testifying to her patriotism: "It was only after I had made several errors in judgement that I was finally alerted to a clearer and more intelligent understanding of the insidious workings of the Communist conspiracy."[71]

The fifth female character in the film is Manya, the immigrant that the women hire as housekeeper. Katina Paxinou, fresh from her Hollywood debut in *For Whom the Bell Tolls*, was originally cast in this role but fell ill on 23 September, six weeks into a shoot beset by delays from the very beginning. The Greek Paxinou was replaced by the Austrian Mady Christians, who had moved to America at the rise of Hitler in 1933 and who lost her career after appearing in *Red Channels* in 1950. She died of a stroke in 1951 at the age of 59. This tragic aftermath casts a darkly ironic pall over her lines in *Tender Comrade*: "Once in Germany, we had a democracy. But they…. Nein, we did not lose it. We let it be murdered, like a little child."

The film was produced at the dawn of systematic audience research for the film industry. RKO employed the Audience Research Institute (ARI) in Princeton to conduct tests into audience reactions to story and title. Jack Sayers of ARI said of *Tender Comrade*, "I believe this is one of the most complete and comprehensive reports we have yet done."[72] As would have been expected for a film about the female home front, the storyline was considerably more attractive to women than men, but also with lower incomes rather than upper or middle incomes. When the survey sample were shown the story without the star mentioned, "the presence of Miss Rogers in the cast improved audience reaction more than the normal amount for a star of her marquee value."[73] It was noted, in October 1943, that the audience grouping that was "tired of any and all war pictures" was "growing steadily,"[74] and that there was a "danger in identification with a tragic theme."[75] *Wherever You Go*, a suggestion from ARI, was the most popular proposed title in the survey, while in both the lists suggested by ARI and RKO, *Tender Comrade* came bottom with the polled audience. The choice of title was clearly becoming an issue, and some days after the initial ARI report was submitted, RKO head office in New York made a list with 108 proposals. These included *Every Inch a Soldier*, *Till Death Us Do Part*, *None but the Lonely Heart*[76] and *Sharing Wives*. Finally, on 20 October the decision was taken—*Tender Comrade*, as originally proposed before the audience research.

The title came from the Robert Louis Stevenson poem *My Wife*:

> "Teacher, tender, comrade, wife,
> A fellow-farer true through life
> Heart-whole and soul-free
> The august father gave to me"

Dalton Trumbo was surely aware of the distinction between "tender, comrade" and "tender comrade" when he removed the comma. The film begins with Jo readying herself for bed in her Los Angeles apartment when she is surprised by the arrival of her drafted husband Chris on one night's furlough before being shipped off. The structure of the film is thereafter the story of Jo's experience living with the four other women interspersed with three lengthy flashbacks to her life with Chris. *Tender Comrade* functions effectively as a hybrid of star-driven women's picture and propagandistic flag-waver. It was intended to speak to the legions of women whose men were in military service and who were keeping the home front functioning. In this respect, the OWI viewed it as a rousing success, sending a message to RKO that read "all cheers and hosannas."[77] Ginger Rogers was to be flagged up on posters as The Chin-Up Girl, taking its cue from the final lines of the version of Trumbo's script dated 25 June 1943: "Her fists are clenched, her head is high. Down she comes, straight into the CAMERA, Pepper Jones taking it on the chin like a good guy; Pepper Jones swinging downstairs as a soldier's wife should, with fire in her soul and thick armor and all guns blazing."

The film showcases the range that made Rogers such a popular star. She displays sass and grit, heart and wit, stopping just short of singing and dancing. In her flashback scenes with Ryan, the register is genial and Jo's comic petulance is defused by Chris' lack of ruffle. The song that soundtracks these reminiscences for Jo is *You Made Me Love You* and that choice gives a flavor of the believable spikiness of their relationship. The first flashback has Chris proposing to Jo, someone he has known since childhood, only for her to accuse him of taking her response for granted and of being a "wolf": "Don't call me babe. Cos it's not very respectful. You lug." Rogers is given humorous business with a hairbrush and slapstick with a hammock and, most unusually, features without immaculately coiffed hair. Her game bluster carries the scene perfectly, as it does in the second flashback when she attempts to arouse Chris' interest when he is trying to read a magazine. She sits flirtatiously in his lap, roughly extricates a splinter from his finger and ostentatiously brings all of his shirts into the room to sew buttons on them. The imperturbability of Ryan, in his first romantic lead role, is a lovely foil to her scene-stealing antics and a sheen of credibility is created by the bumpy nature of their interaction.

The second and the third flashbacks shift from a light tone to Chris impressing on Jo that his serious behavior is due in part to the impending war, and at these moments the propagandistic intent of the piece shines through. One particular scene between the housemates delighted OWI. Barbara (Ruth Hussey) complains about rationing, fails to see the problem with hoarding and admits an isolationist stance. An outraged Doris (Kim Hunter) says she sounds like a "Fifth Columnist" and Jo doesn't hold back: "Do you know where that kind of talk comes from? It comes straight from Berlin.... Mistakes? Sure, we make mistakes, plenty of them. You want a country where they won't stand for mistakes? Go to Germany. Go to Japan." While the scene certainly delivers the required message, the script could be construed as somewhat heavy-handed, though putting the unpatriotic words into the mouth of the appealing character of Barbara is an adept touch. Some in the preview audiences found the message too blunt: "This picture is perfect. Except for one scene in the middle that has too much propaganda."[78] And another: "Too Much Propaganda. The American people are not *stupid*."[79]

The film is distinguished by a quintet of accomplished female performances, their characters representing a cross-section of the American wartime woman: the mobilizer Jo, the good-time girl Barbara, the fledgling Doris, the seasoned Helen and the immigrant Manya. Each woman rises to the challenge of her individual monologue moment, though it is disappointing that the script deprives Patricia Collinge as Helen of the dramatic speech that her talent deserved. Kim Hunter's wide-eyed Doris is an appealing creation, a Stella Kowalski who hasn't yet discovered the textured earthiness that sex can bring to her personality. Ruth Hussey breathes conviction into Barbara, a cynical but attractive character, the one most fundamentally impacted by the cohabitation arrangement, who jettisons her nights at the Cocoanut Grove with their resultant hangovers and gains perspective after she believes her husband has gone down with his ship. Hussey is gifted one very self-aware speech when this news of the sinking comes through: "Ever since I was a kid, I always wanted to be an actress. Guess I've been building my whole life to this moment. I never expected the timing to be so good. And on the staircase too."

Ultimately Barbara's husband is found alive, but the climax of the film brings news via telegram that Chris has been killed in action. Jo ascends the same staircase

A Gal Named Jo: With Ginger Rogers on the set of *Tender Comrade* (1943).

to the bedroom of her baby, who had been conceived on Chris' night of furlough that opened the film. Ginger Rogers delivers an exceptional monologue to her baby about his father, a five-and-a-half-minute unbroken shot in which she is dealing with a breathing infant and genuine emoting. Dmytryk directs this scene beautifully, his camera edging closer to her, embracing her intimacy, then pulling back slightly to show the baby's hand serendipitously clutching that of the actress. The scene is sentimental but merited. Leaving her baby Chris with a photograph of his father Chris, Jo exits the darkened room into the light of the landing and the Chin-Up Girl descends the stairs to rejoin the support network of her housemates and comrades.

This final scene caused much debate. What became known as the "Little Guy Scene" was expanded and contracted in various versions of the script. In one, Jo changed the baby's diaper; in another, it took place just before work the following morning; in several, the speech was considerably shortened. The picture had originally wrapped on 27 October, but after reshooting some scenes during the preview process, it finished on 18 December with a successful showing to the trade on 29 December. At this point, an abbreviated version of the "Little Guy Scene" brought the film to a conclusion but, with the preview audiences polled by Gallup judging the ending to be too abrupt, three extra days were scheduled in January 1944 to reshoot the new longer version. Edward Dmytryk may not have had final say in this tussle between target groups and studio brass but the scene, his imprimatur intact, is a fitting finale, providing both uplift and tragedy.

Murder, My Sweet (1944)

The genesis of *film noir* is a contested landscape. It is a genre that certainly flourished in the post-war years, its fatalistic cynicism matching the prevailing mood as the world licked its wounds after a cataclysmic conflict. But the year 1944 and the author Raymond Chandler are absolutely key to the foundation of the style, with the release that year of two films daubed with the writer's fingerprints: *Double Indemnity*, released in July, written by Chandler and Billy Wilder, based on the book by James M. Cain and directed by Wilder; and *Murder, My Sweet*, previewed at the end of that year, written by John Paxton, based on Chandler's book *Farewell, My Lovely* and directed by Edward Dmytryk. The reviewer in *Time* magazine compared Dmytryk's film very favorably to Wilder's unimpeachable classic: "In some ways, it is even more likeable, for though it is far less tidy, it is more vigorous and less slick, more resourcefully photographed, and even more successfully cast."[80] Both films exhibited flashback structures with cynical voiceovers, a Los Angeles cityscape steeped in shadow, a nefarious blonde female and significant casting against type.

Though a key member of the team that produced the film's style, Dmytryk was not involved in the birth of the project. *Farewell, My Lovely* had been bought by RKO in 1942 for $2,000 but had merely been filleted to produce the plot of *The Falcon*

Takes Over starring George Sanders. *The Falcon Takes Over* was directed by Irving Reis, from whom Dmytryk was to take over directing duties on *Hitler's Children*, and it is a serviceable entry in the *Falcon* series, though lacking the style of Dmytryk's *The Falcon Strikes Back*. Sanders is ineffably suave, and his support Allen Jenkins and James Gleason are reliably wisecracking but it is two uncredited actors who make most impact: Ward Bond as Moose Malloy and particularly Anne Revere as a sleazily pugnacious Jessie Florian.

Adrian Scott had just become a producer at RKO and was seeking rather more promising material than his debut feature *My Pal Wolf*, a tale of devotion between a little girl and

The beginning of a successful working relationship with producer Adrian Scott (left) (July 1943).

her dog. That film was also the debut film of co-screenwriter John Paxton, another graduate from the New York theater scene. Paxton recalled that Scott "understood, as not everybody else did, that Chandler was a marvelous poet,"[81] and he persuaded the studio to give him another shot at adapting the book. Paxton had never heard of Chandler and, after reading the book one rainy Monday morning, worried whether he was up to the task. He remembered that "Scott was intrigued by the possibility of making what he described in our first conversation as a 'good, gritty movie' in the general style or idiom of *The Maltese Falcon*, which we both admired."[82]

Paxton was daunted at the prospect of doing Chandler justice: "I [was] appalled by the difficulties…. Or rather, alternatively appalled (by the complexities, the looseness of plot) and fascinated by the wealth of character, color, and general atmosphere. Eventually, we fashioned the general story line, working together, in close collaboration. I did the actual 'writing,' the screenplay itself. Quite often, I didn't have the foggiest just where I was going. Scott was often working ahead of me."[83] They decided the best way to retain the flavor of Chandler's "outrageous poetry"[84] was to develop a voice-over narration from the central character, Philip Marlowe, and for the narrating of a story to make sense they created the framing structure of Marlowe telling the police about the events up to that point. Consequent to this, they chose to make the film entirely from a first-person perspective, with the audience solely experiencing events as they happened to Marlowe. They approached the novel with the aim of "condensation … simplification … intensification."[85] This involved compacting the conflict that Marlowe had with two sets of police—Los Angeles and Santa Monica (Bay City)—into a single conflict with the forces of law and order, putting Marlowe in jeopardy from the very beginning of the picture and moving Anne Riordan, peripheral in the novel, into the heart of the story and making her Ann Grayle, the daughter of a crucial character. Scott and Paxton "tried to make the plot more coherent by tightening the chain of command"[86] and "were endlessly looking for connective tissue, for ways to make one thing propel us into another."[87]

After his elevation to the studio's A-list with the Ginger Rogers vehicle *Tender Comrade*, Edward Dmytryk was duly assigned Picture 461 on RKO's 1944–45 program. Initially budgeted at $458,000, twice the budget of Scott and Paxton's *My Pal Wolf* but still more than $300,000 less than the final cost of *Tender Comrade*, *Murder, My Sweet* ultimately went over-budget by only $10,000. Cast in the lead female roles were Claire Trevor and Anne Shirley, both veterans of over a decade, with Trevor immortalized as Dallas in *Stagecoach* and Shirley Oscar-nominated for her Laurel Dallas in *Stella Dallas*. Tired of being typecast as willful and winsome respectively, Anne Shirley recalled that "Claire and I put our heads together and conspired to reverse the femme casting. We even ganged up on the producer and director, probably giving better performances for their benefit than we did in the film. But it all did us no good. Claire went back to being bad and fascinating and I went back to being good and dull."[88] Being good and dull was clearly enough to attract the attention of her producer Adrian Scott. The couple were married in Las Vegas on 9 February 1945, a month before *Murder, My Sweet* went on release, but, having had enough of being good and dull, her husband's connections at RKO enabled Shirley to get an early release from her contract and it was her last film. The marriage failed to endure, however. Unable to understand his political stance, they separated over his entanglement with the Hollywood Ten and on 23 August 1948, she announced that they would divorce. Edward Dmytryk's tireless critic, Norma Barzman, who also knew the Scotts, reserved some bitterness for Anne Shirley: "I never forgave Annie for leaving Adrian. He was a brilliant talent, the kindest of men…. Annie, after years of being a mother-driven child actress, found in Adrian a loving person who helped her find herself."[89]

The pivotal casting was naturally that of Philip Marlowe. The production team had initially considered Humphrey Bogart, *The Maltese Falcon*'s Sam Spade, before accepting that he was beyond their budget and aiming instead for John Garfield, who had just made *The Fallen Sparrow* at RKO. They were "frankly appalled"[90] when Charles Koerner gave the script to Dick Powell, the crooner and hoofer in a succession of Warner Bros. musicals who was itching to discard his image. He told an interviewer in 1946, "When the Warner contract ended, Paramount offered to give me the kind of parts I sought, but after several pictures with them, I negotiated my release when I asked for the part of the murderer in *Double Indemnity* and the executives seemed to think I'd lost my senses."[91] Koerner responded to Powell's "little tale of woe"[92] and appealed to Dmytryk and Scott to allocate him the role of Marlowe. Dmytryk wrote: "Adrian and I sat on a bench in the little RKO park and tried to recover from the shock. 'What do you think?' Scott finally asked me. 'It's a challenge,' I finally said."[93] Powell was well aware that he was being cast reluctantly: "My problem was convincing the director, Edward Dmytryk. My box-office appeal was sagging and he could only see me as a singing marine. But I must have begged hard enough because he decided to take a chance on me, and it worked."[94] Work it certainly did. What RKO historian Richard B. Jewell calls arguably Koerner's "most audacious gamble"[95] is one of Hollywood's most successful castings against type.

The moment that most encapsulates what Powell brought to the role of Philip Marlowe is when he is summoned to enter the palatial living quarters of Leuwen Grayle (Miles Mander), his wife Helen (Claire Trevor) and his daughter Ann (Anne Shirley). He skips over several of the polished squares in the vast checker-board atrium as if he were playing hopscotch. It is a display of free-spirited insouciance, at one with the patina of charm with which this Marlowe leavens his toughness, and an act that is almost impossible to imagine Bogart pulling off, or even Garfield. Powell's hitherto feather-light persona, filtered deftly through the punchy poetry of the dialogue, produces a new type of hero—streetwise, resourceful but subtly winking at the audience not to get unduly worried. At one point, Marlowe undercuts his own image in voiceover: "OK Marlowe, I said to myself, you're a tough guy. You've been sapped twice, choked, beaten silly with a gun, shot in the arm until you're as crazy as a couple of waltzing mice. Now let's see you do something really tough—like putting your pants on." The persona that emerged from Powell's performance blends with the description of Marlowe in the Final Script dated 21 April 1944: "It's a contradictory face; both tough and sensitive."

We are first introduced to Philip Marlowe, blindfolded and accused of murder, attempting to plead his innocence to the police. The chosen form of narration, a voiceover that was not merely prosaically descriptive, was termed by John Paxton as "syncopated narration, or narration that is not directly related to the images one is seeing on the screen at the time."[96] He correctly judged it to be "a fairly new idea"[97] and in order to make the reconstructed plotline function, Paxton "found it expedient, for better or worse, to invent some additional Chandler-type language of my own."[98] The convoluted plot concerns Marlowe being enlisted by Moose Malloy (Mike Mazurki), freshly released from prison, to find his previous girlfriend Velma. Subsequently and apparently unrelatedly, he is asked by Lindsay Marriott (Douglas Walton) to help retrieve a stolen jade necklace belonging to Helen Grayle. Marriott is brutally killed and Marlowe is ushered into the criminal circle of Marriott associate Jules Amthor (Otto Kruger). Motivations are suspect and interconnections are concealed and, along with Marlowe, the viewer must navigate the confusing murk. Paxton later conceded that the plot was perplexing: "Many critics still found the film confusing; we contended that we had plugged the holes, and we did—all the questions *were* answered, but things go by pretty fast in a film, particularly this kind of a film. And I think the complaint was justified."[99]

The beginning of the flashback rapidly establishes the visual flair of the piece. Marlowe is sitting in his darkened office as the camera cranes in from outside, a neon sign in Chinese script intermittently illuminating the private detective and providing a subtle foreshadowing of the importance of the Chinese jade necklace. A reverse shot from inside the office provides the sudden reveal of a figure looming over Marlowe which disappears and re-emerges by grace of the neon. It is a bracingly confident introduction to the character of Moose Molloy, hulking and threatening one moment, nebulous and unattainable the next. The shot was complicated to achieve but was performed in camera and not in post-production. Molloy is accorded several of these unexpected entrances—once when the camera pulls back as Marlowe is looking at a photo of the missing Velma to show the familiar bulk observing him; another time an almost imperceptible sidling into view on the other side of a grille that is also casting Ann Grayle in dubious shadow. Molloy was considerably expanded and re-fashioned by Paxton: "I made him more simple-minded than Chandler did, less articulate, more monosyllabic, more unpredictable—and consequently, I think, more menacing."[100] Struggling out of typecasting and determined to make his mark was Mike Mazurki, who had appeared as a Japanese martial arts expert in Dmytryk's *Behind the Rising Sun*. The former wrestler had been spotted in the RKO commissary by studio head Charles Koerner, who recommended him for Moose Malloy. Mazurki remembered that Dmytryk was unconvinced: "He kept telling me that I just didn't fit it. He told me, 'Sure you're an actor—on the [wrestling] mat.' Fortunately for me, he was overruled by Charlie Koerner."[101]

Also gifted a meaningful introduction in Marlowe's office is Marriott. His character is signaled as worryingly effete, from the moment the elevator boy tells of a new client who "smells real nice" to being described by Grayle as a "paltry, foppish man." When he is speaking to Marlowe, the lettering on the window reading 'Philip Marlowe—Criminal and Civil Investigations' fortuitously leaves the shadow of the word "Criminal" emblazoned across his chest. The film is sprinkled with inventive visual touches, such as the black pool of unconsciousness into which Marlowe is regularly propelled and the bubbling up of a water dispenser to disturb what has hitherto been Marlowe's calm-surfaced existence. The bar to which Molloy brings Marlowe being called "FLORIANS," the "L" and "A" of its neon sign lazily flickering to indicate the seamier part of Los Angeles where the detective has ended up. One bravura sequence has Marlowe injected with a hallucinogenic drug and experiencing "a crazy coked-up dream," all vast threatening figures, melting staircases, spinning vortices and dogged pursuit by a man with a hypodermic needle. It is a remarkably effective nightmare, utterly submerged in Marlowe's subjectivity, and rendered with cinematic brio. Powell's performance is accomplished as he attempts to rouse himself from the "grey web woven by a thousand spiders" and sober himself up from the bad trip, and he remembered the ensuing scene with a doctor as the "high point of my enjoyment.... That was the first chance I had had to play anything so dramatic."[102] This is a nuanced portrayal, convincing as a tough guy swimming out of his depth ("I don't know which side anybody's on—I don't even know who's playing today") but possessed of ineffaceable charm, as when he cheekily strikes a match on the rear of a naked statue of Cupid.

With *Murder, My Sweet*, Edward Dmytryk helped inaugurate the panoply of effects and tropes that would come to define *film noir*. Working with cinematographer

Dick Powell and Claire Trevor listen intently to their director on the set of *Murder, My Sweet* **(1944).**

Harry Wild, Dmytryk's Chandleresque universe is suffused with stark overhead light sources, deep enveloping blackness and character-compromising shadows. The director had shown his aptitude for atmospheric shadow in the years leading up to the film—*The Devil Commands, Seven Miles from Alcatraz* and *Hitler's Children* are notable examples. When asked about the style that by 1974 had become known as *film noir*, Dmytryk concurred that this film started a trend of detective *noir*: "[A]s far as RKO is concerned, I think I had a very definite part in it. I think, honestly in a way, we started that style. A cameraman contributes what you ask him to. Before he shot *Murder, My Sweet*, Harry Wild had been doing Westerns and B-pictures with pretty flat lighting. I made a low-key cameraman out of him, and after that he did a lot of low-key work."[103] Director and cameraman produce exquisite effects such as the spotlight introduction of an exotic performer in a nightclub and the concealed figure of Helen Grayle reclining on a sofa, betrayed only by the wisp of smoke emanating from the gloom. Cigarette smoke is used throughout the film as visual embellishment and comment on character. A curtain of smoke drifts past the blindfolded Marlowe at the start of film, an extra layer of opacity that has to be penetrated. Just before Helen is revealed to be the missing Velma, one perfect shot has her embracing Marlowe. We see his face and the back of her head, her hair coiled in tight serpentine tendrils, her hand initially resting on his shoulder then sliding behind his head in a possessive grip, the cigarette smoke continuing to curl upwards. Helen is here at her most diabolical, emitting sulphurous smoke. Marlowe then reveals that he knows she murdered Marriott, takes the cigarette from her hand and stubs it out, extinguishing the demon.

Helen is a delicious creation from Claire Trevor. We are first made aware of her presence by an extended leg visible behind her husband. When he moves and introduces her, she looks up sullenly at Marlowe and notices his gaze sliding down to her leg. Feigning obliviousness to any sexual signal while definitively sending one, she flicks the top of her dress to protect her modesty. In

Anne Shirley steals the headlines from the director—behind her is the script girl for *Murder, My Sweet*, Ellen Corby (1944).

a few wordless seconds, the character of Helen is perfectly established: manipulative, untrustworthy, voracious. When they are left alone in the room, she lures him to the sofa with "Let's dispense with the polite drinking, shall we?" Adopting the same pose, this time the high-cut dress is not adjusted and her full thigh is exposed. Helen knows exactly how to get what she wants. Marlowe is fully aware that this woman with the refined accent and lingering look is toying with him, but he is prepared to endure the sexual attention. Later she admits that she has "gone out with other men. I find men very attractive." Marlowe responds with "I imagine they meet you halfway." He next encounters her when she pays an unexpected visit to his apartment and we see him observe her reflection in his mirror. A joy of the film is to watch the inception of *film noir* tropes such as duplicity being signaled through the use of mirrors, particularly duplicity of a *femme fatale*. Along with Marlowe, we observe the signs and are content to be caught up in their fatalistic undertow.

Helen's lack of integrity is visible to all, even her husband. Ann denounces her to her face as one of those "big league blondes" who are "all bubble bath and dewy morning and moonlight. And inside blue steel. Cold. Cold like that, only not that clean." The duality of Helen is clear, a showgirl called Velma who has had a speech impediment corrected and emerged with a sophisticated accent and a rich husband.

Making sure Dick Powell and Claire Trevor get the point of *Murder, My Sweet* (1944).

During the denouement, having pulled a gun on him, Helen declares, "I could like you, I could like you a lot," and the refined accent momentarily slips and the unsophisticated Velma is laid bare: "This'll be the first time I've ever killed anyone I knew so little and liked so well." We expect her former boyfriend Molloy, loitering outside, to put paid to her plans but before he gets the chance, a gunshot from her cuckolded husband provides retribution for her deception. With the fizz of the *femme fatale* eliminated from the picture, we are soon back in the police interrogation room, Marlowe's blindfold finally explained as his having scorched eyeballs from a gun fired close to his face, before a cutely amusing romantic reconciliation with Ann. It is to Paxton's credit, aided by Powell's performance, that these final minutes provide satisfactory resolution rather than banal anti-climax.

Powell was aware what a career-changing role this was for him, declaring in 1945, "From now on, I'm going to act. I don't care what kind of characters they hand me, just so they don't have anything to do with putting moon together with June and coming out with No 1 on the Hit Parade."[104] His crooner image did not die instantly, however. Late in 1944, the title had been flip-flopping between Chandler's original and *Murder, My Sweet*. Dmytryk told how the film was initially released in New England under the title of *Farewell, My Lovely*, but when the film appeared he recalled that this led audiences to expect another frothy Dick Powell musical, not a dark drama evocatively scored by Roy Webb. Its retitling was wholly successful when it went on general release early in 1945 and ultimately brought RKO a profit of $597,000. Reviews were generally of the rave variety and some writers had the foresight to anticipate that this was the beginning of a new type of "murder melodrama." John Paxton recalled with pride the reaction of the book's author: "Chandler himself was pleased, according to a very complimentary little note he wrote me after seeing the picture—to the effect that he considered the book untranslatable to the screen, or something like that."[105] In fact, Chandler would later say that *Murder, My Sweet* was the best film adaptation of any of his novels. And the opinion of Raymond Chandler, in certain very key respects the godfather of *film noir*, carries considerable weight.

Back to Bataan (1945)

At around the time he signed up to the Communist Party, Edward Dmytryk had his only professional encounter with a future scourge of the American Left, John Wayne. In a notoriously outspoken interview with *Playboy* magazine in 1971, in which, alongside many other contentious matters, Wayne claimed incorrectly to have helped run screenwriter Carl Foreman out of the United States, he was asked why he had taken such a vigorous stand against communism. In response he spoke of social functions becoming "Communist recruitment meetings"[106] and told the following anecdote:

> "Take this colonel [Colonel George S. Clarke] I knew, the last man to leave the Philippines on a submarine in 1942. He came back here and went to work sending food and gifts to U.S. prisoners on Bataan…. The State Department … sent the poor bastard out to be the technical director on my picture *Back to Bataan*, which was being made by Eddie Dmytryk. I knew that he and whole group of actors in the picture were pro–Reds, and when I wasn't there, these pro–Reds went to work on the colonel. He was a Catholic, so they kidded him about his religion. They even sang the *Internationale* at lunchtime. He finally came to me and said, 'Mr. Wayne, I haven't anybody to turn to. These people are doing everything in their power to belittle me.' So I went to Dmytryk and said, 'Hey, are you a Commie?' He said, 'No, I'm not a Commie. My father was a Russian. I was born in Canada. But if the masses of the American people want communism, I think it'd be good for our country.' When he used the word 'masses,' he exposed himself. That word is not a part of Western terminology. So I knew he was a Commie. Well, it later came out that he was."[107]

Dmytryk was presumably aware of the interview when he wrote his autobiography in 1978 but he makes no mention of the alleged exchange. His experience of Colonel Clarke was for the most part cordial: "His accounts of the war in the islands were fascinating, his loyalty to and love for the Philippine troops and citizens were touching, his hatred for MacArthur was unending."[108] As for Wayne, Dmytryk found him to be "truly an amazing man—in some ways"[109] but it was clear that politics remained a bone of contention: "Once, in a charitable mood, he told me that though our methods were different, he considered our political aims were really the same—an interesting

Dmytryk and Anthony Quinn (right) maintain sharp focus in preparing for *Back to Bataan* **(1945).**

comment in light of later events. At that time, due to the network set up by the Hollywood Alliance for the Preservation of American Ideals ... he knew things about me I had no idea he knew. But we got along well during the shooting."[110]

The Philippines had been invaded by Japan three days after Pearl Harbor. American troops led by General MacArthur staged a defense but were forced to withdraw to the Bataan peninsula, enduring an intense three months until MacArthur left in March 1942, abandoning tens of thousands of embattled and embittered American servicemen and Filipino guerrillas. Forced to surrender in April, the men were herded by the Japanese to jungle prison camps more than 60 miles away. That trek became known as the Bataan Death March, during which thousands perished. Dmytryk remembered John Wayne's faith in the General as being unshakeable but Colonel Clarke's disdain for his military superior was backed up by stories of other returned soldiers. One naval chief petty officer told the story of being holed up in the mountains awaiting ammunition reinforcement. They were eventually informed of the night that a submarine would be delivering supplies and they duly hauled the crates on rubber rafts ashore. The only reinforcements that the crates contained were carton after carton of cigarettes, each bearing the words "I shall return—Douglas MacArthur." Dmytryk wrote: "At first they were so shocked and angry that, if they had had the equipment, they would have tried to blow the sub out of the water. Then they just sat down and cried."[111]

Dmytryk found their technical advisor to be naïve with respect to the habits of the Filipinos. Colonel Clarke's idealized perception of the Philippines emerges in a contemporary interview while publicizing the film: "Over here it's hard for us to realize the story book splendour they are heir to. They live like kings…. The homes are like magnificent palaces, million dollar structures. Their living rooms—'salas' they call them—would be ballrooms in any other country…. Nor does this stupendous wealth reflect in the oppression of the simple people…. They have culture, tradition, nobility."[112] He believed that the children played no games apart from baseball and that they would never be seen in clothes that weren't clean, simply because he had never witnessed game-playing or disheveled clothing from his lofty military position. When Dmytryk insisted on dirtying up the clothes of the guerrillas in his film, Clarke stormed off the set and phoned Washington for moral support, which was not forthcoming. Newsreels appeared soon thereafter showing liberated Filipinos in filthy clothing, but Clarke would not admit to having been wrong.

RKO's film was a propaganda piece made during wartime, so criticisms of General MacArthur never made it anywhere near a typewriter. Fellow Communist Party member Ben Barzman was assigned to write a script about the Filipino resistance, initially titled *The Invisible Army*. According to Barzman's wife Norma he was given a meager five weeks to produce the first draft, while the shoot was initially set at ten weeks. With constant rewrites and adaptation to current developments, the shoot eventually lasted from 8 November 1944 until 1 March 1945, a total of 99 days before the camera. Norma Barzman remembered how important it became for the picture to depict the latest developments in the war: "'Believe it or not,' Ben told me, 'RKO is going to synchronize the release of the film with the invasion.'"[113] After the liberation of the prisoners of war, the film was bookended with scenes depicting and naming actual survivors of the campaign, parading cheerfully before the camera as though on a long march back to freedom. It was Edward Dmytryk's most expensive picture yet, budgeted at $1.2 million, for which he received $19,500, while John Wayne, in a big leap of salary from *Tall in the Saddle*, his RKO film of the previous year, took home $87,500.

The film was an important building block in the creation of John Wayne as icon. Cinematographer Nicholas Musuraca was part of RKO's rich talent pool and a master of atmospheric lighting who had already shot *Stranger on the Third Floor*, *Cat People* and *The Seventh Victim*, and who would go on to photograph *The Spiral Staircase* and *Out of the Past*. The standard lamps and focused light sources in the tents and bunkers imbue the military planning scenes with a visual drama and mood that was effectively the RKO house style from the mid– to late 1940s, developed and honed by cinematographers such as Musuraca and directors such as Dmytryk. It was a

John Wayne (right) towers over Filipino extras in *Back to Bataan* while his director (in beard and cap) observes (1945).

style that grew ever more appreciated as *film noir* became recognized as a genre but was taken for granted at the time. Musuraca was nominated for only one Academy Award, for *I Remember Mama* in 1948. The cameraman had photographed Wayne once before in 1939 opposite Claire Trevor in *Allegheny Uprising*, in the same year as their joint triumph *Stagecoach*. The manner in which Wayne is lit in *Back to Bataan* is designed to heighten his status as star, coating him with an aura of heroism, constructing a monolith of masculinity. Towards the conclusion, this idealized combatant is the first to emerge after an attack on a Japanese base, wading alone through water into the lingering smoke of the battle, firing off a round to ensure the enemy is obliterated. It is an exercise in legend-building, all the more ironic given the Leftists who were laying the bricks. With regard to Wayne's later wading into the furor over HUAC, film historian Garry Wills comments on the star not having served during the War itself: "Wayne entered the ideological wars as he did World War II—retrospectively, and with compensatory bravado."[114]

Back to Bataan tells of Colonel Joseph Madden (John Wayne) assembling a guerrilla force after the fall of Bataan, with the assistance of the pupils of school teacher Mrs. Barnes (Beulah Bondi), and involving the rescue of Captain Andres Bonifacio (Anthony Quinn) from the Bataan Death March. It addresses the fact that previously

Where Right and Left meet, there is Coca-Cola: John Wayne (left) with Dmytryk (right) on the set of *Back to Bataan* **(1945).**

the Filipinos had fought against the United States when it took possession of the Philippines from Spain and that the parents of certain characters had waged a guerrilla war at the turn of the century against the American occupier. The complexity behind this shifting of loyalties is underplayed in Barzman's propagandistic script and Mrs. Barnes' class are fully signed up to the American way. From the Spanish colonialists, the class are taught that they gained "the Holy Faith, the Blessed Virgin and the Saints." From the Americans, the children feel the benefit of soda pop, hot dogs, movies and baseball. The school principal corrects them—America has taught them that "men are free—or they are nothing." His faith in America is so unwavering that he refuses to take down the Stars and Stripes when the Japanese come to the school and is hung from the flagpole for his transgression. Allegiance to Uncle Sam is strong. Even the Tokyo Rose–type character broadcasting pro–Japanese propaganda, Dalisay Delgado (Fely Franquelli), is revealed to be a double agent, secretly passing information to the Filipino forces.

A very intriguing, and well-shot, love scene takes place between Delgado and Bonifacio, masquerading as a priest, inside a confessional. Ten years later, there would be much tussling with the Catholic Church over a fake priest pretending to perform sacraments in Dmytryk's *The Left Hand of God*. Wartime meant that greater slack was cut, particularly in the depiction of battlefield violence—a graphic knifing through the neck in *Back to Bataan* would not have made it past the peacetime censors. There is a visceral immediacy to the combat scenes, with the impact of an explosion effectively delivered through a post-production shudder to the camera and a raining down of earth on the actors. One moment in which Wayne's body is thrown into the air after an explosion is so eye-catching that fakery is suspected, but the stunt was genuine—the actor was put in a leather harness, jerked up by a crane and dropped. According to Norma Barzman, "Eddie and Ben invented stunts they hoped would make the Duke cry uncle and ask for a double."[115] Wayne predictably refused a double and performed the stunt twice, with undeniably impressive onscreen results.

Another visually effective sequence is when Wayne, Quinn and the guerrillas conceal themselves in a paddy field, the camera panning along the succession of supine bodies breathing air through reeds. This was shot on a very cold winter's day at Tarzana in the San Fernando Valley and the buoyancy of the actors' bodies kept bringing them to the surface. Several plunges into the freezing water, and several ruined takes, were required before weighting the actors with rocks kept them underwater. Norma Barzman recalls Wayne warming himself with whiskey while glaring at her husband: "This better not be something you dreamed up out of your little head as a goddamned parting gift."[116] According to one source, although Wayne and Dmytryk reached a working rapprochement, a feud developed between the actor and the screenwriter, and "Barzman and Wayne engaged in a private cold war, in which insults and alterations were used as weapons."[117]

The film that had begun production as *The Invisible Army* had its title changed to *Back to Bataan* on 21 March 1945, in order to ride the current headlines. It was Dmytryk's third entry into the theater of war outside North America, and although somewhat less sensational than *Hitler's Children* and *Behind the Rising Sun*, it portrays the Pacific enemy as inscrutably evil. Some attempt had been made to understand the Japanese mindset in *Behind the Rising Sun* but here they bayonet POWs, torture heroic young boys and sadistically dazzle those they are talking to with reflection from a knife. The celebrated war correspondent Ernie Pyle wrote, "In Europe we felt that our enemies, horrible and deadly as they were, were still people. But out here [the Pacific] I soon gathered that the Japanese were looked upon as something subhuman or repulsive; the way some people feel about cockroaches or mice."[118] By contrast, the Filipinos are uniformly heroic and prepared to die for the American flag. Maximo ("Ducky" Louie), the young torture victim, perishes in the arms of Miss Barnes with one regret: "I'm sorry I didn't learn to spell 'Liberty.'" It is a naïve, supremely propagandistic piece but utterly of its time, being released just after V.E. Day to strong success in the United States and overwhelming success in the Philippines. Dmytryk declared himself "a touch embarrassed at its blatant chauvinism"[119] in later years, a failing that he would correct in more nuanced revisits to the Second World War in *Eight Iron Men*, *The Young Lions* and *Anzio*.

Cornered (1945)

Cornered was the reason that Edward Dmytryk left the Communist Party. In 1944, a story treatment from Ben Hecht, Herman Mankiewicz and Czenci Ormonde had been assigned to producer David Hempstead, who had produced *Tender Comrade*. William Dozier, head of RKO's story department, decided he wanted the lightning of *Murder, My Sweet* to strike a second time and so re-assigned the treatment to that film's winning director/producer combination, Dmytryk and Adrian Scott. Neither were impressed with the treatment, titled *Cornered*, that they had inherited: "It was really more like *Key Largo*, laid in the Bahamas, with no content. Now you see, this is one of the things that Marxist attitude did to Hollywood. We wanted to put some purpose in it."[120] The title was retained, the content was retooled.

RKO first assigned someone whom Dmytryk later referred to as "a well-known mystery writer"[121] to script the new *Cornered*. Scott and Dmytryk were both at this point members of the Communist Party, and Scott in particular objected to the strong right-wing views of this screenwriter. Scott let the writer submit the first sequence after a few days and then informed Dozier that it was unusable. The writer was taken off the picture and Scott's friend and comrade in the Party, John Wexley, replaced him. Wexley had written the James Cagney vehicles *Angels with Dirty Faces* and *City for Conquest* and the anti-fascist dramas *Confessions of a Nazi Spy* and *Hangmen Also Die*, so there was confidence that this experienced screenwriter would produce something they could work with. This was not to be.

The plot that the trio of Scott, Dmytryk and Wexley had concocted involved a Canadian airman

With his regular cameraman at RKO, Harry Wild (right) (mid–1940s).

being released from a prisoner-of-war camp and travelling to Argentina to exact vengeance on the Vichy collaborator who had ordered the massacre of his French wife and her Resistance comrades. They wanted to highlight the Nazi sympathies of the Peron regime and the danger of having a proto-fascist police state to the south of the United States. The RKO studio executives were nervous about this choice of location for the film. On 8 February 1945, Dozier was informed that the studio's financial interests in Argentina had to be taken into consideration and it was suggested that the setting be changed to Spain. He was told that the U.S. might soon "come to some understanding"[122] with Juan Peron and that it would be "impractical and highly risky"[123] to proceed with the film. Despite these concerns, it was decided not to inform Scott of the studio's apprehension and Wexley's first full draft was produced on 26 March.

Both producer and director were dissatisfied with this draft, Dmytryk finding it full of "long speeches loaded with Communist propaganda thinly disguised as antifascist rhetoric—manifestoes by the dozen, but little real drama."[124] Scott felt it was too repetitive and lacked clarity, and in an early draft continuity he crossed out swathes, sometimes whole pages, of dialogue. Most crucially, RKO executives were disturbed by the script's political content and requested changes that would remove any element of fascist conspiracy at the heart of Argentine government. One executive, James Francis Crow, wrote to Dozier in April: "I believe Argentina really has been guilty of such things as these…. But does the company wish to do battle with Argentina…? What will the OWI think of this? And the State Department—at a time when the State Department is trying to foster world unity?"[125] Wexley was removed from the project in mid–April and John Paxton took over the scripting reins.

Despite clear evidence that Scott and the studio were also unhappy with his work, Wexley subsequently placed full responsibility for his firing on Dmytryk. Attributing more clout to a mere contract director—not even the film's producer—than Dmytryk surely possessed, he viewed what was ostensibly a research trip rather differently: "Dmytryk had gone to Buenos Aires, preparatory to shooting the picture, to get the government's approval of the script. That's like going to Hitler to get approval of an anti–Hitler story. Dmytryk said he went down there for background shots, but I believe he went down there for their approval."[126] Giving John Paxton no credit whatsoever for the final script, he blamed Dmytryk alone for the film's shortcomings, as he perceived them: "[A melodrama] is what he turned it into. Now little bits and pieces of my ideas remained; he couldn't take out everything. So it still became a fairly good picture."[127]

Dmytryk recalled that "*Cornered* had been cut, dubbed, and was ready for release printing when Adrian and I received a summons from [Communist Party member] John Howard Lawson. We were to meet with him and John Wexley at Wexley's request."[128] At the meeting, they were attacked for destroying the antifascist critique of the film and, to their amazement, instructed to recall the film and reshoot scenes as Wexley had written them. This was clearly an impossible demand, gaining studio permission for such additional expenditure being only the most obvious obstacle. Wexley's recollection of the meeting was that "it had nothing to do with any Party approval or getting consent from Moscow. It was to say to Dmytryk, 'This is a more exciting story than if you take out the juice, if you want to use that word, the substance of it.'"[129] Two further meetings ensued in order to try to reach an accommodation, with Albert Maltz and Ben Barzman on the side of Dmytryk and Scott, but without success. At the third meeting, Dmytryk told Lawson that he wanted out. Lawson left Dmytryk and Scott with the words "For the time being consider yourselves out of the Party. When you decide that you can accept Party discipline, we'll explore the situation further."[130] These words are from Dmytryk's account, and each step along the path to the Hollywood Ten has always been hotly contested by two inflexible sides, but Lawson is generally agreed to have been an obdurate Party loyalist and dubious tactician. Blacklist historian Thom Andersen calls him "the classic American example of the promising writer destroyed by a commitment to Communism."[131] Whether Adrian Scott left the Party after this meeting is unclear, but Dmytryk did, after just over a year of membership.

After Dmytryk's trip to Buenos Aires in April, where he was moved by witnessing a mass gathering to mourn the death of Franklin D. Roosevelt, John Paxton submitted his script on 3 May. On top of producer, writer and director, further winning ingredients from *Murder, My Sweet* were reconstituted. Dick Powell was again to play the lead, Harry Wild was the cameraman and Roy Webb was to provide the score, his sixth and penultimate for Dmytryk. Despite the fact that the $710,000 budget for *Cornered* was $250,000 more than *Murder, My Sweet*, Powell earned the same $50,000 for ten weeks work as he had for the earlier film. Also cast were Walter Slezak, who had acted in Hitchcock's *Lifeboat* the year before, and Luther Adler, one of the original members of New York's progressive Group Theatre alongside Lee Strasberg. Casting the female lead proved tricky, with tests still being made just a week before filming started in June. Ruth Roman and June Duprez were tested but the role was won by Micheline Cheirel, who had acted for Julien Duvivier and Jacques Feyder in her native France.

John Wexley's generous concession that *Cornered* was "a fairly good picture" is damnably faint praise. The film works effectively as a critique of and warning against the fascist elements loitering in the woodwork after the Allied victory, as well as being a grippingly labyrinthine suspense thriller. Dmytryk professed to be not completely satisfied with the end result, "though the last reel and a half is a first-class example of what suspense ought to be."[132] Before that dénouement, Dick Powell's Laurence Gerard plunges into a post-war world devoid of trust, attempting to navigate without the dependable moorings of motive. With Gerard's guard up against everyone he encounters, the viewer is similarly at a loss, deprived of recognizable character actors to assist orientation. With the exception of Walter Slezak, the supporting faces are relatively unfamiliar. Gerard is an even tougher characterization than Powell had given in *Murder, My Sweet*, an unsmiling veteran possessed by his mission to avenge his wife's death. Dmytryk accords him some extreme close-ups, intensity etched into the lines on his hardened face.

Gerard finds his way to Argentina through some lucky detective work in France and Switzerland. Dmytryk's script girl Ellen Corby was given the uncredited role of a Swiss maid, her first appearance on the screen in nine years but the start of an unbroken list of screen appearances that lasted until Grandma Walton in the 1970s. For

June Allyson visits the set of *Cornered* while Dick Powell (right) is on a tea break (1945).

nebulous reasons, Gerard is met at Buenos Aires airport by Melchior Incza, a splendidly slippery performance from Slezak who capably fills the shoes, usually belonging to Sydney Greenstreet, of genial but untrustworthy fat man. Incza introduces him to a set of mostly expatriate Europeans, "a circle of enlightened decadence, a circle without a shred of moral purpose." At a party for this amoral bourgeoisie, Incza comments on the skill required to put on such a refined gathering: "Few people have the talent anymore. My friend Herman Göring had it for one—before the war of course. Ah those were parties!" While the war was still being fought, this line had read, "A few of my Middle European friends had it," but the Allied victory in Europe enabled a more direct reference to the Nazis to be inserted.

The necessity to fight against fascism even after the defeat of the Nazis is a clear clarion call throughout the film. The lawyer Santana (Morris Carnovsky), when he is eventually revealed to be antifascist, spells this out for Gerard: "They are even more than war criminals fleeing a defeated nation. They do not consider themselves defeated. We must destroy not only the individuals but their friends, their very means of existence, wherever they start to entrench themselves. Not only here, but everywhere. In the United States. In England. In France. In Alaska. Or East Africa." Gerard remains obstinately determined to find Marcel Jarnac, his wife's murderer, regardless of whether this obstructs the aims of Santana and his allies. Wondering what group

Dmytryk (center, squatting, wearing cap and with a pipe) looks up from the wartime wreckage at Dick Powell, his star of *Cornered* (1945).

they belong to, he is told, "There is no organisation, Mr. Gerard. Today there is only the right side and the wrong side." The quest that Gerard is pursuing is non-political however and taking sides would only distract him from revenge.

Political content notwithstanding, the style of the film has all the hallmarks of classic *noir*, not least in the type of woman Gerard encounters. Both Madeleine Jarnac (Micheline Cheirel) and Senora Camargo (Nina Vale) are presented as untrustworthy schemers. While Madeleine is ultimately revealed to be an ally forced into a compromising position, Senora Camargo revels in her status as vamp *fatale*. It is a lovely sinuous performance from Nina Vale, an actress with only three screen credits, the first of them under her birth name of Anne Hunter. Vale's introduction is exquisite as she slinks into the room and, in an echo of the beginning of *Murder, My Sweet*, spots Gerard reflected in the glass while checking her make-up. Senora Camargo is the epitome of the European decadence that is the breeding ground for fascist ideology and which is cross-fertilizing with Argentinian corruption. But she also functions as a temptress and in one wittily scripted scene sets out to seduce Gerard. He asks her, "What do you use for morals?" to which she replies, "I think they're a little overrated." But he can't resist the irresistible and having kissed her, several times, he leaves the room with the ultimate brush-off: "Tell your husband I dropped around but I couldn't wait. I got bored."

Dmytryk (center, among unidentified personnel) on the set of *Cornered* with Dick Powell (far right) (1945).

Dmytryk is comfortably in control of the material. Despite the complexities of the plot, he refuses to let bewilderment take hold and keeps propelling the story forward. His collaboration with Harry Wild produces a succession of suspenseful, moodily photographed scenes, such as that between Gerard and Madeleine at a metro station, their conversation constantly and teasingly interrupted by the thunder of passing underground trains. The concluding twenty minutes of the film are a masterful display of *film noir* tropes, with direction, photography, score and performance dovetailing together sublimely. Gerard identifies a waterfront bar as Jarnac's lair and enters it at dead of night. Prowling camerawork conceals the identity of the person who enters the building after him. At several moments, the screen is plunged into pitch blackness, until a match struck by Gerard lights up his face, and an illuminated staircase lures him to the upper floor. It is thrilling cinematography.

Upstairs he finally encounters Jarnac, along with his accomplice Senor Camargo. Jarnac is initially an obscured malign presence lingering in the shadows, refusing to reveal his face except for a teasing glimpse as he lights a cigarette. The sulphurous smoke that rises gives a whiff of the demonic. Jarnac dismisses the responses of Gerard and the Allied forces: "You are a fanatic without real purpose…. I'm afraid the Anglo-Saxon is a poor fanatic. He takes action only when you disturb his visceral

Cornered, a story torn from the headlines: (left to right) Dmytryk, Dick Powell, Walter Slezak (1945).

emotions.... You plastered us off the map once before. You held the fruits of victory in your hands, but you let them decay. We caught the soggy rot that dribbled through your fingers and used it. You didn't understand our methods. You do not understand now." When Jarnac does emerge from the shadows, to reveal the actor Luther Adler, his Luciferian goatee completes the sense of the diabolical. The film concludes with two strikingly violent moments: Jarnac shooting Incza repeatedly in the face so he will be unrecognizable, and, after the inevitable fistfight between Good and Evil, Gerard losing control so utterly that he punches Jarnac to a pulp, and to death. There is an element of bleak victory in this, Gerard ceding some of his humanity to his obsessive quest.

Remarkably, the MPAA waved through this violent conclusion, particularly since in June they had ruled as "unacceptable [the] suggestion that throughout this story Gerard sets out to specifically kill [Jarnac], motivated by personal revenge."[133] They requested the change of Gerard's motivation to "intent to bring [Jarnac] to justice as a war criminal."[134] But the war had changed everything. The violence was more brutal. The themes were much darker. The heroes were more tainted. The scene was set for the flourishing of *film noir*. Dmytryk's *Murder, My Sweet* is rightly acclaimed as a key early example of the style. Less acclaimed but no less accomplished is his darkly layered *Cornered*.

Till the End of Time (1946)

The Best Years of Our Lives is a masterpiece of American cinema. Directed by William Wyler and premiered in November 1946, its depiction of three U.S. military veterans, one of them physically maimed, adjusting to life after conflict is insightful, incisive and emotionally mature. July of 1946 saw the release of another film featuring three U.S. military veterans, one of them physically maimed, adjusting to life after conflict. *Till the End of Time* fails to attain the level of Wyler's classic but it embraces many of the same themes, is intelligent and stirring, and has unfairly languished in the shadow of its bigger brother. Financially, the comparison between the two films was a painful one for RKO. *Till the End of Time* was a partnership picture with David O. Selznick and made a profit for RKO of $490,000. *The Best Years of Our Lives* was a Samuel Goldwyn production released by RKO. It raked in $7,675,000 in domestic film rentals alone but, because RKO charged an inadequate distribution fee to market Goldwyn product, the studio ended up recording a loss of $660,000 on Wyler's Oscar-winning film.

Till the End of Time marked a personal turning point for Edward Dmytryk since it introduced him to the woman with whom he would spend the rest of his life. Jean Porter was a 22-year-old contract player at MGM who had been performing on film since her early teens. In 1944 Porter underwent a memorably unpleasant audition experience with director William Dieterle for *I'll Be Seeing You*. That role was ultimately played by Shirley Temple, to whom she bore a resemblance. The following year Porter received a summons to interview for a teenage role that Temple had dropped out of in order to get married. Believing Dieterle to be the director, she tried to wriggle out of the interview but when forced to attend, she did so having put no effort into her appearance. Only in Dore Schary's office at RKO did Porter realize she had misheard the director's name when she was introduced to Edward Dmytryk.

The attraction was immediate and mutual, but Porter already had a boyfriend, Mel Tormé, and was unaware that Dmytryk was married, though separated. The date of 23 October 1945 was Porter's first day on the film and the painters were on strike. She crossed the picket line and got into make-up and costume, only to discover that nobody was on sound stage ten. She observed Dmytryk outside the studio gates, chatting to those on the picket line. With nothing else to do, she volunteered as a waitress in the canteen, understaffed because of the strike. The production log records, "Director arrived on stage 2:45 due to strike." When Dmytryk went to get a sandwich, he encountered "the world's prettiest waitress, all made up and dressed to look like the girl next door."[135] He gave her a gentle lecture on the reasons behind the strike and why it was important not to cross a picket line.

While on 48-hour leave from the Navy in November 1943, Guy Madison—then Robert Moseley—had been discovered in the audience of a *Lux Radio Theatre* broadcast in Los Angeles by David O. Selznick's talent scout Henry Willson. Cast on the strength of his looks alone, he was given a small role as a sailor in *Since You Went*

Dore Schary (right) visits the set of *Till the End of Time*, starring Dorothy McGuire (center) (1945).

Away and caused a minor sensation, encouraged by shirtless shots in the likes of *Photoplay*. Madison was the first of a new breed of All-American pin-up boy with single-syllable forenames, as well as the inspiration behind a new word coined by Hollywood columnist Sidney Skolsky: beefcake. Guy Madison was extremely good at looking handsome, but his talent did not extend beyond the aesthetic, and he required dance lessons for a jiving scene with Porter. Despite his obvious lack of acting ability, Selznick placed him under contract and as soon as the war was over loaned him to RKO for *Till the End of Time*, "which I demanded that he play only because it was written for him and written from his own inexperience and natural limitations as an actor."[136]

The director who had this non-actor forced into a leading role in his seriously intentioned film was obliged to talk him through every scene, line by line: "[H]e simply couldn't act. It didn't seem to bother him any. Where many a more accomplished player would have worried himself sick, Guy, after a ridiculous rehearsal, would go to his dressing room and conk off until the assistant called him back to the set. It was probably just as well. A bad actor was trouble enough—a bad and frightened actor might have made things impossible."[137] Dmytryk felt the film could have been "exceptionally good"[138] with a decent actor in the lead, even, somewhat perversely given their fraught relationship, mentioning Kirk Douglas as someone he would have liked in the role. Selznick may well have insisted on the casting of Madison if RKO were to be loaned his contractee Dorothy McGuire for the picture. Dmytryk later told an interviewer, "I love Dorothy McGuire but I resent this about her, but she was under instructions, she said, 'Oh, I think he's fine, I think he's wonderful.' She knew better than that. She knew he stank."[139]

Also on the film fresh from the forces and preparing for his close-up was Robert Mitchum. In his first of three films for Dmytryk, Mitchum was cast in the type of role he would trademark—a wry individualist, wise to the ways of the world but seemingly above its concerns, spare with words but rich in integrity. Mitchum had been onscreen since 1943 in a couple of dozen pictures but had really made an impact in *Story of G.I. Joe* which had been released that summer and which would earn him his only Oscar nomination. After seven months of military service, Mitchum was discharged from the Army on 12 October and rushed to the marine base at San Diego where Dmytryk's film was already on location: "I came out of Fort MacArthur, I had a suit and a bottle of Scotch in my locker, and I put on both of them. The next thing I knew I was in a Marine uniform and we were up to take twelve."[140] Dmytryk and Mitchum hit it off together, both professionally and personally: "I saw right away that he was going to be very good. And he had the greatest photographic memory of any actor I ever worked with. If you changed lines, cut out lines, it didn't matter. He could adjust without hesitation. He was the most cooperative guy I've ever known."[141] Dmytryk was impressed at how intelligent and articulate Mitchum was and enjoyed the freedom of his spirit, but he noticed a change when the actor was in front of the camera—an internal switch was flicked that held something back and kept him under control.

The film was originally titled *They Dream of Home*, from the novel by Niven Busch, and the title only changed to *Till the End of Time* on 7 November, well into the shooting schedule. Unusually for a Dmytryk picture, it ran over-schedule by 31 days, finishing on 22 January 1946, and went over-budget by $130,000, with a final cost of just over $1 million. A large proportion of the budget went on the headline female star. Dorothy McGuire is on the books as receiving $75,000, an astonishing sum given that Robert Mitchum and Jean Porter were receiving $10,000 each, and Guy Madison, the male lead, was getting $3,233. Even the director was only paid one third

Jean Porter teaches Guy Madison some moves for *Till the End of Time* (1945).

of McGuire's salary. The figures begin to make sense when a comment from Dmytryk is taken into account: "Selznick often collected ten times as much for a star as he was paying out in salary."[142] Sound and photographic tests had been made in July of Lizabeth Scott for the part but the quality of Dorothy McGuire's performance would leave no-one in doubt that she was worth the money.

The proof of that quality is that she is able to create such a vibrant, fresh character while acting opposite an actor who can give her almost nothing in return. Patricia Ruscomb is the most fascinating character in the film. As a war widow, she could almost be Jo Jones, the Ginger Rogers character from *Tender Comrade*, adjusting to peace time several years later. When we first encounter Patricia, along with homecoming Marine Cliff Harper (Madison), her lingering gaze on the serviceman tells him all he needs to know and, one brief intimate dance later, they leave for her place without saying goodbye to their friends. This is no shy wallflower—this woman knows what she wants. She is spikey and independent, tender and wounded, a combination

Already a fan: Jean Porter with her husband-to-be on the set of *Till the End of Time* (1945).

of characteristics that McGuire brings to life with subtle shading. Patricia has to deal with the overly enthusiastic and emotionally immature Cliff. She assures him that what he is feeling isn't love, adopting the role of experienced older woman: "You're pretty grown up—for a kid your age."

In one shocking outburst, Cliff calls her a tramp for going on a date with someone else. This stinging insult almost terminates the relationship, but Cliff's contrition causes some of Patricia's reserve to crack and she breaks down while recalling her marriage: "John married me because when he went to war, he wanted to able to dream of home. That's why I married him, I wanted him to have that dream. The thing I didn't count on was at the end of the war, John's coming home would be my dream. The war is over, and John isn't coming home. And I'm stuck with my dream." It is a beautifully played scene by McGuire. She realized the potential of Patricia but was disappointed with the result: "I've fought for things and sometimes I have been right. I fought the hardest for this role and it was my least successful. I went right back to playing nice girls and faithful wives."[143] Dmytryk was very fond of McGuire, "but she gave me nothing but trouble,"[144] constantly disagreeing with his suggestions on blocking. Ultimately, he would suggest the opposite to what he wanted in order to achieve his desired staging. This on-set behavior combined with her pursuit of a

Dmytryk (front left) directs Guy Madison and Jean Porter in *Till the End of Time* (1945).

non-stereotypical role suggests an insecurity that the necessity of carrying her inexperienced leading man can only have deepened.

Cliff's confusion at his inability to possess Patricia the way he wants is just one element of a confused and fraught homecoming for him. When he left three and a half years previously, he was in the middle of his freshman year at college and now his parents, in particular his mother, still regard the war veteran to be a boy. The night he arrives home, Cliff's parents steal into his bedroom while he is pretending to sleep, and his mother gently puts his protruding foot back under the bedclothes. When they leave, Dmytryk's camera lingers on his weeping face before panning down to catch him sticking his foot back out again. The scene is silent but eloquent about this readjusted family. When he starts to tell his mother of the sordid realities of combat, she changes the subject, unwilling to let the war poison her ordered suburban bubble. While his father and his cronies keep harking back to *their* war, the Great War, highlighting the gap between generational experiences, Cliff also feels a disconnect with those younger than him, untouched by conflict. Next-door neighbor Helen (Jean Porter) makes her interest in him abundantly clear but her blithe inexperience makes of their four-year age difference an unbridgeable chasm.

It is only with fellow veterans that Cliff is able to recalibrate to civilian life. While in a café with Patricia, he notices a serviceman with the shakes and immediately

Robert Mitchum and Jean Porter in *Till the End of Time* (1945).

goes over to offer support. The scene of solace indicates the depth of Cliff's loyalty and of Patricia's empathy. Another veteran, Perry Kincheloe (Bill Williams), has lost both his legs and is unable to muster the strength to attempt to overcome his disability by wearing his artificial limbs. He can't bear what his former boxer's body has become: "I'm 21 and I'm dead." Cliff and Bill Tabeshaw (Robert Mitchum) try to bolster his self-esteem but it is only when Cliff phones him appealing for help for Bill, that Perry finds the courage to go and assist his friends. This leads to a very moving scene between Perry and his mother (Selena Royle) where she encourages him to rediscover his spirit ("There are different kinds of fighting") and he emerges from his bedroom in uniform with his artificial legs: "Son, it's good to see you in your fighting clothes." Allen Rivken, the screenwriter of the film, recalled in an interview, "I got a call one night from a soldier who had also lost both his legs. He just wanted to tell me that he had been planning to commit suicide and then he saw the picture, and on account of that he had changed his mind."[145]

Bill is Cliff's main buddy, a man who will change all immediate plans for a pretty girl and lose a fortune in Las Vegas on a whim. Mitchum's performance is excellent, giving Bill an air of overwhelming ease with life that masks not only an inability to find his position in the post-war landscape but also a severe physical pain from the silver plate that has been inserted into his skull. Dmytryk felt that Mitchum "identified with this character, sure,"[146] and he let him rework some of his dialogue to infuse aspects of Mitchum into Bill. The heavy-lidded high-living notwithstanding, the integrity of Bill is never in doubt and is crystallized in the climactic scene when Bill, Cliff and Perry are approached in a bar by members of a racist veterans' association. The year before *Crossfire* would attack the issue frontally, this Dmytryk film slips in its comment that all is not perfect in post-war America. The racists criticize the unions as being composed of "foreign-born labour racketeers" and inform the trio that their organization permits "no Catholics, Jews or Negroes." The black serviceman with whom our heroes have been friendly chooses this moment to wander off.

Dmytryk commented about the lack of agency of this subsidiary character in 1974, "As I look back on that now, I realize that the whole thing was handled in a patronizing way ... but you could not confront the issue openly."[147] Bill's moral compass is unwavering and, on behalf of the black man and a Jewish fellow Marine killed in action, he spits in the eye of one of the racists and initiates an ethically charged barroom brawl. This action climax is all the more satisfying since a revitalized Perry is able to use his boxing skills and land some knockout blows: "Push them to me!"

The closing seconds of the film unfortunately chime more with the banality of its title than with the political and psychological content that has buoyed the film. *Till the End of Time* was chosen to replace *They Dream of Home* when it was decided to lace the film with a song of that title, based on Chopin's Polonaise Op. 53. It is the love theme for Cliff and Patricia, and it swells on the soundtrack at the film's conclusion as they run to each other and embrace, brushing away neatly in that clinch all of the relationship complexities that the viewer has observed. It is a regrettably trite final image.

And yet happy endings of a kind do exist. The infatuation that Eddie felt for Jean is discernible onscreen, in the two scenes showcasing the ice-skating and dancing prowess of his supporting actress. In the dance sequence, Jean's jitterbugging ability carries Guy in much the same way as Dorothy carried him in the dialogue scenes, but it is a charming routine—as is Porter's performance overall, aided by the adoring camera lens of her director. Mel Tormé fell by the wayside and Eddie and Jean became an enduring couple, still together upon his death in 1999.

So Well Remembered (1947)

Over images of rainy North of England townscapes, the voice of James Hilton intones the prologue: "In the mill town of Browdley, as elsewhere, the people heard Hitler's death rattle in the throat of the wireless, listened to each violent convulsion. They would have preferred one clean dramatic note of triumph, but they took what they got and made the best of it—as they had been doing for six years—and for years before that." Hilton's novels had provided Hollywood with the raw material for several notable successes since the mid–1930s—*Lost Horizon, Goodbye, Mr. Chips* and

Dmytryk, Martha Scott and John Mills (seated left to right) receive a toast from an unidentified celebrant while making *So Well Remembered* (1946).

Random Harvest. The Lancashire-born author drew upon his youth in the mill town of Leigh for *So Well Remembered*, a family saga with a political edge, published in 1945 and hewn from the same socially progressive coalface as *The Stars Look Down* and *Love on the Dole*. The film version was the first in what was intended to be a series of co-productions between RKO and the Rank Organisation. RKO chief Charles Koerner had travelled to England just after the war had ended and had struck a deal with J. Arthur Rank that enabled RKO to utilize some of its English assets and gave the British studio the benefit of American distribution. Adrian Scott then developed the production with John Paxton as writer and Irving Reis as director. When Reis decided he didn't want to travel to Europe, Scott invited his old comrade onboard, and Dmytryk made his first trip to England.

Dmytryk found Rank a refreshing alternative to the Hollywood studio heads: "The great industrialist and revitalizer of the British motion-picture industry was a very down-to-earth man. Though he had been to the United States several times since the war and could have outfitted himself completely, he still wore the shirts with frayed collars and cuffs and the frayed ties that adorned the other Britishers who had still to practice austerity at home."[148] The relationship with Rank was cordial and the Methodist mogul would later become Dmytryk's savior during his enforced sojourn in England. Studio work on *So Well Remembered* was performed on the soundstages of Denham, at the same time as another political saga of the Left was being filmed by the Boulting Brothers at the same studios. *Fame is the Spur* is the tale of a Labour politician who, through the course of a long career between the 1880s and the 1930s, loses the socialist fervor that initially fired him and succumbs to a life of accommodation with the Right. The Boultings' film is less successful than Dmytryk's, but with the nightmare of HUAC looming on the horizon, there is a certain irony that the social idealism of *So Well Remembered*, which would be used against Edward Dmytryk in those hearings, is less representative of the director's journey than the story arc of the protagonist of *Fame is the Spur*.

A suitable location had to be found as backdrop to the saga which stretched from 1919 to 1945. Unfortunately, by 1945 the Nazi Blitz had permanently altered the urban landscape of many industrial towns in the North of England. In July 1946 Dmytryk scouted for locations with the production team but the bomb damage put paid to Birmingham, Leeds and Manchester. When they arrived in Macclesfield, Dmytryk asked a policeman where they could find a slum section: "He looked at me with a very small smile on his face. 'I don't think you'll find anything else in Macclesfield,' he said."[149] It was, and is, a great source of civic pride to Maxonians that their town was chosen as location for a large-scale Hollywood production, the RKO radio mast being inherently more impressive to Brits than the Rank man with the gong. A book glancing back affectionately at the town's history is titled *Macclesfield—So Well Remembered* and relates the excitement of being an extra on the film. Extras were paid "ten shillings, or perhaps even two pounds or so,"[150] a Hollywood extravagance since "they would have done it for nowt."[151] Dmytryk found "the unfailing good nature of the townspeople"[152] extraordinary, and even when the Macclesfield fire brigade dowsed a crowd of extras by turning their hosepipes up in the air on an inconveniently sunny day, "it was a lark."[153]

Somewhat echoing the plot of *The Stars Look Down*, Martha Scott plays Olivia Channing, the upwardly focused wife of George Boswell (John Mills), a crusading newspaper editor, whose zeal in addressing local deprivation with his friend Dr. Richard Whiteside (Trevor Howard) drives a wedge into his marriage and exposes the ruthlessness of his spouse. The script is a showcase for John Paxton's skill at adaptation. The James Hilton novel is soused in bald prose, its narrative a stream of incident without insight. Paxton has filleted the most interesting of these incidents from the book and constructed a persuasive, dramatically coherent screenplay from them. The film's most compelling character, Dr. Whiteside, barely features in the novel, is tangential to the action and is dead before the midpoint. Trevor Howard, in the middle of his purple patch of classics that stretched from *Brief Encounter* in 1945 to *The Third Man* in 1949, produces the finest acting in the film with an impassioned, inspired performance as Whiteside. His delivery of Paxton's astute speech about alcoholism ("the dire bubonic plague of the soul") is riveting:

> "I shall quickly outline the etiology of alcoholism, how the disease begins. First the weight of the world settles on you. A heavy depression, like the soft underbelly of an elephant. In the distance you see a way out, a promising little exit, small and round, about the right size to fit a cork. It's cosy inside the bottle. The light is soft and green. What happens gradually is that the alcohol breaks down the fatty tissue between the cells and they run together like raspberry jam.

Dmytryk (far left) directs John Mills (center) on location in Macclesfield for *So Well Remembered* (1946).

> One cell that had character blends into another that hasn't. It happens so slowly you don't even know it's going on. And you like it while it's happening, that's the worst of it. You love it, the exhilarating process of decay."

Perhaps Howard was able to bring some of his own issues with alcohol to the role. It is to the film's credit that even when Whiteside overcomes momentary crises with the bottle, it is acknowledged that this is a battle not won but constantly being fought. Certainly, the suggestion that a doctor could proceed with his career as a functioning alcoholic was problematic to the Production Code office, whose recommendation was to "tone down considerably, if not to omit entirely, the suggestion that Doctor Whiteside is drunk through a considerable portion of the story."[154]

The film's strong sense of place is partially attributable to Freddie Young's masterly skill at photographing the environs of Browdley's dark satanic mills. The cobbled hills and terraced streets of Macclesfield are captured through veils of rainfall and form the perfect backdrop for a story of urban deprivation. Young's work slots into the rich monochrome continuum of Northern English industrial photography stretching from the John Grierson school of documentarists in the early 1930s through to the 1960s with Freddie Francis on *Sons and Lovers* and Walter Lassally on *A Taste of Honey*. The documentary tradition is referenced in a sharply edited

John Mills and Patricia Roc on set among supporting professionals at Denham Studios for *So Well Remembered* (1946).

sequence when the silent cotton mills of the town are pushed back into service at the onset of war and the workers are observed at their skilled and, as it turns out, hazardous work. Young enjoyed the change of style and the efficiency of the American directors he worked with at British studios in the late 1940s (Dmytryk, George Cukor, Joseph L. Mankiewicz) and the art director on the film, Laurence Williams, was specifically requested by RKO, presumably impressed with his work on his previous film, *Brief Encounter*. Williams' sets of the backstreets of Browdley and the interiors of mansions and newspaper offices are impressive and merge perfectly with the location work in Macclesfield. Dmytryk and Williams remained lifelong friends.

Two of the most striking moments in *So Well Remembered* arise from the fluidity of Dmytryk's direction in capturing the scale of Williams' sets. A storm of import has been signaled by a smooth pan up to rain falling on a skylight. At the Channing manor house, the camera watches Olivia enter via the front door and slowly cranes rightwards up the ivy-covered masonry to stop at the first-floor window of Olivia's bedroom. Her father enters and they have a disagreement, unheard but witnessed by the viewer through the rain-streaked glass, before he leaves in a temper and she comes towards the window and towards the camera. Her father is about to drive off to his death. Hilton is given narration voiceover, but the power of the moment lies in the dialogue-free visuals. Later in the film, George is given the news that his and Olivia's

Dmytryk, Patricia Roc and Richard Carlson on location for *So Well Remembered* (1946).

son has contracted diphtheria after she failed to get him vaccinated. In a beautifully executed shot, a mirror image of the one just described, the camera starts seemingly inside the child's bedroom as he is being examined with some urgency by Dr. Whiteside. It then pulls away from the upper window and makes a very slow movement rightwards down the much more modest facade of the Boswells' home to ground level where it pulls in on George looking mournfully out the window. Whiteside enters and, again unheard through the glass, informs George that his child has died. Blinking away tears, George leaves the room to meet his disconsolate wife, watched by Whiteside and by the viewer on the other side of the window. Camerawork, acting, Freddie Young's lighting and Hanns Eisler's music coalesce to effect a most moving moment.

John Mills is dependably excellent as George Boswell, a man with ramrod straight morality which is only partially bent by the blind spot of his love for Olivia. Dmytryk loved working with him and remembered their playing pool, at the very beginning of their acquaintance, in their hotel at Buxton, when the director pulled off a tricky shot: "'Why, you lucky sonofabitch!' screamed Mills, with typical British understatement. I knew we were going to get along just fine. I have since done a few other films with John. I will never work with a finer actor or a better man."[155] The performance of Martha Scott is more problematic. The script attempts to deal with

Dmytryk (with pipe) captures working-class life in Macclesfield for *So Well Remembered* (1946).

Scott's American-tinged accent by explaining that she received part of her education in the United States but the excuse rings hollow and her tightly wound, occasionally histrionic Olivia is an awkward match with the ease of Mills' George. Scott's inability to convince as a member of the North of England gentry is matched by Patricia Roc's lack of credibility as member of the lower classes. Julie is a girl adopted by Whiteside when her mother dies in childbirth and is played as a toddler in one brief scene by John Mills' daughter Juliet. Roc's refined accent as the adult Julie is utterly at odds with the humble circumstances in which she was raised and the film squanders conviction in its final third when it focuses on the romance between Julie and Charles, Olivia's son by a second marriage, played by American Richard Carlson. The transatlantic casting is understandable given the production circumstances of the film, but it is at the cost of authenticity.

Paxton's scripting skill is clearest in the first two thirds of the film, where the combination of social comment with domestic drama is most successful. George and Whiteside's crusade for better housing in the town is stymied by the intransigence of the ruling class epitomized by the Channings. From their vantage point high above Browdley, John Channing (Frederick Leister) fools himself into visualizing the spires and chimneys as cathedrals, while his daughter Olivia is repelled by the urban sprawl that her family helped create and that resembles "a filthy sludge eating at the fringes of the green hills." The lack of proper housing and sanitation leads to an outbreak of diphtheria, announced by a dramatic camera move from George making a speech in the rain into the bedroom of the worried mother (Joan Hickson) of a sickly child. The passages depicting the progress of the disease are well directed and scripted with social conscience worn on sleeve. Whiteside gives his reason for taking on the infant Julie: "This is a clinical experiment of mine—to see if it's possible to get a child past the age of ten in this town." The treatment of the war wounded becomes a theme in the latter part of the picture, when Charles suffers facial scarring after his RAF plane crashes. The tussle for control of him between Julie and the domineering Olivia comes to a head on another stormy night, that of V.E. Day. When Olivia discovers that the couple have married against her wishes, the whistles and sirens suddenly signaling the end of the war are a cacophonous assault on her scheming, as sharp a rebuke as the slaps that uncharacteristically erupt from George. It is a strong denouement, nicely offset by Whiteside's toast: "We'll drink to victory, however sad it tastes." The PCA objected to the penultimate line of the film, which indicated that a honeymoon couple might be enjoying themselves: "I don't suppose the young folks upstairs will be wanting their tea too early in the morning, will they?" Fortunately, the line was preserved, as much for its sly humor as for its confirmation that John Paxton had grasped the centrality of tea to British existence.

Despite its qualities, *So Well Remembered* is the least of the three films Edward Dmytryk made in England in the 1940s, perhaps partially due to his frustration at the working practices which he compared unfavorably to studio practices in Hollywood. The film is bold in its espousal of social issues but could scarcely be called a communist tract. It was shot between July and October 1946, and 1947 swept in with a whiff of red hysteria in its nostrils. Gossip columnist Hedda Hopper took heavily against the film, and though it was released in the UK in July, its release in the U.S. was pushed back until November, long after *Crossfire*. By that stage, the HUAC hearings had taken place and it became terminally tainted by the blackened reputation of its makers. In May 1948, Howard Hughes took controlling interest in RKO and oversaw an edit of *So Well Remembered* that Dmytryk disowned. The film ultimately lost $378,000 in a particularly rough year for RKO: "Not a single picture released between January and April 1948 earned a profit"[156] and *I Remember Mama* lost over $1 million. The title of the film proved to be rather ironic and it disappeared from circulation for decades. It did however receive its Macclesfield premiere at the Majestic cinema in 1948, and for a contingent in that town it is still fondly remembered.

Crossfire (1947)

"I like you, Mr. Edwards," Monty said, and slapped Mr. Edwards on the knee familiarly. Jeff saw the man's face go white. Floyd nudged Jeff and whispered: "We're set, buddy. Set. I ain't beaten up a queer in I don't know how long."[157]

Dmytryk (second from right with three other attentive film professionals) directs a close-up on Robert Young, speaking to Robert Mitchum (both seated) in *Crossfire* (1947).

The murder that is committed in *The Brick Foxhole*, a 1945 novel by fledgling screenwriter and future director Richard Brooks, is a homophobic hate crime, but the book seethes with racial hatred and religious vitriol. The Floyd who is so excited about the prospective queer-bashing digs deeper into prejudice later at the home of their gay host Mr. Edwards: "Well, the war'll be over, won't it? An' we'll be a-comin' home. An' we'll be a-comin' home with our rifles and things. An' we'll put the nigger in his place for good. You watch. First nigger looks cross-eyed at anybody, we string the bastard up."[158] At a boxing match between Whitey ("They were proud of him because he was one of them"[159]) and a Jewish fighter called Max Brock, Monty is braying for blood: "I hope the little sheeny gets murdered. That'll teach him a lesson. Him and his kike father…. Let's go early and get a couple of close seats. I want to see little Maxie's blood splash."[160]

Brooks paints a brutal and discomfiting picture of ennui and prejudice among the soldiers holed up in the brick foxhole of a barracks near Washington, D.C., at the tail end of the war. They yearn for the combat taking place in faraway continents, if only to relieve the tedium of their regimented existence. On weekend release, they head for the city on the hunt for available women, renting hotel rooms as a trio and assigning rotating half hour slots to use the room with their pick-ups. One soldier,

Jeff Mitchell, consumed with jealousy at the imagined infidelity of his wife, visits a brothel and has sad, unfulfilling sex with a prostitute called Ginny ("He thought she couldn't be any more than sixteen"[161]) while in the next room another prostitute is being whipped with a rubber switch by a regular client, a naval officer ("'His money's good,' she said. 'He pays plenty'"[162]). A Catholic is a "Papist bastid,"[163] a homosexual is a "sexual pervert,"[164] Jews are "Christ-killers."[165] This is an unvarnished view of military life, related by someone who had experienced it first-hand. It is no wonder Joseph Breen of the Production Code wrote to RKO after the studio had purchased the rights, "We have read the novel, *The Brick Foxhole*, and, as you can well understand, the story is thoroughly and completely unacceptable, on a dozen or more counts. It, also, goes without saying that any motion picture following, even remotely, along the lines in the novel, could not be approved."[166]

From such an inauspicious root grew the first Hollywood film to address anti–Semitism and one of the very first to even have the word "Jew" uttered onscreen. The novel was brought to the attention of Adrian Scott by Edmund North, future screenwriter of *In a Lonely Place*, *The Day the Earth Stood Still* and *Patton*, but then still a major in the U.S. Signal Corps. North recognized in the book the true tang of wartime military existence, but Scott latched onto the seam of prejudice so rawly exposed and cajoled John Paxton into adapting the second half of the book into a screenplay. Paxton produced a First Rough Draft Continuity script on 27 December 1946 that was titled *Cradle of Fear*. The story centered around the killing of a Jewish civilian called Samuels and, in the initial treatment, the action that took place in Samuels' apartment was related from three perspectives. This structure was explored fully in *Rashomon* three years later, and it is something of a missed opportunity that this novel narrative style was not developed in *Crossfire*, though an element of it remains in two slightly conflicting flashbacks and in the script direction that makes unreliable narrator Monty appear more attractive in his flashback. Early versions of the script display Monty's wide-ranging racism more openly, signaling earlier that he is the murderer of Samuels. They also add an element of gay pick-up in Samuels' interaction with Mitchell, who will be suspected of the murder and pursued, even though there is no pick-up in *The Brick Foxhole*. Mitchell says in voiceover, "Suddenly the most important thing in the world [to Samuels] was for me to hear some records he had. It seemed important to me too."[167] The script adds, "Samuels puts his arm around Mitchell's shoulder, saying something to Miss Lewis, who answers, nods, smiles, turns back and starts for the lobby entrance."[168]

Initially RKO President R. Peter Rathvon was unenthusiastic about Scott's proposal and Paxton's refashioning of *The Brick Foxhole* into *Cradle of Fear*, suggesting it would make a "good exploitation picture."[169] He told incoming production chief Dore Schary, who was Jewish, "I doubt that it has the least value as a document against racial intolerance and I think there is a chance it might backfire and have an effect opposite to that intended."[170] This attitude reflected the decades-long reluctance of studio heads, most of whom were Jewish, to address this particular prejudice and draw attention to themselves. Schary saw the potential of the film to be a socially progressive crowd-pleaser and, fired by the information that Elia Kazan was preparing *Gentleman's Agreement*, with anti–Semitism as its subject-matter, at 20th

Century–Fox, pushed it rapidly into production.[171] John Paxton later recalled the heady days of early 1947: "The single most important factor in the making of *Crossfire*, to me, was the speed and excitement with which it was made. The day Schary approved the project, a little parade went off around the lot (the writer just tagged along) looking for sets that could be borrowed or adapted, or stolen. An unusual procedure with front office blessing.... Because of the competitive rush (to beat out *Gentleman's Agreement*) there really wasn't time for a lot of the heavy thinking and consideration that normally went into a film. Consequently—fortunately from my particular point of view—there was much less mucking about with the script than anything else I have ever been involved with."[172]

Joseph Breen reacted positively to the submitted screenplay, but in a letter of 27 February 1947 suggested a toning down of expressions of racism—"nigger," "kikes" and "Yid" were all recommended to be changed, though notably not forbidden. All these usages were cut from the final script. The released film came under some criticism for not addressing racism against African Americans, and for not mentioning blacks in a speech about various forms of prejudice, and Breen's blue-pencil appears to have been strictly adhered to. It is noteworthy, however, that playing in the background in the dance bar where Ginny works is *Shine*, a song tied to the African American experience. Paxton attributes this choice, "an intentional bitter irony,"[173] to Dmytryk, "the jazz buff and very knowledgeable."[174] Explicit portrayal of prostitution had obviously been erased from the script and Ginny was made over into a dance hostess. Yet gently suggestive dialogue between Mitchell and Ginny still had to be omitted (to Mitchell's "You know what I'd like to do?" Ginny's response of "keep it clean"[175] was changed into a knowing snort), as had any "suggestion of a 'pansy' characterization about Samuels or his relationship with the soldiers."[176] Along with objections to over-depiction of the act of drinking and to the words "lousy" and "nuts," Breen also suggested "changing Mary's line, 'everything will be all right,' so as to avoid any possible flavor of condonation [of her husband's flirtation with Ginny]."[177] Far better, according to the Production Code, to have a husband languish in guilt than to have a wife forgive.

Crossfire scurried into production in March 1947. Initial casting suggestions had included James Cagney or Pat O'Brien for the detective Captain Finlay, John Garfield for the level-headed Sergeant Keeley and for Ginny, Jane Greer or "Betty"—perhaps, given the type of role, Betty meaning Lauren Bacall. The urgency of mounting the film meant no time for courting stars from other studios and RKO contract players filled the cast list. Robert Young played Finlay, Robert Mitchum played Keeley and Gloria Grahame played Ginny. Robert Ryan had approached Richard Brooks in 1945 when they were both in the Marines and expressed the desire to play the bigoted Sergeant Montgomery if the book were made into a film, claiming to understand the character better than anyone.

Paxton recalled, "Scott and Dmytryk wanted the script as tight as possible, as pre-planned as possible. Together, we went over every shot, particularly from the standpoint of cost."[178] It was decided to minimize expenditure below the line (sets, materials, labor, short shooting schedule) and spend considerably more on the acting talent in order to "strengthen its box-office potential and ensure quality performances."[179] The film ultimately cost $600,000, of which roughly half went on the cast,[180] and began its 23-day schedule on 4 March with the scene between Mitchell and "The Man" at Ginny's apartment. Two days previously, *Cradle of Fear* had become *Crossfire*, at the behest of Dore Schary. John Paxton wrote: "I remember that. Sunday morning, in the big rush. At his house. He wanted a one-word, 'catchy' title. He pulled *Crossfire* out of his hat, out of thin air. He liked it, meaningless as it was, and it stuck."[181]

One reason why *Crossfire* is among Edward Dmytryk's very best films is its concision. The production's economy of scale and timing pulled the essential elements into sharp focus and pared away superfluous matter down to an 85-minute running time. The decision to discard the first half of *The Brick Foxhole* was a sound one, concentrating almost all of the events into one long night, and the film does not set foot off the RKO lot. Dmytryk does an exemplary job at propelling plot and maintaining grip. His direction is supple and his camerawork is sinuous, and the film is suffused with moments that display a man who is master of his art. A scene from the perspective of Mitchell is a woozily accurate rendering of the sensation of being inebriated. When Mitchell (George Cooper) leaves the dance bar, there is a long slow cross-fade from the downcast image of Ginny, at the very end of which, with sublime timing, her eyes look up at his departing figure. The scene where Leroy is used to entrap Monty at the hotel washroom makes excellent use of mirrors, the camera observing what the characters cannot. The coffee that bubbles up and spills over to relieve the tension of the wonderfully off-kilter scene between Mitchell and The Man (Paul Kelly) at Ginny's apartment. The humorous touch of the characters going to a cinema that is showing Dmytryk's *Cornered*. Such confidence of handling raises *Crossfire* to the top rank of *films noirs*, exactly the sort of escapism with content that Dore Schary was aiming for. As entertainment, it trounces its competitor as 1947's anti–Semitism chief consciousness raiser, *Gentleman's Agreement* being wordy, worthy and muddled of message.

As the opening credits fade, Dmytryk and cameraman J. Roy Hunt instantly propel the viewer into a struggle to the death, a shadow on the wall pummeled with fists, until a lamp is overturned and the screen remains pitch black for nine seconds. The lamp is switched back on and two pairs of feet scurry from the room leaving a motionless body behind. It is a daring beginning, confident in its ability to engage the viewer with blackness from the outset. Hunt's lighting throughout is exemplary, single light sources piercing the gloom, shadows looming with ominous intent, etching lines of tension into the faces of the characters. This darkness feeds very well into the portrayal of the murderer Monty. Dmytryk accords Robert Ryan several extreme close-ups, his face semi-obscured, the darkness within Monty unable to conceal itself. Ryan's performance is excellent, a bullying cockiness teetering on the edge of paranoia, and it is helped in no small measure by how he is shot. Roy Hunt was a veteran of some thirty years when *Crossfire* was made and Dmytryk was full of praise for his abilities and personal qualities: "one hell of a photographer—and one of the sweetest men ever created."[182]

Dmytryk draws accomplished performances from his entire cast, many of them below-the-radar contract players among whose best work this was. Robert Mitchum displays his habitual unbuttoned integrity in the role of Keeley, a dependable and unflappable foil to anyone acting opposite him. Alongside him and Ryan, the standout performance comes from Gloria Grahame, a piece of adroit casting. Ginny is described in the script as "a mixture of innocence and sinful sophistication"[183] and in interactions she "looks around professionally bored."[184] Grahame captures this aura of wounded diffidence perfectly. Ginny is gifted a memorable onscreen entrance, emerging from Mitchell's drunken haze to soft lighting accompanied by a strident blast on the trumpet and responding to his fresh come-ons with a "Drink up and be nice." She bats away his attention with an earthy laugh and a self-conscious adjustment of her hair ("Sure, I know, I remind you of your sister") before reminding him to "Be nice." And that is precisely what he does do to her and it cracks her protective carapace. Grahame is marvelous in the touching scene where Mitchell dances with her in the yard at the back of the bar and in her eyes we can witness her defenses seeping away. Later, under interrogation from Finlay and Mary Mitchell, the guard snaps back up and she is almost unreachable: "Tonight was a long time ago. I wouldn't be able to remember." The ebb and flow between these facets of Ginny, and her peculiar dynamic towards the man who may or not be her husband, are conveyed perfectly by Gloria Grahame, and the Oscar nomination she received was wholly deserved. She lost out to Celeste Holm in *Gentleman's Agreement*'s near-clean sweep but would attribute her later Oscar win for *The Bad and the Beautiful* to the lingering goodwill towards her performance as Ginny, which established her onscreen persona.

Robert Young was the headline Robert of *Crossfire*'s starring trio, and the most generously remunerated, his $125,000 being almost ten times as much as Robert Ryan's salary on the picture. His Finlay is a calm, modulated performance, combining concentration with lassitude and coaxing information from the suspects with the subtlest of touches. Monty's explicit racism may have been toned down by the censor, but he still can't help referring to Samuels as a "Jew-boy" and it is clear that Finlay suspects him from the outset. Another butt of Monty's bullying humor is Leroy (an effective performance from William Phipps), whom Monty derides as a stupid Tennessee hillbilly. It is to Leroy that Finlay delivers a speech denouncing religious and racial prejudice, surrounded by symbols of American democracy: a photo of Franklin D Roosevelt and a copy of the Declaration of Independence on the walls, the Capitol visible through the window. There was criticism from some quarters that the speech was overly simplistic and didactic, but the choice of Leroy as its target was a canny one. Wringing understanding from him was addressing the least informed members of the audience: "Hate, Monty's kind of hate, is like a gun. If you carry it around with you, it can go off and kill somebody. It killed Samuels last night." The original script featured a visual flashback to Finlay's grandfather being the victim of anti–Catholic prejudice, but the decision was wisely taken to convey this through Young's performance alone and it is a moving and persuasive speech. Some nervousness about the potential reception of the film still persisted though—a mention of negro lynching was for some reason excised and there was discussion about redubbing a reference to "American history" into "history."

Paxton generously attributed to Adrian Scott the subsequent clever plot device of using Leroy to lure Monty to the "right-house-but-the-wrong-address," the scene of his second murder: "I think it was inspired and a wonderful example of his talent. Neither of us thought of it as an 'entrapment,' I don't think of it as that now; it was a dramatic device, a quick, economical, and surprising way of getting from Monty an instantaneous, unspoken, irrefutable confession."[185] The ending of *Crossfire* became a source of contention between the film's creators. Monty escapes from the police and, in the original script, is shot dead by a military policeman with a tommy gun while making a run for it. Dore Schary said in an interview, "We looked at the first couple of shots of that sequence—we never completed the sequence—and, as I remember, it was Dmytryk who first brought up the question that he thought we might get a totally different reaction from the one intended, that it would look overpowering."[186] Schary agreed that it would look like the murderer was cornered by Nazi stormtroopers and the audience would feel sorry for him. He suggested that Finlay order him to stop and "with one shot knock him off. It's legitimate. He's going to escape but Bob Young warned him."[187] Schary was asked why Monty wasn't captured and brought to trial, to which he responded, "Well, you just didn't have enough time. See, the boat has sailed."[188]

John Paxton, re-watching the film decades later, was appalled at this alteration of his script: "I had forgotten that Finlay shot Monty. I was shocked, flinched along with other members of the audience at the Los Feliz. I say it is terribly wrong, was terribly wrong, even in its own time, because it was dramatically crude, in lousy taste, and improbable marksmanship."[189] Paxton accepted that the convention of the day was to resolve matters within the span of the film's timeframe but felt that his solution with the military police was less objectionable than the resolution chosen. He suspected that Schary did not want such a decisive action to be taken by an extra off-screen but should be an intentional act by a leading character. Amidst the praise heaped upon *Crossfire* at its release, this misstep did provoke critical comment. An editorial in *Life* magazine remarked on the ending's "strange callousness: the murderer never gets a trial and the new moral impression of the picture is that it is okay for a man wearing what Mr. Schary describes as 'the equivalent of a sheriff's badge' to shoot a fleeing anti–Semite in the street."[190] The ending is the film's sole serious misjudgment, bringing a flavor of wild west law enforcement to the modern streets of Washington, D.C., and shifting the coda out of kilter. The originally scripted speech while driving past the Lincoln Memorial was jettisoned for the anti-climax of Keeley's final line to Leroy: "Well, how about a cup of coffee, soldier?"

Four years previously, Dmytryk's *Tender Comrade* had been subjected to one of the most detailed audience testing procedures to that date. RKO's hope in testing *Crossfire* was to establish that a socially concerned piece could be commercially viable. Two previews were held—one in New York at RKO's 86th Street Theater (approximately 600 comment cards from around 2000 audience members), and the other, on 16 May 1947, in Los Angeles at Hill Street Theater (500 cards from 1700 attendees). The results of the Los Angeles screening were incredibly encouraging: 246 found the film Outstanding/Excellent/Very Good; 74 judged it Good/Fair; and only five registered it as Poor. The number of audience members that said they would recommend it was 187, against 25 who would not. Any doubt that there existed a current of anti–Semitism in American society was dispelled by various of the responses to

Gloria Grahame and George Cooper in *Crossfire* **(1947).**

the question as what the patron would remember about *Crossfire*. A handful called it "Jewish propaganda," while even a few supportive voices expressed disquiet: "Bad taste in embarrassing Jewish patrons"; "A queer sense of embarrassment of hearing the word Jew said out loud and a DEEP sense of shame that we should all need this." The vast majority of responses as to whether the film served an educational function were positive ("Yes indeed. One of the best pictures we have seen in a long time and we see all of them") but again dissenting voices were registered ("Yes. Jews should correct their obnoxious ways, brazen ideas etc. if they want to be liked in this world"; "No. I think that this picture will not help in erasing hatred. It will probably increase it more"). In response to criticism that the film was heavy-handed in preaching to the audience, Dmytryk used the result of these previews as his defense in a letter to the *New York Times*: "None of us has ever considered our audiences as unintelligent. But it cannot be denied by anyone who has followed public opinion polls that the people who make up our audiences are certainly uninformed ... we got a far higher return of [preview] cards than any picture has ever gotten. Ninety per cent of these were completely in favor of the picture; only four per cent, most of these openly anti–Semitic, were against it. Specifically these cards indicated that by long odds the favorite scene in the picture was the very scene to which you object—the scene with Leroy."[191]

According to the prominent film critic Cecelia Ager, *Crossfire* broke the taboo of verbal acknowledgment of Jewishness in American cinema: "It feels fine, hearing at last 'Jew-boy' and 'Jew' and 'Jewish person' from the screen. It's like hard rain after a long-brooding thunder storm. It clears the air."[192] This is not strictly accurate. Vincent Sherman's *Mr. Skeffington* of 1944 deals with prejudice against the firm Skeffington & Co., and has Claude Rains admitting to his daughter that "I'm Jewish." In Dmytryk's own *Till the End of Time*, released in 1946, Robert Mitchum instigates a fist-fight on behalf of his fallen Jewish army buddy, Maxie Klein, when a veterans' group declares their membership policy of "No Catholics, Jews or Negroes." *Crossfire* was nevertheless a landmark film in the depiction of prejudice on the American screen, and the very first to address anti–Semitism with any rigor. It beat *Gentleman's Agreement* to the cinemas by four months and was for the most part garlanded with praise, including winning Best Social Picture at Cannes and Albert Einstein judging it a "very useful picture and ... would like Hollywood to make more of the kind."[193] The film was an extremely successful attraction wherever it played, making a $1.27 million profit for RKO and its biggest hit of the year, a success that was sustained in the South to the surprise of commentators.

When the Academy Award nominations were announced in early 1948, *Crossfire* earned five nods—for Picture (Adrian Scott), Edward Dmytryk, John Paxton, Robert Ryan and Gloria Grahame. The world had altered irrevocably in the twelve months since the heady days of preparing the picture. In May 1947, the month that *Crossfire* began previewing, HUAC had dipped its toe into the Hollywood pond, and followed up with the main Washington, D.C., hearings in October. In November, Dmytryk and Scott were cited for contempt of Congress and December saw the release of the Waldorf Statement, the "gentleman's agreement" of the Hollywood studios that instigated the blacklist. In March 1948, *Gentleman's Agreement* won Oscars for Best Picture, Best Director (Elia Kazan) and Celeste Holm got the trophy that should have had Gloria Grahame's name on it. The fact that *Crossfire* lost in all categories was a foregone conclusion. Edward Dmytryk and Adrian Scott had been sacked by the studio four months previously, their RKO careers terminated right at the very pinnacle of their success.

III

The HUAC Nightmare
(1947–1951)

Humphrey Bogart's change of heart is as vivid an indication as any of the ideological and moral maelstrom that engulfed Hollywood in the wake of the war. When, in May 1947, the House Un-American Activities Committee (HUAC) announced its investigation to prove that "card-carrying [Communist] party members dominated the Screen Writers Guild, that Communists had succeeded in introducing subversive propaganda into motion pictures and that President Roosevelt had brought improper pressure to bear upon the industry to produce pro–Soviet films during the war"[1] and summoned nineteen politically suspect or "unfriendly" witnesses to testify, liberal Hollywood rushed to the barricades to defend freedom of speech and thought. In a radio broadcast, Bogart questioned, "Is democracy so feeble that it can be subverted merely by a look or a line, an inflection or gesture?"[2] and was one of a flock of stars who flew to Washington that October in support of those subpoenaed. Within a few months, the pressure that was exerted upon Bogart led to his public declarations of "I detest Communism"[3] and of being "a foolish and impetuous American" who had been "duped.... No, sir. I'll never forget the lesson that was taught to me in the year 1947 in Washington DC."[4] Lessons are certainly to be learnt from the saga of the Hollywood Ten and the whole wretched period that followed, but perhaps not those that Bogart was claiming to have been taught.

HUAC had been set up in 1938, initially to investigate corrosive communist and fascist elements in American society. From the very beginning however, the emphasis was clearly on the communist threat, to the extent that James Scott, the Imperial Wizard of the Ku Klux Klan, declared: "The programme of the Committee mostly parallels the programme of the Klan."[5] The first chairman of the Committee claimed that there were more than 2,000 "outright communists and party-liners"[6] working for the government in Washington and perceived the performing arts to be ripe for investigation due to the fear that communist propaganda could be disseminated in the guise of innocuous entertainment. The Committee's initial findings on Hollywood were somewhat lacking in credibility. Bogart, James Cagney and Fredric March, among others, were named as communists, only to have that judgment withdrawn, though the nadir had earlier been reached when the ten-year-old Shirley Temple was similarly embroiled.

In reality, this period did witness a flourishing of politically progressive thinking in the film community and the formation of socially engaged groups such as the

Spanish Refugee Committee and the Anti-Nazi League. The Communist Party set up a Hollywood branch in 1936 to benefit from the prestige and funding that west coast left-wingers could supply. Although influencing the content of films may have been desired by the Party, the leader of the Hollywood branch, John Howard Lawson, realized that the screenwriter, not to mention the mere performer, was not a sizeable enough cog in the movie-making machine to be able to steer films in any political direction. This was acknowledged in 1946 by the Party national chairman: "We can't expect to put any propaganda in the films, but we can try to keep anti–Soviet agit-prop out."[7]

By 1946 of course, the Soviet Union had reverted from wartime ally to enemy. When it returned to the fray in 1947 to re-focus on Hollywood, HUAC was seeking the publicity that open sessions with such high-profile, glamorous individuals would provide. Franklin D Roosevelt, whose Federal Theater Project had been an early subject of investigation, had recognized this craven aspect of the process back in 1938: "Most fair-minded Americans hope that this committee will abandon the practice of merely providing a forum to those who, for political purposes or otherwise, seek headlines which they could not otherwise obtain."[8] The new chairman of the Committee, J. Parnell Thomas, was nothing if not publicity-seeking. Among the members of the Committee were the fervently anti–Semitic, anti-black Representative John Rankin of Mississippi and a young Richard Nixon.

Edward Dmytryk received the pink slip of his subpoena on 19 September 1947, along with Adrian Scott at RKO. Scott was working on *The Boy with Green Hair* at the time, and the co-scriptwriter of that film, Alfred Lewis Levitt, recalled the moment: "I remember when Adrian and Eddie Dmytryk got their subpoenas. I was with Adrian when Eddie came into Adrian's office and said, 'They can't prove anything on me.' That was his total reaction at the time."[9] Dmytryk himself remembered he and Scott feeling a degree of elation. They had been waiting for this moment to arrive and were eager to take on the Hollywood right-wingers who had been flashing their fangs since the preliminary Hollywood hearings that spring. Dmytryk and Scott decided to get representation from Bartley Crum, a San Francisco attorney who was both Roman Catholic and Republican, and therefore anything but a Communist apologist, but "he had the typical liberal Republican's attitude toward HUAC and its continuing attempts to censor by intimidation—he was shocked."[10]

Nineteen had been summoned to appear in Washington in October, many Communists or former Communists, some merely liberals such as Lewis Milestone, director of *All Quiet on the Western Front* and *The Front Page*. The first meeting to coordinate a common defense for the witnesses was held at Milestone's house, one of the lawyers present being Ben Margolis. Of Dmytryk, Margolis said in an interview thirty years later: "I would say that he was one of the least vocal, least important persons in forming policy, not because he was or wasn't a Marxist, but just because there were other people who were more vocal, who had sharper minds, who spoke better…. He was no fool, but I would certainly not put him down as an extraordinary person … this was a remarkable group as a whole. Strong people."[11] Dmytryk and Scott would hold on to their lawyer Crum but would form a united front with the larger group, and it was agreed to make decisions by unanimous consent. Of unanimity, Dmytryk later wrote: "I have been allergic to it ever since. Where unanimity is required, freedom ceases to exist."[12] The group flew to Washington, D.C., and settled themselves in the Sheraton Park Hotel, confident of success in front of the Committee, given the oratorial and intellectual abilities of most of their number.

The hearings opened on 20 October 1947. As well as the nineteen "unfriendly" witnesses, twenty-four "friendly" witnesses were called—either former Communists prepared to purge themselves of their impure thoughts or upstanding citizens who heartily disapproved of all of that Commie stuff. Under the adoring glare of the newsreel cameras, Robert Taylor, Ronald Reagan and Robert Montgomery were among those who confirmed the Committee's assumptions that Hollywood was a seething cesspool of suspect politics, although the contribution of Adolphe Menjou is instructive as to how effective such testimony was: "I believe that under certain circumstances a communistic director, a communistic writer, or a communistic actor, even if he were under orders from the head of the studio not to inject communism or un–Americanism or subversion into pictures, could easily subvert that order, under the proper circumstances, by a look, by an inflection, by a change in the voice. I think it could be easily done. I have never seen it done, but I think it could be done."[13] Gary Cooper was sufficiently down-home in his musings on communism—"From what I hear, I don't like because it isn't on the level"[14]—though he would later redeem himself in his defense of the writer Carl Foreman over *High Noon*, an incisive allegory of the period.

While the friendly witnesses were permitted to read statements, the unfriendly nineteen were not granted that courtesy. When Dmytryk took the stand on 29 October, he referred to this discrepancy when he was refused permission to make a statement: "Mr. Chairman, if you let me I will answer the question. However, most other witnesses, certainly the witnesses the first week, were given the right to answer as they pleased. Some went on at great length."[15] It had been decided in strategy meetings for the nineteen to read a prepared statement denouncing the proceedings and to refuse to answer questions under the protection of the First Amendment, which defends the right to free speech. The decision had been taken that to invoke the Fifth Amendment, which protects against self-incrimination, would indicate that they had something to hide. At no stage, of course, had membership of the Communist Party been illegal but this was proving to be a somewhat academic point. The one point that Dmytryk did manage to make was in confirming he had been an officer of the Screen Actors Guild: "I think that this kind of questioning is designed to bring about a split in many of the guilds among the members of the guilds at a time when we have just succeeded in getting unity between the guilds."[16]

The approach of the nineteen proved tactically self-destructive: only writer Albert Maltz, on 28 October, was permitted to read his statement, and the proceedings rapidly degenerated into a cacophony of bellowed demands, frustrated retorts and gavel poundings, with the recurring refrain "Are you now, or have you ever been, a member of the Communist Party?" Chairman Thomas's treatment of the witnesses was undeniably hostile and belligerent, but the aggressive rhetoric that was fired back in response failed to win public sympathy. John Huston, one of the phalanx of supporters who had flown in from Hollywood, wrote later: "One after another, they were knocked down. It was a sorry performance. You felt your skin crawl and your stomach turn. I disapproved of what was being done to the Ten, but I also disapproved of their response. They had lost a chance to defend a most important principle. It struck me as a case of thoroughly bad generalship."[17] Dmytryk recalled sitting beside his boss Dore Schary when John Howard Lawson took the stand on 27 October and feeling his spirits sink as Lawson and Thomas engaged in an unwinnable shouting match. He asked Schary about his chances at the studio now: "'You have an ironclad contract,' he replied. And that is what made Dore Schary a rather wonderful man, though an uncertain executive; he really believed in corporate integrity."[18]

Ten days after they had begun, the hearings were abruptly terminated, with only eleven of the subpoenaed unfriendly nineteen having been called. Had Bertolt Brecht not fled the country within hours after testifying "No, no, no, no, no, never"[19] to the question of whether he had ever applied to join the Communist Party, we might now be recalling the Hollywood Eleven. The strategy employed had backfired, antagonizing the Committee, and Dmytryk's disillusionment was accompanied by a sense of isolation. On 24 November, the House of Representatives voted contempt indictments against the Ten by a margin of 346 to 17, and the studios quickly responded. Despite the misgivings of producers such as Schary, Harry Cohn, Samuel Goldwyn and David O. Selznick, the moguls assembled the day of the Congress vote at the Waldorf-Astoria hotel in New York and agreed on their Declaration the day after: "We will not knowingly employ a Communist, or a member of any party or group which advocates the overthrow of the Government of the United States by force, or by any illegal or unconstitutional methods."[20] HUAC may have initiated the hearings but it was Hollywood that instigated the blacklist.

A fundamental failure of nerve from the studios facilitated the nightmare of the following years, a state of affairs that they anticipated: "We are frank to recognise that such a policy involves dangers and risks. There is the danger of hurting innocent people. There is the risk of creating an atmosphere of fear. Creative work at its best cannot be carried on in an atmosphere of fear."[21] Convening in the same city as their Wall Street backers, they buckled under the financial pressure. What was even more cowardly than putting the bottom line ahead of their employees' rights, was the willful blindness of this group of mostly Jewish movie executives regarding the anti–Semitic nature of much of the enquiries. Congressman John Rankin relished referring to movie stars by their original Jewish names, both at the HUAC hearings and on the floor of the House of Representatives. A few years later, in October 1950, a chaotic meeting of the Directors' Guild of America called to discuss HUAC witnessed the same bigotry when Cecil B. DeMille pronounced the names of the liberal-leaning Fred Zinnemann and William Wyler so as to emphasize their foreignness, their Jewishness. This led John Ford at the same meeting to declare: "I don't agree with C.B. DeMille. I admire him. I don't like him, but I admire him."[22]

Once the studio moguls had adopted their position and their employees realized the danger to their contracts of maintaining old allegiances, support rapidly seeped away from the Ten and their cause. Bogart wasn't the only one to perform a volte-face. Mere months after declaring in a radio broadcast, "If this committee gets a green light from the American people now, will it be possible to make a broadcast like this a year from today?,"[23] John Garfield wrote a piece called "I'm a Sucker for a Left Hook," while Edward G. Robinson wrote one titled "How the Reds Made a Sucker out of Me." Such statements would save neither of them from future entanglements with HUAC. The President of the Screen Actors Guild had already made that organization's standpoint clear in a telegram on 19 August: "IMPERATIVE THAT GUILD RECEIVE AT ONCE SIGNED AFFIDAVIT RE NO AFFILIATION WITH COMMUNIST PARTY IN ORDER THAT WE MAY FILE FRIDAY FOR ELECTIONS. RONNIE REAGAN."[24]

On 26 November 1947, the day before Thanksgiving, Dmytryk and Scott were fired by N. Peter Rathvon, President of RKO, since production chief Schary refused to be their executioner. The contempt trials were months away and Dmytryk's finances had run dry. Prior to being served with his subpoena, he had settled a divorce from Madeleine and had given her "literally everything except a small bank account and my car."[25] His financial future had seemed rock-solid at that point, sitting at the top of the directors' pack at RKO, earning $2,500 a week, 52 weeks a year. He and Jean had bought a hundred acres near Agoura Hills in Los Angeles County where they were planning to build a house and start a horse farm. Madeline and Michael moved into the apartment house in Beverly Hills that was part of the divorce settlement, so on top of it all, Dmytryk was effectively homeless. In the bleak days of early 1948, fear led some of the Left to flee to Mexico and the future loomed dismally for all.

Dmytryk's temporary savior appeared in January. Rod Geiger was setting up a film based on the novel *Christ in Concrete* and was convinced that Dmytryk was the man to direct, despite the latter's assurances that distribution in the United States would be a problem with his name attached. Shooting in America also proved impossible, and, while Geiger set up a deal with British-based producer Nat Bronsten, Bronsten offered Dmytryk another project. Prior to leaving for England, Dmytryk and Jean moved in with Geiger and his girlfriend Katya. That spring saw a reconnaissance trip to London via Stockholm, the Ten being found guilty of contempt of Congress and, on 12 May, an unassuming wedding between Edward and Jean in Ellicott City, Maryland, with Albert Maltz as the only witness to whom they had prior acquaintance. On their honeymoon night, Dmytryk, Maltz, Paul Robeson and others of the Ten spoke to a crowd of supporters in Philadelphia: "The applause was roof-shaking, but I didn't hear Jean. The bride had gone to bed."[26] The couple returned to England, settled in August at 47 Glebe Place, Chelsea, just around the corner from Carol Reed, and Dmytryk made his "exile films," **Obsession** and **Give Us This Day**. The Dmytryk's son Richard was born in a private nursing home in July 1949, after a birth that nearly proved fatal for Jean, and not long after, the family returned to Los Angeles to await the result of the Ten's Supreme Court appeal.

Dmytryk took some script doctoring jobs which he could perform under the radar of the blacklist, but his financial situation was precarious. Albert Maltz recalled that "there was an attitude in Hollywood, that I'm sure Dmytryk shared, that of course we would win our case. It was unthinkable that ten such individuals would go to jail.... [After] he was ordered by the court to return [from England] ... from that time he became active in the affairs of the Ten.... He became especially militant after we were turned down by the Supreme Court.... Dmytryk was especially active, especially militant in that and aroused and indignant."[27] This indignance did not prevent his growing disillusionment with the workings of the Ten. He was appalled when Robert Rossen[28] was roundly attacked for the punchy statement about the corruption of power in his film *All the King's Men*, criticism that Rossen's daughter Carol characterized as "How dare he do this picture because people might think that Hughie Long was a little too like Stalin?"[29] Violent dissent within the group was not uncommon. Alvah Bessie recalled an incident in 1946: "Albert [Maltz] wrote an article called 'What Shall We Ask of Writers?' in which he objected to the strict criticism the Party made of writers for not following the line and promoting the interests of the Party in the way it felt the Party should be promoted. There was a meeting that was very hostile to Albert, and I myself attacked Albert.... I said, 'We need more Party writers, and we need more writers who are more closely identified, not less closely identified, with the Party.'"[30] For Dmytryk, the final straw came when it was decided, after lengthy debate, that freedom of speech did not apply to fascists, "'because what they say is a lie.' ...that was when I decided that, sooner or later, I had to part company with the Hollywood Ten."[31]

The appeal of the Ten was turned down by the Supreme Court in April and on 29 June 1950 Dmytryk was sentenced to six months in prison and a $1,000 fine. While eight of the Ten received the same fine but a prison sentence of double the length, he and Herbert Biberman were sentenced by a more lenient judge. Biberman believed this was because Dmytryk had already turned informer prior to prison, but this version is not credible, since there would then be no necessity to go to prison at all. Maltz, with whom Dmytryk served his prison sentence at Mill Point, West Virginia, was certain Biberman was wrong: "[The] first place we were was the Washington jail.... Biberman left a little before we did,[32] but Dmytryk and I left together after 18 days.... I remember Eddie saying, 'I'm going to be able to face my grandchildren. I'm glad I'm here.' Well, that was I think very sincerely a man trying to feel comfortable about a very uncomfortable situation."[33] On the drive to West Virginia, the marshals lost their way and Dmytryk, an experienced pilot and navigator, ended up directing his own way to prison. Deprived of their liberty and their careers, it can only have provided scant solace for the Hollywood Ten when their chief inquisitor Congressman J. Parnell Thomas was convicted of taking bribes. Two of them, Lester Cole and Ring Lardner, Jr., found him working in the chicken farm at their Connecticut prison. The poetic justice wasn't lost on Cole: "I see you are still shovelling chicken shit around."[34]

The prison camp regime at Mill Point was mild on discipline and low on security, with no wall or fence, and Dmytryk maintained a good relationship with the guards and warden. Around half of the inmates, varying between 600 and 750, were serving time for making or selling moonshine, around half were illiterate and around two-thirds were black, with segregation employed apart from work and leisure activities. They discovered that Clifford Odets was already an inmate, having been given a three-month sentence for contempt of Congress. Maltz was made an orderly at the four-bed hospital and Dmytryk was made garage clerk, servicing and fueling the trucks that were used for the camp's lumbering activities. This role required long hours but incurred additional privileges, and Dmytryk was permitted to organize an evening weightlifting class.

Dmytryk maintained constant written contact with Jean and the letters the new parents exchanged could be extremely touching: "It's going to be hard for me to forgive the government, missing my son's first birthday. I try hard not to get bitter. But perhaps that's why I always think about England when I think about us being together after I get out. I'm really so homesick for the place."[35] The letters bear witness that Dmytryk was attempting to set up a film project in England with the assistance of Dick Powell but that some form of contrition was required in order for Dmytryk to lose his untouchable status. The preamble to this was a statement to the press that immediately cooled the relationship with Maltz: "Dmytryk had given out a statement that the papers had run … that he was supporting the government in the Korean War, our government, and it implied that those who did not were somehow traitorous."[36] Dmytryk's true accusation of treachery was reserved for the hardline Communists whom he blamed for his current predicament: "My 'comrades' proclamations of carrying the torch for freedom of speech and thought were proven frauds, and it became obvious the Ten had been sacrificed to the Party's purpose as a pipeline for the Comintern's propaganda."[37]

Buoyed by this sense of having been a pawn, he made an official statement on 9 September that he was not a communist or communist sympathizer, nor had he been at the time of the Congressional hearings. On 13 September, he wrote to Jean: "Dick [Powell] sent me a wonderful wire, and if his reaction is general in Hollywood, I'm well satisfied."[38] Dmytryk was released from prison in mid–November, after serving four and a half months: "No more of this. Next time the Constitution can go take a jump in the lake. My Baby comes first."[39] His fervent hope was that his official statement would be sufficient to resurrect his Hollywood career. It soon became clear, however, that a more conclusive distancing from his former associates would be necessary. A tentative deal with Harry Cohn of Columbia fell through when Dmytryk's name appeared in the press, against his wishes, in support of parole for the remaining Eight of the Ten still in prison, and Jean decided she didn't want to move to Europe where he had offers of work. In order to break the blacklist on which he unexpectedly found himself, and with financial demands from the tax authorities and his ex-wife pressing heavily upon him, he was left in no doubt that the absolute requirement was "a second appearance before the House Un-American Activities Committee, with full and open answers to all questions asked."[40]

By the time the Committee reconvened in March 1951, liberal Hollywood had grown accustomed to the watchful eye of the FBI, conspicuous in the Californian sunshine in their hats and grey flannel suits, and had come to fear the deposition of the pink subpoena slip, sometimes enacting elaborate schemes to avoid receiving one. Having witnessed the abject failure of the Ten's First Amendment defense, many of those summoned took what became known as the Diminished Fifth, admitting their own deeds but refusing to incriminate others. Lillian Hellman wrote to the Committee: "I cannot and will not cut my conscience to fit this year's fashions."[41] Dmytryk tussled with his conscience, weighed it up against his family situation, with Jean now pregnant with their second child, and financial predicament, and made his decision: "I would have to name names and I knew the problems this would cause…. [My] decision was made easier by the fact that my experience as a party member had been rather meager, and I couldn't name anybody who hadn't already been identified as a party member. Weighing everything, pro and con, I knew I had to testify."[42] Ultimately, "I did not want to remain a martyr to something that I absolutely believed was immoral and wrong."[43]

On 25 April 1951, after the appearance of the writer Abraham Polonsky, Edward Dmytryk testified before the Committee. He was questioned about the objective of Communist Party—"[My] opinion is they had probably three chief purposes … to get money … to get prestige. And the third and most important one, was, through the infiltration and eventual taking over of Hollywood guilds and unions, to control the content of pictures."[44] With regard to which specific guilds—"Communists were successful for a time in … controlling … the Screen Writers' Guild. They were not successful at all in the Screen Directors' Guild."[45] He was asked how many Communists were in the Directors' Guild: "As far as I know there were seven, and as far as I know that was just about all…. Frank Tuttle…. Herbert Biberman…. Jack Berry…. Bernard Vorhaus…. Jules Dassin … and myself."[46] The Committee did not draw attention to the fact that he only mentioned six directors. The following month, an extensive interview with and profile of Dmytryk titled "What Makes a Hollywood Communist?" appeared in *The Saturday Evening Post*. Richard English, who had coincidentally been the screenwriter for one of Dmytryk's first shots at directing, *Million Dollar Legs*, spent a few weeks interviewing Dmytryk for the article, the pair staying at the Coronado hotel for some days.

Criticism from the Left to this public recanting was instant and intense. In *The Hollywood Reporter*, Maltz wrote a riposte to "that lying article by Richard English, which infuriated me,"[47] which asserted that it would correct the lies but which failed to offer evidence to that effect. Dmytryk was sad that it was Maltz who made the public attack on him, since he considered the best man at his wedding "almost a Christ-like figure … very nice, very sweet and very honest and very fair. And this article was so obviously dishonest, and it was full of the usual thing, which is what they do so goddamn well, half-truths."[48] However, despite asserting many times that he had only given the Committee names that had already been named, Dmytryk belatedly admitted, or became aware, that one of those he mentioned had not previously featured in testimony—Bernard Vorhaus. Vorhaus, who was shooting a film in Italy, became "very depressed. I just loved filmmaking, and there was no point coming back to America to appear before the Committee."[49]

The antipathy against Dmytryk endured down the decades. The son of Lester Cole said his father regarded Dmytryk as "a total shit. He could never abide people who turned. You did not do that."[50] John Berry called him "a typical hack. His pipe-smoking pose used to drive me up the wall."[51] Norma Barzman was "put off by Eddie's steely eyes."[52] Joan LaCourt, who would become Mrs. Adrian Scott, also focused on Dmytryk's physicality: "My first contact with Adrian Scott came when I was working as the stage manager of a mass meeting in support of the Hollywood Ten. One of my jobs was lining up the Hollywood Ten alphabetically. I remember that I took a dislike to Dmytryk right away. He was an antsy-pantsy guy. If he'd had a couple more feet on him, he might have been more confident and a winning flirt. As it was, he was just this little man always trying to impress. He was very short so he would always sit on a table in a group photo in order that he would appear as tall as the others."[53] At 5'7" Dmytryk's lack of height became his defining, and somehow condemnatory, characteristic for LaCourt in other interviews: "He would always sit on the table when the photographers came through so that his shortness would not show."[54]

The attitude of others on the Left was more nuanced. The blacklisted actress Lee Grant did not "put him in the same camp as Kazan. I am sure that Dmytryk found a *raison d'être* for what his actions are. He wasn't one of the Ten anymore."[55] His foe at the time of *Cornered*, John Wexley, appreciated that "one of his motivations was to continue to work. It was not that he changed his principles. They made him what Whittaker Chambers, in his book *Witness*, called 'a running hound for a bone.' They can do whatever they like with you, once you have informed. So they trotted him around to American Legion meetings and other places where he could talk about the evils of Communism, Socialism, and the fifth column."[56] Ring Lardner, Jr., understood that, as the only director in the Ten, Dmytryk would not be able to continue his career under a pseudonym as the other writers in the group could. Historian of the blacklist period Larry Ceplair cites the family pressure that he was under: "Dmytryk, I think, went back and informed because his wife was on the verge of a nervous breakdown, thinking he wouldn't work again."[57]

Edward Dmytryk's prison time and subsequent recanting places a rather gauzy filter in front of certain received monochrome certainties of the horrendous blacklisting era. His attitude was unrepentant from 1951 until his death in 1999 but his daughter Vicky, born in November 1951, just at the peak of the controversy surrounding him, told this author that he "regretted it later and said he would have done things differently if he had it to do over again."[58]

Dalton Trumbo's retrospective view on the era was contentious: "[T]he blacklist was a time of evil ... no one on either side who survived it came through untouched by evil.... [I]t will do no good to search for villains or heroes or saints or devils because there were none. There were only victims."[59] It's difficult to equate the soul-searching Louis B. Mayer may possibly have endured with the torment of Philip Loeb, the actor who committed suicide after his name appeared in the publication *Red Channels*. While there was never an official studio blacklist, the closest thing was this pamphlet, first published in 1950, which listed not only Communist Party members but many whose crime had been to attend the wrong rally or to support a suspect cause. In our era of "alternative facts," it is sobering to discover that this was when being considered a "premature anti-fascist" was enough to have one blacklisted. Fighting against fascism during the war was noble and all-American; doing so in the 1930s was treasonable. Lillian Hellman was an acute chronicler of the whole sorry business: "The McCarthy group—a loose term for all the boys, lobbyists, congressmen, State Department bureaucrats, CIA operators—chose the anti–Red scare with perhaps more cynicism than Hitler picked anti–Semitism."[60]

And all the while, the blacklist robbed the viewing public of some glorious talent. The luminous character actresses Gale Sondergaard and Anne Revere, formerly so respected by their peers that they had been awarded Oscars, disappeared from the screen. Lee Grant, acclaimed for her debut in *Detective Story*, had her cinema career snatched from her for a decade and a half. Larry Parks, eviscerated by the Committee, never regained his. Vincent Sherman, the favored director of Bette Davis at Warner Bros, didn't work from 1952 to 1956. Betsy Blair, once she was no longer under the protection of her respected husband Gene Kelly, watched the work dry up. Zero Mostel, Lionel Stander, Paul Robeson, strong characters all: unemployable. The even more insidious "greylist" made quality work very difficult to come by for artists of the caliber of Edward G. Robinson and James Wong Howe. A brief list culled from a long litany. Despite what Trumbo may have asserted, these were the real victims.

At the outset of the hysteria, in one of the radio broadcasts of 1947, William Wyler asserted: "I wouldn't be allowed to make *The Best Years of Our Lives* today. They are making decent people afraid to express their opinions. They are creating fear in Hollywood. Fear will result in self-censorship. Self-censorship will paralyse the screen. In the last analysis, you will suffer."[61] Cecil B. DeMille's reviled "Herr Vyler" predicted well. As the screens got wider and more colorful, the content faded into sepia. The challenging *noirs* of the 1940s were replaced with bloated Cinemascope epics and bowdlerized Broadway adaptations, with Paddy Chayefsky–esque realism providing occasional respite. The blunting of novelty and the dominance of conformity in the 1950s meant the status quo remained resolutely unrocked. Edward Dmytryk was to regain his career, but in a landscape parched of pluck.

Obsession (1949)

Obsession is a remarkably effective transposition of *noir* sensibility to the soundstages of Pinewood. After his experience of working in an English studio on *So Well Remembered*, this Nat Bronsten production reinforced Dmytryk's attitude toward the British film industry. While working on the film, he told *Variety* that he felt that inadequate incentives and lack of promotion prospects made the British studio technician less efficient that his opposite number in Hollywood. Having himself started in the industry as a messenger, he was able to rise through the ranks by displaying initiative. "That is unlikely to happen in Britain, asserts Dmytryk. Anyone starting in the props department would probably stay there, and consequently the wrong type of person is being attracted to the industry."[62] He was assigned 30 days to shoot *Obsession*, a tight schedule, but, using his short-day technique[63] from *Crossfire*, the shoot finished on time.

American-born Nat Bronsten had been a plastics engineer during the war and had made his producing debut with Cavalcanti's *They Made Me a Fugitive* in 1947. He purchased Alec Coppel's unpublished book *A Man About a Dog* intending it to be the film debut of his girlfriend, a Russian opera singer called Marushka. Concealing this fact from his collaborators, Bronsten proposed that he, Coppel and Dmytryk, along with their female significant others, convene at a resort hotel on Lake Annecy to develop the screenplay. Coppel, who would go on to script *Vertigo*, did most of the work after discussion with Dmytryk, while the rest of the party lived the high life in the French Alps. After three or four weeks, Coppel had a draft ready but when Bronsten read it, he realized that there was no part for an opera singer. He suggested a scene in a cabaret. "After a few very uncomfortable hours, we finally convinced our producer that Marushka would have to wait a little longer for her big break."[64] The following morning, they discovered that Bronsten and Marushka had departed without them, leaving their bills unpaid. Money had to be cabled from Coppel's agent in London before the group could afford to leave their lakeside lair and return to England.

The script explicitly highlights U.S.–British tensions, both in the dialogue at a gentlemen's club expressing contemporary concern at British dependence on American dollars to finance post-war recovery, and in the casting of Brits Robert Newton and Sally Gray against Yank Phil Brown, in roles in descending order of nefariousness. Coppel avoids pulp convention in adapting his book for the screen and creates a believably perverse triangle. As an experienced Oscar-nominated director, Dmytryk was undoubtedly the senior artistic partner in the production of *Obsession* for Independent Sovereign Films, but his team more than rose to the challenge of recreating *noir*ish textures on the £150,000 budget of a minor British production company. Some of Bronsten's other productions (*They Made Me a Fugitive*, *Silent Dust*) are veined with a squarely British *noir* sensibility and look, and the cross-fertilization of British and American strains of dark drama yields strong results in *Obsession*. Dmytryk's maintains a tight grip on his material, pacing it fluidly and charging it with tension. His camerawork provides some neat flourishes, as when a bullet-hole is discovered in a doorframe, a moment with Hitchcockian inflections.

Sandwiched between his iconic roles of Bill Sikes in *Oliver Twist* and Long John Silver in *Treasure Island*, Newton's Dr. Clive Riordan is a vivid example of the English archetype of the urbane gentleman murderer, or in this case would-be murderer. Vivid the characterization may be, but the performance is not afflicted by some of Newton's unpalatable eye-rolling tics. It is rather a subtly modulated portrayal of polite menace with only an occasional sulphurous look betraying the passions underneath. Newton was another in the long line of talented alcoholics that Dmytryk directed: "One of the nicest, most considerate, most sensitive of men when sober, he was a holy terror when drunk, though sometimes amusing."[65] This assessment chimes exactly with that of his biographer: "boozy and destructive, subtle and passionate … thunderously boisterous and quietly private … full of laughter."[66] Such was his unruly reputation that he was required to post a £20,000 bond to guarantee that he would remain sober for the duration of production, and luckily the film ran to schedule. On the final day of the shoot, he started drinking ale at lunchtime, was rosy-cheeked when the last scene wrapped and, "by the time our set party was over, he was already Mr. Hyde."[67]

Bill Kronin, the object of Dr. Riordan's obsession, is the latest in his wife's sequence of adulterous liaisons and is played by Dmytryk's fellow greylistee Phil Brown, a graduate of the Group Theatre in New York and the Actors' Laboratory in Los Angeles. Brown and Dmytryk had made the trip to Britain at around the same time and their collaboration was close on both *Obsession* and *Give Us This Day*. That connection was ruptured after Dmytryk testified before HUAC. Years later Brown would express his disappointment at those who had caved into HUAC, and may even have been speaking about Dmytryk in the following quotation: "The day one of my closest friends reeled off his list, all mutual close friends, I felt the first sharp tinge in my guts. What a terrifying dilemma to be faced with! How could I be angry with him? Do you get angry with someone you love because they have fallen victim to an illness? Can you hate a man who you knew was finding the simplest act of facing himself in the mirror to shave an almost unbearable experience? Can you castigate a man who must keep away from his familiar haunts for fear of running into friends whose lives he has wrecked? Can you forgive him?"[68] Dmytryk for his part, writing in 1996 and responding directly to Brown's quote, dismissed opinions from the Left that he was living a miserable existence as "axioms taken from the communist 'Handbook on Wishful Thinking.'"[69]

The fact that Newton and Brown's divergent acting styles prove complementary is indicative of the film's happy marriage of Hollywood director to British milieu. The third member of the twisted triangle is Riordan's wife Storm, a woman who has had a succession of lovers, silently tolerated by her husband. When he spots her meeting Kronin at a cocktail party, Riordan observes, "Storm's under full sail again. The calm has lifted." Waiting for the couple to arrive back from an illicit rendezvous, Riordan places his handgun on *The Times* newspaper. In a deft display of the passing of time, he decides to do the crossword while waiting and the next shot shows the crossword completed as their taxi pulls up outside. The scene in which he confronts the lovers as they frantically endeavor to lie their way out of a compromising situation, is a beautifully played game of cat and mouse. Kronin pleads his case that the affair is merely a harmless little flirtation, to which Riordan responds, "There have been so many harmless little flirtations. You've heard of the last straw, haven't you, Bill? Well, you're it." The devious irony is that, although Kronin professes his love for Storm and almost loses his life on her account, for her it clearly is just another flirtation. Storm visits Kronin in hospital at the film's conclusion, apologizes for not having been to see him previously and announces that she is going on a long sea trip on the advice of her doctors. The look that she casts his way, a nicely supercilious performance from Sally Gray, makes it clear that her travelling companion is another in her long line of men.

The plot exhibits a gothic gruesomeness which belies the fact that it was filmed in 1948. Riordan imprisons Kronin in a dank inaccessible cellar for months on end, with the ultimate intention, once Scotland Yard interest has died down, of dismembering his corpse, dissolving it in an acid bath and flushing it away. Scenes of the psychopath at work in his chemical laboratory or preparing his cutting instruments for use are familiar from the twenty-first century serial killer movie but must have been morbidly thrilling to a contemporary audience. The script acknowledges the British fascination for macabre murder, referencing Dr. Crippen and the "Brides in the Bath" case of 1915. The film cocks its eyebrow cheekily with censor-baiting dialogue regarding body disposal:

> "Why not chop me up in little pieces and sort of sprinkle me around?"
> "Oh no, I can't feel remotely attracted."

"Didn't I read of a case of a guy who shoved his victim into a trunk and checked the trunk in a cloakroom? How about that?"

"Oh no, most old-fashioned. It's almost an English institution."

Riordan's urbane civility, bringing his intended murder victim a daily flask of martini, is humorously inappropriate in the circumstances and perfectly portrayed by Newton.

The appearance halfway through of the law in the form of Superintendent Finsbury, played with characteristic nonchalance by Naunton Wayne, initiates a witty intellectual tussle as the policeman circles around Riordan, laying snares. Finsbury's initial appearance is preceded by a whiff of smoke and he is braced to play devilish tricks to catch the demon doctor. His relaxed style of non-interrogation unsettles Riordan in its off-handedness, a style that many a successive detective would adopt— Colombo would recognize Finsbury's use of "There was one small point I completely forgot...." Given the production circumstances of the film, it is entirely apt that the good doctor is eventually snagged by the occasional Americanism ("Thanks, pal") in his speech, indicating that he has been exposing himself to accents less cut-glass than those of the reactionary codgers in his gentlemen's club. Much club chatter is about the post-war decline of Empire and Britain's diminished standing in the world. Riordan, a man whose wife has made a cuckold of him and who is not the criminal mastermind he thought he was, is really only master of his own destiny when controlling the engines in the room-sized Empire of his train set.

Dmytryk makes fine use of Nino Rota's score, chronologically equidistant between his *Rome, Open City* for Rossellini and his first film for Fellini, *The White Sheik*. He knows when to silence the music completely, as when Riordan is up to no good with his chemistry set, and Rota produces a jaunty theme for Monty the dog, ultimately Kronin's savior. If the audience had been wavering as to whether or not to give Riordan their sympathy, all chance of that is dashed when it becomes clear that he is prepared to kill Monty. Audiences will accept anything, but the dog can't die. Riordan's fate is thus sealed. The entire animal kingdom appears to have been conscripted to ensure this outcome, and a cat is instrumental in a policeman spotting Riordan's car and eventually rescuing Kronin.

The cinematographer C. Pennington-Richards was known for the realism of his debut, Humphrey Jennings's *Fires Were Started*, though by this stage he had detoured via such melodramas as *Esther Waters*. His lighting manages to imbue bomb-scarred London sites[70] with something of the dreadful beauty that monochrome wrought from devastated continental cities in *Germany Year Zero* and *The Third Man*. Dmytryk's choice of stark overhead bulbs in ineffectual shades predominates in *Obsession*, casting morally murky Dr. Riordan in incongruous illumination, as all around him is shadow. Dmytryk loved working with "Penny" ("Cheerful, witty, hard-working, and ingenious"[71]) and was more than satisfied with the result of their collaboration: "When we walked on the set in the morning, a pull on the lamp cords lit the set. When an actor walked close to a light, he was hot; when he backed too far away, he nearly disappeared in the background. But God, did it look real!"[72] The glowering looks of Newton, dark eyes under heavy brows, respond well to Pennington-Richards' shadow play, as in the close-up of the cuckold eavesdropping on the lovers from behind a curtain. It is only appropriate that the police locate Kronin by the discovery of an unexplained extra light switch. The tonal palette is especially effective in the descent to Kronin's dungeon, a single torchlight piercing the darkness to reveal the ghastly lair. The high key flippancy of the film's final scene in the hospital fails to dispel the crepuscular nightmare that Dmytryk has evoked.

By an incredible twist of timing, the production of *Obsession* coincided with the apprehension of a genuine acid-bath murderer. John George Haigh had murdered his victims and dissolved their bodies in sulphuric acid, carrying out his crimes in Gloucester Road, Kensington, just across Hyde Park from the Mayfair locations of the film, as well as in Crawley, Sussex. He is confirmed to have disposed of six bodies by this method, though he claimed more victims. His final victim Olive Durand-Deacon was murdered on 18 February 1949. As Haigh awaited trial, with the details of his case *sub judice*, publicity packs were dispatched prior to the release of *Obsession*. The *Daily Mirror* relished the coincidence of art imitating life and splashed with photos from the film as well as details of Haigh's case. Not only was the newspaper's editor jailed for three months for contempt of court, but Pinewood was banned from publicizing the film and the release date was pushed back from April. Resolution came at the height of summer. The film was released to much public curiosity on 3 August. Haigh was hanged by executioner Albert Pierrepoint exactly a week later.

Give Us This Day (1949)

Give Us This Day is a tantalizing glimpse of the direction that Edward Dmytryk's career might have taken if he had stayed in England and chosen exile rather than surrendering to the hounds of HUAC. It is a socially engaged piece of work, a lament to the proletariat, occupying the sparsely populated terrain at the intersection between social realism and *film noir*. Its hero Geremio confronts the moral dilemmas and agonizing self-doubt familiar in the *noir* universe, languishing under bleakly expressionistic lighting, but the mean streets of this metropolis are filled with decent Italian-American construction workers trying to survive the Depression and the bad guys are their mostly unseen bosses. The subject-matter seems tailor-made for Dmytryk, who never relinquished his liberal convictions, and he attacks it with a vigor and conviction emerging from recognition that the unfamiliar class-bound Britishness of *So Well Remembered* was unable to provide: "All of us believed in the film so much that it was almost a crusade."[73]

Rod Geiger was an American soldier who had fallen in with Roberto Rossellini while serving in Italy and who had been instrumental in the making of *Rome Open City* and *Paisan*.

The Geiger project that brought Dmytryk to England was the adaptation of a semi-autobiographical, stylistically modernist novel by Pietro di Donato, *Christ in Concrete*, to which Rossellini and Luchino Visconti had previously been attached, as director and producer respectively. Geiger, something of a wheeler-dealer, displayed

Dmytryk (center) and Sam Wanamaker (right) examine model New York City trains with an unidentified collaborator for *Give Us This Day* (1949).

a lavish façade that disguised a lack of assets. He wanted Dmytryk to direct his newly acquired property but quickly discovered that, post–HUAC, American money could not be raised for a film with one of the Ten attached. Pre-empting what would become a talent drain of blacklisted and greylisted artists to Europe, Geiger found a British-based backer, Nat Bronsten, and the production of this very American tale shifted to England. The original scriptwriter, John Penn, was proving unsatisfactory, so Dmytryk approached Ben Barzman with whom he had worked on *Back to Bataan*. Barzman was scripting a Lana Turner vehicle at MGM but was convinced that making *Christ in Concrete* successfully would help break the rapidly solidifying blacklist. He apologized to Dore Schary, who had got him the job at MGM, for abandoning his scripting duties, to which Schary replied, "If you do, even if you're not blacklisted, you'll never work in Hollywood again!"[74]

In seeking finance for the film that would become *Give Us This Day*, Dmytryk became reacquainted with one figure in the industry whose motives he judged to be more philanthropic than mercenary: "If ever there was an example of a good capitalist, it was J. Arthur Rank. I have never met an executive with a more open mind. He listened attentively as I explained my situation, then dismissed my communist background as of no real consequence. My political views, he said, were no business of his."[75] Dmytryk and Rank had worked together two and a half years previously on *So Well Remembered*, and the director was inclined to believe that Rank was being charitable in putting up half the money for the film in return for distribution rights, since he must have been aware that an American boycott of the next Edward Dmytryk picture was a distinct possibility. He did however ask Dmytryk an unexpected question, whether he believed in God: "I sat there for a moment quietly. I am an agnostic. I don't *know* whether a God exists.... So I stretched a point and said yes. I have been lucky in the people who have crossed my path in critical moments of my life. J. Arthur Rank almost made a believer out of me."[76]

Rod Geiger was a rather less ethically motivated financial partner. Ben Barzman, his wife Norma and children were promised first-class tickets on the *Queen Mary* from New York to Southampton. When they arrived in New York and the tickets were not forthcoming, Barzman threatened to leave the picture with his finished script, despite having already burnt his bridges in Hollywood. Tickets were procured overnight and the Barzmans arrived in England early in 1949. Norma Barzman, in a memoir exhibiting incredible recall of detailed conversations, claims Dmytryk met them with the news that the Bank of England was refusing to release expense money for Americans in London and Geiger was unable to provide the funds: "Geiger hadn't paid Ben, so he didn't have a signed release allowing him to use the screenplay, a document the bank considered critical.... 'If I sign a statement saying I've been paid in full,' Ben said, 'I'll never be paid.'"[77] Barzman prevaricated for weeks, constantly unable to secure money from the producer. At one point, Dmytryk recalled Geiger triumphantly presenting a briefcase full of money—money so fresh off the printing press that green ink came off on his hands. On another occasion, gunfire was heard on the street where Geiger was staying, an apparent ruse to get him out into the open to face his creditors. Ben Barzman ultimately signed the necessary piece of paper on 23 March 1949, the day before shooting began. "Barzman was paid,"[78] wrote Dmytryk. "Of course, we were never paid for the screenplay,"[79] wrote Norma Barzman.

Norma Barzman makes one verifiably untrue assertion in *The Red and the Blacklist*: that just prior to the shoot commencing, the production team met with John Trevelyan, the head of the British Board of Film Censors. Trevelyan only joined the BBFC as a part-time examiner in 1951. Assuming that she did attend a meeting with someone at the BBFC and misremembered him as being Trevelyan, she writes that objections were made about a scene where Geremio's wife is washing in a tin bath in the kitchen and about Geremio, at the moment of his death, calling on the saints in prayer: "We cannot have prayers unanswered."[80] It was indicated that if the couple were shown in bed in their tenement flat, single beds would be necessary in order to meet the requirements of the Production Code, American distribution being essential for the commercial success of the film. One point where Barzman and Dmytryk concur in their accounts of the making of the film is that the British censor forbade the use of the word "Christ" in the title. The production was retitled *Give Us This Day*.

Sam Wanamaker, who had appeared on Broadway earlier in the decade opposite Ingrid Bergman's *Joan of Lorraine* and had just made his film debut in *My Girl Tisa*, was cast as Geremio. The following year, he also found himself a victim of blacklisting and permanently relocated to England. For the role of Geremio's wife Annuziata (20 and Italian), Geiger had secured a tentative commitment from the retired Luise Rainer (39 and Austrian). Despite her pedigree, Dmytryk felt she was unsuitable due to age and accent. She invited him and Geiger to her home to express her disappointment and treated them to "a thirty-minute recital of decapitated expectations, fancied slights, and delicately revealed hurts,"[81] concluded by a tearful dismissal when a bellboy serendipitously arrived with a letter from her husband. Luise Rainer was not a double-Oscar winner for nothing. They decided instead on Lea Padovani, who had begun shooting *Othello* with Orson Welles as his Desdemona, the role that would eventually be played by Suzanne Cloutier in that troubled production. Prefiguring what would happen with Maximilian Schell on the set of *The Young Lions*, when Padovani arrived in London it was immediately obvious that she spoke no English. Fully expecting to have to send her back to Italy but not wanting her trip to have been completely fruitless, Dmytryk filmed a test of her and had Phil Brown coach her dialogue. As she progressed from initial nervousness to wide-eyed passion, the character of Annuziata took shape on the sound stage at Denham. Padovani gives a beautiful performance in the film and worked hard on her English, though her strong accent works perfectly as the young bride-to-be fresh off the boat from Italy. Her instinctive feel for the character was in sharp contrast to the cerebral approach of Wanamaker. He had charts in his dressing room that mapped the emotional peaks and troughs of Geremio through the film, as an aid to pitching his performance at the correct level. Dmytryk recalled Padovani's reaction: "You're full of shit. I understood Annuziata when I first read the script."[82]

An interesting profile of Dmytryk at work on the film appeared that summer in the British magazine *Film Illustrated Monthly*, in an article titled "Give Us This Guy": "We've got a soft spot for Eddy Dmytryk. And it's not only because he's a nice guy to talk to, and happens to like Jelly Roll Morton's *New Orleans Memories*, either.... We don't by any means agree with all his way-left-of-centre views—but you can't help admiring someone who turns down two million dollars because of them.... 'I've starved before, and I'll starve again,' he told us over lunch at Denham. 'But I've noticed that each time I starve it's on a higher level.'"[83] The article contends that RKO wanted to settle Dmytryk's firing out of court but that he was "determined to stick with the rest of the gang."[84] He was bound to be welcomed back in Hollywood before long, the reader is assured, but even in that case Dmytryk was intending to make one film a year in Britain. Sam Wanamaker asserts that *Give Us This Day* could never have been made in Hollywood, "because Hollywood is not interested in the truth."[85]

The article is full of praise for the realism of the building-site set and notes Dmytryk's drive for detail: "We were standing watching the camera crew setting up for a shot of Wanamaker when we overheard this discussion. 'But I don't want it all to come down in one go,' said Dmytryk. 'I want the building to collapse in three sections. I want to be able to shoot the big fall in stages, so I can cut from shot to shot and build up a big scene, cutting from a close shot of bricks and beams falling, to a medium shot, and then back to a long shot of the place coming down.' The people concerned with the set construction seemed immovable in their conviction that once the place started coming down, it was going to come down all at once. 'Look,' said Dmytryk, jumping out of his chair beside the camera, 'Let's go up and discuss it there.' And he started dashing up ladders to the third half-built floor of the building, followed, somewhat reluctantly, by members of the production side. 'That's Eddy for you,' said someone as he disappeared in the gloom towards the roof of Denham's towering Stage 5."[86]

After their work together on *Obsession*, his collaboration with cinematographer Pennington-Richards (Penny) is even more successful the second time around. As indicated in the magazine article, the huge building site comprised a four-story structure which was to collapse at the conclusion of the picture. The decision to erect this on a soundstage was chiefly determined by the unpredictability of the British weather, but the difficulty that arose was making the set look like it was lit by a single light source, the sun, rather than a multitude of studio lights with their resulting shadows. Director and cinematographer discussed the problem, and Penny watched the construction of the set, formulating his solution. He obtained the four largest sun arcs available, clustered them in a clover formation and placed them in the most distant ceiling corner of the soundstage. The heat emitted by this arrangement was so intense that each scene would be set up and rehearsed under the relatively low light of the ceiling lamps. When the cameras were ready to roll, the arc lights would be struck and the set would receive its brilliant illumination. Dmytryk wrote: "But, by God, we had only one shadow! Even now, when I sometimes run my 16-millimeter print, I marvel at Penny's skill. I'd swear we shot those scenes out of doors."[87] The respect between the two was mutual, as Pennington-Richards indicated many years later in an interview: "Now you need co-operation to a certain extent from a director, you need a director who knows what you're trying to do, and Eddie Dmytryk did know. He knew where he had to leave me a little bit where I could put something in, you know. And we worked wonderfully together, no question whatever."[88]

Behind the credits of *Give Us This Day* roll a series of New York cityscapes, culminating in a view of slum housing overlaid with the wording "Directed by Edward Dmytryk," as if setting out his stall that this will be a socially committed piece of work. The wonderfully atmospheric opening sequence is saturated in *noir* tropes. Geremio staggers drunkenly through the shadowy streets of Manhattan via Denham, steam gushing from the subway vents into the blustery night air. He ascends a shadowy stairwell to the dizzy summit of a tenement building, only to find his front door locked on him. Breaking it open, he finds his wife Annuziata in furious reproach. After lashing out and slapping her, his children burst into the room singing "Happy Birthday" and he flees to the home of his mistress, Kathleen (Kathleen Ryan). There commences a lengthy flashback to show the compromises and betrayals that have brought our hero to this dark night of the soul. It is a bravura beginning, bearing *noir*'s familiar sense of fatalism, reinforced by Pennington-Richards' moody lighting and Benjamin Frankel's urgent score.

The standout performance in the film is Lea Padovani who delivers a finely textured portrayal of Annuziata. We first encounter her as a shy young woman, shipped over from Italy to meet and marry Geremio. Dmytryk constructs a marvelous sequence depicting a core ritual in the working-class experience—the community wedding of Geremio and Annuziata. It is the most joyous expression in the film of the social bond among the common people, all united in a feast of food, wine and song. The couple are serenaded with a song having the refrain "Without love you're nothing at all," while Annuziata gazes at her groom, her eyes glistening with the promise of the future. Under duress, she falteringly makes a speech: "I didn't know what I would find when I came here. Now I know. I am among my people." Padovani perfectly captures the wide-eyed vulnerability of the arranged bride, and as her character is ground down by disappointment, Annuziata's disillusionment is palpable in Padovani's expressive face, only to be replaced with the fiery refusal to give up the dream of a house of her own. It is a deeply affecting performance.

The setbacks that Geremio is forced to endure bring to mind the trials of Job and indeed, considering its makers were a band of atheistic or agnostic Communists, the film is heavy in religious symbolism. When Geremio leaves his home after the confrontation with Annuziata at the beginning of the film, he deliberately impales his hand on a railing, creating a bleeding stigmata on his palm and prefiguring his martyrdom by the end of the film. Returning home contrite and seeking forgiveness, Geremio falls to his knees and Annuziata cradles his head in her lap, a Madonna bearing her suffering man like a Pietà. But the God that is being referenced is a cruel God and inflicts disasters on the undeserving. During a difficult childbirth, Annuziata's friends circle her bed intoning "Salt to the devil, water to Hellfire," and at another point she dismisses her husband with "Why don't you go to the devil?" The devil appears to have gained the upper hand in 1920s New York. After the Wall Street Crash puts paid to their livelihoods, one of Geremio's workmates laments, "Heaven has forgotten us."

This scene of the laborers post–Crash discussing their fates is one of the clearest examples of Barzman's tendency to florid dialogue. Julio (Bonar Colleano) speaks of himself in the third person: "In the house of Julio, the air is become hunger. Stomachs have become wounds. In the house of Julio, children's hearts have become swollen vessels." Geremio responds, "In the house of Geremio, the dream is dying, and it is worse than hunger. Money was saved for a house, money torn from our food and comforts. Now we are eating our dream." The aim is clearly to give the proletarian man, for it almost always the language between the working men, a nobility and a dignity, an intellect and a poetry. The intention is pure, but the language occasionally suffers from grandiosity when set against its social-realist backdrop. Such stylistic flourishes draw a sharp contrast with the neorealist aesthetic that Rossellini and Visconti, both originally attached to *Christ in Concrete*, were developing at the time in Italy.

As with the social cohesion during the wedding party, the film celebrates working-class solidarity and co-operation between laborers. The central group of five talk of their pride of being bricklayers and builders and when they collaborate, as with a competition set up to pit workman against workman, they succeed and are able to divide the prize money among the quintet. When someone tries to shift from the bedrock level of the pure proletariat, they lose their bearings and begin to lose their soul. The owners of the building-sites remain the unseen capitalists but when a character moves from laborer to foreman or developer, the film judges him harshly. Murdin (Sid James), once nearly involved in a fatal accident, endangers the men on his site when he wins a demolition job by cutting back on safety measures. He takes Geremio on as foreman, which chips away at his integrity and leaves him side-lined by his workmates. After Geremio berates his closest friend Luigi (a very good performance from Charles Goldner) for not working hard enough, Luigi suffers a fall which renders him unemployable. Straying from one's roots will only result in punishment, either for oneself or for those closest.

The climax of the film is shockingly bleak. Having reconciled himself to his wife and resolved to practice solidarity with his workmates, a building site accident, caused by Murdin's corner-cutting, has Geremio buried alive in concrete, begging for forgiveness as he sinks to his death. The religious imagery recurs emphatically at this point: the accident takes place on Good Friday and is prefigured by Geremio draped on a wooden cross. The working man is martyred by an unseeing God and an uncaring capitalist system. When informed in the final scene that she will receive the amount of money he would have earned in his lifetime, his widow laments, "How much he earns? Is that the value of a man's life?" The final shot of her family's silhouettes walking away from camera is accompanied by silence on the soundtrack and by a wrenching poignancy that admits very little hope.

Give Us This Day exhibits a potency that overcomes its minor defects and the passion involved in bringing it to life communicates itself onscreen. Dmytryk recalled its executive showing for Rank, Bronsten, Geiger and others: "When the film was over and the lights came on, nobody moved for a full five minutes. No word was spoken. I had never had such a successful showing, and I never would again. When my guests could finally speak, their compliments were effusive."[89] The film's critical reception was equally effusive—it won the First Grand Masterpiece Award at the Venice Film Festival and prizes at Vichy, Prague and other festivals. It was listed in *Cahiers du Cinéma* as one of the best films of the year. The American Legion was of a different opinion and threatened a boycott of future releases if exhibitors refused to pull the film, and they duly complied. The title was changed to *Salt to the Devil* in an attempt to outwit the boycotters but the ruse failed, and the film limped into cinemas.

Where it was shown, it was received rapturously. *Salt to the Devil* received its first showing in the San Francisco area on 12 October 1950. The review in the *San Francisco Chronicle* was a rave: "There aren't many pictures in the uppermost shelf of this reviewer's esteem, and sometimes they get mighty lonesome up there, high above the run-of-the-projector stuff. But yesterday they had company."[90] Even more vindicating was a letter to Dmytryk from the owner of the Vogue Theatre where it was shown: "I knew that you would be pleased to hear that when your credit was flashed on the screen, the audience broke into spontaneous applause. In all my years as a Motion Picture Exhibitor, I cannot recall that this has ever happened before. All in all the picture is being well-received and we are looking forward to the pleasure of housing it for a long run."[91] By the time of this showing, Edward Dmytryk had served his time in Mill Point Prison, West Virginia, and liberal public opinion was clearly behind him. Before long, he would achieve pariah status from both Left and Right.

IV

Stanley Kramer, Career Savior
(1951–1954)

Prior to his release from prison, Dmytryk's agents, Charles Feldman and Jack Gordean, had used the statement he made from Mill Point in September 1950 to set up a deal with Columbia Pictures. Harry Cohn was a strong opponent of HUAC who had not wanted to sign the Waldorf Declaration and was willing to separate himself from the pack in employing one of the Hollywood Ten who had expressed contrition. The figure being discussed between agents and mogul was $60,000 per picture. Upon release, Dmytryk was approached by Herbert Biberman, who had received the same shorter sentence as him, with a request to support the application for parole being made by the Eight still in prison. Dmytryk agreed to write to the parole board on the condition that his name be kept confidential, realizing it might jeopardize the negotiations with Columbia. Within days, Dmytryk's name was leaked to the trade papers and Harry Cohn withdrew his offer. It was this incident that propelled Dmytryk to make his appearance before the Committee but the public purging that he was forced to undergo did not lead to the hoped-for avalanche of offers. His agents kept trying but, with the second Hollywood HUAC hearings in full swing, the studio bosses clustered together, unwilling to risk the negative publicity that might result in employing the declared ex-Communist.

In March 1951, independent producers the King Brothers employed Dmytryk to overhaul the script for their upcoming crime film titled *The Syndicate*. He produced a three-page document with ten points such as "Strengthen the point that gambling is the mainstay of crime today, as rum-running was during Prohibition days"; "Focus more on the big final race.... Mickey has to catch the field and pass them in the stretch to win. But Penny is still actually in danger. She is saved after the race"; and "Put back the opening as previously written, showing the far-flung activities of the Syndicate."[1] *The Syndicate* was never produced. Also that March, Stanley Kramer set up an unprecedented production deal with Harry Cohn, who was determined to beef up the Columbia Pictures release schedule with product that was externally produced. The agreement, brokered by Kramer's new partner Sam Katz, was worth $25 million, requiring Kramer to deliver thirty films, six a year, financed and released by Columbia and with profits being shared. Within months, the fates of Edward Dmytryk and Stanley Kramer would be intertwined.

On 13 May, Dmytryk was announced as director of the upcoming King Brothers swashbuckler, **Mutiny**.[2] *The Hollywood Reporter* wrote: "Move by the Kings marks them as the first to respond to urgings of the Un-American Activities Committee that the film industry put back to work those who have co-operated with the Committee. This will be Dmytryk's first job in Hollywood in three-and-a-half years."[3] It was a financially astute move by the King Brothers, who made a sizeable profit from the film, and a politically acceptable one from Dmytryk, whose re-appearance in the director's chair did not provoke tumultuous headlines. Indicative of the nervousness of the time however, and rather ominously for the future, the *Variety* review of *Mutiny* does not mention Edward Dmytryk or refer to the direction at all.

The Dmytryk family, Eddie, Jean and Rick, rented a small house in Sherman Oaks in the San Fernando Valley and, while waiting for a further offer of work, the man of the house spent three hours a day lifting weights: "I was in the pink, but also in the red. I just couldn't get rid of that damned color."[4] Jean was pregnant again and put two-year-old Rick in a nursery school for three hours every morning. The little boy was involved in a traffic accident in October which was initially hugely worrying for them, but he made a complete recovery and the following month, on 27 November, Victoria Jean was born.

By this stage, Dmytryk had been approached by Stanley Kramer and was in the middle of a four-picture deal for him, which had begun with the shooting of **The Sniper** in September. Kramer later explained, "I was a producer, and I always wanted to be a director. And Eddie was one of the people who was efficient, knew film, could edit, and was reasonably always on schedule.... To make the kind of pictures you wanted to make—and I made a lot of unsuccessful ones—...you had to be the producer, the boss.... It changed then into a director's medium.... I was not cut out to be Darryl F. Zanuck or his counterpart, and that's what I was doing, and I just was no good at it."[5] Dmytryk disagreed, feeling that Kramer "would have been another Selznick or another Thalberg if he hadn't had this tremendous driving ego that wanted to do everything, most of which he does not do very well. Except produce, actually."[6]

Kramer was sympathetic to Dmytryk's plight, calling him "the Hollywood One.... I think Dmytryk once he had become what was termed by that Hollywood group 'a cooperative witness' was called upon all the time to make statements. It must have worn him down to a frazzle.... To continually protest 'I am an American' can wear you down as much as anything."[7] Kramer had just finished producing *High Noon* at United Artists, with its clear message of doing the right thing, regardless of the judgment of one's peers. Though he later denied the political factors in employing Dmytryk, he cannot have been blind to the possible repercussions. It was therefore a brave and admirable move on the producer's part to fully rehabilitate the director, and it was a lifeline for Dmytryk, for whom Kramer "was very fair as you noticed, because he hired me. It also indicates that he's not an extreme liberal or extreme progressive or he wouldn't have, because by that time I had purged myself obviously. He hired me because he thought I was a good filmmaker."[8]

In March 1952, with their financial future looking secure and while shooting his second film for Kramer, **Eight Iron Men**, the Dmytryks moved into a new home in Bel-Air, leased with an option to purchase. It was a two-story house on St. Cloud Road, built around 1912, where Carole Lombard was living when she met Clark

Gable, and where they lived together while building a ranch house in Encino. The Dmytryks would live there for the next nineteen years.

In June 1952, while he was scouting locations in Israel for his next picture, *The Juggler*, Dmytryk's first wife Madeleine died. Madeleine had maintained tangential involvement with the film industry, picking up three credits at RKO: dialogue director on *The Falcon's Alibi* (1946) and *The Master Race* (directed by Herbert Biberman in 1944); and researcher on *Youth Runs Wild*, a film directed by Mark Robson in 1944, to which Edward Dmytryk had originally been attached. The circumstances around Madeleine's death by drug overdose are unclear but aroused some press speculation at the time. Mitch Tuchman, in his interview with Albert Maltz in 1976, asked Dmytryk's prison-mate about the matter: "[In] 1952 [Madeleine] lived in an apartment house in Beverly Hills where [Adrian] Scott and Mrs. Alvah Bessie [lived too].… And the way the newspaper reported it was that it was an overdose, but they called in Adrian Scott for some questioning.… The paper implied that she had been having an affair with Scott and that he was about to go off with Mrs. [Helen] Bessie and that over that she had committed suicide."[9] Maltz replied, "I think that's all absolute nonsense. But I don't know."[10] Joan LaCour, who married Adrian Scott in 1955, confirmed that Scott had been dating Madeleine.

Madeleine had put her and Dmytryk's son Michael in the Chadwick boarding school in Los Angeles county, and when Jean went to fetch the eleven-year-old boy, Madeleine's sister and Adrian Scott were there, both also wanting to take the boy home with them. Jean later wrote: "I hadn't seen him in six years.… He went up to his Aunt Barbara and hugged her, and to my astonishment, he came over and hugged me. He nodded to Adrian. He had been told that we all wanted him, and that his dad would be home tomorrow. He chose to come home with me, to be with his dad."[11] The newly enlarged family began its readjustment process and Jean acknowledged the efforts of her husband: "He is a proud and brilliant man and finds it difficult to be soft. He wanted to be a good father but didn't know how. It did not come naturally."[12]

The Juggler was shot in Israel in the autumn of 1952, the first feature film to do so, and the following year Dmytryk directed a short portmanteau film called *Three Lives*. It was a non-commercial film produced by the United Jewish Appeal, scripted by Edward and Edna Anhalt, presented by Charlton Heston and featured Jane Wyman, Randolph Scott and Arthur Franz. Though minor, it continued the theme of the Jewish experience in Dmytryk's work.

Moreover, Kramer was so satisfied with Dmytryk's work on his previous three films that he entrusted him with his most important property and what would become the jewel in the Kramer-Columbia crown, *The Caine Mutiny*. The biggest star that Dmytryk had yet directed, Humphrey Bogart, had begun working on the film in June 1953. When the first six films produced by Kramer in his deal with Harry Cohn—the non–Dmytryk titles of these six being *Death of a Salesman* starring Fredric March, *The Happy Time* directed by Richard Fleischer, *My Six Convicts* written by Michael Blankfort and *The Member of the Wedding* directed by Fred Zinnemann—were financial failures, Columbia reduced the number of films per year to three, but after ten failures, the agreement was terminated on 24 November 1954. The supreme irony was that the eleventh picture, *The Caine Mutiny*, the only commercial hit of the bunch, was so successful that it wiped out the losses on the previous ten. The relationship between Cohn and Kramer was fraught and their parting frosty but about a year later, they found themselves on the same plane, just as Kramer's first film as director, *Not as a Stranger*, was shaping itself into a hit. Kramer recalled that Cohn "approached with a smile on his face, put an arm on my shoulder, and said, 'I hear you've got a great picture. I want you to know I'm proud of you.' If there's anyone who can figure out Harry Cohn, I wish he'd explain the man to me."[13]

Just three years after his bargain-basement stint on *Mutiny*, Edward Dmytryk enjoyed one of the biggest hits of his career in *The Caine Mutiny*. The years of bounty had returned but the grumblings below deck continued and full acceptance remained elusive.

Mutiny (1952)

The King Brothers knew how to take advantage of a situation. Frank, Maury and Herman King (born Kozinsky) had been bootleggers during the Prohibition era. When that well ran dry, they eventually entered the motion picture business, initially with Producers Releasing Corporation (PRC) in the late 1930s, and subsequently with Monogram, for which they made *Dillinger* in 1945. The film was budgeted at $193,000 and made over $4 million worldwide. With their self-confidence thus fortified, they went independent with *The Gangster* in 1947, to unimpressive box-office receipts. Fortuitously for them, all hell was breaking loose in Washington just then with the HUAC hearings. Frank King called Dalton Trumbo, gaining infamy as one of the Hollywood Ten alongside Edward Dmytryk, and offered him $3,750 for a year and a half's work with them. Trumbo started work on *Gun Crazy* the next day.

The blacklist became a golden opportunity for the King Brothers, enabling them to hire talent at rates slashed from what had been earned pre–HUAC. For the next 20 years, they employed writers such as John Howard Lawson, Ring Lardner, Jr., Michael Wilson and Lester Cole, fronted by other names. The brothers were sanguine about their involvement in this black market. "Politics didn't enter into it at all. We were just interested in making pictures,"[14] was Frank King's justification. While many would replace the word "pictures" with the word "money," Dalton Trumbo was defensive of the producers: "When I and others plummeted in value, we naturally found ourselves in this new market, and naturally these independent producers availed themselves of our services because they felt that for this money they could get better work. So there wasn't really this brutal exploitation of black-market writers that has sometimes been referred to."[15]

Edward Dmytryk's brush with the King Brothers had kicked off in March 1951 with a scripting advisory role but only became public after his testimony before the Committee in April. His rehabilitation began the following month with the publication of "What Makes a Hollywood Communist?" in the *Saturday Evening Post* and his signing to the King Brothers for $5,000 for one swashbuckler, though the King Brothers inaccurately informed the press that he was receiving $2,500 a week. The trio of lead actors earned more than him—$22,000 for Mark Stevens, $7,916 for Angela Lansbury and $5,250 for Patric Knowles—as did music director Dimitri Tiomkin. It was a rock-bottom rate for an Oscar-nominated, commercially successful director. Grateful for the work, no matter the level of renumeration, Dmytryk began filming on the Sam Goldwyn lot on 22 June and wrapped on 16 July.

Mutiny is a potboiler on the high seas of 1812. With war declared between the USA and England and American ports blockaded, Captain Jim Marshall (Mark Stevens) is dispatched by President Madison to France to secure $10 million in gold bullion in order to fund the war effort. As second-in-command he enlists his old friend Ben Waldridge (Patric Knowles), a former Royal Navy captain who has fallen from his rank in disgrace and is now leading a dissolute life. The film is at core a paean to male loyalty, despite the vicissitudes that fate and females bring to bear on the friendship. The bond between these two brothers-in-arms is contrasted against two other unstable relationships. The mutinous duo that foments the crew, Hook (Gene Evans) and Redlegs (Rhys Williams), are well-drawn subsidiary characters, ruthless sailors propelled by lust for gold and grog. They more than meet their match when at Le Havre they are joined on board by Ben's estranged wife Leslie, another in the serpentine succession of villainesses played by Angela Lansbury.

Though the script is not of the standard one could wish for such a skilled actress, Lansbury attacks it vigorously. Suspecting that the gold bullion has been smuggled onboard as an anchor, she is initially dissuaded by Hook and Redlegs from entering the anchor room since it is no place for a lady. To which she retorts, "If that anchor is what I think it is, I can forget I'm a lady." Discovering that her suspicions about the anchor are correct, her allegiance is clear: "You're dirty, you smell of tar and you haven't shaved for weeks, but I think I love you both!" It falls to her to persuade her still besotted husband to mutiny and make off with the gold: "Take your choice, Ben: ten million in gold—and me. Or nothing." Having been twice Oscar-nominated less than a decade earlier, Lansbury was also somewhat slumming it by signing with the King Brothers. Her retrospective attitude to the film was dismissive: "Don't wait up for it on the late show."[16]

Mutiny is not a swashbuckler of the top rank and displays its meager budget and lack of ambition too clearly. It is set almost entirely on board the *Concord,* whereas scenes onshore would have provided respite and a more interesting rhythm. This is particularly true regarding the introduction of the character of Leslie. She is met in France by Jim and Ben and proves instrumental in enabling a difficult, presumably exciting escape with the gold bullion. Alas this adventure all happens onshore, off-screen. The script is credited to Philip Yordan, who had been nominated for an Oscar for *Dillinger* in 1945, received a second nomination for William Wyler's *Detective Story* the year before *Mutiny* and would ultimately win for Dmytryk's *Broken Lance.* Yordan later relocated to Europe where he would operate as the King Brothers did the United States, employing blacklisted writers on various productions and claiming the screenwriting credit for himself, a subject of frequent resentment. One of his closest associates was Bernard Gordon, who was subpoenaed to appear before HUAC in 1952, was not called when the Committee ran out of time but was nevertheless blacklisted. In an interview about his friend Yordan, Gordon admitted that "most of the people who worked for him were seriously underpaid … people did feel exploited,"[17] and in a later interview, conceded that he was "notorious"[18] for using the work of others under his own name.

Mutiny is scored stirringly by Dimitri Tiomkin and photographed in Technicolor—a first for the King Brothers—by Ernest Laszlo. Patric Knowles gives good account of the moral weakness of Ben, prepared for the second time in his career to put desire for his wife ahead of loyalty to friend and country. Redemption is his when he shoots Leslie rather than have her shoot Jim, and volunteers for what ends up as a suicide mission to sink a British ship with a prototype submarine, here called "submersible." Publicity for the film declared it to be modeled after the first ever submersible that was built under the operation of Robert Fulton's steamboat, and also boasted the use of an 18-gun, 94-foot brig. For most of the duration of the film, Dmytryk is unable to stretch himself with the raw material at his disposal but with a full-blooded combat scene using cutlass, dagger and hook against the mutineers and, particularly, with the final submersible sequence, he wrests an exciting denouement from the script that bears Philip Yordan's name. It may not be historically accurate but having its nineteenth century heroes pedaling furiously in a wooden crate to torpedo an enemy vessel certainly earns points for originality.

The King Brothers knew their business and made a financial success of the film. The swashbuckler received its premiere in Seattle on 27 February 1952 and was particularly popular in Atlanta, Dallas, Los Angeles and New York. On a final budget of $445,000, *Mutiny* delivered a profit of $310,000 from all territories. Having endured the boycott of *Give Us This Day*, Dmytryk needed to know if the Communist mud would stick: "It served as a finger in the wind for me. Nobody protested my employment; the American Legion remained quiescent; no theaters were picketed. I had demonstrated that I was no longer 'unclean.'"[19]

The Sniper (1952)

On 26 July 1951, Joseph Breen of the Production Code Administration (PCA) wrote to Stanley Kramer:

Dear Mr. Kramer:

We have read with very great care the first draft screenplay for your proposed production titled, THE SNIPER, and regret to be compelled to advise you that this material, both basically and in detail, is so thoroughly and completely unacceptable from the standpoint of the Production Code that a motion picture based upon it could not be approved by us.

You will have in mind that provision of the Production Code which states quite clearly that "*sex perversion or any inference of it is forbidden.*"

In addition, we are of the opinion that the over-all flavor of this story is such as to make it most repellent. It is our considered unanimous judgement that this is a type of story which does not lend itself to screen dramatization for mixed audiences in theaters.

It is our further thought that this is not the kind of story which, by some careful rewriting, might be salvaged. We could not, by the wildest stretch of the imagination, approve anything even remotely suggestive of the present story.[20]

The bark of the Production Code was frequently worse than its bite but such a decisive rejection of the concept behind this proposed film, pre-publicized in *Variety* two months earlier as "the story of a sex maniac,"[21] would have deterred many a producer. And yet *The Sniper* was made.

The originators of the story were Edward and Edna Anhalt, who had also provided the story for Elia Kazan's *Panic in the Streets*. Edward found the germ of an idea when he spotted a steeplejack on a smokestack in San Diego and thought about what a great vantage point it was. This image would work its way into the climax of the picture and from it developed the plotline of a murderer who "got his kicks out of shooting women."[22] The Anhalts gave a rather more measured explanation of the rationale behind the film in an article for the *New York Times* in May 1952: "We had four purposes in writing and producing the film with Stanley Kramer. One, to expose the shocking inability of our present social machinery to protect the individual citizen against the sex criminal. Two, to do so with a maximum of suspense and excitement, i.e., entertainment. Third, to use the correct psychological vocabulary of the situations to make our points, regardless of traditional censorship. Four, to do a completely straight story line without jazzing up or gimmicking for cinematic effects or relief."[23]

The Anhalts sold the story to Kramer who employed Harry Brown to write the screenplay. In response to Breen's letter in July, a meeting was arranged for 2 August between Kramer's team, including Brown and Edward Anhalt, and Breen with a PCA colleague. Anhalt remembered convincing them to reverse their decision through the unusual method of highlighting the fact that it was women that the sniper targeted: "I proved he was a heterosexual sniper, he didn't get his kicks off shooting *men*, therefore it was not about *perversion*, as they called it."[24] Whatever the tactics deployed, the production team agreed to eliminate all inferences of sex perversion, and a revised script with "very extensive changes"[25] was deemed acceptable on 14 August, albeit with further amendments to be made.

Particular attention was drawn to the scenes where Eddie Miller (Arthur Franz) deliberately maims himself to prevent him from using his rifle, where he meets May (Marlo Dwyer) in a bar, and where a police line-up of sex offenders is interrogated. For the first, the original script described "Eddie pressing his hand down on the electric burner."[26] Dmytryk stylishly resolved this problem by shooting Eddie from below, the glowing ring of the electric stove reflected on the ceiling behind his head and the shadow of his hand moving in and obscuring the reflection. It is a visually striking and dramatically effective moment. In the original bar scene, May invites him to "come around and see me some night. But ring the bell first." This was construed as clearly soliciting, and thus unacceptable, though the replacement dialogue where May says, "You know I like you, you got a nice face," while slipping a beermat with her name and address on it into his pocket, seems equally forward behavior for a lone woman in a bar.

The PCA relaxed its squeamishness about even referring to sex offenders. The original reference in the script to "every registered offender of this type" was objected to, with "every potential killer of this type"[27] suggested as an alternative, yet the line in the finished film has changed to "every registered sex offender of this type." Similarly, the words "molesters" and "peeping Toms" were requested to be eliminated in a police inspector's speech, but Frank Faylen instead speaks the words "rapists, defilers, peeping Toms." Certain lines were beyond the pale, however. Reference to a man in the line-up who "only buys candy for small children"[28] was cut, as was mention of "sex nuts."[29] While the PCA issued its approval on 10 December 1951, the film encountered censorship issues in other territories. The British censor initially rejected *The Sniper* but after performing additional edits on four reels, including removal of the line-up sequence and of the phrase "peeping Toms," it was given an X certificate.

Stanley Kramer chose, somewhat mischievously, the famously fastidious dresser Adolphe Menjou for the role of the scruffy police detective assigned to the sniper's case. Menjou had been a leading actor in the 1930s but by the early 1950s his career was on a downward trajectory. He was also a leading right-wing figure within the Hollywood community, unashamedly admitting, "I'm a Red-baiter. I'm a witch-hunter if the witches are Communists."[30] He had been a friendly witness before HUAC in October 1947, his testimony including some rather extraordinary statements: "I believe that under certain circumstances a communistic director, a communistic writer, or a communistic actor, even if he were under orders from the head of the studio not to inject Communism or un–Americanism or subversion into pictures, could easily subvert that order, under the proper circumstances, by a look, by an inflection, by a change in the voice. I think it could be easily done. I have never seen it done, but I think it could be done."[31] This made him a *bête noire* for the political spectrum between the Communists and the progressive liberals, Dore Schary describing him as a "creep."[32]

From the other side of the political spectrum, Kramer chose Edward Dmytryk to be director of *The Sniper*, because Kramer was supervising concurrent productions at Columbia and needed a capable deputy: "I found him particularly appropriate because he could be depended on to be on or near schedule. He was a competent, knowing film director and a very good editor, and it took a lot of the responsibility from me, because I was making multiple films, which I didn't want to be making and which really I wasn't too talented at."[33] Dmytryk had survived a feared boycott of his first post-prison picture *Mutiny* and thus seemed to have weathered the HUAC storm, at least commercially. Kramer's decision to put a jailed ex-Communist and a torchbearer for the Right on the same picture was perverse: "I didn't make these choices capriciously.... Well aware of the political differences between Dmytryk and Menjou, I called both of them into my office before the filming began. 'Remember one thing while you're making this picture,' I said. 'We're here to do a job. We want to do it as thoroughly and truthfully as possible, so let's submerge any personal or political resentments and get on with it.'"[34] Both director and actor proved to be professionals and there was no discord on set. Both however experienced flak for this collaboration. The *Daily Worker* fumed on 15 November that Dmytryk was "now palsy-walsy with his erstwhile foe—the rabid witch-hunter and haberdasher's gentleman—Adolphe Menjou."[35] Menjou responded pithily to one outraged associate's query as to why he had accepted the job: "Because I'm a whore!"[36]

In the skilled hands of Edward Dmytryk, the Anhalts achieve the four aims that they had outlined in the *New York Times*: *The Sniper* is a plea for criminal reform providing key generic pleasures with a patina of realistic jargon, in a relatively unsensational manner. The film is the first to attempt to understand the psychology of a sexually motivated killer, and among the first to take a serious approach to the social origins of the criminal. For the first 24 minutes, we view the world almost totally from the perspective of Eddie Miller, apart from a short scene in the bar where his first victim Jean Darr (Marie Windsor) plays the piano, and a conversation about him between two hospital employees. Dmytryk pulls his camera tight into Miller's face, as he looks through the viewfinder of his rifle at a young woman and as he makes a desperate abortive phone call to the doctor at the prison from which he has been released. We observe him flinch at signs of female aggression (a mother slapping her child, his domineering work supervisor) or sexuality (a flirtatious cash register attendant, a succession of courting couples). When he accidentally bumps into an elderly woman, her husband berates him, "You might have hurt this lady. Young fool!" Miller is tempted to react physically but just then a traffic signal chimes STOP, and he thinks better of it. Miller very much does want to stop, and we are sympathetic to his attempts—trying to get himself committed back to a psychiatric ward; burning his hand to prevent him from using his rifle.

But sympathy only goes so far, and Miller's crimes are chilling. Marie Windsor gives an engaging performance as Jean, a customer of the cleaning firm for which Miller is a driver, who is friendly without being flirtatious but who makes the fatal error of pushing him out the back door when her jealous boyfriend turns up. In a sharply filmed sequence, with accomplished twilight photography from Burnett Guffey, Miller stalks Jean along the San Francisco streets and takes up position on a roof opposite the Paper Doll Club. When she leaves the bar after her shift, we are prepared for Miller to shoot at her, but Dmytryk still produces a shocking moment. Jean pauses to look at her photo in a display case, a shot rings out and she is propelled into the display, shattering its glass, before falling to the ground. At the time it would not have been possible to show any element of impact of the bullet itself, but the ingenious solution to show a pane of glass utterly smashed is vivid testimony to the violence that has occurred.

The second killing is perhaps even more startling despite its absolute inevitability. Marlo Dwyer was a supporting actress who made four films with Dmytryk, most notably as the girlfriend of the murdered Samuels in *Crossfire*. May Nelson in *The Sniper* may have been softened by the Production Code into a more innocuous figure drinking in a bar than originally written, but she brushes off Miller, sensing that his stories of Hawaii are fanciful, though not before providing him with her address. The tension is again well built as she staggers home alone at night, kicking a tin can which clatters ceaselessly down the steep San Francisco street. Dmytryk's camera observes her enter her house and pans up to the first-floor apartment where a light is switched on. He cuts to a view outside her window and watches her ready herself for bed, where she will sleep with a doll, and pour herself a drink, all the while composer

George Antheil has his orchestra hold a single note. The tension built up is acute and the resolution is dramatic. Once again, we hear a shot and see May fall to the floor inside her bedroom, and the focus then pulls back to pinpoint the bullet hole that has pierced the window. It is a remarkably executed scene.

The scenes that depict the police pursuit of Miller are less successfully handled in Harry Brown's screenplay. Menjou is pleasingly rumpled as Lt. Frank Kafka and Richard Kiley is effective as the psychiatrist Dr. Kent, but Kiley's speeches advocating tolerance and treatment of sexual offenders have a tendency to preachify. After a society woman has been killed by Miller, City Hall takes the serial killer seriously and a meeting is called between politicians, press and businessmen. Kent appeals to them: "Put these people away when they're first caught. And those who can be cured will be cured. And those who can't, well, at least they'll never get out to try it again." His entreaties are dismissed as "psychiatric mumbo-jumbo" due to the cost of effecting such a scheme. The scene is important in explaining the reforms that the film is propounding but it lacks energy and feels labored when compared to the much more vital sequences focusing on Miller. Certain of the police scenes exhibit verve, however, such as the rooftop pursuit of a would-be copycat killer, the presence of the police revealed by the pulling back of some laundry on a line. Another smartly shot scene which combines the story of Miller with the police procedure against him has him pull up in his van at the home of his victim Jean while the police are in her apartment. We watch Kafka performing his investigation in the foreground while, through the window, we witness Miller reverse his van out of sight.

In probably his best role, Dmytryk regular Arthur Franz gives a committed performance as Miller, the tight close-ups scrutinizing his doubts and frustrations and flashes of anger. As he burns Jean's dress to destroy evidence, we watch his face illuminated by flickering flames morph from delight to disgust. Edward Anhalt called Franz "a wonderful actor"[37] and judged Dmytryk to be "marvelous with actors."[38] As the film progresses, Miller's volatility increases and his attitude to women becomes ever more unstable. Phallic symbolism can be overplayed in film criticism but Miller's fetishistic handling of his rifle seems a meaningful inclusion on the part of the Anhalts. We suspect that his antagonistic work supervisor (Geraldine Carr) may end up a victim but ultimately she is a crucial element in his capture. At an amusement park, Miller is baited by a woman to throw balls at a target in order to drop her into a barrel of water. The enthusiasm of her taunting increases the accuracy of his throwing and he loses composure, throwing balls at her instead of at the target. The misogyny consuming Miller is writ large on Franz's face.

As critical as *The Sniper* is of the political realm, it also treats the public consumption of sensational news stories with distaste. Throughout the film we are treated to a Greek chorus of those excited, disgusted and frightened by the sniper on the loose, reveling in the salacious aspects and delivering judgment on the perpetrator. There are gawpers at every crime scene, appealing for the police to let them get a little closer. When the police have Miller cornered at the end of the film, we hear one woman declare, "I hope they kill him!" with bloodthirsty relish. At the very first crime scene, Dmytryk fades from the display case smashed by the victim to a young girl among the voyeuristic onlookers staring at the corpse. This is a crime scene clearly unsuitable for a young child, yet her mother is unrepentant when a policeman points this out. The film makes it implicit that Miller's mental imbalance is due to a damaged relationship with his mother. The effects of this young girl witnessing such a disturbing event will only become apparent in the years to come.

The film was shot between 27 September and 23 October 1951, its Los Angeles locations including Long Beach Amusement Park and Hollywood Alpine Cleaners, which gained considerable advertising as the cleaning firm for which Miller worked. What really distinguishes the film, however, is the excellent location shooting performed in San Francisco. The life of its inhabitants is sensed—commuters on the streetcar, revelers on the night-time streets—and most of all the unique topography of the city is captured, the steep hills forming a vivid backdrop to the action. This is especially true at the conclusion of the picture. After the arresting visual sequence of shooting a steeplejack on a chimney—the image that provided the inspiration for the script—Miller flees the scene and we follow his dogged progress up and down the steep gradients of the city in a lengthy series of shots that indicate his exhaustion, physical and emotional. Dmytryk commented on the fact that Miller keeps running, despite the fact that nobody is actually in pursuit: "My intent was to indicate that he was trying to escape his own conscience."[39] Once he reaches his room, he is palpably relieved. He draws the blinds, assembles his rifle and waits. There is a bravery to the final four minutes of the film. Eschewing a violent resolution and leaving Miller alone in his room, we join the crowds outside and follow Kafka and the police as they enter his building and shoot open his bedroom door. As Kafka enters the room, the camera adopts his perspective and slowly rounds the corner, coming to rest on Miller cradling his gun on the bed. He looks straight to camera, which pulls in with a very tight close-up, and we see his tear-streaked cheeks and a look of gentle resignation. "All right, Eddie, let's go," says Kafka. It is a subdued, humane ending, quite at one with the film's appeal for understanding in place of retribution.

The Sniper can be appreciated today as a sober appeal for reform in the guise of a tightly constructed, sharply executed thriller. It premiered in March 1952, with the distinction of having Saul Bass design its trade advertisements, and obtained very good reviews in *Variety*, *The Hollywood Reporter* and other publications. Harry Cohn, head of Columbia, was not among the admirers. After a studio screening, Kramer remembered him saying, "This thing stinks. I hate it, and it'll never make a nickel."[40] Without the support of the top office, the Columbia distribution and publicity departments practically ignored it and the film failed to make a profit. Bosley Crowther of the *New York Times* disliked the film and was upbraided by Edward Anhalt at a cocktail party for his very critical review. Anhalt objected to Crowther treating "any piece of shit that comes from Twentieth Century–Fox, which is purely Twentieth Century–Fox, a musical, with great tolerance"[41] and for not treating an experimental film such as *The Sniper* with the same indulgence. Anhalt recalled that Crowther "blew up to twice his size! I probably hit some sort of a button with him."[42]

The film managed to gain a certain notoriety when, much as *Obsession* had done four years earlier, the title of the film made the leap from the entertainment pages to the news section. On 17 November 1952, the *Hollywood Citizen-News* reported an incident in Toronto: "An eighteen-year-old youth faced attempted murder charges here today after sitting through twelve showings of the movie thriller *The Sniper*, and then firing at five persons in his own sniping spree…. 'I shouldn't have seen that picture. I seen it too much, too,' the short, slender Fisher told the police."[43] A script that had mentioned the phenomenon of copycat killers became rather too prescient. The original aspects of the script may not have appealed to Bosley Crowther, but the Academy recognized them and nominated Edna and Edward Anhalt for Best Motion Picture Story. Alas, they suffered the ignominy of losing to the screenwriters of one of the worst Best Picture winners of all time: Cecil B. DeMille's *The Greatest Show on Earth*.

Eight Iron Men (1952)

Eight Iron Men was filmed under the working title of *The Dirty Dozen*, the title that coincidentally would provide Lee Marvin with a huge hit fifteen years later. Here Marvin was at the start of his career and one of a relatively unknown ensemble, both then and now. The lack of name actors bothered the director, but producer Stanley Kramer reassured him: "You can bring it off—I know you can do it."[44] Dmytryk certainly did bring it off and the film stands up remarkably well as a contained chamber-of-war piece, dealing with the reaction of seven GIs when the eighth member of their squad becomes trapped under enemy fire. The director's concerns about marquee appeal were not unfounded though and it was unsuccessful at the box-office. "*Eight Iron Men* was well liked by the critics. Unfortunately, they got in free."[45]

A Sound of Hunting by Harry Brown had opened at the Lyceum Theatre on Broadway in November 1945 but, failing to find an audience that wasn't worn out by war, closed after only twenty-three performances. It did however prove a successful springboard for a 32-year-old actor called Burton Lancaster, who won good notices, a Theatre World award and an agent in Harold Hecht. Lancaster lost a syllable to become the more masculine Burt, and together with Hecht forged a unique career in Hollywood. Stanley Kramer eventually picked up the scent of the play through his association with Harry Brown and Frank Lovejoy, one of the cast of what Kramer embellishes in his autobiography into a "Broadway hit…. I was delighted with the prospect of working with [Lovejoy] again. Lancaster had never worked for me, but I got indications from his camp that he was willing to repeat his stage role on film. What I didn't anticipate was that by the time I was able to get a shooting date and hire a cast, both Lovejoy and Lancaster were committed to other projects. There went my chance to make a picture with a certifiable star, Lancaster, and an excellent, well-known costar."[46]

When he came to assemble his crew and cast, Kramer reconvened the talent from his recent success, to Dmytryk's advantage and relief. Brown, the screenwriter on *The Sniper*, was to adapt his own play, while Edward and Edna Anhalt from the same film became associate producers. In a deliberate effort to avoid typecasting,

Arthur Frantz, the Sniper himself, was cast as the mediating presence of Private Carter, while the police psychiatrist in that film, Richard Kiley, was to play the twitchy, trigger-happy Coke. The cast was completed by a non-stellar but thoroughly competent group of actors, their lack of familiarity bolstering credibility in this troop of archetypes as everymen. Bonar Colleano, born in New York but a well-known face on post-war British screen (*A Matter of Life and Death*, *The Way to the Stars*, *Pool of London*) and stage (Stanley Kowalski opposite Vivien Leigh), made his American film debut here in the central role of the womanizing Collucci. Dmytryk requested George Cooper, who had inhabited the pivotal role of Mitchell in *Crossfire*, to play Private Small, and embraced the recommendation of the Anhalts after they saw Lee Marvin in *Dragnet* on TV. Following in Lancaster's footsteps, Marvin was cast as Sergeant Mooney, in what was obviously something of a star-making part.

Marvin had served in the 4th Marine Division in the Central Pacific and had been wounded at Saipan. His film career began in 1952, and *Eight Iron Men* was the last of the five films of his released that year. His military service not only informed his performance but proved invaluable to the production. The machine gun used in the film was not a mere prop but was an authentic German piece, with an unfortunate capacity to jam. After a few days of frustration, during which the experts who had rented the gun were unable to solve the problem, Marvin, who had never served in Europe, only in the Pacific, "spread out a sheet, took the gun completely apart in a few minutes, then reassembled it. It never jammed again."[47]

Marvin and Colleano would bond on all-night drinking sessions, despite Dmytryk's efforts to prevent them, but Marvin's focus on set could not be faulted: "He was very much with it. If he did it, believe me it was done by that kind of character because he did his study. He studied his character and he knew his people."[48] He taught his fellow cast members how to realistically age their uniforms and "when he put on his clothes, they were believable, the shoes that were half-laced, everything about him was. We used him as a hint for how to dress the other actors who hadn't been in the war."[49] Dmytryk was effusive in his praise for Marvin: "Oh, he was a wonder. He did one thing that was very important. He showed me how people died at the front. He said, 'They didn't just all throw up their arms and land flat on their face or on their back. Sometimes you're up against a tree. Sometimes their legs are turned a certain way.' Obviously [he was] a great observer.... I should have known that people don't die the way they do in the movies, big dramatic pirouettes!"[50]

The play is set in Monte Cassino during the Italian campaign, but Kramer decided not to specify the location in the film. The architecture of the bombed village in which the squad are holed up has something of a Mediterranean feel, while the incessant rain and inclement conditions bring to mind Northern France or Belgium. The whiff of soggy realism for any inhabitant of Northern Europe was partly due to some very un–Los Angeles weather. Heavy storms emptied up to three inches of rainfall onto the exterior set at the RKO-Pathé facility in Culver City, "breaking all Southern California records,"[51] according to the production notes. With the entire crew braving the storm in regulation black rubberwear, it was suggested that Dmytryk distinguish and identify himself by donning a yellow raincoat, providing a dash of Technicolor amidst the monochrome mud. Reversing the usual procedure of keeping a cover set prepared and available in case of bad weather, a sound stage duplicate of the exterior set was built at the Columbia Ranch at Burbank for use when the Californian climate reverted to type.

Undoubtedly wary of having a film composed exclusively of a dozen dirty men, containing its eight-strong squad of iron, several dream sequences were written to feature the type of women the GIs can only fantasize about. With an eye to whipping up interest around their low-key film, Kramer's publicity department placed the following advertisement in the Hollywood trade papers:

> "DREAM GIRLS WANTED—There is a lack of callipygian sex appeal in Hollywood. 20 luscious lovelies are needed for a major studio production. Must be the type who would appear in a lonesome man's drooling dream of romantic Paradise. Gorgeous looks PLUS sex appeal essential. Dress for interview as you think you should look in such a dream."[52]

This appears to have had the desired effect and reportedly sixty actress/models were ultimately cast, whether or not they knew what "callipygian" meant.

The three fantasy sequences do provide glamorous respite from the grit of the soldiers' reality, though whether these dream girls constitute female characters is best left unaddressed. Two of the dreams come from the subconscious of the perennially amorous and utterly frustrated Collucci ("I get hair on the palms of my hands. The beast rises in me"). The most memorable sequence, neatly choreographed, features an urban street entirely populated by the afore-mentioned "luscious lovelies"—postwomen, policewomen, removal women. The camera glides along, adopting Collucci's point of view, and attracts admiring smiles from each of the women he encounters, until he is stopped short by one of them. That Mary Castle should so strikingly resemble Rita Hayworth, at that time still a huge sex symbol and Columbia contract star, is hardly coincidental, and that her image was misleadingly front and center in posters for the film must surely have been a ploy for naive patrons to believe Hayworth was in the picture. The fantasy figure lures the camera inside and upstairs towards a bedroom, only for the dream to be, understandably, rudely ruptured.

Collucci, the most comically vivid character, perfectly embodied in the broad open features of Bonar Colleano, also provides the punchline to the third dream sequence, imaginatively shot and cleverly photographed by J. Roy Hunt. Ferguson (James Griffith) manages to lead the Hayworthian goddess to the altar, only for Collucci to snatch her from him as he carries her over the threshold.

The echoes of *The Sniper* in *Eight Iron Men* were not confined to the casting. The film begins with the unseen enemy setting up position in a bunker amidst the rain-drenched ruins of the frontline town. The opponents are never referred to by nationality, nor do we ever see more of them than the barrel of a machine gun or a rifle. The threat of being picked off by the malevolent eye of the sniper hangs over every excursion from the large basement bunker where the squad has been sequestered for the last seventeen days.

Harry Brown, later an Oscar winner for *A Place in the Sun*, displays a sure sense of character and dialogue in a military context. While the clash between Mooney and Coke forms the backbone of the film, with Collucci providing frequent comic relief, all eight members of the squad are clearly differentiated. The acting ensemble spark very well off each other, prepped by ten days' rehearsal. Even the subsidiary role of Captain Trelawny (Barney Phillips) is sharply delineated; the granite-faced former car salesman laments the days when "I used to smile all the time."

When Private Small trips and ends up trapped in a muddy ditch, just as the company is about to abandon the town and pull back, the squad squabbles over whether to disobey orders and launch a daytime rescue mission. Though dismissive of Small as a combatant ("He's the kind of dope that if it was raining soup, he'd have a fork. And he'd drop that"), Mooney reflects the loyalty that ties these men together: "We came up here with eight men, and we're going back with eight men." The film is strong in depicting this bond, despite the grievances and aggression that inevitably bubble up during tight confinement. The moderating figure of Carter explains to Trelawny towards the conclusion of the film why orders have been broken to rescue Small: "You think in terms of a company. I think in terms of eight men. I live with these guys. I may die with them. I'm closer to them than I ever was to anybody in my family." Trelawny, battered by the intolerable exigencies of his role, can only respond: "For ten seconds there, you just ran this company."

The delivery of a fruitcake to Muller (former child star Dickie Moore) provides a visual metaphor for the squad. Divided into eight slices, the solitary slice left over for Small is a constant reminder that they are not whole. After Mooney, Muller and Coke fail to effect a rescue, it is discovered that Collucci, until now viewed (not least by himself) as lazy and self-centered, has gone it alone. In an excitingly staged sequence, he disables the enemy foxhole by grenade and carries Small back to safety—only for the revelation that the comrade who has caused so much consternation has been comfortably comatose all day after giving himself a painkilling shot for his sprained ankle. Small's ingratitude sparks an angry tirade from Coke, while Collucci defiantly wolfs down the final saved piece of fruitcake: "All you did was ruin me, that's all you did! Collucci the goof-off, they used to call me. Now things are gonna be expected of me!"

It's a sharply ironic denouement. The strength of the film lies in its celebration of military spirit, the bond between the band of brothers, but veined with the messiness of reality, the fact that many of these men really do not like each other. The aggression between Mooney and Coke keeps threatening to boil over into violence but is mostly contained by the strength of character of the Sergeant, an impressively bottled performance from Lee Marvin. The lack of jingoism is also apparent in the scant respect the men have for authority—orders are constantly questioned and, if necessary, ignored. Harry Brown wrote cogently about military life, having lived it. He had, according to Edward Anhalt, been a captain whose company had to walk across the plains from Anzio to the Roman hills, and whose novel about the experience, *A Walk in the Sun*, was the best of World War II. Dmytryk would deliver his own take on the incident in 1968 with *Anzio*.

Eight Iron Men is one of the clearest examples of Dmytryk's skill at camera placement. The play has been opened out effectively and the production design of the ruined town is amply showcased. However, much of the film does take place in the constricted space of the basement bunker and Dmytryk marshals his cast impressively within the frame. His choice of angle ensures that the set never becomes a mere backdrop but possesses genuine depth of field as characters are placed strategically throughout. An actor will appear in extreme close-up while a conversation between others is in shot; another will crop up in the distance while five other characters are clustered in frame. It's a masterclass in how to maintain visual interest in a confined space, a knack Dmytryk had gained in his years at RKO.

The film abounds in telling imagery, sometimes to chilling effect (a pan from a helmet pierced by a sniper's bullet to a slumped soldier's body), sometimes humorous (Collucci on his rescue mission appears from behind the shattered almost-nude statue of a female). Most telling, and bitterly indicative of the film's realistic perspective, is the image saved till the conclusion. The squad has pulled out and Mooney takes one last look at their base for the last three weeks. The camera pans around from his point of view, taking in the rubble, the squalor, the rainwater cascading in the background. Mooney spits and leaves.

The Juggler (1953)

On the cover of the first British edition of Kirk Douglas' first autobiography *The Ragman's Son*, he faces the camera with a quietly confident smile, dressed in shabby overcoat and hat and carrying a backpack. That this itinerant version of Douglas chosen to represent him should be a promotional image for *The Juggler* is somewhat ironic, given the antipathy that developed between Douglas and his director Dmytryk during the production of this film, and which even, according to Douglas, predated it. Douglas relates that after Dmytryk's release from prison, "Charlie Feldman asked me if I would help Eddie get a job. I didn't just help get him a job. I gave him one. I paid Eddie a weekly salary and had him work on scripts. I took him to restaurants, football games. I brought him to my house, despite many, many people telling me I was foolish to associate with him and could ruin myself."[53]

When it came to working together on *The Juggler*, Douglas claimed that "this man I had befriended when he needed help looked at me as if I were a total stranger."[54] Dmytryk never gave any indication in published material of having met Douglas prior to this production, though he did tell of script doctoring work during the difficult period between returning from England and going to prison. In an interview given for an Oral History project in 1979, Dmytryk didn't hold back: "The only actor I've ever had any trouble with, as an actor, because of temperament, was Kirk Douglas. Who is a shit, and difficult to work with, he admits it. But that's the way his insecurity shows itself."[55] In his autobiography of the year previous, he was more circumspect but still critical, writing that he only once saw anger from his cinematographer J. Roy Hunt, with whom he had also worked on *Crossfire* and *Eight Iron Men*: "That was during my Kirk Douglas film and Kirk could crack the patience of Job."[56]

Dmytryk wrote how the usual order of shooting, location first followed by studio interiors, had been reversed since Douglas wanted to take advantage of an 18-month tax-free break that was then available to Americans living abroad. After shooting in Israel, the first feature film ever to do so, Douglas planned to stay on in Europe with his fiancée Pier Angeli. The Hollywood shoot was consequently running to a strict schedule, departure date for Israel firmly set. The film was again a Stanley Kramer production and days for rehearsal were allocated, during which dialogue was honed, to the apparent satisfaction of Douglas. Once they started shooting, however, Douglas viewed the script with fresh eyes and recommenced the procedure of reworking it. Moreover, Dmytryk wrote, "like a man putting on a heavy diving suit, the minute we were ready to shoot, he had to go, and he was a very slow goer."[57] The production started to slip behind schedule.

Dmytryk had always been adept at picking up slack by employing time-saving techniques from his B-movie days. The climax of the film wherein Douglas' character performs a juggling show for the children of a kibbutz was filmed towards the end of the studio schedule. He recalled, "In order to save lighting time, I was finishing all scenes in one direction without regard to direct continuity. This meant a couple of Kirk's close-ups had to be put off until late in the afternoon."[58] By mid-afternoon, Douglas was furious at being made to wait but was placated, dismissed and eventually called back on set, the lights having been set with his stand-in. When he started to complain again, Dmytryk lost his cool: "I pointed out that I was trying to save time, which he had largely been responsible for losing, so we could get him to Europe in time for some effective tax-dodging. He was outraged and stormed off the set."[59] Bridges were built overnight by an apologetic delivery of flowers and cigars from the star to his director but, by Dmytryk's own admission, their working relationship was permanently soured.

For whatever reason—the perceived slight of Dmytryk not acknowledging their prior relationship or his autobiographical revelations from 1978 about the star's tax arrangements and toilet habits—Douglas had his revenge. In his own book, published in 1988, he called Dmytryk a fink for recanting and naming names, even while admitting that he hadn't had the courage, in order to make *Lust for Life*, to refuse MGM in signing a statement that he had never been a Communist. Rather more outrageously, he dishes sexual gossip on Dmytryk: "Eddie didn't ignore the female lead, a very young, pretty Italian girl named Milly Vitale. They were very close."[60] Douglas told of Jean Porter Dmytryk coming from America towards the end of the shoot and Dmytryk terminating the affair: "When the picture was over, we all left on the same plane—Eddie holding hands and cuddling with his wife; Milly sitting next to me and crying on my shoulder. Milly was a casualty of location shooting."[61] As with his judgment of Dmytryk before HUAC, Douglas bizarrely attempts to deflect from his criticism of the director's behavior by revealing that he also had location affairs with the "attractive, tough"[62] Israeli girls while being engaged to Pier Angeli.

Stanley Kramer felt that the personality clash between the two arose from different approaches to the material, the director's calm and unemotional, the star's fired by righteous passion. The script of *The Juggler*, adapted by Michael Blankfort from his own novel, told of Hans Müller, a psychologically scarred German-Jewish juggler who had survived the Nazi death camps and was seeking a new life in the fledgling state of Israel in 1949. The subject-matter resounded with Douglas whose parents had emigrated from Russia, his mother having seen one of her brothers killed on the street in an anti–Semitic attack. His visceral response to and enthusiasm for the script enabled Kramer to work with him for the first time since Douglas' breakthrough in one of his productions in 1949: "One reason I hadn't used him since *Champion* was that I couldn't afford him."[63] Once he had signed Douglas to the film, Kramer was able to travel to Israel to seek the cooperation of the authorities, which was enthusi-astically forthcoming.

Michael Blankfort had been nominated for an Oscar for the screenplay of *Broken Arrow* in 1950. In reality, he was a front on that script for Albert Maltz, one of the Hollywood Ten along with Edward Dmytryk. The close friendship between Blank-fort and Maltz was definitively ruptured when Blankfort testified before HUAC in 1951 and 1952. He denied ever having been a member of the Communist Party, being therefore unable to name names, and he also repudiated or apologized for having been involved with Communist front organizations. Despite being not technically a "friendly witness," the fact of his cooperation with the Committee meant that Maltz never responded to friendly overtures from Blankfort for the rest of his life. Decades later, Blankfort recalled, "that was one of the things that turned me off about the Party—when they saw old friends they'd cross the street in order to avoid saying hello to each other, because one had become a Trotskyite."[64]

The irony of this situation is that Blankfort nevertheless missed the opportunity to direct *The Juggler* because of his political connections. In May 1952, four months after his second appearance before HUAC, he was refused the renewal of his U.S. passport. His application stated that he wished to travel to Israel in order to direct the film to which he was contracted. Blankfort was not blacklisted but he was viewed as politically questionable, the State Department not appearing to recognize the legiti-macy of HUAC, which had thanked him for his cooperation. Pre-production on the film proceeded without him, and Dmytryk flew to Tel Aviv in June to scout loca-tions for the film he was now directing. However, Blankfort's problems with the State Department continued after the film was in the can. He reapplied for a passport in February 1953 but was indicted with the allegation that "he was a member of the Communist Party as recently as 1945"[65] and in December was confronted with a Kaf-kaesque notification that the Department had "definitely decided to tentatively refuse a passport."[66] In September 1955, he made a fresh passport application. There was some truth to comments from blacklistees Anne Revere and Dalton Trumbo about the negative repercussions whether or not one cooperated with the Committee.

Despite the screenwriter being prevented from travelling to Israel, the film ben-efits greatly from its location shooting in the fledgling state. There is a keen contrast between the ancient steep streets of Haifa and the sprawling new residential devel-opments for which building labor from newly arrived refugees is urgently sought. The character and temperament of the Israelis is reflected in the film from the lived experiences of the filmmakers. Douglas found them "strong, outspoken.... Some-times quite exasperating"[67] and Dmytryk recalled a pipe being slapped out of the mouth of the art director when he unwittingly smoked on the street in Jaffa on the Sabbath. Authority is portrayed as invested with strength, and we are encouraged to view the police though the eyes of Hans Müller. His crippling horror at men in uniform leads him to attack a police officer requesting his ID and causes him to go on the run to evade authority figures entirely. The police detective Karney (Paul Stewart) firmly insists that a Dutch tourist eyewitness not leave the country until he has assisted them fully in their pursuit of Müller. A poster in Karney's office prominently displays a verse from Deuteronomy, "THEY SHALL DEFEND THE RIGHTEOUS … AND CONDEMN THE WICKED," replacing a differently nuanced verse from Deuteronomy that had been specified in the script: "DO NOT DESPISE JUSTICE … AND TAKE CARE NOT TO PERVERT JUSTICE, FOR BY SO DOING YOU SHAKE THE WORLD." The necessity for absolute adherence to the law is reinforced when a father encourages his daughter to assist the police by giving them her photo of Müller: "Sometimes for the sake of the law, we have to give up our friends." This line of dialogue is doubly resonant, evoking not only the horrors of Nazi Germany but also Dmytryk's experience with HUAC.

The country where the refugee boats are docking is fresh from its own conflict. The new arrivals at the camp near Haifa where they are housed are informed that the Israelis "finished our war just three months ago." It is an environment where rifles are carried, excursions too close to the Syrian border are to be feared and ruined Arab villages bear silent witness to recent bombardment. The parallels with the shattered Europe that the refugees are leaving behind are sharply etched. Streets in Jerusalem are pock-marked with ruined buildings, fields around a kibbutz are still mined, demilitarization is an ongoing process. The accommodation camp is encircled with barbed wire, an echo of concentration camp that is lost on nobody, not least composer George Antheil, whose jaunty underscoring of the refugees' initial optimism hits somber chords when they arrive at the camp. Müller is one of the most damaged of the new arrivals, formerly an internationally celebrated performer from Munich, now a psychologically scarred shell of a man, unable to reconcile himself to the loss of his wife and children at the hands of the Nazis. His lack of self-worth feels confirmed when those new arrivals with trades are quickly summoned away to a meeting while he, master of juggling balls and entertaining children, is left behind in the dormitory with the old and the blind.

Müller is a man struggling to wrench himself from the darkness into the light. In the blinding brightness of an Israeli summer, he continually retreats into shade. At a news kiosk, when he fears he is about be apprehended, he finds deep shadow within and withdraws to it. His luminous savior comes in the form of Ya'El (Milly Vitale), a spirited kibbutz worker. When he first sees her, she is operating a heliograph, signaling by light flashes to a neighboring settlement. The following scene has him consumed by a dark nightmare before she opens the door and allows a shaft of light to awaken him. Müller is resistant to being rescued, however. At a communal dance, centered around a huge bonfire, he pulls her away into the darkness to inform her that he will be leaving. Ya'El recognizes the consuming blackness that he is unable to shake off but confesses her love for him and wants him to stay with her and make their home in the kibbutz, in defiance of his belief that "home is a place you lose." In the final scene, he barricades himself into a hut, his pursuer Karney outside, and retreats into a dark corner. As his demons overwhelm him, Dmytryk pulls into an ultra-tight close-up on Douglas, the screen swallowed up by the intensity of his fear.

It is the voice of Ya'El that convinces Müller to finally emerge from his shadows and step into the sunlight to receive her embrace and accept her help. The performance of Kirk Douglas is not as shaded as J. Roy Hunt's lighting design. At times his broken man destroyed by survivor's guilt is wrenchingly effective, at others his acting is overwrought. Kramer made a similar assessment: "Douglas was so wrapped up in the role, he sometimes became too intense."[68]

Decades later, the judgment of author Michael Blankfort on his own script was "Tendentious and contrived but in its time not as bad as it seems."[69] The script certainly has its deficiencies, in particular too much attention being paid to the police pursuit of Müller after he has attacked the policeman. These sequences are frequently shot on location and provide additional flavors of the country, but they are centered around Paul Stewart, whose performance is stolid and stiff, and the rather uninteresting police procedure breaks up the rhythm of the much more compelling journey of Müller. Dmytryk has improved on Blankfort's raw material. The concluding pages of the script, which underwent multiple rewrites between the final draft on 10 July 1952 and the final shooting version on 30 August, have Müller emerge from the hut, rifle in hand, while a succession of voices from the last few days replay in his head ("Every person is precious to us," "I prayed that you wouldn't destroy yourself"). He drops the rifle, falls to the ground and, as Ya'El embraces him, the character of Yehoshua (Joey Walsh) makes a quip in his eccentric English. Dmytryk improves on this ending by removing the flashback voices and the humor and tightening it to an embrace between the lovers. The existing ending is not wholly satisfactory, feeling underwritten, but is preferable to the overwritten bathos of the script.

The film's most successful element is the relationship between Müller and Yehoshua, an orphaned teenage boy whom he has met on the road between Haifa and Nazareth. Yehoshua, or Joshua, was the assistant to Moses who led the Jews into the Land of Milk and Honey, and this modern-day acolyte ultimately performs the same function for Müller, after insisting on accompanying him on his travels and becoming his apprentice. Müller has abandoned the skill that made him famous but, in an attempt to cheer Yehoshua up, he performs some juggling, impressively mastered by Kirk Douglas after months of practice. Thereafter Yehoshua insists he be trained to become the "First Israeli Juggler." It is a winning performance from Joey Walsh, touching in his need for this father figure not to disappear and humorous in his self-taught English phraseology—"You're precisely magnificent!"

The uplifting kibbutz communal dance scene comes immediately after Müller has burnt a newspaper to prevent others from knowing he is a wanted man. He blows the ashes from his hand, an unwitting gesture that he is about to move on from this troubled period of his life. The dancing around the fire is a sign of rebirth. The harmony on the kibbutz is represented as hope for the future, a community sharing and pulling together, moving on from the literal minefields that surround them. The following day, as Müller puts on a juggling show for the children of the kibbutz, we witness the formation of a family. Müller presents Yehoshua, who has broken a leg in a mine accident, as the First Israeli Juggler and watches his protégé perform with paternal pride. He exchanges a look with Ya'El, their meaningful smiles embracing a future together. It is the new Israel in microcosm, a hope for an idyllic future.

The father-figure has passed his skill onto the son and is preparing to move on from his troubled past. Here it is Ya'El, who habitually carries a rifle, that is the figure of strength. This woman has clearly expressed her determination to hold onto this man and it is she who will ensure that man and boy, damaged mentally and physically, will heal.

After *Crossfire* had been the first American film to confront anti–Semitism head on, *The Juggler* was Edward Dmytryk's second seminal film pertaining to the Jewish experience. Michael Blankfort termed the period of the late 1940s and early 1950s as "the 'shush years' when Jews didn't want to make themselves too obvious for fear of anti–Semitism."[70] He asserted that the film was only made due to the Jewish guilt felt by Stanley Kramer and Kirk Douglas. While Kramer would likely not have agreed with this characterization, he felt that the subject-matter was the reason why Columbia boss Harry Cohn made no effort to promote the film: "Jewish old-timers in the film industry … had suffered through so much anti–Semitism and heard so many derogatory stories about 'the Jews' owning Hollywood that they played down as much as possible the Jewish influence and participation in filmmaking."[71] Despite strong reviews, particularly from *Variety* and Bosley Crowther in *The New York Times*, *The Juggler*'s ground-breaking elements went unheralded and gravity brought it back to earth with merely modest success.

The Caine Mutiny (1954)

Captain Philip Francis Queeg was a role that Humphrey Bogart was desperate to play. "Captain Queeg … had surprisingly narrow, sloping shoulders, and was hollow-chested and potbellied. His forehead was furrowed, and there were three deep vertical wrinkles in the center; his eyes squinted as though he were trying to see a long distance."[72] The character was clearly no romantic lead, and the only physical characteristics that Bogart seemed to have in common with him were the quizzical brow and the squinting eyes, but Queeg was the pivotal figure in Herman Wouk's hugely successful 1951 novel *The Caine Mutiny*. The psychologically unstable martinet captain of a World War II U.S. minesweeper was a peach of a role for any actor in Bogart's age bracket, and he was determined to land it: "I liked Captain Queeg. I felt I understood him."[73]

The early 1950s saw many established stars break free of their contracts to the studios that had made them, saving the studios money by removing the obligation to pay salary to stars who were between assignments, and enabling the stars to demand more money per short-term contract. In the next few years Edward Dmytryk would work with several actors in this position, most notably Clark Gable and Spencer Tracy, and by the end of 1952 it was Bogart itching to get out of his Warner Bros. contract. When the actor would not commit to a proposed film directed by Nicholas Ray, the studio attempted to veto him making the Wouk adaptation at Columbia, scribbling at the bottom of the memo to him, "Do ours first, then *Caine Mutiny*!"[74] Bogart, however, knew that he held the upper hand, since refusing assigned projects might entail loss of compensation from Warners but it would shorten his contract with them and hasten a lucrative life as an independent. Warner Bros. was forced to concede.

Bogart made his enthusiasm for the role only too apparent. When the sale of the movie rights to the book was announced, he immediately expressed an interest and made an appointment to meet producer Stanley Kramer. Fred MacMurray, Jose Ferrer and Van Johnson had already been lined up but the crucial role of Queeg was as yet uncast. Bogart brought along some steel balls to the meeting and manipulated them while speaking, just as Queeg in the book had memorably done in order to placate his inner demons. It was a foolhardy performative gesture. When Kramer related this story to Columbia studio boss Harry Cohn, Cohn informed Bogart's agent that he was "not going to pay $200,000 because he knew that Bogart wanted this role."[75] This time Bogart was forced to concede: "Damn it, Harry knows I want to play it and will come down in my price rather than see them give it to somebody else."[76]

The U.S. Navy was proving an obstacle to producing a film of the novel. Two studios had already attempted to set something up but had been denied the blessing of the Navy, who were wary of the negative public relations effect of suggesting that the armed forces could permit an unstable character like Queeg to rise in its ranks. Without the supply of naval ships and hardware, the credibility of any film would suffer and the cost would make it unviable. Stanley Kramer was on the last film of his production deal with Columbia Pictures. It had not been a lucrative arrangement for the studio, for Kramer had produced a succession of artistically interesting films that had made little or no money. The latest had been *The 5,000 Fingers of Dr. T*, which had cost $1.6 million and had grossed $0.25 million. Kramer was impatient to move on and harbored barely concealed contempt for his boss: "What I liked best about *The Caine Mutiny* was that it was the last picture I had to make for Harry Cohn."[77] Cohn scoffed when Kramer promised him that this final production would win back all the money that had been lost on the previous ten Kramer productions, since he didn't even believe that Navy consent was possible.

Kramer found himself summoned to Washington, D.C., to outline his plans to a panel of admirals: "These were the men who had refused navy cooperation on this venture to the two biggest and most powerful studios in the film industry— MGM and Fox. Were they likely to change their minds for a young producer at a middle-sized studio who had just made ten flops in a row and wanted now to film a story all of them no doubt hated? Maybe they were counting on this to become my eleventh flop in a row."[78] Encountering a marked hostility to the book, in particular its title, since the Navy contended that there had never been a mutiny in the United States Navy, Kramer insisted that he would go ahead with the production with or without their consent. He told them, "[U]nless we can use a reasonable amount of the navy's resources, including some vessels, we'll have to mock up facsimiles that wouldn't please you any more than it would please me…. The way to make the navy look real and powerful is to show some real ships. That will impress anyone who sees

the picture." His argumentation worked and he left the meeting with their full cooperation and the promise of a qualified officer as technical adviser.

The Navy were aware that co-operation with the filmmakers was very much in
their interest. The film showed every sign of being commercially successful. Not only
had the book been an enormous bestseller, receiving fourteen hardback reprints in
1951 alone and winning the Pulitzer Prize, but a play version had been adapted from
the novel by Wouk himself and was being produced by Charles Laughton's artistic
partner Paul Gregory. The deals for play, titled *The Caine Mutiny Court-Martial*, and
film were being set up at the same time, on the understanding that the play would be
performed before the film was released. Dmytryk's friend Dick Powell was initially
assigned as director of the play and attempted unsuccessfully to hack back Wouk's
four-hour version of the novel's courtroom sequence into something that could
actually be performed on stage. The task was beyond him and he was sacked, to be
replaced by Laughton. Laughton's text editing and directing abilities rescued the production, which opened on Broadway early in 1954 to great success, with Henry Fonda
in the role of the defending lawyer. Laughton's methods did not mesh with Fonda's,
the actor sensing that his role had been diminished. At one point on tour he burst out
at the director with "'What do you know about men, you fat, ugly faggot?' Laughton
never spoke to him again, even when, in *Advise and Consent*, they acted together."[79]

Wouk's inability to adapt his novel also became apparent when he was hired by
Kramer to write the film script and produced something unworkable. Stanley Roberts, who had written Dmytryk's *Under Age* a decade previously and had just adapted
Death of a Salesman for the screen, confirmed his reputation as an adept literary editor and delivered a 190-page script. Both Kramer and Dmytryk were happy with his
work but Cohn was insisting on a two-hour running time and on the inclusion of "the
girl." Columbia would not accept the film without some love interest, so a romantic
strand had to be inserted while "exceptional material"[80] had to be excised. Roberts
could not accept making cuts to his script and quit. Finally, Kramer engaged Michael
Blankfort, with whom he and Dmytryk had worked on *The Juggler*, and together they
pruned away 50 pages. The result is a fair contraction of a weighty novel, though
shading has clearly been lost in the abridgement. Bogart sought advice from his
friend John Huston, who felt that "Queeg loses face all too quickly. I would like to see
him … in a good light for a while longer.… At first he should appear to be the perfect
and complete officer. Then something ever so slight should make us wonder briefly.
Then something else should cause us to put away our doubts.… And then, when we
least expect it, those doubts should be sickeningly confirmed."[81]

One can only speculate that this degree of character depth was what Dmytryk's
preferred three-hour version of *The Caine Mutiny* would have provided. Nevertheless, Bogart produces a beautifully textured characterization. When the Captain is
first introduced, half an hour into the film, he does indeed appear to be Huston's
"perfect and complete officer," one who has gained his position on the minesweeper
Caine through rigorous adherence to rules: "As anyone who knows me will tell you,
I'm a book man. I believe everything in it was put in for a purpose. When in doubt,
remember on board this ship we do things by the book. Deviate from the book and
you'd better have a half a dozen good reasons. And you'll still get an argument from

me." The audience surrogate, freshly graduated Ensign Keith (Robert Francis[82]), exudes contentment at this change of command and Queeg's promise of a tight ship: "On board my ship, excellent performance is standard. Standard performance is sub-standard. Sub-standard performance is not permitted to exist, that I warn you. K?" Just as Queeg fingers the steel balls he carries around whenever he starts to feel uncomfortable about a situation, the tell that he is at ease and in control is his use of the casual "K?" to underline his authority.

The first time Queeg encounters an untucked shirt, the steel balls are plucked from his pocket, prompting furtive exchanged glances among his subordinates. But Bogart paces his performance well, and this is the only external sign of disquiet. It is only later, when Queeg's inability simultaneously to follow orders and maintain discipline causes the ship to cut adrift one of the targets it is towing in a drill with other ships, that Bogart permits the first manic glint to enter his eye. The actor controls his reactions, subsuming almost all the panic that Queeg is feeling, only letting a trace of it seep out in that panicked look. The dam breaks, however, when the *Caine* must escort a wave of landing craft under enemy fire. Queeg's fear is apparent to all, as he flinches at the impact of explosions and orders a quicker than expected retreat. After this apparent cowardice, he summons his officers to a meeting and appeals for their "constructive loyalty." Dmytryk accords Bogart a huge close-up and the actor delivers. We are able to observe each flutter of facial muscle as Queeg exposes his vulnerability, all the while fingering the steel balls to focus his will: "A ship is like a family. We all have our ideas of right and wrong, but we have to pitch in for the good of the family. If there was only some way we could help each other."

This is a pivotal moment in the film. From a modern perspective, it would appear that Queeg is suffering from some degree of post-trauma. He has served "seven tough years in the Atlantic," with the last couple of years being particularly brutal due to U-boot attacks. Skippering a "beaten-up tub" minesweeper would likely have been perceived as a gentler posting in comparison, but Queeg is not up to the task. None of his officers knows how to deal with this self-exposure from their Captain and his appeal to them is met with uncomfortable silence. When Queeg leaves the room, Keefer (Fred MacMurray) quips, "This is what is known in literature as the pregnant pause." The failure to seize the situation and assist Queeg at this point prolongs his captaincy and ultimately leads to the mutiny, as well as provoking a moment at the climax of the film that rankled with Kramer: the defense lawyer Greenwald (Jose Ferrer) drunkenly haranguing the officers for their failure of nerve, in a speech that the Navy insisted upon. Kramer wrote, "I agreed to the insertion because I felt I had to concede on something to prove my sincerity, and this was actually harmless because by the time the remarks are made at the end of the picture, the audience has seen the whole story and everyone has come to his or her own conclusion."[83] This speech, along with the opening declaration that "There has never been a mutiny in a ship of the United States Navy," weights the film heavily in the favor of the Naval top brass, but such was the cost of full co-operation.

John Huston recalled that Bogart was "rather well satisfied with [his] performance as Queeg, but didn't think so highly of Van Johnson and MacMurray."[84] This is unfair since both actors gave textured performances that were out of their habitual zone. Johnson, languishing in light fare at MGM, was overjoyed: "A role like Maryk after all these years! Believe me, I'm grateful. Nobody can say it wasn't time for a change."[85] Critics had been dismissive of him, as in C.A. Lejeune's putdown two years before *The Caine Mutiny*: "Van Johnson does his best: appears."[86] Under Dmytryk's direction, he produces perhaps the best work of his career as Lt. Stephen Maryk, who overcomes his own doubts about challenging authority by keeping a journal on Queeg's erratic behavior, wrests control of the *Caine* from him during a typhoon and faces a court-martial. He convincingly conveys a man riven with uncertainty and whose eventual victory tastes sour. For the first time, he instructed that his facial scarring from an early accident not be covered by make-up, a sign of how firmly he grasped this opportunity. Later Johnson would comment, "I was in a rut, Stanley Kramer saved my life."[87]

At the moment that the *Caine*'s previous Captain DeVriess (Tom Tully[88]) leaves the ship under command of Queeg, Dmytryk employs a clever shot to indicate the real clash to come, with the profiles of Maryk and Lt. Keefer presenting a literal face-off to each other. Keefer is the novel-writing intellectual on the *Caine*, quipping sardonically about the captain's eccentricities. When Keith comments that at least Queeg is "certainly Navy," Keefer responds with "Yeah, so was Captain Bligh." If ultimately Maryk is the *Caine*'s Fletcher Christian, Keefer is the one who planted the mutinous seed. Having "diagnosed" Queeg's paranoia, Keefer urges Keith to take action but, lacking the courage of his convictions, leaves Maryk and Keith to face the charge of subversion alone once he realizes that co-operation would also make him a mutineer. This cowardice creates a villain of Keefer, and Greenwald shows his disdain by throwing a glass of champagne in his face at the film's climax. All the other characters exit the room, leaving Keefer in a pregnant pause of his own making. The film has pitted the aphorism-spouting Keefer against the self-confessedly under-achieving Keith, and the intellectual has lost. MacMurray acquits himself extremely well in the role and had played morally dubious characters before, most notably in *Double Indemnity*. Nevertheless, he considered the champagne scene "a little extreme" while recognizing that his apprehensions "were based on the fact that I wasn't used to be treated like a villain after playing so many nice guys."[89] To Kramer, MacMurray, whose wife died just before the actor flew to Honolulu to join the production, "was a spectator in the scene of life, both in his work and in personal relations. He seemed strangely to have retired within himself."[90]

The dramatic peak of the film is when Queeg takes the stand at Maryk's court-martial and slowly buckles under Greenwald's questioning. It is a masterly display from Bogart, who begins the scene with righteous assurance. As the probing shifts the sands beneath him, the cracks appear in the façade and his paranoid state reveals itself. Dmytryk judged his display of transition in the scene to be "one of the finest I have ever witnessed—and transition is what acting is all about."[91] The camerawork meshes perfectly with the performance. Dmytryk starts with a medium shot of Bogart composed and confident. The first sign of defensiveness is when Queeg quickly crosses his legs in response to a question. Gradually Dmytryk's choice of shot edges closer as Queeg's discomfort grows, culminating in an extreme close-up when his paranoid instability becomes obvious. Beautifully played and directed, the long silent reaction shots that follow are edited and timed adroitly, anticipating how gripped the audience would be by the preceding bravura display. Kramer recalled, "Bogart's performance electrified the crew. There was utter silence and then they applauded. They were suddenly galvanised into a condition which I don't think they had expected, or if they knew about Bogart, at least they hadn't witnessed it firsthand."[92] Bogart's instinct in pursuing the role had been sound. The performance was one of the finest of his career, fully earning him his final Oscar nomination for Best Actor.

Cohn's insistence on depicting a romance between Keith and May Wynn (the actress Donna Lee Hickey adopted her character's name professionally from this film onwards) is a miscalculation. Although it permitted location shooting at Yosemite National Park, which interjects visual variety amidst so many scenes at sea, momentum is squandered by banal script content and two of the least interesting presences on screen. Otherwise the direction navigates its course with assurance and paces it effectively. Kramer was generous with praise for his director: "Dmytryk did a superb job on *The Caine Mutiny*, not only in difficult scenes involving warships, but also in the management of the cast. There were several marvelous performances in that picture, and he, as the director, deserves a lot of credit for that, even though he was working with highly skilled actors. Sometimes great actors work very badly together, either because of ego problems or poor direction. When you put Bogart, MacMurray, Ferrer, and Van Johnson in the same picture, you have an interesting mix of personalities. They might not have blended, but under Dmytryk's direction they did, and I didn't hear any of them complain about him."[93]

Harry Cohn and Stanley Kramer enthusiastically parted company after *The Caine Mutiny*, despite the fact that it performed more successfully than either could have anticipated: $20.4 million at the U.S. box office alone and Columbia's biggest hit of 1954. The day he left the studio, Kramer told Cohn, "'This has been the worst experience of my life'.... He didn't even rise to shake my hand. After an awkward moment of silence, I turned and walked out of the room."[94] Hollywood rewards success as much as quality and the film received seven Academy Award nominations, including Best Picture. That Edward Dmytryk was not nominated could be perceived as industry bias against him, but that must be set against the fact that the nominated directors that year included Billy Wilder (*Sabrina*) and Alfred Hitchcock (*Rear Window*), neither of whose films got nominated for Best Picture. The winner that year was the utterly deserving Elia Kazan for *On the Waterfront*. Kazan famously testified before HUAC and, like Dmytryk, was never forgiven by many. Comparisons have been drawn between the content of *On the Waterfront* and *The Caine Mutiny* with the inference that both had defense of the informer as their theme. This was undoubtedly so in Kazan's case, working from Budd Schulberg's script—Kazan wrote in his autobiography: "When Brando, at the end, yells at Lee Cobb, the mob boss, 'I'm glad what I done, you hear me?—glad what I done!' that was me saying, with identical heat, that I was glad I'd testified as I had."[95] Dmytryk, however, had not originated his project. It had come from an established book and was a property that Kramer had entrusted to a director with whom he already had a good working relationship. The thematic retrofitting may have provided echoes of Dmytryk's political history, but they were almost entirely coincidental.

V

Consolidation Across Continents
(1954–1960)

The Juggler proved to be the shape of things to come in the 1950s. As the political atmosphere remained dark in the wake of the second HUAC hearings and the blacklist became entrenched, Hollywood studios were bursting to escape the soundstage and find colorful and exotic locations that would fill the new wider screens. Dmytryk's location shoot in Israel was the first of a string of reconnaissance trips and foreign shoots that he made throughout the decade, reflecting his regained status as bankable director.

His financial situation rapidly improved, "though solvency was still some years in the future,"[1] and in 1954 the Dmytryks were able to purchase the Bel-Air property they had been leasing since 1952. He enjoyed the physical exertion of taming the grounds of the property as a post-production recovery mechanism: "When I've

finished a film, it takes me at least six weeks to recover, during which time I find it impossible to read a book or carry on an intelligent conversation. Production drains me, as I believe it does most persons in the so-called creative arts, and chopping brush is an ideal activity for a body controlled by a depleted mind."[2] When Dmytryk made his film with Clark Gable in 1955, the star confirmed that he and Carole Lombard had lived in the Dmytryks' property together and that he had commissioned the tennis court that Dmytryk was at that point busy deconstructing.

After the enormous success of *The Caine Mutiny*, Dmytryk found himself at 20th Century–Fox to make **Broken Lance** for Sol Siegel, thirteen years after being fired from Paramount by Sol Siegel. The western was

Edward Dmytryk in the 1950s.

a triumph in CinemaScope, a format that Dmytryk had tried to get Kramer to use on *The Caine Mutiny* but which the producer had rejected due to a pictorial conservatism. *Broken Lance* was so successful that the majority of the films Dmytryk made for the remainder of the decade were for Fox. Inaugurating a successful relationship in 1955 with another studio, Paramount, he made the short *Bing Presents Oreste*, a promotional push for the Maltese singer Oreste Kirkop that was introduced by Bing Crosby. The Dmytryks returned to London to make **The End of the Affair**, Jean looking after the two younger children for a few months in a flat in Kensington while Eddie was at Shepperton Studios. The grey London skies ultimately propelled the family back to sunny California and Dmytryk finished editing the film while comfortably holed up at Claridge's.

As a Sinophile, who had studied written Chinese and adored its cuisine, Dmytryk overlooked the scripting deficiencies of **Soldier of Fortune** and accepted the project since it would mean working with Clark Gable and entail location shooting in Hong Kong. Gable and Dmytryk also visited Tokyo, where a press conference was held at which the star insisted the TV cameras be removed: "'You are my competitors,' he told the TV crewmen, 'and I will not work hand-in-glove with my competition.'"[3] They also visited an all-girl musical theater where the star of the show, a famous kabuki dancer, requested a meeting with Gable. The star and director were brought backstage where the tiny performer looked up at the six-foot King of Hollywood, holding his hand and silently weeping: "It's the only time I have ever seen Rhett Butler nonplussed. Like a frozen frame, they stood there for what seemed like a full minute…. Then she broke away and glided into her dressing room. I had seen the power of the King."[4]

Manufacturing hits with the old guard of Bogart, Tracy and Gable brought Dmytryk right back onto the A-list, higher than he had been in his RKO days, with his former studio languishing and heading for dissolution after the disaster of Howard Hughes' ownership. Those widescreen vehicles of the 1950s were not only a visual break but often a thematic rupture from the tighter focus that the Academy ratio frequently imposed. Dmytryk himself described the change in the type of film he was making as a shift away from the sugar coating—the reliance on camera tricks and building of suspense—to the pill—the kernel of humanistic concern: "Though I still felt some satisfaction in contriving an unusual setup or photographic effect, it was of no importance to me unless it helped accentuate a point about some human characteristic or conflict of relationship…. I also began to understand why so little attention was paid to this approach by filmmakers. It is damned difficult."[5] Thus he took on projects with troubled pre-production histories like *The End of the Affair* and **The Left Hand of God**, accentuating human dilemma over spectacle. Remuneration for these star vehicles was generous enough that Dmytryk was able to buy a 37-acre farm in Kona on Hawaii and he flew there with the family as often as possible.

Spencer Tracy enjoyed working with Dmytryk on *Broken Lance* so much that he entrusted a cherished project to him and arranged with Paramount for him to produce and direct **The Mountain**. This involved a location scouting trip to Europe in June 1955, reviving memories of the similar reconnaissance trip he had made in 1946 for *The White Tower*. The shoot at Chamonix took place later that summer and Dmytryk spent a stopover evening in London with Tracy and Katharine Hepburn, eating at an Italian restaurant in Soho. When they returned to Claridge's where the men were staying, Hepburn entered from the rear of the building and took the service elevator up to Tracy's suite. After coffee she exited via the same route and Dmytryk walked her back to her hotel, the Connaught. On an earlier occasion, the management of Claridge's had objected to Hepburn wearing slacks, she had moved out immediately and never again went through the lobby of Claridge's, even when wearing a dress. While her husband was shooting in France, Jean Dmytryk recalled a boozy evening in Los Angeles with Frank Sinatra, Humphrey Bogart and Lauren Bacall, the latter two of whom had become good friends with the Dmytryks, where the men used subterfuge to send a telegram with risqué content to *The Mountain*. After multiple refusals from the operator, they finally succeeded with a coded version, which they triumphantly toasted with more Scotch.

Though *The Mountain* fell short of its peak of expectation, Paramount were satisfied enough to offer Dmytryk a play-or-pay four-film contract. The deal was non-exclusive, so he was able to accept the offer from Dore Schary at MGM to make **Raintree County**. Though the shoot involved more location work, the Southern states of the U.S. were considerably less far-flung than Europe. Nevertheless, the production proved extremely arduous and Dmytryk withdrew to his Hawaiian retreat to recharge his batteries: "My distaste for the business slowly dripped away, and after about four months, I could think of films again without a tic or a tremor—which was lucky, because 20th was sending smoke signals in my direction."[6] **The Young Lions** sent him back to Europe again, and this expansive, finely acted production, despite being "one of the most trying jobs of my entire career,"[7] became the film of which the director was most proud.

In 1958, Paramount reported its largest annual profit since 1949, $12.5 million, which was considerably more than its rivals, but its production schedule was moving very slowly. Dmytryk therefore stayed at Fox for his next film, **Warlock**, which he also produced, and which is one of the very best films to his name. By the time it had finished shooting, but before he performed the final edit, Dmytryk was off on another reconnaissance trip for Paramount, leaving for Nepal on 16 January 1959. For $250,000, the studio had purchased *The Mountain is Young*, a novel by Han Suyin, the Chinese-Flemish author of *A Many-Splendoured Thing*. 20th Century–Fox had prefixed the title with *Love Is* and produced a huge hit in 1955. Paramount were hoping for the same success with her latest book and wanted Dmytryk to produce and direct it. Another tale of interracial love, the story tells of a married female writer who falls for an engineer in Kathmandu in 1956. Since Nepal had only recently opened itself up to the wider world, it was necessary to develop a sense of the place before it could be convincingly put on screen.

Among those travelling with Dmytryk to the Himalayan kingdom were screenwriter Robert Aurthur, after their successful collaboration on *Warlock*, and Jean. The trip was mostly made by propeller plane and entailed two days in Hawaii, one in Tokyo, one and a half days in Hong Kong, three days in Singapore, one day in Calcutta and two weeks in Nepal. In Singapore they stayed in the Royal Suite, with its built-in waterfall, at the Raffles hotel and met with Han Suyin, who was reluctant to explain exactly what degrees of meaning lay behind her novel. Dmytryk was bowled over by the beauty of Nepal and the hospitality of the Nepalese: "The country was almost completely untouched and unspoiled. The only hotel in Kathmandu was a renovated Rana palace, operated by an aging Russian ex-ballet dancer and his attractive young Scandinavian wife."[8] They flew by the king's private plane to Pokhara and Dmytryk, a pilot himself and familiar with the Alps and the Rockies, was left speechless by the grandeur of the Himalayas. There they spent an evening with the Indian ambassador, with Ravi Shankar playing sitar with a small troupe for four hours.

Excited at the prospect of making a film against this exotic backdrop, Dmytryk and Jean left a few days early for Patna and, after all the luxury that the trip had thus far entailed, were thumped back to earth with a decidedly un-luxurious and somewhat threatening night train to Calcutta. In Bombay, they visited the studio of Mehboob Khan, director of *Mother India*, where Dmytryk was impressed by the production facilities but nonplussed by the wholly alien manner of operating a production schedule. They returned to Los Angeles via London, and Aurthur set to work on the script for their Nepalese epic. Paramount were enthusiastic and requested the producer/director to make himself available as soon as the script was finished. Dmytryk had one more film left on his deal with 20th Century–Fox and rashly accepted the first project that was offered to him. *The Blue Angel* is one of Dmytryk's weakest films, galling since it was the follow-up to one of his strongest, and in its indifferent handling one can almost sense that the director's mind is more on his enticing next project than the one in hand.

That enticing next project, however, never happened. The script for *The Mountain is Young* was completed, much to its producer's satisfaction, but the studio refused to move forward with it. The silence regarding the project was variously construed at the time as nervousness about the interracial angle, balking at the cost or doubts about the feasibility of the remote location, and it was only much later that Dmytryk realized why the film had quietly slipped off the production slate. It was his old enemy, a change of administration at Paramount. Control had passed from Y. Frank Freeman, a risk-taker, to Jack Karp, a conservative executive. Han Suyin's novel remained in print for the rest of the century; the film has remained unmade.

Paramount instead offered Dmytryk a fresh property, *Appointment in Zahrain*, to be made with his friend Clark Gable. Dmytryk employed Richard Matheson, author up to that point of the novels *I Am Legend*, *The Shrinking Man* and *A Stir of Echoes* along with many short stories, to write the script. At the beginning of November 1960, Dmytryk met with Gable when the star was finishing his scenes on *The Misfits*, they discussed the nearly completed script and looked forward to a second collaboration. But Clark Gable died on 16 November. Matheson found himself unable to finish the script now that it had lost its star, and ultimately Dmytryk dropped out of the project too.[9] At the dawn of the 1960s, two of the stars who had helped make the previous decade so successful for Edward Dmytryk, Humphrey Bogart and Clark Gable, were dead and the old guard was beginning to feel old hat. The director continued to have success in the 1960s, in a seesaw between permissiveness and piety, but the peaks were fewer, as were the opportunities. The King of Hollywood was dead, and to an extent Old Hollywood died with him.

Broken Lance (1954)

The year of 1953 was the year of CinemaScope. 20th Century–Fox premiered its patented process with *The Robe* in September and followed up with the release of *How to Marry a Millionaire* in November. The financial returns were so phenomenal that Fox immediately pushed all of its A productions into the process and reaped the rewards. In 1954 the studio's profits shot up to $8 million, and Fox claimed eleven of the top 35 hits of the year, all of them in CinemaScope. One of the eleven was *Broken Lance*. This in the same year that Dmytryk's *The Caine Mutiny* was a huge hit for Columbia and the second highest-grossing film of the year.

The early days of CinemaScope necessitated a recalibration in film grammar. The vast envelope of the screen was ideal for vista and spectacle, but less well-suited to close-up and intimacy. As with Henry Koster's efforts on *The Robe*, many early films were static and failed to exploit the potential of the new format. Visually accomplished films such as *Bad Day at Black Rock* and *It's Always Fair Weather* were on the horizon, but Dmytryk's contribution with *Broken Lance* displays brio in its confident use of widescreen composition. This did not go unnoticed at the time, as in a rave review from *The Hollywood Reporter*: "Sol Siegel has assembled an almost perfect cast and Edward Dmytryk directs them with a skill that may set a historic milestone in the development of the wide-screen technique."[10]

Dmytryk found himself energized by the new format: "Ordinarily, I prefer the 'Golden Mean' frame, but in semidesert Arizona I felt the old experimental thrill. The soft, distant mountains formed a low, broad horizon; men on horseback filled more screen horizontally than vertically; even the squat, spreading architecture of the American West suited the new dimensions perfectly."[11] His collaboration with cinematographer Joe MacDonald captures the majesty of these vistas and imbues the skies with commentary on his characters. Piercing blue for the hope of young love; deadening grey for the finality of a funeral; a vast canopy of pregnant clouds for the dormant familial bitterness preparing to burst forth. *Broken Lance* employs its visual splendor intelligently.

Composition within frame had always been a Dmytryk strength, and the release of breath permitted by the corset-loosening of the expanded screen gave him a fresh canvas on which to deploy his skill. The Devereaux father and sons quintet provide the ideal number of characters to arrange across this shape of screen, and there is pleasure in recognizing when members of the family are literally taking sides. The opening of the film uses the expanse of the screen beautifully. Joe Devereaux is being released from a three-year jail sentence, and behind him the prison interior recedes into darkness, shadows slashing across the field of vision. As he exits the building, the camera is behind him and, observing the brightness of freedom beyond, dollies in for this sunny freedom to swallow up the screen. The camera movement and contrast to the jailhouse gloom imparts a delirious sense of liberation.

Broken Lance is a Western reworking of *House of Strangers*, scripted by Philip

Yordan and directed by Joseph L Mankiewicz for Fox in 1949. The film had been a box-office disappointment, but producer Sol Siegel felt there was some mileage in the story of a bitterly riven Italian-American banking family and he employed Richard Murphy to Westernize it. Studio head Darryl Zanuck feared that the script adhered too closely to the original and suggested a racial divide in the family, rather than the financial feud that had split Edward G. Robinson's offspring in *House of Strangers*. Matt Devereaux the father would have three elder sons by his first marriage, while Joe, the fourth and youngest, would have a Native American mother. Zanuck saw Jeffrey Hunter in the role of Joe, and "I can only see Spencer Tracy as Matt."[12] MGM were given $250,000 to loan Tracy for this single film, while the star earned $165,000 plus a percentage of the profit. This disparity only aggravated Tracy's itch to get out of his MGM contract.

Also riding out the tail-end of an unsatisfactory contract was Richard Widmark: "I was tired of being shot from one movie to another—finishing one on a Saturday and starting another on Monday. I could get more money on the outside and get a wider variety of stuff."[13] He refused to sign a new contract with Fox and his punishment was the fourth-billed role of Matt's eldest son Ben on *Broken Lance*. He left the studio after completing the film. Dolores Del Rio had been sought for the role of Señora, Matt's Native American wife, but her visa was delayed in Washington "pending investigation of her political affiliations."[14] The role went instead to Katy Jurado, the Mexican actress who had made a splash in *High Noon* but who was nineteen years younger than her compatriot Del Rio and only six years older than the actor who would play her son. This was not Zanuck's choice of Hunter, but Tracy's choice, the emerging Fox contract player Robert Wagner. Tracy had seen Wagner in *Beneath the 12-Mile Reef* and specifically requested him for the film.

Broken Lance began its 55-day shoot near Nogales, Arizona, at the beginning of March 1954. Dmytryk had been fired by Sol Siegel at Paramount during a purge in 1940, but it was Siegel who now hired him to direct this $2 million movie for Fox. Dmytryk considered Siegel "the director's perfect producer,"[15] an efficient organizer who would then leave the director well alone, but he was nervous about the interfering reputation of Zanuck. Aside from some unwelcome input at the editing stage, whereupon Dmytryk was defended by his producer, his experience with Zanuck was benign enough to initiate a fruitful collaboration throughout the rest of the decade. Dmytryk's assessment of the mogul was a jumble of contradictions: "sophisticated yet extremely naïve, independent yet subject to the importuning of sycophants, possessing limited taste yet recognizing and appreciating taste in others."[16]

Spencer Tracy, curtailing his problem drinking for the duration of the shoot, was for the most part a popular colleague. E.G. Marshall, playing the part of state governor, recalled that the star "always knew his lines. Never had to be prompted. One take was the norm. In my judgement, he was the quintessential film actor (I never saw him on stage). Everyone respected him and, dare I say it, loved him."[17] Robert Wagner loved him so much that after filming he placed an advertisement thanking Tracy for his help and advice. The advice could however be delivered irascibly. Wagner recalled Tracy taking him aside in irritation after the young actor admitted trying to underplay him: "Do you really think you could underplay me? ... Because you could *never* underplay me…. Why don't you think about playing the scene and being honest in it and bringing something of yourself to it and taking all this other stuff out of the way? Why don't you think about *that* instead of being a smartass son of a bitch and trying to underplay me?"[18]

Richard Widmark also remembered the benevolence seeping away on occasion: "It was Spence's scene; he was doing all the talking. I happened to be standing in the wrong place or something, and he looked up and said, 'Who the fuck do you think is the star of this picture?' I said, 'Oh, Spence, come on.' Then he got embarrassed. That's the other side of Tracy. He could be very petty and egomaniacal."[19] His old friend Clark Gable agreed with this assessment when talking to Hedda Hopper about the film: "Spence *is* the part. The old rancher is mean, unreasonable, and vain. All he has to do is show up and be photographed."[20]

Tracy's ease onscreen exerts a magnetism that makes it hard to disagree with Marshall's assessment of him being the quintessential screen actor. His every breath, glance, hesitation enriches the reality of the character. As effortless as he made it look, Tracy worked hard in preparing his speech cadences. Dmytryk realized that at times his naturalistic vocal tics were covering momentary memory lapses, and once asked for another take when he felt the delivery was too woolly. Tracy asked why. "You flubbed just a touch too much on that one." The actor retorted, "Young fella, I've spent a lifetime perfecting that flub."[21] With good humor, he consented to the extra take. On another occasion, Dmytryk rewrote a scene that he felt didn't flow well. Tracy asked if he could play the scene as written, having learnt the lines, and broke up the phrasing so naturally that the scene flowed perfectly, without changing a single word. Dmytryk compared his ability to wring truth from text to that of Louis Armstrong: "Louis could make a ricky-tick lyric sound like poetry, and Tracy could make a leaden line shine like gold."[22]

As in many great Westerns, *Broken Lance* focuses on a moment of transition for the Old West. By 1886 Matt Devereaux is omnipotent cattle baron of his own domain, having trekked from the east with his wife and three sons a quarter of a century previously. After her death he married and had a fourth son by the daughter of a Native American chief, whom he calls Princess and the local community call Señora, in a feeble attempt to disguise her origins. The elder brothers feel aggrieved at being treated like underpaid hired hands while the youngest, Joe, clearly benefits from favoritism. The eldest, Ben, wants to be granted some degree of autonomy to open an office in the nearest town and broaden the scope of the family business.

It is this clash of pioneer autonomy with business-minded modernity that forms the bedrock of resentment within the family. Ben wants to lease tracts of their huge expanse of land for mineral and oil exploration while Matt stubbornly refuses to diversify from what has enriched him and given him his power. This collision of ideas is expressed physically in one bravura sequence. Realizing that their cattle are being poisoned by deposits from a copper mine on a distant part of their land, the Devereauxs ride 40 miles across their unspoiled terrain to challenge the mining company. The mineshaft equipment rises starkly from the landscape, belching black smoke into the blue sky, a foretaste of how the landscape will be despoiled when fully exploited. Here the five men stand off against dozens of mineworkers, with tension built adroitly, until reinforcements from the Devereaux ranch ride up and Matt orders the mining constructions to be burnt. This act of destruction will land him in court and seal the family's fate.

With a certain irony, the roles are reversed within the family with regard to racism. Ben harbors resentment for his "half-breed" half-brother and has barely concealed disdain for Native Americans. Matt relates the story of his Irish father moving to America after the ravages of the Famine and, having presumably himself suffered some prejudice along the way, displays no racism and adores his Princess. Tracy and Jurado have a fine chemistry in their scenes together, one where they are preparing for a dinner party being especially sweet. E.G. Marshall's state governor is one of the guests at this dinner party. A letter written by Marshall to Katharine Hepburn, although misremembering the details of the script (it is not he but Carl Benton Reid who has the line "Her bad back"), recalls how the shooting of this scene demonstrates how fondly Hepburn was held in Tracy's mind: "I and my wife were invited to a dinner party, Spencer had remarried an Indian. My wife, Kate, disapproved and didn't show up. 'Her bad back,' I said lamely. Spence said, 'Let's change the name to Grace, if it was Kate she'd be here.'"[23] In the film, the absent wife is indeed called Grace.

Broken Lance won plaudits for its treatment of racism, and a Golden Globe as Best Film Promoting International Understanding. The antagonism of the community towards the interracial marriage ranges from the insidious pretense that she is Spanish to the blatant hostility when Joe and Barbara (Jean Peters), the daughter of the governor, express romantic interest in each other. Matt is wounded by the lack of loyalty of his old friend the governor ("Not you after all these years!") and is aggressive in his rejection of this racism: "I'm gonna tell my boy that if he wants that girl of yours to take her, if he has to pull her out of the house by the hair of her head."

Matt also finds himself at odds with modern ways when he ends up in court. He contemptuously calls the attorney from the east "Sonny" and defends his recourse to violent methods, the ways of the Old West, to protect his holdings. When challenged over shooting a man some years previously over water rights, he is defiant: "Every drop that's on my ranch, I either dug for or channelled it in." But the courtroom scene reveals sharply how out of time he is. Matt is placed in contempt of court and, to avoid having his father put in jail, Joe takes the blame for the riot at the mine and accepts a jail sentence himself. A lovely shot has Matt alone in a courtroom ante-chamber, looking through a doorway as the proceedings against his son conclude. He has been left behind by the progress of civilization and is now an impotent observer of the force of the law. He closes the door on the society to which he is unable to adapt.

The subsequent scenes display Tracy's utter mastery of technique. Matt summons his three elder sons in a bid to release Joe from jail. "You wanted us?" asks Ben. Matt replies, "No I don't want you. I told you to come here. Sit down!" When Ben refuses to sign the necessary papers, Matt whips him and suffers a stroke. The beauty of Tracy's performance is in the gentle foreshadowing of the stroke. It can be observed but incredibly subtly. Tracy feeds in unusual gestures that in retrospect are entirely apposite.

His post-stroke performance is also perfectly observed, and the final scene between Tracy and Widmark led the critic Jack Moffitt to hail it "one of the finest coordinated pieces of screen acting I've ever seen."[24] Ben is now in charge of financial affairs and his father asks him not to put land up for sale for oil exploration. "It's just a little late for asking now, Pa." Dmytryk holds the camera back in a two-shot, observing the rhythmic interplay between the actors, Widmark more than holding his own with the Master. Matt, a husk of his former self, is forced to look up to the resistant figure of his resurgent son when Ben refuses to sit: "I always used to think there was too much of me in you for us to hit it off. But I know now that I was wrong. There wasn't enough of me in you." Darryl Zanuck had originally conceived the death of Matt in melodramatic terms ("lightning, thunder, galloping horses"[25]) but the reworked version from Murphy and Dmytryk of him quietly sliding from his horse, having just died in defense of his world, is infinitely more powerful.

A fratricidal fight between Joe and Ben is an excitingly shot climax to the film but the closing minutes really belong to Katy Jurado. The stillness of her performance now takes center stage and becomes mesmerically moving. Having laid flowers on her husband's grave, she watches her son do the same, before riding off in a wagon with his bride. She will slip back to her own people, or possibly slip away altogether ("There is no longer need for me, my son"), and she smiles contentedly at the appearance on an outcrop of a lone wolf, a creature that Matt had always refused to shoot, and now potentially his reincarnation. It is a beautiful, elegiac conclusion.

Jurado's contribution won her a richly deserved Oscar nomination. She spoke of her happiness for homeland Mexico by being in contention for the award and on the night of the ceremony provided more Latin fire than observers were prepared for. She "created what the *Los Angeles Mirror-News* called 'a minor sensation' in her 'flame-colored gown which had at least four enormous red roses blooming across her shoulder.' When the forecourt emcee complimented Jurado on the outfit, she elaborated, 'It's a Dior and the bra and panties that came with it are flame-colored, too.'"[26] She lost to the rather more demure Eva Marie Saint in *On the Waterfront*. The film's only other nomination was Philip Yordan for Motion Picture Story, which won. The irony that Yordan should win an award for originality for a film based on his own work of five years previous seems to have passed the Academy by.

The End of the Affair (1955)

"A story has no beginning or end: arbitrarily one chooses that moment of experience from which to look back or from which to look ahead."[27] The opening sentence of Graham Greene's 1951 novel *The End of the Affair* displays the author's typically acute understanding of the nature of narrative. It also reflects on the particularly circuitous route that the novel made towards its first screen adaptation and refracts some irony onto the chronology within the film, given the two edits that emerged.

David Lean appears to have been the first director to express an interest in adapting the book. In February 1952 he wrote a letter to Gregory Peck, having heard from one of the Woolf brothers at Romulus Films of Peck's interest. He wrote that he was immensely moved by the book and found it "a first class piece of writing, but how one gets a film out of it which has that curious magic of the writing and makes [Production Code head] Mr. Breen happy, I can't quite see at the moment. But I do see that somewhere there is a mighty fine movie to be made along the lines of two very intimate character studies."[28] Three weeks later, Lean was forced to withdraw from the running. He wrote to Peck: "Over here, the rumour was that the film was going to be made in the early summer, and the damnable thing is that by the autumn it looks very much as if I shall be at work on a pet subject of my own."[29] In reply, Peck confirmed that "it looks like *The End of the Affair* deal has fallen through. I held out for a completed screenplay and approval of director and co-star before making a definite commitment.... I know you will agree that it is much too tricky a picture to go into without knowing how the adaptation will turn out. It could be ghastly, and very well might be, since I understand that Graham Greene will have nothing to do with the adaptation except in a kind of advisory capacity."[30] Greene later made his feelings about Peck playing Maurice Bendrix clear: "I was very much against him."[31]

Peck was to remain a presence in successive attempts to set the film up, but at this point the producer David Lewis picked up the baton, employed Lenore Coffee to write a first form draft script and attempted to engage William Wyler as director. In August, Lewis sent the script to Wyler in Rome where the director was shooting *Roman Holiday*, mentioning that "Olivia de Havilland has accepted and wants very much to do [it]."[32] Since Wyler had directed de Havilland to an Oscar for *The Heiress* in 1949, the producer and actress were keen for a reunion between director and star: "Talked [to] Olivia last night. She [is] certain when you read script *Affair* you will see some great possibilities she feels and that with only you will [it] be [a] truly memorable picture."[33] Despite his continued interest in the project, Wyler prevaricated over committing, leading the agent Ray Stark of Famous Artists Agency to express his frustration in November: "Writing to you is like talking to a Freudian analyst—a fellow can really slip into free association quickly by writing you and never getting an answer."[34] In December, de Havilland was still "v anxious to do it"[35] and Wyler expressed his terms: a deposit of $250,000, all expenses and possible payment for an American writer. His proposed fee was a considerable step up from the $155,000 he was receiving for *Roman Holiday*. Ray Stark responded that a quarter of a million dollars "is a lot of dough in cash to dig up for an independent project these days, but we are certainly going to do our best."[36]

The issues of basic incompatibility with the Production Code that David Lean had highlighted early in 1952 were to plague the pre-production of the film. The plot told of an adulterous affair that is terminated by Sarah, a married woman, when, mistakenly believing her lover Maurice to have died in a bombing raid, she promises God to relinquish Maurice for good if his life is saved. 20th Century–Fox expressed interest in producing *The End of the Affair* throughout 1952, despite the reservation expressed by Darryl Zanuck that he "cannot see how you could get it by the Code and retain the full value of the story itself."[37] A Production Code of America (PCA) memo in March crystallized their objections: "After much discussion it was decided that

there was no treatment which we could see of fitting this story under the Code....
The problem lies in the deep absorption of this story in lust.... Part of the problem
springs from the fact that the man is a cynical and sensual atheist."[38] That the plot has
Maurice develop a morality and change his character was strangely not an ameliorat-
ing factor since this aspect "in addition to the grossness of the sex relationship seems
to be the main stumbling block in the story."[39] Script revisions by November had not
solved the problems of depicting "an adulterous sex affair that is far too *detailed*, too
prolonged, and too *gross*."[40] A new script was submitted on 2 December, which David
Lewis assured William Wyler had cleared the PCA, who were giving "their assurance
full cooperation to keep vitality of material based on excellent reworking flashback
first fifty pages."[41] It is likely there was an element of producer bluster in this reassurance since the hot property rapidly went cold for over a year.

In early 1953, David Lewis was talking to other directors and studios, including
Howard Hughes at RKO, but Wyler's agent thought that the project "looks very dubious"[42] and informed Wyler of "possibility acquiring *Affair* for 85 thousand outright
Lewis requiring guarantee production."[43] At that point, despite the fact that Wyler
had wanted to stay on and make another film in Europe for tax reasons, he withdrew
from the proposed project, most likely due to insufficient recompense, and produced
his next film *The Desperate Hours* in Hollywood.

Lenore Coffee had been a screenwriter in Hollywood since the 1920s, reaching
her peak in the 1930s and 1940s as a contract writer at Warner Bros. and MGM. She
was particularly adept at tailoring vehicles for the female titans of the day, including
Bette Davis and Joan Crawford: "Bette's talent was basically intellectual, Joan's emotional."[44] Regardless of talent, Coffee was an apt choice to script *The End of the Affair*,
which probes belief from a singularly Catholic perspective, since she had converted
to Catholicism when she was nearly twenty: "I like Graham Greene very much. He's
a convert to Catholicism, too. He said something once that I will always remember,
'I wouldn't want a God I could understand.' I have never forgotten that. That's rather
true."[45] She enthusiastically accepted he project that David Lewis offered her: "*The
End of the Affair* is a very good book. I wrote a beautiful script, but they got somebody in England to rewrite it, and it wasn't an improvement. I opened with the ending, the separation—after they had already stopped seeing each other—and then I
backtracked to show what led to the separation. I reversed the order of the novel."[46]
This is not strictly accurate since Greene also toys with the chronology of the plotline. The book, narrated by Maurice Bendrix, begins with his chance meeting in January 1946 with Henry Miles, the husband of Sarah, a year and a half after an affair
between Maurice and Sarah had abruptly terminated. Maurice is a novelist whose
self-reflexive narration dips back into the past, revealing glimpses of the beginning
of the affair, teasing the reader with concealed information, until a change of narrator in the middle of the book, in the form of Sarah's stolen diary, reveals the reason
for her breaking off the affair. According to Quentin Falk in his study of film adaptations of Greene's work, and contrary to what the screenwriter asserted, the film was
originally shot as Coffee had written it, with a lengthy opening flashback. However,
Columbia was afraid of confusing the audience and re-assembled it into generally
chronological order. Falk quotes Dmytryk as saying that Greene liked the original

pre-release version very much, and both director and author were disappointed with the imposed new edit.

The part of Sarah, which Olivia de Havilland had pursued so enthusiastically, went to Deborah Kerr. In the wake of her image-shattering role in *From Here to Eternity* and an extremely successful run on Broadway in *Tea and Sympathy*, Kerr resolved to continue to seek out nuanced characters: "In the future parts I choose are going to be about real women; they may not be pleasant, but they will be real people."[47] Kerr succeeds magnificently in breathing life into the complex character of Sarah, a woman unfulfilled by marriage and morally riven when one of her affairs destabilizes her bedrock beliefs on religion and existence. Years later Kerr would express some disappointment with the material: "Today, or even just a few years after we filmed it, the screenplay could have benefited from being more explicit. I loved the book, but that's sometimes a trap you fall into: when you come to do the film you find so much is interior thought that it can't be put into dialogue."[48] These were the doubts behind adaptation that concerned everyone from the inception of the project, not least the author and the screenwriter. Coffee related, "Later I met Graham Greene in England—only once. I said to him, 'I had the dubious pleasure of writing the script for one of your films.' He laughed and said, 'Dubious pleasure! I like that very much.'"[49]

Greene derived no pleasure, dubious or otherwise, from the casting of Van Johnson as Maurice: "I stymied Gregory Peck. But then to find that Van Johnson took his place was a disaster."[50] Greene visited the set during the shoot and recalled with distaste how Johnson would chew gum during romantic scenes while the camera was on his lover in a reverse shot: "It didn't seem to me that it would have inspired very good acting from Deborah Kerr."[51] This unsuitable casting is the film's major blemish. Dmytryk had directed Johnson to give a very effective supporting performance in *The Caine Mutiny* which lifted him out of the frothy roles where he had been languishing. But Johnson is unable to match the caliber of his leading lady whose performance is rich with nuance, in a leading role that requires the viewer to observe the moral maelstrom seething within Maurice. Johnson can only manage a superficial reading of this anti-hero, his soul remaining obscured despite the script's attempts to illuminate it. The reviewer in the *New York Post* was particularly scathing in his assessment: "What's really bad is Johnson's tendency to look like a St Bernard when he becomes thoughtful."[52] The actor himself looked back fondly on Maurice Bendrix: "What a dream part. It was probably the happiest picture experience of my entire career."[53]

The thundering piano chords that open the film evoke the Second Piano Concerto from Rachmaninov that memorably underscored David Lean's *Brief Encounter*. Benjamin Frankel's accomplished score, his second for Dmytryk after *Give Us This Day*, provides a passionate counterpoint to the emotional turmoil of Sarah and Maurice. Further echoes of *Brief Encounter* are present, though less than resoundingly, in the character of Sarah. Unlike Celia Johnson's Laura, Sarah has conducted adulterous trysts before, and on our first encounter with her, Maurice spots her kissing a guest at a cocktail party. The affair with Maurice is implicitly consummated, although the censorship laws would not permit a realistic depiction of an adulterous liaison until four years later in *Room at the Top*. The filmmakers performed a skillful job in subtly conveying the sexual aspect of the affair within the bounds of what was permissible.

The figure that most invokes *Brief Encounter* is that of Henry, Sarah's husband, played with devastating understatement by Peter Cushing. In the earlier film, Laura's husband Fred is gifted the line "Thank you for coming back to me" after Laura has ended her affair. Henry is a fleshed-out version of Fred and we are privy to his pain. A senior civil servant, fastidious and precise, he is unable to engage with Sarah on the emotional level that she requires. Henry is visibly uncomfortable when Sarah asks about his belief in God and whether he prays. "One is taught to" is his response. But his love for Sarah, his need for her, is just as intense as her passions, only expressed in a different register. With her bags packed to leave him, Henry makes a desperate appeal for her to stay. In a scene that is beautifully acted and directed, Sarah massages Henry's temples as his composure crumbles. Initially staring straight ahead and deliberately not making eye contact, his aching desperation is exposed and, responding to this unfamiliar vulnerability, Sarah promises to stay with him. Cushing and Kerr match each other perfectly and movingly. Dmytryk found Cushing to be "completely professional, utterly charming…. British artists are more disciplined, more versatile, and much less self-indulgent than their American counterparts."[54]

The other man in Sarah's life is much more volatile, his emotions never far from the surface. Maurice's dark glances from their first encounter betray his jealousy for all the men who have come before in Sarah's life, never mind those who might currently be waiting in the wings. Looking at his reflection in a barroom mirror, Sarah seems intuitively aware of this and says, "Trust is a variable quality." He then instructs her to wipe her mouth so that he can kiss her, in a gesture that is domineering, not romantic. Later, when he is rude to someone who assumes that he is Sarah's husband and he condemns her ease at concealing the truth, her initial suspicion is confirmed. "You have no real trust in me," she says. In a single facial expression, Deborah Kerr skillfully conveys Sarah's depth of love for this man despite full awareness of his many faults. Maurice behaves poorly when with her and reprehensibly when without her. Once Sarah has ended the affair, Maurice tells us in voiceover, "My jealousy turned to hate." He engages a private detective (John Mills) when Henry confides his fears of her infidelity, and cruelly confronts Henry with the evidence, inaccurate as it turns out, that she is romantically involved with another man. Despite knowing that she is seriously ill in bed, he threatens to come and see her, making her flee to the sanctuary of a church on a rainy night, with ultimately fatal consequences. Maurice crosses so many ethical boundaries in the film that there is a cruelty in it being Sarah who bears the moral burden of their affair, finding her independence of spirit challenged by internal tussles of fidelity and faith.

The war has literally thrust Sarah and Maurice together. On their first evening alone, they take shelter from an air raid in a doorway and, in a strong moment of camera choreography, Dmytryk dollies in on the couple, closer and closer, until the intimacy between them is overwhelming. Sarah later remarks, "We're not the only ones living from day to day," betraying that perhaps the intensity of this liaison for her is a reaction to the unpredictability of the conflict around them. Imminent change is prefigured by her arriving at Maurice's flat on 18 June 1944, five days after the Germans commenced attacking London with V-1 flying bombs, with a bunch of flowers which give her "a kind of faith" in the midst of wartime turmoil. She had passed a soapbox speaker in the park who was railing about God: "It seemed so, well, risky at a time like this being rude to God." Having spent the day together, a bomb hits the house in an impressively rendered scene and Maurice is trapped under a doorway. Believing he has been killed, she feels impelled to pray and promises that she will renounce their relationship if God will bring him back to life. When he emerges, speaking of experiencing "a terrific sense of space and distance, like I'd been on a long journey," Sarah's look of fearful incredulity, beautifully expressed by Kerr, signifies the weight of the promise she has made.

Sarah seeks guidance from religious and secular sources in an attempt to navigate this unknown territory. The first time she speaks to a Catholic priest, she almost swallows the word "God," so unfamiliar is it for her to be speaking in these terms. This scene is akin to a confession, taking place in a church with the subtle shadow of a cross placed across her heart. To a humanist preacher, she appeals for help in extricating herself from her promise: "Convince me! I'm the most willing convert you ever had." But God, or the fateful hand of the scenarist, thwarts her best efforts: "Whenever I have a good impulse, I get punished. I prayed once and promised once and see what happened to me." *The End of the Affair* is remarkable as a Hollywood production of its era that seriously addresses faith and one woman's struggle with the existence of God. It is intelligently scripted by Coffee, with much dialogue taken from Greene's novel, and sensitively handled by Dmytryk, who extracts strong performances from almost everyone. It also nuances its denouement, drawing a less clear-cut conclusion than the novel.

When Sarah dies, in a scene where the departure of life is elegantly indicated by the cessation of movement of a chandelier on the ceiling, it is revealed that her mother had her baptized as a Catholic while a toddler. Sarah had finally accepted the existence of God, partly due to the intensity of her atheist advisor's disbelief: "You can't hate something that isn't there." The film has constantly teased that the hand of God is guiding matters, such as the moment when the lovers are about to kiss, and her sudden cough prevents them. Sarah's final words to Maurice, changed from a church interior to the church foyer after an objection from the Production Code, are "God bless." Coffee's script does however stop short of the two "miracles" that Sarah seems to have caused at the end of Greene's book and Neil Jordan's 1999 remake. With the outcome of the film, the Production Code has acted as God's surrogate—the illicit love affair has been punished, one lover is dead, and the other is consumed with regret. Dmytryk's camera ascends in the final shot to a deity-eye view, observing a bereft Maurice, battered into belief.

The End of the Affair may have been too cerebral to set the box-office alight, but it lingered positively in the memories of its participants, especially with respect to the leading lady. Lenore Coffee found it a "happy experience, my only one with Deborah Kerr,"[55] while for Dmytryk the actress was "a revelation. A superb artist, sensitive and passionate on the screen, she seemed to have no trace of temperament or ego."[56] Coffee blamed finances for the shortcomings of the film, as she perceived them: "It should have been a much better picture than it was, due in large part to considerable cheese-paring by the company which financed it."[57] The film was entered in competition at Cannes and Kerr received a nomination from the British Academy for her performance. When asked in 1984 which of the adaptations of his religious novels he was most satisfied with, the notoriously critical Graham Greene responded, "I suppose the least unsatisfactory was *The End of the Affair*. Deborah Kerr gave an extremely good performance in that."[58] This assessment is very different to that of Maurice Bendrix in Greene's book when he and Sarah watch a screen adaptation of one of Maurice's novels: "The film was not a good film, and at moments, it was actually painful to see situations that had been so real to me twisted into stock clichés of the screen."[59] Edward Dmytryk's *The End of the Affair* is indeed a good film that manages, for the most part, to transcend cliché.

Soldier of Fortune (1955)

On 2 March 1954, while his old colleague Spencer Tracy was shooting his first scenes for Edward Dmytryk on *Broken Lance*, Clark Gable left the MGM studios for the last time. Gable had been at MGM since 1930 but the new regime under Dore Schary compounded his disillusionment and hastened his departure. He had been offered a new two-year contract but without his desired percentage share in profit, which newly freelance stars now expected. He still smarted from the fact that he had had no share of the unprecedented success of *Gone with the Wind*, fuming that they had never even given him the 16 mm print of the film that he requested. Over a script disagreement, Schary handed him a suspension, to which Gable responded, "Imagine that. Suspending a guy for the first time in his life after twenty-three years with the studio."[60] Despite the huge success of *Mogambo* in late 1953, Gable struck out on his own, with one final MGM picture *Betrayed* released after his departure.

Spencer Tracy was making *Broken Lance* on loan to Fox but was also desperate to leave MGM. After one more picture for them, *Bad Day at Black Rock*, his first film as a free agent was Dmytryk's *The Mountain*. Dmytryk provided precisely the same service to Clark Gable, whose first post–MGM movie was *Soldier of Fortune*. Fox were happy to give Gable an attractive deal that made him the most expensive freelance actor in the industry: two pictures per year with $400,000 in salary and 10 percent of the gross. Dmytryk had just been given a five-picture deal at the same studio and was the only contracted director at Fox on Gable's approved directors list. The actor read and liked the *Soldier of Fortune* script that Ernest Gann had adapted from his own novel, even if the director considered it "a potboiler, though possibly one of the better ones. It wasn't up to the quality of the films I'd been doing lately, but—there was Clark Gable … Susan Hayward … and Hong Kong."[61] Thus, despite a lack of enthusiasm about the project from both Dmytryk and producer Buddy Adler, *Soldier of Fortune* went into production.

Susan Hayward was not an actress who inspired enthusiasm from her colleagues.

Clark Gable (left) at the studio with his director on *Soldier of Fortune* (1955).

Robert Preston, who had appeared in three films with her, responded to an interview request with "Anything I have to say about Susan Hayward you couldn't print."[62] Marsha Hunt, her co-star in *Smash-Up, the Story of a Woman*, said: "This was a person so private and so closely involved with her job at hand that all relationships with others are non-existent."[63]

Gable accepted Darryl Zanuck's choice of Hayward for *Soldier of Fortune*, though his first choice had been Grace Kelly who turned down the role. The closest Hayward and Gable had gotten to appearing in the same picture was when the actress had been one of several dozen to get a screen test for Scarlett O'Hara. Hayward had recently divorced Jess Barker and she was obliged to file a court petition on 13 October 1954 to bring their twins Timothy and Gregory with her to the location shoot in Hong Kong: "I don't think a mother should be away from her children for long, and the trip would help broaden the boys' education."[64] Barker objected to their removal from school and the fact that Hong Kong was not a safe destination due to being "invested [*sic*] with Communists and disease."[65] The judge found in Barker's favor, and Hayward refused to make the trip without her sons. Zanuck considered Hayward's box-office prospects to be so strong that he took the highly unusual decision of sending the necessary cast and crew to shoot in Hong Kong, using long shot and body double[66] for the female lead. All of the actress's close-up work was shot on Fox sound stages, with rear projection used when necessary. The result is a fatally compromised film, rich in local color and exotic locale—until Susan Hayward appears onscreen.

Ernest Gann's plot had Jane Hoyt (Hayward) arriving in Hong Kong in search of her photographer husband Louis (Gene Barry) who has been missing for three months. Hank Lee (Gable), an American entrepreneur of dubious provenance, locates Louis in China and, despite having fallen in love with Jane, sets out to rescue him. The storyline caused problems with Joseph Breen of the Production Code, who in October 1954 decreed that the "basic story is unacceptable"[67]: "The difficulty in this story stems from the fact that the leading man sets out with the avowed intention of breaking up the marriage of the leading woman and her husband and the conclusion of the story is that he succeeded in this intention…. [W]hen the two lovers part a proper expression of their mutual regard for the sanctity of marriage [should] be written."[68] As usual, any kink in the cloth of marital fidelity had to be ironed out, but a few weeks later the offensive points had been addressed and the "breakup of the marriage will be pinned upon Louis."[69] The censor in Australia was even less inclined to break up the Hoyts. When the film was released there in November 1955, the ending wherein "Miss Hayworth [sic] returns to Clark Gable"[70] was deleted, leaving the unhappy couple of Jane and Louis on the airport bus, about to fly back to a compromised life together.

Where CinemaScope had been a vitalizing experience for Dmytryk on *Broken Lance*, with its liberating Arizona vistas stretched across the screen, the format was more problematic in *Soldier of Fortune*. The locations in Hong Kong are vividly captured, the streets vibrant, the harbor filled with junks. Hank Lee is introduced at a viewpoint along the Peak Tram funicular railway and his hilltop villa gives onto a spectacular vista. The interior scenes, however, filmed at 20th Century–Fox in Hollywood, suffer from the common widescreen malady of the day: hotel lobbies the size of an aircraft hangar; living rooms the size of a comfortable apartment; the resultant sacrifice of intimacy for scale. Dmytryk's camerawork fails to rise to the challenge of energizing these expanses.

Gable's character is sketched inconsistently. Hank Lee is initially described to Jane Hoyt by marine policeman Inspector Merryweather (Michael Rennie) as "a disgrace to your country … a gangster. Smuggling is one of his lesser vices. He'd do anything to make a dollar—and has." Later an old flame, we can only assume, gushes, "I think he's the most wonderful man in the world." He is clearly an aggressive force to be reckoned with in business, proudly points out a military gun on his boat as "the biggest thing I ever stole," has books lying around his home in a fervor of self-improvement and, though a bachelor, has adopted three children out of the goodness of his heart. It's a mishmash of characteristics that don't fully cohere. Gable's ease as an actor enables him to dominate the screen but not to bridge the gaps in Hank. The performance is most effective when the problematic shackles of personality are thrown off and he becomes an action hero, pushing into Communist China to rescue the husband of his love, firing off rounds at the foe in his white t-shirt.

Jane Hoyt is a woman so alluring that, on the first two occasions she appears, normal business ceases and all characters in a hotel lobby and in a rough bar turn to ogle her. She is able to inspire adoration in Hank, who tells her, "All my life I wanted to meet someone like you. Someone I could believe in. I was beginning to think there wasn't anyone. I never thought I'd find out the hard way." Unfortunately, Susan

Hayward is unable to incarnate this mesmerizing creature adequately. Dmytryk did not rate her as an actress and felt that her insecurity about acting opposite Gable left her "scared, scared to death."[71] Hayward won her Oscar and had most success when required to emote violently but her limitations reveal themselves when she is required to listen to another actor, her face often a mask devoid of reaction. For Jane, Hank is prepared to leave his adopted country and risk his life to rescue Louis: "I want your husband out of China more than you do. I wish he was sitting here right now so I could stand a chance with you. I can't fight a ghost." Hayward's performance does little to explain this degree of dedication.

One positive feature of *Soldier of Fortune* is that Hong Kong and Chinese characters are portrayed by Oriental actors, which is not the case in Dmytryk's following film *The Left Hand of God* and its regrettable casting of Lee J. Cobb. Less satisfactory is their cursory representation. One of the most interesting figures is a Chinese general, exiled from his homeland and down on his luck, eking out a meager living as a tour guide for hire. This is a mature performance from Richard Loo but the General appears in only a few scenes and, just as we are appreciating some depth of characterization, he is arrested by the Chinese authorities while escorting Jane to Macau and never seen again. The intriguing figures of an aged underworld contact (Soo Yong) and Hank's old flame (an uncredited Frances Fong) are given similarly short shrift. In their place we have an uninspiring group of Occidentals, broadly written and indifferently acted. Alex D'Arcy plays René, a Frenchman who blacks out seconds after downing two whiskies and who engages in a farcical fistfight with two Australian sailors. The action around Tweedie's bar is intended to inject some colorful characters into the film but is so tonally out of kilter that it merely seems absurd.

The rescue of Louis was hampered by censorship constraints regarding a fight sequence: "[T]here should be no kicking or kneeing. In addition, of course, the set should not contain an open latrine, as presently described."[72] The result is a remarkably easy springing from captivity. Once onboard Hank's boat, our heroes are pursued by the Chinese Communists,[73] but a friendly flotilla of junks, assembled by bribing with wristwatches, ensures their escape. Dmytryk was particularly pleased with this final sequence: "The first shot of the fleet of nearly a thousand vessels, with their myriad-colored sails, silently but swiftly gliding toward and then past us was electrifying…. Like a flock of pigeons, all the boats came about as one and sailed back towards us for the next shot…. I have worked in almost every country of the so-called technically superior Western world, but I have never seen planning, organization, or execution anywhere near that shown by this group of fishermen, lightermen, and smugglers."[74] In the decades after 1978, when this was written, nobody would accuse China of being technically inferior.

Dmytryk's experience with his leading man was positive: "Gable was a director's dream. Never a moment late, always well prepared."[75] There was an attempt by studio publicists to suggest romance between Gable and Hayward, and they were pictured together on 2 February, celebrating his 54th birthday. It was to be their sole onscreen pairing. *Soldier of Fortune*, released in May, was a hit with audiences ($7.9 million at the domestic box office) and generally well-received by the critics: "Edward Dmytryk's very able direction keeps the high adventure always on a believable plane."[76]

The film's success may be attributable to the fact that CinemaScope, Gable and Hayward were all hot properties that year—the actors' other films in 1955, *The Tall Men* and *I'll Cry Tomorrow*, were even bigger hits. Unfortunately, *Soldier of Fortune* has not endured well and it is hard to disagree with the director's dismissal of it as a "potboiler." For Gable, however, the grass was indeed greener on the other side. When MGM saw how successful his films were after he had left the studio, they made overtures to rehire him, provoking the following instruction from Gable to his agent: "See how high you can get those sons of bitches to go. When you get their very best offer, tell them to take all the money, their studio, their cameras and their lighting equipment, and shove it all up their ass."[77]

The Left Hand of God (1955)

From the mid–1930s onwards, Monsignor John J. Devlin was a Catholic priest in Los Angeles who became technical advisor to the office of the Production Code on all matters of Catholic concern, and ultimately the arbiter of what was acceptable to the Catholic Church for portrayal onscreen. The genesis of the film project *The Left Hand of God* provoked a clash between three Catholics: on one side, Monsignor Devlin and Joseph Breen, Director of the Motion Picture Association of America (MPAA), and on the other, William E. Barrett, the author of the book, and later provider of the source material for the film *Lilies of the Field*.

Barrett's book told of an American pilot, James Carmody, shot down over China who becomes right-hand man to a bandit chief, Mieh Yang. After falling from favor with Yang, Carmody escapes in the guise of Father O'Shea, a Catholic priest who has been murdered by the gang, and ends up at a mission where he must continue his masquerade as the clergyman. In 1950 *The Left Hand of God* was serialized in the magazine *Redbook* and, prior to its publication as a book, Barrett sounded out the interest of the Hollywood studios.

That July, Paramount, despite their interest, decided that it was "inconceivable that the Catholic church will accept without protest and eventual condemnation of the picture the spectacle of the holiest of their sacraments being performed by a layman posing as a priest."[78] The MPAA agreed that "this subject matter would be utterly and totally impossible under the Code."[79] Warner Bros. were very keen on the property and, sensing "an almost certain sale to one or another of the studios in town,"[80] spoke up for the inspiration the picture could provide to Catholics and non–Catholics alike "at this particular time when world attention is focused on the conflict in the Far East."[81] The suggestion had been made to change the status of the priest to a lay brother, as in the Edward G. Robinson vehicle *Brother Orchid*, but Finlay McDermid of Warner Bros. suggested another solution: "would it be possible to tell the story without having the camera show specific cases in which the masquerading priest performed marriages, gave absolution, etc.?"[82]

Jean Porter and Lee J. Cobb on *The Left Hand of God* (1955).

By September the studios had stopped chasing the property, either through the anticipated insurmountable hurdles that the MPAA would place in the path of production, or, as an internal MPAA communication whispered, that they didn't think the book was good enough: "I don't have to tell you that, if they thought it had a real chance, they would have left nothing unturned to grab it, and whip it into shape."[83] Unofficial word had got back to Barrett that the studios had passed and that the damning opinion of Monsignor Devlin was to blame. The four months from September witnessed a tetchy exchange of letters between Barrett, Breen and Devlin, with Barrett fulminating that the opinion of one unaccountable priest had stymied negotiations for the sale of his book when other members of the Catholic clergy had embraced it, and with Breen defending the reputation of his office, and of his unpaid advisor Devlin, vigorously and at length. Barrett, with the paranoia of an author who fears his ideas have been stolen, suggested underhand behavior on the part of Devlin by quoting a Louella Parsons column in August, to the effect that an MGM proposal with the same basic premise as his book had been cleared for production. This film, then under the working title of *Roman Holiday* but eventually released in 1952 under the title of *When in Rome*, was a comedy starring Van Johnson which had Paul Douglas as a con-man disguising himself as a priest on pilgrimage to Rome.

Breen was dismissive of Barrett's implications ("The Metro story no more resembles Mr. Barrett's story, than does the moon resemble your grandmother"[84]) and grew tired of the accusations of impropriety: "The gentleman is obviously quite a contentious citizen, who is very greatly upset because he has not, as yet, succeeded in selling his story to one of our companies."[85] Barrett had reined back on his accusations by the beginning of 1951, and, realizing that having Breen as an enemy was counter-productive, accepted his suggestion that, as long as the priest was not shown performing holy sacramental rites, then the premise of his story should be allowable for the screen. By January, Breen had also amended his opinion on the quality of Barrett's work. After speaking to Howard Hawks ("He is interested in your story, and told me, quite frankly, that he felt he might be able to develop a good screenplay from it"[86]), he wrote Hawks a letter to encourage his engagement with the project "based upon this very excellent novel."[87]

Hawks' interest waned and the project lay dormant for a few years until 20th Century–Fox produced a draft treatment of the novel on 16 March 1954. By this stage, "while Twentieth Century–Fox had first option on this material, there was nevertheless the possibility that it would be taken over by Metro, should Fox not choose to exercise its priority."[88] Monsignor Devlin felt that the MGM proposal was to introduce "more shocking" material into the story, "such as, possibly, pretending to say Mass, or pretending to hear Confessions."[89] Fox however exercised its option and started to pursue Gregory Peck to star. A decade previously, Peck's second film had been a Fox hit about a Catholic priest in China, *The Keys to the Kingdom*, and Hollywood studios have an unerring enthusiasm for the obvious choice.

Peck, also a Roman Catholic, was not enthusiastic about the script. In September he wrote to producer Buddy Adler at Fox to explain his reservations—avoiding the depiction of the moral struggle of a layman performing religious ceremonies would rob him of acting opportunities; the love story with the nurse at the mission was both conventional and distasteful; Carmody's speech to God lacked conviction. Most revealing was his reason for finding the Chinese setting dramatically uninteresting: "I think the prospect of seeing so many Chinese faces crowded together in the Church, the hospital and the village is not an exciting one. There is a heaviness about these people and a lack of individuality for Western audiences that fosters dullness."[90] His sign-off was forthright: "I don't think that the script measures up."[91]

Darryl Zanuck was not going to let the box-office potential of Peck, fresh from smash hits *Roman Holiday* and *The Snows of Kilimanjaro*, slip away from him without a fight. He sent Peck a last-ditch telegram on 4 December 1954: "We are scheduled to start photography [on The] *Left Hand of God* middle of February and I have deliberately held off signing anyone for role in hope that you would reconsider as you apparently are the only important actor in the world who does not want to play the role and does not appreciate the script STOP Personally I feel that you should do this role but before closing elsewhere I wanted you to have first refusal STOP Dmytryk is set to direct.... I am trying to give you priority on every important story we purchase.... I would hate you later on to feel that I tempted you and then gave the role to someone else." Peck's response was terse and final: "Darryl, Grateful for first refusal on *Left Hand* but still do not [feel] attracted to role." Zanuck conceded defeat and Humphrey Bogart was signed to the role.

All of the tussling over the representation of the sacraments becomes rather irrelevant when watching the finished film. As had been suggested during the discussions, the film opens with Carmody in clerical guise losing the suitcase containing his priestly accouterments to a fast-flowing river. He mentions this fact when he arrives at the mission, but he is informed how many converts are waiting to have their confession heard and later is shown preaching to a congregation from the altar. Anne Scott (Gene Tierney), a nurse at the mission, says, "If you say a High Mass, Father, perhaps I could be your soloist," and tries to explain why she hasn't been to confession. So, though he is not explicitly shown performing the sacraments, the clear implication is that this is happening offscreen. This fudging of the issue was standard with the MPAA. The producer Val Lewton "thought that Breen barked more than he bit: the Production Code director always allowed 'greater leeway' than his letters indicated."[92]

Red lines were breached in the depiction of a brothel, or the Yellow House of the district. Despite Breen's prohibition of showing Carmody entering the Yellow House or even of viewing the prostitutes themselves, both occur in a scene where Carmody fetches a parishioner from the brothel. The prostitutes remain a presence in the community and at the very end of the film they are standing just outside the gates of the village to bid farewell to Carmody. Lewton, who at one point was in charge of censorship at Selznick International, summarized Breen's attitude in a letter to David O. Selznick: "Mr. Breen goes to the bathroom every morning. He does not deny that he does so or that there is such a place as the bathroom, but he feels that neither his actions nor the bathroom are fit subjects for screen entertainment. This is the essence of the Hays' office attitude to prostitution, at least as Joe told it to me in somewhat cruder language."[93] A stronger stance was taken with the character of Mary Yin, a concubine of Mieh Yang (Lee J. Cobb). Her role as Carmody's sexual partner was effectively deleted, and Jean Porter Dmytryk, in her final film appearance, is left with a single scene in the final cut.

Bogart naturally gives an entirely different inflection to the role than Peck would have done. The initial sight we have of a priest carrying a gun has its own particular resonance when the actor is Humphrey Bogart. Given their respective star personas, we would be more inclined to believe that Bogart is a bandit masquerading as a priest, whereas with Peck it would be a priest masquerading as a bandit. Bogart adroitly downplays the clergyman in his character, always slightly embarrassed to be asked to perform a blessing. Being unable to deliver a High Church sermon at his first time in the pulpit, Carmody's Father O'Shea simply addresses the congregation in Chinese, instantly endearing himself to the locals. Bogart's lack of ease in clerical garb feeds well into the awkwardness that Carmody feels at suddenly being perceived as a priest of the people. It is not one of his most textured performances, since the script itself lacks texture, but his persona glides over the inconsistencies. When Yang is threatening to attack the village, Carmody goes into the church and Dmytryk gives us a crucifix-eye view of the fake priest and we hear Carmody's thoughts in voiceover: "Here I am, Lord. I'm not going to pray. What I have to say I'd like to stay standing on my feet. These people think I'm a priest. I'd nothing to offer but faith in a God I didn't believe in or think existed." It is a joy to watch the expressions flicker over Bogart's weathered, soulful face as Carmody looks up and confronts the contradictions of his nascent faith.

"That man has magnetism," says mission nurse Beryl (Agnes Moorehead) of Father O'Shea, adding that his eyes are "so beautifully unhappy," a neat summation of Bogart's appeal. Beryl is the sage presence in the film. She can't quite see through Carmody's masquerade, but she mentions several times to her husband Dr. Sigman (E.G. Marshall) that there is "so much in O'Shea that isn't meant to be a priest." Moorehead and Marshall play off each other beautifully, two consummate supporting actors portraying the rhythms of married life with studied ease, in particular one scene in which they discuss Anne's infatuation with Father O'Shea. As Sigman lights a cigarette for Beryl and casually hands it to her, she rebuffs his suggestion that women can't understand celibacy with a defense of Anne's behavior: "Females are simple biological structures. Their bodies pay very little attention to their minds." Such a rationale has more usually been deployed to defend male sexual behavior, but screenwriter Alfred Hayes upends convention. Here, as so often throughout the film, Hayes' script struggles for a profundity that remains elusive. The contribution of Moorehead and Marshall, however, provides ballast for some of the less successful elements. Moorehead would work for Dmytryk again in *Raintree County* and would regard him as one of her favorite directors, while Marshall would be cast in four Dmytryk films. The director was full of praise for their work together on *The Left Hand of God*, calling their scenes "a total delight. I've often wished that the thrill of watching superb actors practicing their art could somehow be 'laid under' the finished scene, like a music track, to add to the audience's enjoyment. For me it is a rare bonus."[94]

When Carmody encounters the ravishing beauty of Anne, his dog-collar is insufficient to prevent him from flirting with her ("It's been a long time since I went walking out with a pretty girl"), unsettling the religious certainties of the nurse. Their rapport is an aid to their work with the villagers as she "checks their temperatures" while he "checks their souls" but her attraction for him soon destabilizes the working relationship. The suppressed romance is less than persuasive due to an awkward chemistry between Bogart and Tierney, his earthiness and her ethereal air proving an abrasive combination. Considering the circumstances, an absent onscreen chemistry is more than understandable. Tierney's mental health was under severe strain at this point in her life and Darryl Zanuck, aware of her fragility, asked Dmytryk and Bogart for their approval to cast her. It was a difficult shoot for her: "When I think of that time it is like watching a silent movie. There are no sounds, no words. I told my doctor I could observe myself, as though I were outside my own body, all during the filming of *The Left Hand of God*."[95] She was extremely grateful for Bogart taking her under his wing, helping her with lines and encouraging her to seek medical treatment. Gene Tierney would not make another film for seven years and this would be her last starring role.

One casting choice is fatally compromising. Despite the best efforts of Ben Nye and his make-up team, Lee J. Cobb utterly fails to convince under heavy eyelid prosthetics as Yang, his aura more Lower East Side than Far East. The script tries to explain this away with the line "I'm a graduate of one of your universities," but to the modern viewer the tendency of classical Hollywood cinema to cast occidental actors as other ethnicities is a severe obstacle to engagement. Yang and Carmody frequently resort to throwing dice to resolve differences and late in the film they wager the safety of the mission and the future of Carmody on the rolling of five dice. Yang throws "three sixes—Father, Son and Holy Ghost." The dice appear more loaded with faith than fate, however, and Carmody throws "four threes. You lose. You shouldn't have invoked the Trinity." Yang concedes defeat to the mysterious ways of the Catholic God: "I'll have to act benevolent and create a legend. I've been touched by the Holy Spirit and have decided to spare these villages. You'll become the most celebrated priest in China."

Lee J. Cobb was yet another performer who endured an uncomfortable entanglement with HUAC. He had been named as a Communist Party member by Larry Parks in his testimony in March 1951 and experienced an instant career decline. He felt deserted by former friends: "All of this time I was out of touch with my colleagues—the people with whom I had shared these ideological tenets. When the chips were down, you were abandoned. They ran when I was named. The very people I was protecting were beneath contempt."[96] He finally testified in June 1953, confirmed that he had joined the Party in 1940 or 1941, named various names and took leave of the committee with the words "I would like to thank you for the privilege of setting the record straight."[97]

The Left Hand of God is one of a trilogy of 20th Century–Fox films spanning three decades that concern themselves with Catholic missionary priests in China: *The Keys of the Kingdom* was directed by John M. Stahl in 1944 and *Satan Never Sleeps* was directed by Leo McCarey in 1962. Despite a script that tussles with theological issues without coming to grips with them, Edward Dmytryk's film compares favorably to the other two. *The Keys of the Kingdom* is the most epic in scope, covering the decades of Gregory Peck's missionary career, and is lustrously photographed but its huge timespan renders it frustratingly episodic. *Satan Never Sleeps* is unconvincing—in particular the central casting of William Holden—shoddy and terminated Leo McCarey's career.

Dmytryk handles his imperfect raw material well, keeping the pace brisk, ensuring the 85-minute film doesn't overstay its welcome and providing an emotional kick at its conclusion. His use of the CinemaScope format is astute, employing clever composition for the interior dialogue scenes, so often ill-suited to the ultra-wide frame. The fake Father O'Shea frequently has a judgmental crucifix or Da Vinci *Last Supper* or statue of Christ hovering just over his shoulder, physical manifestations of his conscience assessing his actions. Carmody had said, "I haven't been in church since I was an altar boy," and Dmytryk's camera placement ensures that the Catholic iconography of his youth silently witnesses his moral quandaries. The exterior landscapes, filmed at the Fox ranch at Malibu, are very well photographed by Franz Planer, whom Dmytryk called a true artist: "He was one of the first to bring out pastel shades or the soft, warm colors of the great Dutch and Flemish painters. Of course, that was on the negative, and we usually saw it only in the rushes. The finished product was as hard and postcardy as Herbert and Natalie Kalmus, who originated Technicolor, could make it."[98]

The Left Hand of God continued Dmytryk's mid–1950s run of box-office successes. The film ultimately earned $11.4 million, making it the 25th most success-ful Hollywood release of 1955, ahead of Humphrey Bogart's other two releases from that year—*We're No Angels* ($8.6 million) and *The Desperate Hours* ($7.1 million). Bogart and Dmytryk enjoyed a cordial and mutually beneficial working relation-ship through their two films together, and the director was concerned when the actor would cough uncontrollably before starting a scene: "At one time or another, nearly everyone on the set begged him to cut down on his smoking, but Bogey would just shrug his shoulders and light another cigarette."[99] During the making of film, Bog-art suffered from severe back pain which, when tested, led to the discovery of cancer of the esophagus. He shot one final film at the end of 1955, *The Harder They Fall*, and died in January 1957.

The Mountain (1956)

The Mountain had to be a Paramount picture. The titular peak, the site of frater-nal psychodrama, bears more than a passing resemblance to the studio's logo. Spen-cer Tracy had loved *La Neige en Deuil* ("Snow in Mourning," a rather more poetic title than the prosaic English choice), a book by Russian-born French author Henri Troyat and had suggested it to MGM as a vehicle for him. When they balked at the potential cost of location filming in the Alps, Tracy for the first time contemplated leaving the studio that had made him. The property was snapped up by Paramount and he was signed to star in the film as a freelance for $250,000, as with *Broken Lance*. Before his scheduled start of filming on 1 August 1955, he had a showdown with MGM over his last picture for them, *Tribute to a Bad Man*. Tracy was unhappy with his co-star Irene Papas, with scarring from the removal of a malignant growth on his face and with the high-altitude location shoot in Colorado. After five days on location, an increas-ingly irascible Tracy announced that filming at this altitude was impossible for him. The director Robert Wise called Sam Zimbalist at the studio, "and told him I couldn't continue with Tracy. An hour later he called me back and said that Tracy was out of the picture."[100] Less than a week later, Tracy wrote in his diary, "Finished at Metro! June 18 last salary day.... The end of 20 years."[101] That he should have been released from one picture on account of altitude issues only to commence work on another at much higher altitudes is the summit of irony.

Tracy had given the book to Dmytryk while they were making *Broken Lance* together and it was on the actor's request that Paramount contracted the director to make *The Mountain*. The year 1955 was a financially comfortable one. Dmytryk's pro-ducer/director package from Paramount netted him $5,700 per week for the 26 weeks commencing 5 July 1955. His contract also stipulated "a location survey in France, Italy and Switzerland" with first class travel for him and his wife Jean "including sleeper if by air and drawing room if by train." Included in the deal were first class liv-ing expenses up to $500 per week, not counting automobile expense which was also provided by the Corporation. The reconnaissance trip, also involving production manager Harry Caplan, cinematographer Franz Planer, art director John Goodman and scriptwriter Ranald MacDougall, began on 18 May, lasted until the beginning of June and took in Interlaken, St Moritz, Bolzano and Chamonix. Chamonix was the obvious choice as the center of operations due to its close proximity to all of the required locations—village, pastures, glacier, snowscapes, rockfaces.

MacDougall's script adaptation tells of the Teller brothers living in the French Alps. The elder Zachary had been an exceptional climber but gave it up some years pre-

Spencer Tracy yodels from *The Mountain* (1956).

viously after the death of a climber in his care, while the much younger Chris simmers in resentment at his status as guide to much wealthier tourists. When a plane crashes at the summit with all onboard assumed dead, and a salvage party is unable to reach the wreckage, Chris persuades a reluctant Zachary to accompany him to the plane via a precarious route, with the intention of looting valuables. Their discovery of a single survivor causes a clash between the brothers, with Zachary intent on saving her and Chris fearing that this will jeopardize his get-rich-quick scheme.

In the book, the elder brother is 52 while the younger is "barely thirty."[102] After the positive experience of working with Robert Wagner (25 years old in 1955) on *Broken Lance*, and aware that his own marquee value might not be sufficient to make a hit of *The Mountain* with a younger audience, Tracy (55) approached him to play his brother. Wagner remembered how Tracy's support provided him with direction at a moment when he lacked it: "He believed in me very much and turned me around and made me look at myself…. At that time I had nothing on my mind but my hair…. As long as I had my name in the paper and my hair was combed I felt everything was fine…. I'm sitting there doing nothing and Spence wanted me for *The Mountain*. He gave me co-star billing above the title. That got me swinging again."[103] MacDougall was unhappy with this casting, having written the part with Charlton Heston (31) in mind: "To me, as a primal contest between simple good and simple evil, it called for an equality of forces involved. Wagner seemed to me to be a born loser in a contest with Tracy.... As an antagonist for Tracy, it seemed to me the outcome of the contest would be in doubt with a stronger man. With Wagner, I felt that the younger man would emerge as being petulant rather than powerfully evil."[104] Dmytryk deferred to Tracy and accepted his choice of Wagner, to the ultimate detriment of the film. If there is one element of *The Mountain* that capsizes credibility, it is this fundamentally inappropriate casting.

Dmytryk relished being his own producer for the second time after *Behind the Rising Sun*: "People sometimes comment that wearing two hats must require twice as much work. On the contrary, I think most—if not all—director-producers will agree it makes the whole job much easier. It eliminates the need for compromise, and that's a great advantage, both mentally and artistically."[105] He cast known and reliable actors such as E.G. Marshall and Claire Trevor in supporting roles. Trevor, on a weekly salary one hundredth of Spencer Tracy's for four weeks work, was only signed to the role on 17 August, a week after the director and main cast had flown with TWA out of Los Angeles. This plane flight, as well as nerves about the location demands of the film, caused Tracy such anxiety that he attempted to pull out of the picture, telling Dmytryk, "I can't do it. It's just not the part for me. How about Gable? I think he's free, and he'd be perfect. Or Robert Young?"[106] After rearranging the flights once, and on the verge of having to cancel them again, Dmytryk realized that the actor needed him to assume control: "When he stalled again, I simply said the car and driver would be calling to take him to the airport at a certain time, and I would expect to see him there. That was it. He showed up."[107]

The advance guard stopped first in London and then Paris, where Indian actresses were interviewed for the role of the plane crash survivor. Anna Kashfi, a 20-year-old model from Calcutta[108] with no acting experience, had been approached in London by Richard Mealand, the Paramount executive who had "discovered" Audrey Hepburn. She recalled being introduced to Spencer Tracy in his suite at the Hotel Raphael: "Before I had a chance to collapse from fright—no one had told me the star's name—he surrounded me in a smothering embrace, lifted me off my feet, turned to Edward Dmytryk, and proclaimed: 'She's the one. Pack the bags. We're rolling.'"[109] Kashfi became close with Tracy and they would socialize together long after the film wrapped, but she was frank about his temperament: "He would tolerate no laxity … his rage could be volcanic."[110] He never told her why he chose her so spontaneously but since the role involved him carrying her down a mountain, lifting her up and testing her weight was perhaps a factor. When the production moved to Hollywood for studio work, Kashfi was sitting in the Paramount commissary one day in October, observing the amusement of Pearl Bailey and George Sanders at the antics of an actor at a nearby table. He was "kissing and nibbling at the nape of a blonde (subsequently identified to me as Eva Marie Saint)"[111] but he noticed Kashfi and asked to be introduced to her. She misheard his name as Marilyn Bongo. Two years later Anna Kashfi became the first Mrs. Marlon Brando.[112]

In early August, Dmytryk, Tracy and Wagner drove from Paris to Chamonix via Geneva. The director spent the next few weeks pinpointing locations while the stars

Robert Wagner takes a snapshot of his director upon *The Mountain* (1956).

acclimatized and trained with guide Charles Balmat, a descendant of Jacques Balmat who had made the first ascent of Mont Blanc in 1786. Wagner had brought his
own kitchen equipment, fearing a lack of Hollywood-level comforts. Tracy mocked
him with "Are you here for light housekeeping or to act?"[113] There is some hypocrisy
in Tracy's comment since Harry Caplan reported back to head office that the star was
very dissatisfied with the accommodation that had been assigned to him and proposed a chateau being hired for his use, before a more acceptable hotel was found:
"Tracy is one of those artistic people who is a complainer. The room is filthy, the rugs,
beds are dirty, and the food (being pension plan) has no variety or selection to it."[114]
Caplan reported that "Eddie kowtows to his every wish,"[115] and wrote that he feared
what Tracy had promised he could physically achieve was beyond the actor's capa-
bility. A later communication made clear the compromises that had to be struck:

Spencer Tracy performs hair duty on Anna Kashfi while Dmytryk (kneeling, in front of unidentified actor) is otherwise occupied on *The Mountain* (1956).

"It is to be noted that the glacier is accessible only by foot and took the crew carrying equipment between 2 to 2½ hours walk each way. On this basis it would have taken Mr. Tracy at least 2½ hours each way. In a conference held by Messrs. Dmytryk, Tracy and Caplan it was mutually decided that it would be inadvisable for Mr. Tracy to make this trip as it would jeopardise his health and could conceivably shut down production on location. One day only was used for the glacier to make key shots with doubles and plates. It is also to be noted that Robert Wagner made the trip and was photographed. Mr. Tracy at no time refused to go to the glacier or any other location."[116]

There was a certain bravado in Dmytryk choosing *The Mountain* for his first non-studio-based film as producer, since it entailed extensive location shooting at inaccessible spots. Fortunately the Paramount camera department rescued him from the necessity of hauling VistaVision cameras up mountain sides by designing and building two small hand cameras, replacing the extremely heavy blimps that were usually required for Paramount's proprietary widescreen process. The film began shooting in Chamonix on 29 August and on that same day, Caplan fell and wrenched both knees on the rocky mountain terrain. The Alpine weather frequently proved unaccommodating, with bad light in the morning and poor conditions in the

On a clear day, you can see Beverly Hills: Edward Dmytryk (center, right of unidentified actors) on *The Mountain* (1956).

afternoon, and the days between 13 and 15 September were completely rained out. Dmytryk suffered a slipped disc on 22 September but, aware how crucial he was in keeping the production on its rails, soldiered on through the pain.

Most dramatic was an incident at the workmen's téléphérique which was used to gain access to Les Bossons glacier. Wagner was required for shooting on the

Climb Every Mountain: Edward Dmytryk on *The Mountain* (1956).

glacier and, because he had a fear of the vertiginous cable-car journey, Tracy said he would accompany him, despite not being needed on camera. Mid-journey, the car wrenched to a halt so forcibly that it hit the cable, smashing the glass, and was left suspended at 11,000 feet. Makeup man Frank Westmore recalled: "From our viewpoint on the Aiguille du Midi, we could see the little car below us, swinging wildly from side-to-side and bouncing frighteningly against a now-slack cable."[117] Eventually the stars and crewmen in the cable-car were rescued and brought to the summit, Westmore commenting that Tracy looked twenty years older than earlier that day. After some ineffective hours waiting for decent light, everyone went back down via the same mode of transport. That evening, Tracy's good behavior regarding alcohol was violently ruptured when, in a drunken rage, he smashed a glass and gashed Wagner's hand.

By the time the film wrapped on location on 26 September, *The Mountain* was eleven days behind schedule but worse was to come when Tracy's alcoholic wobble descended into an all-out bender. It started with celebratory drinks for the end of location shooting, then drinks in Paris to calm his nerves for the delayed flight, then drinks on the plane to New York. Dmytryk said that they "got on another plane to come to L.A., and he was out of control."[118] He was to be met at the airport by his family but when he was whisked away in a limousine, his daughter Susie was made aware for the first time of the extent of her father's drinking problem. He went AWOL for six days, with Dmytryk getting progress reports of his drunken exploits, and the film had to be shut down. On the seventh day, he ended up in hospital with a bleeding ulcer, and a week later a contrite Spencer Tracy was back on set. Between 3 and 13 October the production had been shut down for ten days due to what the official record described as "illness." The picture wrapped on 21 November.

Certain of its contributors did not look back at *The Mountain* fondly. In 1983, Claire Trevor said, "Oh, God, that was a terrible picture! It goes on forever and it's bad.... [Wagner] looked like he was twelve years old, and Spence had already gotten heavy and old-looking. It was ludicrous."[119] After watching the completed film in February 1956, Tracy declared himself "disappointed"[120] and wrote in his diary, "*Mountain* is failure. Think must be [the] ending. Wrong—always thought wrong. Phony."[121] Such judgments are unnecessarily harsh. The film certainly has disruptive elements but its reception at the time was at least partially enthusiastic, garnering positive reviews from, among others, *The Hollywood Reporter*, the *Herald Tribune*, the *New Yorker* and *Time*. The film ultimately made $5.1 million domestically which made it a merely moderate hit. Proof that it has endured came at a busy public screening in London early in 2020, where the film exerted a palpable tension and was received with audible appreciation.

Where *The Mountain* falters is in script deficiency and, inevitably, casting. Claire Trevor was correct in so far as Tracy looks considerably older than his actual age while Wagner could potentially have passed for his grandson. More fundamental though is MacDougall's attribution of "simple good" and "simple evil" to the two main characters. These are impossibly unrealistic archetypes that make for dull creations on screen. The thrill of observing multi-faceted characters in the hands of skilled actors is one of the core pleasures of cinema. Not unsurprisingly, Tracy comes closest to creating a breathing person. His weathered face of crags and crevices, a snowy mop of hair at the summit, has the monumental aspect of a Mount Rushmore, but his Zachary is a simple man, unburdened by intellectual complexities. He may have to consult a textbook to confirm the location of India, but his moral compass is secure and only wavers when it conflicts with his protective instinct for his brother. Wagner is a much less proficient actor and struggles to make Chris more than indulged and peevish, spectacularly ungrateful when Zachary risks his life for him during their perilous ascent. He is particularly weak when MacDougall's script flips his character into psychopathic mode, prepared to murder the crash survivor in order to safeguard his booty. It is a character progression that is beyond his range. When Tracy expressed disappointment with the end of the film, he must have been contemplating this element, although, since the casting of Wagner was his idea, he was not prepared to admit it even to his diary.

The hardships endured during the location shoot reap rewards. Franz Planer and his camera operator Til Gabani, who photographed at the higher altitudes that Planer's heart condition prevented him from reaching, stretch the majesty of the Mont Blanc region across the VistaVision screen. The scenery is spectacular and Paramount's widescreen process has rarely been more aptly named. There appears to have been a certain naivety regarding what could be shot on location, with a studio missive reporting that various sets for locations would have to be constructed at the studio "because we could not find them or which were physically impossible to reach."[122] The glacier "originally was visualised as a tremendous hillside glacier on which Mr. Tracy or his double would glissade down the glacier preceded by the sled carrying the girl,"[123] which indicates that a more rigorous logging of the actual available locations should have been performed.

The necessity to build rock faces in the studio pays unexpected dividends, however. The Paramount set-builders managed to create a particularly credible sheer of rock that the brothers must traverse and notably effective is the moment when Dmytryk's camera pulls slowly back to reveal the expanse that is to be crossed via crevice and tiny ledge. Such a shot would have been impossible to achieve on location. Acting as mountaineers on these sets provoked injury, with the studio logging that Wagner was left with bleeding fingers on his right hand from climbing and hanging from a rope on 29 October and Tracy also cut the fingers on his right hand on 31 October. The studio climbing scenes demonstrate the unparalleled skill of Spencer Tracy. Wordlessly and with a compelling intensity, Tracy edges along the rock face, his tongue jabbing from his face as his fingers probe for the next icy crevice. The tension with which he and his director invest these scenes renders the viewer's knuckles as white as the performer's. Dmytryk commented on this superlative display of screen appropriation: "Throughout the scene, shot in close-up, he was standing on the bottom of an upturned apple box, perhaps eight inches off the ground, but you would have sworn it was a matter of life and death on Everest. That's acting. In the final film I let the scene run without a cut, except for a couple of foot inserts—it must have lasted a full four minutes. Only an actor of Tracy's caliber could have sustained a scene of this kind for so long."[124]

If the climbing scenes were not sufficient to make Tracy's demanding behavior and drunken disappearance tolerable, then his final scene dispels all doubt. Having rescued the "Indian lady" and with Chris having fallen to his death due to his all-consuming greed, Zachary tells the story of the expedition to the authorities, whitewashing his brother's motives and painting himself as the greedy party. In a visual echo from his previous film, *The Left Hand of God*, Dmytryk places an image of

Christ just above Zachary, judging him for his dishonesty, as with the Bogart figure in that film, but forgiving him for his pure intentions. Naturally nobody in the room believes his story, but it is exquisitely acted by Tracy—perfectly paced, subtly structured and devastatingly moving. It is mostly a monologue with a few interjections from Claire Trevor and E.G. Marshall, and Dmytryk shot Tracy's close-up first so that the bedrock of the scene would be fresh and firm: "As usual, Spence nailed it on the first take. At the finish, most of the crew was crying. I said, 'Cut,' and looked over at E.G. Tears were streaming down his face. 'I wish all the method actors could watch this man work—just once!' he said."[125]

An interesting side-note to the production is the logging in the studio records on 16 November of the following line: "Music credit should read 'MUSIC SCORE BY BERNARD HERRMANN.'"[126] Herrmann was at Paramount in 1955 for *The Trouble with Harry*, *The Kentuckian* and *The Man Who Knew Too Much*, and the reason for him not scoring *The Mountain* can only be a source of conjecture. The film's music was ultimately written by Daniele Amfitheatrof but it is tantalizing to contemplate Tracy's intensity played out against an Alpine visual and Herrmannesque aural backdrop.

Raintree County (1957)

On 12 May 1956, Elizabeth Taylor and Michael Wilding hosted a dinner party for Edward and Jean Dmytryk, Rock Hudson, Kevin McCarthy and Montgomery Clift. Clift reportedly only had a couple of half-glasses of wine but at one point "went to the bathroom and took 'two downers.'"[127] The party broke up around midnight and Clift followed McCarthy down the twisting Benedict Canyon Drive in his Chevrolet, driving erratically. Shortly after, McCarthy arrived back at Taylor and Wilding's house in great distress: "Monty's dead. I think he's dead."[128] Elizabeth Taylor later wrote about that night: "We finally made out [from McCarthy] that Monty's car had crashed into a telephone pole about a block and half down the hill.... The doors were jammed shut, but we could see that Monty's head looked like it had been mashed right into the steering wheel.... He was bleeding from the head so much that it looked like his face had been halved.... I crawled into the car and lifted him away from the steering wheel. I found that he was breathing and moaning. All my revulsion about blood absolutely left me. I held his head and he started coming to. You could hardly see his face. It was like pulp. He was suffering terribly from shock, but he was absolutely lucid. There was a tooth hanging on his lip by a few shreds of flesh, and he asked me to pull it off because it was cutting his tongue.... It wasn't till the doctors took him away that there was the shock of finding myself covered with somebody else's blood. The sick, sweet smell of it made me want to vomit.... His jaw had been broken in four places, his nose in two places, and he was badly cut around the eyes. And his upper lip—it was like a spoon had gouged a great big hunk out of his mouth and teeth."[129]

Together Clift and Taylor had been shooting *Raintree County* for Edward

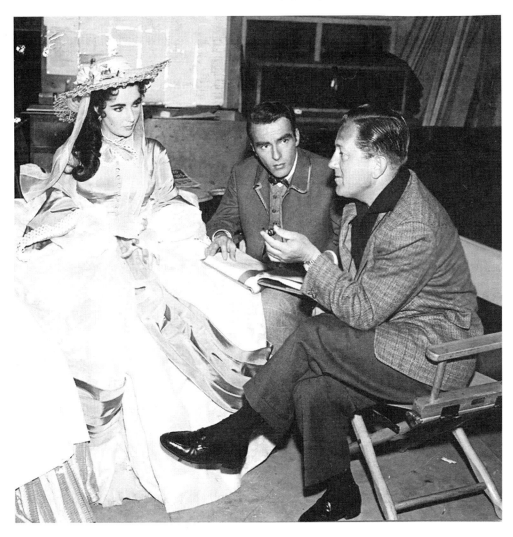

Elizabeth Taylor and Montgomery Clift on set with their director during the early studio sequences of *Raintree County* **(1956).**

Dmytryk since 2 April. The film had just completed studio work at MGM and was about to go on location to Mississippi. Clift's torso had been spared in the accident, with all of the damage facial. The reconstructive work required was mostly healing of the bone fractures and involved wiring his jaws together, though since his appearance did alter there was unfounded conjecture that the actor had received plastic surgery. When the film was released, morbid comparisons were made between Clift's scenes shot before and after the car crash. The accepted narrative that Clift's looks were irrevocably lost due the accident was challenged by two people who were in a position to know. Clift's doctor Rex Kennamer was the first on the scene of the accident after members of the dinner party: "After Monty's face healed, the residual damage was mostly dental. Many people who went to see *Raintree County* came away saying, 'Oh, what a terrible thing happened to his face.' But that was because the Montgomery Clift they remembered was the one in *From Here to Eternity*. A great change came over him in the three years after that. I know that there were parts of *Raintree County* shot before the accident that people attribute to after the accident."[130] Edward Dmytryk agreed: "Falling off the wagon can be more damaging than hitting a telephone pole. I've seen greater physical changes in Richard Burton after a few weeks on the booze."[131] "And this is what happened to Monty Clift. You cannot drink and take dope and retain your physical firmness, your muscle texture, none of those things. Your face falls apart. It's as simple as that. Nobody wants to believe it, because it isn't dramatic enough."[132]

Raintree County was MGM's attempt to revive the glory that was *Gone with the Wind* in the era of the ultra-wide screen and was to be the first shot using a new process called MGM Camera 65, which would eventually be renamed Ultra Panavision 70. The publicity for the process grandly dubbed it "The Window on the World" and promised "a high-fidelity image in keeping with 'road show presentation.' The reproduction is sharper, brighter, clearer."[133] To achieve this trumpeted improvement required a camera weighing 200 lbs., a soundproof blimp covering it that weighed another 200 lbs. and four grips to move the contraption. The size of the camera matched the heft of the novel on which the film was based. Ross Lockridge's Civil War epic had been published in January 1948 and became an instant sensation. The author had endured pressure from publishers and film rights holder MGM to cut over 150,000 words prior to publication, a stressful process that compounded Lockridge's mental fragility. In March 1948, at what should have been his moment of greatest triumph, Lockridge committed suicide.

The film adaptation lay fallow until 1955 when it was revived by MGM production chief Dore Schary, who assigned David Lewis to produce. Lewis' working experience with Edward Dmytryk had been positive on *The End of the Affair* and so he was approached to be director. Dmytryk's unusual perspective on the project, which would end up costing $6 million, a huge expenditure at the time, viewed it as an experimental film: "It didn't concern itself with great battles or the burning of cities, but with the unfulfilled hopes and unrealized dreams of a small number of rather unremarkable people. That's why I considered it experimental, though I would never have used that word within the hearing of any of the studio management."[134] The stars chosen to carry this costly experiment were Elizabeth Taylor and Montgomery Clift, five years after their luminous pairing in *A Place in the Sun* in which George Stevens had granted them a succession of deifying close-ups. Clift was returning to films after a three-year break and Taylor, coming off another Stevens production *Giant*, was just entering her period of peak stardom. Dmytryk was initially cautious about Clift's reputation as a heavy drinker but at a casual pre-production lunch, the actor assured him, "I'm on the wagon."[135] The third member of the film's romantic triangle was played by Eva Marie Saint, fresh from her Oscar-winning role in *On the Waterfront* and acclaimed performance in *A Hatful of Rain*, and a meaty supporting cast included Agnes Moorehead, Lee Marvin, Nigel Patrick and Rod Taylor.

The working practices at MGM were different from the other studios at which Dmytryk had worked. He found the priority given to publicity overwhelming and the studio organization anachronistic and inefficient: "The production department set up shooting procedures and schedules without much feedback from the director or producer, and the art department still designed huge sets that could be shot from only one position, conveniently staked out by the set designer."[136] He learnt that Metro female stars tended to sleep late in the morning, among them Taylor and particularly Greer Garson, and the reading rehearsal was a ritual that Dore Schary forced him and Clift to undergo, only for Schary to be appalled at Clift's "method" of hesitant character building. Nevertheless, the first six weeks of the shoot on sound stage and at the extensive backlot set built of the fictional Indiana town of Freehaven ran smoothly. Moods were buoyant when the first part of the schedule concluded, and flights were booked to New Orleans the following Monday while the studio trucks started out for Mississippi. And Elizabeth Taylor threw her fateful Saturday night dinner party.

Initial press reports after the accident indicated a two- to three-week postponement of shooting but in reality, Clift did not return to the lot until 23 July and location shooting did not begin until a week later, at the height of a Southern summer. The locations chosen for Civil War–era Indiana in the film were in Mississippi, Louisiana and chiefly around Danville, Kentucky, since the march of industrialization in the Southern states at the time had trampled less underfoot than further north. The first working location was at Natchez, Mississippi, site of the "Windsor Ruin," a mansion that had been burnt to the ground leaving only huge stone colonnades as a memorial to its glory, and the crucial scene shot there was revelatory of Taylor's character Susanna. The day of shooting was particularly hot and humid and Taylor, corseted tightly and burdened with a costume weighing nearly 90 lbs., impressed with her emotional grasp of the scene, and promptly collapsed at the end of the take. A doctor quickly diagnosed tachycardia, an excessive heart rate. Dmytryk recalled, "When Monty heard the word 'tachycardia' he understood at once what was needed. He disappeared into his trailer and in less than a minute he returned and handed the doctor a small leather case. When the doctor opened it I was close enough to see it contained two vials of Demerol and at least a couple of shiny unused syringes, all neatly stowed in their appropriate crannies…. Monty had exposed himself courageously, and without a moment's hesitation, to help a friend in trouble."[137]

It became clear over the course of the shoot that Clift was in acute and constant pain with the healing of his jaw, but he never complained about it and resorted to concealed medication in order to cope with it. After the tachycardia incident, Taylor was forced by the insurance doctor to stay in bed for an extended period, and to alleviate her boredom, Dmytryk, Clift and the writer Millard Kaufman agreed to have dinner in her room every evening. One evening, Clift was late and not responding to the phone, and when Kaufman and Dmytryk went to check on him, they found him passed out on the bed and unrousable, with the remnants of a cigarette burnt out in his fingers. Returning to Taylor's room, they discovered that of a full bottle of the sedative chloral hydrate that the doctor had left for her, two of the 24 capsules were missing. Dmytryk wrote, "Elizabeth's reassurance that she had used none of them left us with only one reasonable answer, and in about fifteen minutes our prime suspect showed up, wide-awake, smiling, and 'all there,' including fresh band-aids on two fingers of his right hand."[138] While Clift ate his dinner, Dmytryk and Kaufman returned to search the actor's room and eventually found the missing capsules. The situation was delicate but the making of the film was paramount. Kaufman purchased vitamin capsules of the same shape and color as the chloral hydrate and they performed a substitution. Whether or not Clift noticed, nothing further was said.

After two weeks of a bedridden leading lady, the production was able to move to Danville, Kentucky, where the West Coast contingent were assailed by insects, in particular chiggers, and the locals were assailed by a late-night excursion from an intoxicated and naked Montgomery Clift. To prevent a repeat performance from the actor, an off-duty policeman was posted nights on Clift's porch. When they left town, Dmytryk asked him how he had found his duty: "'Oh,' he said, 'it was quite interesting. I had to stop Mr. Clift a number of times, but he didn't seem to mind. We would sit down and talk until he was ready to go back to bed. A wonderful talker! Although it wasn't always clear what he was talking about. But he was always friendly and seemed to enjoy our chats. By the way, your drunks are a lot less belligerent than ours.'"[139] As filming progressed, Clift's capacity to cope with the pain diminished and he would take to pharmaceutical means earlier each day, to the point when shooting a picnic scene that he could barely speak. Dmytryk was forced to go to Clift's trailer, with an assistant director as witness, and dismiss him for the day. Unbeknownst to anyone until Clift summoned a doctor later that day, he had worked stoically through the picnic scene after breaking a toe, which he then proceeded to further injure by falling off his bed. Yet the next day, he was happily on set without a limp. Dmytryk mused that "Monty's 'use' was rendering him insensitive to physical pain. Inflicting damage to his self-esteem was another matter. I never 'sent him home' again."[140]

The screenwriter Millard Kaufman, whose previous two scripts, *Bad Day at Black Rock* and *Take the High Ground*, had been Oscar-nominated, managed to whittle down Lockridge's 1,000-page tome to a 200-page script, still the foundation for a lengthy film. The central character is John Shawnessy (Clift) who, upon graduation from Freehaven college in 1859, appears set for a life with his sweetheart Nell Gaither (Eva Marie Saint) until the arrival in town of Southern belle Susanna Drake (Taylor). Susanna fakes a pregnancy in order to trap John into marriage and her mental instability quickly becomes obvious. Her attempt to relocate with him to the South is unsuccessful since John fails to adapt to the cultural differences, and back in Freehaven, they do eventually have a child. When the Civil War breaks out, Susanna flees back South with their four-year-old boy Jim, and John enlists in order to cross into Confederate territory and find his family.

Dmytryk's own analysis of the script is accurate. The film has a very tight focus on merely three characters with insufficient incident to justify its three-hour running time. In the first half, a Fourth of July race and an attempt by John to find the mythical Raintree are the only non-dialogue driven scenes, while the second half features some battle sequences but without the epic sweep that the genre usually promises. Dmytryk's handling is sturdy but uninspired, his camera remaining tethered to the dialogue rather than finding a way to soar above it. The heaviness of the blimp-like camera and the solidity of Kaufman's script, striving for the profound without attaining it, are too weighty a combination. Johnny Green had been Music Director at MGM but he resigned his post in order to score *Raintree County*. His music provides a constant counterpoint, to an oppressive degree. Dmytryk, who was no longer part of this process after delivering his first cut, agreed with this assessment: "That was a lovely score, by the way, but I think we used just a little too much. There would have been a little less of it if I had been on it."[141] The early scenes place too much emphasis on the Chinese Golden Raintree that legend has Johnny Appleseed planting in this Indiana county. According to John and Nell's teacher Professor Stiles (Nigel Patrick), this tree is "not of gold, but of fulfilment, whose flower is accomplishment and whose fruit is love." John's quest to find the tree is unlikely and the continual recourse to the legend is labored. It is a poetic symbol that fails to bear fruit, even when the Raintree makes a belated appearance in the final shot of the film.

A major failing is the lack of character coloration. There are only two personalities outside of the central trio who make an impact, both due to the skill of the performers—Nigel Patrick's slippery Professor Stiles and, particularly, Flash Perkins, played with attention-grabbing ease by Lee Marvin. Marvin makes of Perkins' death scene the most emotionally resonant moment that does not involve Elizabeth Taylor. To cast Agnes Moorehead as John's mother, only for her to feature in a mere five scenes with scant number of lines, appears perverse. A comparison with *Raintree County*'s prototype *Gone with the Wind* is illuminating. The earlier film is richly populated with minor characters, providing comic relief and dramatic ballast. *Gone with the Wind* also features two enduring performances by African American actresses, Hattie McDaniel and Butterfly McQueen. As complicated as the legacy of these roles may be, the representation of race appears to have gone into reverse gear in the decade and a half between the two films. Susanna has two female slaves who are granted names, Soona and Bessie (Isabel Cooley and Rosalind Hayes, both uncredited), but not personalities. One scene was shot in which Barbara Drake (Jarma Lewis) shows too much leg when getting out of a carriage and a black footman is chased by her husband with an axe after looking at her leg. The studio cut the scene out of nervousness with how it would play in the South.[142] The only black actor granted an appreciable number of lines is Ruth Attaway as Parthenia, who delivers one lovely speech to John about Susanna's mental illness: "As long as I knowed that child, there's been a war going on inside her." Ruth Attaway is also uncredited.

Eva Marie Saint is not given enough material to display her range, her Nell passively pining on the sidelines for her lost sweetheart and enduring the waspish barbs of her victorious love rival. Montgomery Clift's intensity provides occasional lift to the character of John, but in the early scenes the 36 year old is unable to project the freshness of a 20 year old, and overall his pharmaceutical intake undoubtedly stifled his capabilities. The one exceptional element is the performance of Elizabeth Taylor. Though Leslie in *Giant* is a Texan, Susanna is the first of her truly mercurial Southern characters, with *Cat on a Hot Tin Roof* and *Suddenly, Last Summer* still to flare before the decade was out. Susanna is a challenging role, snapping from coquettish to vengeful, the flickers of self-doubt ever ready to creep into her eyes. Taylor rises to the challenge superbly and the film loses color when she is off-screen. Her mesmerizing grip is maintained throughout one six-minute monologue when Susanna tells John about the childhood fire at her family home. In the years before the dilution of the word, Dmytryk found her performance "awesome"[143] and felt that in that particular scene Taylor "famous for her beauty, but somewhat suspect as an actress, delivered more versatility and virtuosity than I had ever seen."[144] He also judged it to be the scene that clinched her first Oscar nomination, the sixth performer that he had directed to that achievement.

By the time *Raintree County* was sneak previewed in Santa Barbara, at a cinema where the audience was known to be selective and in a three-hour-45-minute cut, both Dore Schary and David Lewis had lost their positions and Sol Siegel had been installed. Dmytryk recalled that the film "just played absolutely beautifully, beautifully from beginning to end,"[145] and the opinion cards were overwhelmingly positive. He recalled Eddie Mannix, one of the studio's top executives and its chief disciplinarian, exclaiming that the audience had liked it: "As though that was the most horrible thing that could possibly happen to the picture. Now if the film came out and it was a big success, the stockholders would say, 'Why did you fire Dore Schary who made this picture?' So they *wanted* the picture to be bad."[146] Siegel, also in attendance and according to Dmytryk "a very honest man,"[147] instructed the film to be wrapped up and quickly dispatched to cinemas, but not before the inevitable retakes which MGM relied upon to achieve perfection, more than any other studio in Hollywood. Dmytryk refused to participate in preparations for 25 pages of retakes without the input of his stars, and ultimately five pages were reshot and cut into the shortened film. "I never entered MGM's gates again."[148]

Despite the grumblings from his underlings, Siegel had a picture to sell and MGM's ballyhoo machine went into overdrive to promote the $6 million film, the studio's costliest to that date and over-budget by upwards of $700,000. Lavish publicity brochures were published, trumpeting the new MGM Camera 65 process, the fact that the film was the new longest MGM production, beating the two hours 48 minutes of *Quo Vadis*, and the 119 speaking parts, a record number for MGM. The world premiere of *Raintree County* took place on 2 October 1957 at the Brown Theatre in Louisville, Kentucky, with an estimated 50,000 people reportedly lining the streets. The Hollywood premiere was at Warner Bros Beverly Hills six days later with ten members of the cast present. The publicity pushers ensured that Montgomery Clift attended with May Britt who, although she had just shot *The Young Lions* alongside him, did not appear with him in any scenes. Reviews were mixed to positive and business boomed. *Raintree County* became the fifth most successful release of 1957, ultimately earning $17 million at the U.S. box office. Edwin Schallert's review in the *Los Angeles Times* was fairly representative of the critical reception. While declaring it to have "many elements of great interest, even though it is something less than [a] masterpiece,"[149] Schallert also found it to be "pretentious,"[150] a word which is not a million miles away from Dmytryk's own "experimental."

The Young Lions (1958)

In 1948, Irwin Shaw published *The Young Lions*, a novel inspired by his observations while serving in the Signal Corps during the Second World War. Shaw had

had his first Broadway play produced when he was 23 years old and subsequently earned an Oscar nomination as co-scriptwriter of *The Talk of the Town,* directed by George Stevens and starring Cary Grant and Jean Arthur. He was initially sought by William Wyler to be part of the filmmaking team that the director was assembling in the Signal Corps, but ultimately ended up in George Stevens' unit instead. Shaw was listed in *Red Channels* in 1950, experienced blacklisting and settled in Europe. *The Young Lions* tells the intertwined stories of three conscripts: Noah Ackerman, a rootless American Jew; Michael Whiteacre, an East Coast sophisticate; and Christian Diestl, an Austrian ski-instructor.

Blonds have more fun—Marlon Brando with Dmytryk on the set of *The Young Lions* (1958).

It was Fred Zinnemann who originated the film's casting. In late 1951, he corresponded with Irwin Shaw about taking on the project as director, with Shaw as screenwriter. Shaw declined: "[The] whole book seems so remote to me at this time that I really don't think I could do it in another form. I'm sorry."[151] Early in 1952, Zinnemann declared that "the project is now dead…. I met with considerable apathy in several instances, when I tried to outline the project. Everyone had high respect for the book, but there were a number of objections raised—how can you condense all this material into one picture; the cost of production will be staggering…. At any rate, no one got excited until I mentioned my idea for casting: Monty Clift to play Noah, Marlon Brando for Christian and Julie Harris for Hope. After some persuasion, I succeeded in getting Monty and Brando to read the book. Both were very much interested … even though both Clift and Brando are known to be very elusive characters when it comes to making a firm commitment."[152] Zinnemann had directed Clift in *The Search* in 1948, Brando in *The Men* in 1950 and was about to direct Harris in *The Member of the Wedding.* The idea foundered however when it appeared that Irwin Shaw was not prepared to finance a script treatment to attract stars that were not firmly attached, and Zinnemann withdrew from the project: "All that remains to be said is that I was thrilled at the prospect of making *The Young Lions*—that I was aware of the enormous difficulties of getting the project organized, but hopeful of overcoming them, especially in view of Monty's keen interest—and that I regret the premature and inevitable ending…. P.S. I will always have the faith that this will be a great film someday."[153]

The rights to the book ended up being bought by Al Lichtman, who had been a 20th Century–Fox distribution executive. Lichtman convinced his old studio to finance the production, initially envisaged at $2 million, a 64-day shoot and with a cast of contract players. When Dmytryk was approached to direct, Edward Anhalt was completing the first draft of the script. Anhalt, with his then wife Edna, had originated the story of *The Sniper* for Dmytryk, and had been associate producer on *Eight Iron Men*. Anhalt recalled that he was just the latest in a succession of writers to be assigned to essay adaptation of Lichtman's pet project. One of Fred Zinnemann's literary advisors had isolated the issue in adapting a 700-page book with lead characters operating in different realms: "[T]he dialog is ready-made for screening as is. The adaptation problem is incident-selection, not rewriting of dialog in this book."[154] Anhalt also recognized the importance of event sequencing and careful shifting between perspectives and continents.

Core to Anhalt's interpretation of the story was a recalibration of the morality of Christian Diestl. The book had examined the corruption of Christian, his humanity destroyed by the depravities of war and the Nazi regime. Anhalt felt it was not only more interesting but ethically correct to depict Christian's dawning realization that he had been duped by the national socialist promises and rendered blind to the extent of the evil around him. The screenwriter also believed that the U.S. Defense Department would sanitize American involvement in the war and wanted to counterbalance this by demonstrating that the whole German race was not culpable for the evils perpetrated in their name and that evil recognized no national borders.

This interpretation of Christian's character was grasped enthusiastically by Marlon Brando when the role was once again brought to his attention. His agent approached Dmytryk, and a meeting was set up at Brando's home. After talking for two hours, Brando agreed to do the film. Dmytryk later admitted to Montgomery Clift that, although he agreed with the thrust of the changes to Christian's character, he had consented to rewrites of the part in order to get Brando to commit. After reading the script, Brando told his friend and acting coach Carlo Fiore that he was going to "turn this Nazi heel into a tragic hero."[155] He decided to dye his hair Aryan blond, inspired by a beautiful boy he had seen in an old German film. To complete the look of nobility, he wanted his make-up man Phil Rhodes to give him a "John Barrymore nose."[156] Brando's vision of Christian went further than Anhalt or Dmytryk had envisaged. His friend Maureen Stapleton, who disagreed violently with him over the interpretation of the role, was told about how he had forced Dmytryk to permit the changes. Brando told her, "If it had been Gadg [Elia Kazan], he wouldn't have let me do it."[157] The originator of the character, moreover, was vocally opposed to making Christian sympathetic. In a debate on CBS television, Irwin Shaw clashed with Brando, who declared that he didn't want to play a vicious cliché of evil and that Shaw knew nothing about Christian. Shaw contended, "It's my character. I created him."[158] To which Brando replied, "Nobody creates a character but an actor. I play the role; now he exists. He's my creation."[159]

By the time Brando committed to the film, Montgomery Clift had already been cast in the role of Noah Ackerman. With his interest aroused by Zinnemann some years previously and having experienced a positive working relationship with Dmytryk under the most trying of circumstances on *Raintree County*, his response to Dmytryk sending him the script was "the shortest telegram I ever received: 'Yes.'"[160] While Brando was adopting an image of Aryan perfection, Clift's physical preparations went sharply in the opposite direction. He lost weight to emaciate his frame, he altered the shape of his nose with putty and made his ears stick out with wax lodged behind them. It was a defiant deglamorisation, a riposte to the critics and public who had bemoaned the loss of his matinee idol looks, a change in his appearance which most attributed to his car accident but which was in reality due to his alcohol and medication dependencies.

The third lead role in *The Young Lions*, that of the suave, service-shy Broadway star Michael Whiteacre, seemed a perfect fit for Dean Martin, but he was not the first choice, nor remotely under consideration according to Edward Anhalt. Tony Randall was scheduled to play the part, but Anhalt was appalled when he read about the casting in the *Hollywood Reporter* since Michael Whiteacre was envisaged as a cocky lothario, which didn't square with the general perception of Randall. Anhalt said Dominick Mazzie, who owned a nightclub in Los Angeles, suggested Dean Martin to him, and he promptly relayed the suggestion to Buddy Adler at the studio. MCA, the agency that represented Clift, Brando and Martin, offered Martin to Dmytryk at a bargain rate. Martin's career was in the doldrums, having split with his partner Jerry Lewis and coming off the flop of *Ten Thousand Bedrooms*. An effective straight role could resuscitate his career and Dmytryk enjoyed the challenge of offbeat casting. Dmytryk knew from experience that Clift needed to be treated considerately, so phoned him and suggested that Martin take the role opposite him. "Good God, no!"[161] was the response. Dmytryk brought up Randall's name next and, not knowing his work, Clift decided to go see him in the film *Oh Men! Oh Women!* that was showing in New York that evening. Early the next day, Clift phoned Dmytryk: "If it's still all right, I'll go with Dean Martin."[162] To save Randall's face, his agent spread the story to several publications that MCA had insisted that Martin be cast, in order to provide their clients Clift and Brando. Years later at an anti-trust investigation into MCA, Dmytryk had to swear under oath that this had not been the case and that it was "only a jealous agent's bit of gossip."[163]

The female roles in the film were filled by new discovery May Britt, Barbara Rush and, about to have a very good year with the upcoming *Peyton Place*, Hope Lange. When the crew left for Paris in May 1957 to prepare for the European part of the shoot, the key role of Captain Hardenberg, Christian's superior, was still uncast. Among many other options, Dmytryk was given a brochure for the actor Carl Schell, whom the director initially rejected as unsuitable. Ultimately, in desperation, he called Schell's agent asking if he was available and was told that the actor could be in Paris by midnight that evening. Dmytryk consented to the meeting, only to let it escape his mind, returning to his hotel after midnight to be confronted with an unknown face—Maximilian Schell, the brother of Carl. Maximilian Schell found the whole scenario humiliating, having to wait for hours outside a hotel, only to realize it was a case of mistaken identity and having no English with which to communicate with the director who hadn't asked for him in the first place. Fortunately, Dmytryk recognized Schell's face from a film he had seen in Munich and decided to take the risk that he would be able to learn English quickly enough under the tutelage of Walter Roberts, his dialogue coach. After more chaotic misunderstandings the following day, including waiting in central Paris at the Fox offices before finally being informed that the film was already shooting on location outside the city, Schell recalled how within two hours of arriving at the shoot, he was signed to the film script-unseen and was in a uniform before his signature on the contract was dry.

A chemistry sparked between Schell and Brando rapidly, and while the Austrian actor found the star surprisingly unpretentious, he was aware that on set Brando's word went. When Brando commented that Schell's uniform did not match his character because "Hardenberg … is the most correct and best-dressed officer in the army!"[164] the uniform was promptly altered. Schell noted that Dmytryk was able to cope with such stellar posturing while other directors he had worked with would have found this impossible. Brando was generous with the young actor, six years his junior but playing his superior, as when during a scene of photographs being taken in front of Sacré Coeur, Brando suggested that at the last moment Hardenberg put himself on the step above Christian to express his dominance. Dmytryk commented that in this, Schell's first big moment before the camera, his English had attained such a good level that none of the scene needed to be post-dubbed. His performance matched the level of his diction, was noted in the upper echelons of Hollywood and a mere five years after standing on a Parisian street, without the linguistic ability to converse with Edward Dmytryk, he was standing at the podium in the Santa Monica Civic Auditorium, making an acceptance speech as Best Actor for Stanley Kramer's *Judgment at Nuremberg*.

Schell's connection with Brando endured throughout the shoot and intensified when they returned to Hollywood, Brando throwing a party for him. They womanized and they philosophized. The star loved when Schell's fledgling English, lines learnt by rote, would sneak into his acting, as when he mispronounced "I should have shot you" as "I should have coot you," to Brando's enduring amusement. After one evening of intense soul unburdening, Brando took a book of Indian philosophy from the shelf and wrote inside, "Max—Maybe thinking is better than fucking. I should have coot you! My best always, Marlon."[165] Others noted the change in Brando around this time, a period when, as in Paris in June, his clothes could be ripped from his back by rabid fans and when his aggression towards photographers escalated. A friend Pat Cox observed: "His eyes changed. No more shyness, no more vulnerability. He looked at everybody with a lot of confidence. But also pity too. Like he felt sorry for you."[166] Close friends such as Christian Marquand and makeup man Phil Rhodes provided a security cocoon for him, and since Rhodes would not travel without his wife Marie, she became Brando's stand-in, a role she fulfilled for many years.

In one respect it is unfortunate that the two most exciting actors of their generation share no screen time, since the creative fireworks between Brando and Clift might have been dazzling. Realistically that was unlikely to have happened since a personal rapport never developed. Dmytryk recalled a meal at a restaurant in Paris, designed for the leading men to get to know each other and the first time that Brando and Clift had met. Clift was garrulous and propelled the evening's conversation, Martin provided dry quips and Brando, Clift's junior by four years, for the most part observed. Dmytryk later wrote: "Finally, Marlon opened his mouth. 'You ought to see a shrink,' he told Monty, quite seriously. And that was the end of a possibly beautiful friendship."[167] Dmytryk relished the creativity of the two actors, though acknowledged their different methods of producing magic: "Monty's ideas flashed like sparks from a pinwheel, while Marlon wrestles with his interminably."[168]

One myth has arisen over the only moment at which Clift and Brando share the screen, right at the very end. Prior to an uplifting coda, the film concludes with the demise of Christian, shot dead by Michael after he and Noah have witnessed the horrors of a concentration camp. According to a persistently related account, Clift and Brando clashed over this death scene in which Brando wanted to tumble dramatically down a hill with arms outstretched, in a visual echo of Christ crucified. In one version, he was to become entangled in barbed wire and thus evoke a crown of thorns. Patricia Bosworth, the biographer of both Clift and Brando in two separate books, reports Clift saying, "If he does that, I walk off the movie."[169] In a 1979 interview, Ronald L. Davis asked Dmytryk about Bosworth's account that had been published the year before. Dmytryk replied, "None of this ever happened. I don't know where the hell she got the story."[170]

Dmytryk realized from the outset that the assigned budget and shooting schedule were not going to be sufficient for a film of this scale, even before taking into consideration the demanding and mercurial presences of Clift and Brando. As he predicted, the cost rose from $2 million to $3 million and the shoot wrapped after 125 days, twice the original estimate. The usual location headaches had to be endured—substandard crew, torrential downpours, broken legs—but one unusual off-set incident put Marlon Brando in a Parisian hospital when a pot of scalding tea was accidentally poured into his lap at the Hotel George V. His treatment for a scalded scrotum took him out of action for a few days but the conception of a child later during the shoot proved there was no lasting damage to the Brando brand. Dmytryk was worn down by Brando's initial style of working—unfocused goofing around preceding dozens of takes before alighting on the way he wanted to play the scene. On Brando's first day on set Dmytryk recalled that a simple scene with little dialogue required 18 rehearsals and a succession of botched takes before Brando exclaimed, "Oh, *that's* what the scene is about!"[171] Brando did settle into the role after some days and the number of takes diminished, particularly when he was playing opposite Schell whose talent was obvious to all.

Clift's technique was completely different. He would be preoccupied with a scene days or even weeks before it was due to be shot and would avidly discuss interpretation of character with his director, several times waking Dmytryk at 3 a.m. or 4 a.m. to thrash out some point with him. When he arrived on set, he was utterly prepared: "Like Spencer Tracy, Monty was a one-take man."[172] If more than three or four takes became necessary, his acting suffered and lost its spontaneity. Clift mastered his drinking for the duration of the film, Dmytryk only recalling one time that work had to be stopped for that reason, and his good relationship with Dean Martin kept him buoyant. Martin called Clift "Spider" due to his physical tics and the pair developed a jocular buddy bond. After Clift's death, Martin spoke fondly of their time on *The Young Lions*: "Nobody wanted him around, nobody would eat with him. So I took him to dinner, or I would have a drink with him, or I would put him to bed 'cause he was always on pills you know. He was such a sad, sad man, and he was like a boy, so unhappy and rejected, and so I'd say, 'Come on, Clift, let's go.'"[173]

It is exactly this boyish quality, carried over from real life into his interpretation of Noah Ackerman, that distinguishes Clift's performance in *The Young Lions*, providing us with some of his best moments onscreen in any film. A scene between Noah and Hope on the evening of their meeting is exquisitely performed—an aching uncertainty seeping through an attempted bravado, the little boy peering through the man's eyes, desperate to salvage the disaster of her rebuffing his advances: "I'm going to say something to you. I'm not opinionated. I don't think I've a single opinion in the whole world. I don't know why I kissed you, I just couldn't help it. I guess, I guess I wanted to impress you. I was afraid that if I was myself, you wouldn't look at me twice. It's been a very confusing night. I don't think I've been through anything so confusing." Hope Lange rises to challenge of performing opposite an actor on such tremendous form and provides a gentle foil to Noah's vulnerability. After she has to explain how he will find his way home, Noah repeats the directions but his mind is elsewhere: "The bus to Eastern Parkway. And then…. I love you. I love you." And elation starts to bubble through his confusion.

In a film with many echoes and reflections between its American and German soldiers, an equivalent scene which illuminates Brando's character is between Christian and a woman who had initially rejected his advances, Françoise (Liliane Montevecchi). When they first meet, the Frenchwoman treats the German soldier with derision: "Are you still the conqueror? The young golden god of war?" When asked if he might see her again, she replies, "Perhaps when the gold has worn off a little." Towards the end of the film, Christian has been battered by the horrors of war and when he encounters Françoise again, she remarks, "Christian, you're not the golden warrior anymore." In the scene that followed between the two of them over a dinner table, Edward Anhalt had written a long speech from Christian, explaining the sources of his disillusionment. On the set Brando was unhappy, believing the speech to be overly explicative and sensing that Christian should not be able to articulate his feelings at this point. He indicated the table decoration, a revolving trinket with a star and heraldic angels propelled by candle flame, and declared that it should be the star of the scene. His speech was almost entirely dropped, with only the line "I think I've come too far" indicating his depth of desperation, and Dmytryk keeps the revolving metal star constantly in shot, mesmerizing Christian into silence. It is a beautiful scene, with Brando communicating so much wordlessly, and proof of what an instinctive innovator he could be.

The Young Lions is a sprawling picture, epic in feel at two and three-quarter hours. The first cut was half an hour longer but president of 20th Century–Fox, Spyros Skouras, despite finding it "so beautiful, so perfect"[174] at its first studio showing, demanded that it be shortened. It is tantalizing to think of those scenes from Clift and Brando that were lost forever in the process. While Anhalt's script only rarely strikes the profundity it strives for, he weaves the parallel stories very effectively, deftly achieving the job of condensation that had worried Fred Zinnemann. Dmytryk is in full command of his material, maintaining pace throughout the lengthy running time, drawing strong performances from the entire cast and ensuring theme is not submerged by incident. His ability to mount strong action sequences is much in evidence, immersing the audience with the post-production camera judder that had characterized his battle explosions since *Back to Bataan*. His widescreen framing is eloquent, while his camera is fluid and lacking in ostentation, as is the crisp photography of one of his favorite collaborators, Joe MacDonald. Dmytryk is at his strongest in the intimacy he conjures in quieter scenes, both Brando and Clift praising him for his ability to inspire confidence from his actors. At one moment, his camera gracefully visualizes this intimacy. Hope is visiting Noah in a military prison and, while they are speaking to each other through the glass divider, Noah's face and the reflection of Hope's merge into one and become indistinguishable.

The film is Dmytryk's third, after *Crossfire* and *The Juggler*, direct attack on anti–Semitism. Noah experiences prejudice from both Hope's father and his fellow conscripts, and in both cases is able to prove his worth to the anti–Semites. With Hope's father ("I never knew a Jew before") the acceptance is rapid; with the soldiers, it takes a series of brutal fistfights for them to treat him with respect. In the latter case, the prejudice is institutional and Captain Colclough (Herbert Rudley) instigates the abuse of Noah. In an interesting echo of Dmytryk's earlier film, when Colclough is upbraided and court-martialed for his mistreatment of Noah, there is a photo of Franklin D. Roosevelt on the wall of his colonel, just as there was on the wall of the exposer of prejudice in *Crossfire*, Finlay (Robert Young). Noah's moral superiority is not only expressed in defiance towards the enemies who wear the same uniform as him, but later in combat when he rescues two of his erstwhile tormentors in crossing a river from hostile territory. This same incident exposes the backbone of Michael Whiteacre, for whom the war and friendship to Noah reveal the reserves of decency under his flip façade.

In the climax of the novel, Noah is shot dead by Christian who is in turn killed by Michael. Anhalt altered the ending and has Christian destroy his weapon before being shot dead by Michael. Brando performed his dying tumble down a hillside to end in a pool of water in a single take. The film wisely keeps Noah, the moral center of the film and its most compelling character, alive in order to reunite with Hope, his pointedly named wife. While the film is clearly centered around three men, it is noteworthy that in their relationships with women, the females display the upper hand. In their first love scenes, both Hope and Françoise control the outcome of the date and decide when to bestow a kiss on Noah and Christian respectively. Margaret (Barbara Rush) has a stronger sense of character than her fickle boyfriend Michael. Gretchen Hardenberg (May Britt), with whom Christian has a fling, is initially sexually voracious, though when her morality sinks below his, Christian has no hesitation in rejecting her violently. It is in comparison to the immorality of the Hardenbergs, the captain and his wife, that Christian is able to divine the strength of his own ethics.

The incident in North Africa where Christian refuses to shoot a British prisoner and Hardenberg performs the act is a key moment in questioning the principles that have been guiding him.

The Young Lions was released in April 1958, to generally very strong reviews and robust box-office. It became the eighth biggest Hollywood release that year, earning $12.8 million domestically, but its producer, Al Lichtman, was not to enjoy its success, having died just over a month earlier. After the New York premiere at the Paramount Theatre, Monty Clift was satisfied with his performance and ecstatic at the positive responses of those around him. The review that night from Bosley Crowther in the *New York Times* was lukewarm about the film and scathing about Clift, so his friends tried to conceal the newspaper from him. When he managed to read it, he was crestfallen. He believed it was the best performance he had given onscreen and the lack of recognition of this achievement contributed to his resurgent alcohol abuse. Marlon Brando's hangover from *The Young Lions* was rather more positive. In October 1957, he married Anna Kashfi, Dmytryk's discovery from *The Mountain*, who was pregnant and who gave birth on 16 May 1958 to Christian Devi, conceived while Brando was playing Christian Diestl.

Warlock (1959)

Edward Dmytryk made four westerns during his career, stretching from his very first film, *The Hawk*, to one of the last, *Shalako*. In 1959, his career reached a certain apotheosis with his third western, *Warlock*, which Phil Hardy, author of *The Aurum Film Encyclopedia* on *The Western*, has called "Dmytryk's masterpiece."[175] The elements wound together fortuitously. Dmytryk was approaching the end of a very successful decade, at the beginning of which he had been *persona non grata*, hired cheaply by the King Brothers to make the undistinguished *Mutiny*, and by the end of which he had overseen the two most lavish productions of his career, *Raintree County* and *The Young Lions*. As *Warlock*'s producer-director, he was closely involved in the development of a script that gleams with complexity and lack of cliché, was given a sizeable budget from 20th Century–Fox to realize his vision and was able to muster an impressive cast to breathe life into his characters. Looking back over his career, the memories of this high watermark were fond: "I enjoyed [*Warlock*] tremendously."[176]

Dmytryk had been expecting an offer from Paramount after completing his epic effort on *The Young Lions* but production there was in the doldrums. Instead he was approached by Buddy Adler at Fox with the proposal to produce and direct an adaptation of Oakley Hall's novel *Warlock*, which examined aspects of the Old West that hadn't been done to death onscreen. The choice of writer was completely Dmytryk's and since he wanted to forge distinction from the source material, he "wanted someone with original ideas—a risk taker."[177] Robert Alan Aurthur was a New York–based writer with many television credits, who would ultimately write *All That Jazz* for Bob

Fosse but whose only produced screenplay to that point had been *Edge of the City*, a gritty drama for Martin Ritt in 1957. Dmytryk's approach was "to discuss the story and the characters in fairly broad terms, arrive at some tentative decision on the story's main thrust, and then let the writer retire to do his work, keeping only the lightest rein on progress."[178] The first draft was overlong but together they fashioned a script with bracingly original relationships that also revealed underexamined aspects of social history in a late nineteenth century frontier mining town.

Henry Fonda was experiencing his own purple patch in the late 1950s, his immediately preceding films being for Alfred Hitchcock (*The Wrong Man*), Sidney Lumet (*12 Angry Men*, *Stage Struck*), King Vidor (*War and Peace*) and Anthony Mann (*The Tin Star*). Richard Widmark's most recent run of directors was more modest (Norman Panama, Gene Kelly, John Sturges, Karl Malden) and he had been a star for a decade less than Fonda. Yet for *Warlock*, a film with effectively two lead male roles, Widmark was paid $200,000 and Fonda $175,000, both for ten weeks work. The other three actors making up the fascinating quintet at the story's core were Anthony Quinn ($125,000), Dorothy Malone ($75,000) and Dolores Michaels ($3,700). This was Quinn's fourth time acting in a Dmytryk film, though the first since *Back to Bataan* in 1945. Quinn clearly had the measure of the man after multiple experiences of working with him, yet he felt the peculiar compulsion to open his 1995 autobiography with reminiscences about *Warlock*, providing a self-justification for working with the pariah of the Hollywood Ten: "I did not know what to make of this man, and I passed many long nights with Fonda and Widmark, worrying what kind of signal we were sending by working with him. It was a confusing time. Everyone was cutting his own deals, doing what he had to do. There was no separating the way we lived from the way we worked. Dmytryk was actually a nice man, or at least I had known him to be a nice man, and when I sounded him out, I came away thinking he still might be one."[179] He, along with Widmark and Fonda, notable Hollywood liberals, clearly disagreed with the decision that Dmytryk had made to testify before HUAC but it was bizarre to surmise that the director had actually changed his personality through making that decision. In the end, his nights of soul searching on the set of the film he had signed to make led to him granting his director some leeway: "After all he had been through, Dmytryk could not see that he had any other course, and I could not see that our condemnation would accomplish anything except to pacify ourselves. He had suffered enough. Too many of our friends had suffered enough. And so, we worked."[180]

Dmytryk was extremely satisfied with the cast he assembled: "Henry [Fonda] is a beautiful actor"[181]; Dorothy Malone was "a woman of immense understanding.... She had a *real* instinct for acting"[182]; Anthony Quinn, "always an excellent actor, was getting better and better and did a beautiful job."[183] Dmytryk had suffered Richard Widmark's insecurity on *Broken Lance* but this time he was top-billed and confident of his position. The director found him to be "an extremely conscientious workman, a study in concentration and creative irritability, and [with] a very short fuse."[184] These characteristics led to a notable incident on the set of *Warlock* involving a scene that was truncated for the final cut. Dorothy Malone was at the beginning of a relationship with Jacques Bergerac, previously Mr. Ginger Rogers, soon to be

Mr. Dorothy Malone. Her depth of passion affected her depth of concentration and according to Dmytryk she "was not up to doing her homework."[185] Late one afternoon she and Widmark were rehearsing a complicated moving shot for filming the next morning. Both Widmark and Dmytryk were getting impatient with her lack of pre-paredness and at the end of the third rehearsal, when her character was meant to slap his, Malone whacked Widmark hard on his left ear. Grabbing her hand, Widmark pointed out that it was a rehearsal, so punches were normally pulled, and that his left ear was his bad ear, so please would she hit the other one, if she had to hit any at all. The next morning, Dmytryk had a final rehearsal for the camera, which went well until the slap, when Malone again delivered a full blow to her co-star's left ear. "Wid-mark's arm shot up in instantaneous reaction, landing a terrific clout on the side of Dorothy's head. Tears popped out of her eyes—not from crying but from the concus-sion—and she flew backward clear across the set."[186] Widmark yelled at her, calling her a "no-talent bum,"[187] until a break was called, and cooler heads prevailed. Cam-eraman Joe MacDonald broke the tension on the first take by putting crossed boxing gloves above the on-set saloon door with a sign reading "Hail the Champ!" Widmark and Malone burst out laughing while the camera was rolling, spoiling the first take but rescuing camaraderie.

Joe MacDonald, cameraman for Dmytryk on multiple occasions, was a noted cinematographer of westerns—the exquisite black and white of Ford's *My Darling Clementine* and Wellman's *Yellow Sky*, and the widescreen splendor of Dmytryk's *Broken Lance* and *Warlock*. MacDonald's photography in *Warlock* inhales the stun-ning Utah scenery and breathes life into the film most vibrantly in those scenes shot against this backdrop or on the extensive exterior set built on the Fox backlot. That the title of the film is also the name of the town is appropriate since we are given a tangible sense of Warlock's geography and environment. At the summit of a hill sits a respectable large house where weddings are conducted and hymns are sung. The saloon, initially called The Glass Slipper, rebranded The French Palace when a new coarsening wind sweeps into town, is the center for disreputable behavior at the base of the hill, literally in the downtown area. Our first introduction to the town is the sight of a water cart dampening the red dust of the streets that swirls and chokes and soaks up the incessant, fierce heat of the sun. Warlock has been established in a beautiful but hostile environment that is only endured due to its proximity to mines. Dmytryk renders the dry heat palpable and orchestrates billows of dust at moments of transition, as at the moment that the new form of law-keeping in the shape of Clay Blaisedell (Henry Fonda) and Tom Morgan (Anthony Quinn) enters the saloon for the first time. When permanent change does come to town at the film's climax, we are forewarned by a flash of lightning followed by a torrential downpour that washes away the old order. The final scene takes place the morning after the storm, with the last two lines of the film being: "Chilly out"—"Yep." The change to Warlock is so fun-damental that even the elements recognize it.

The shift that occurs within Warlock in 1881 depicts in microcosm the general trend of western pioneer society from the old ways of the frontier to the adoption of law and order. The town is being terrorized by a lawless band of cowboys from the San Pablo ranch who have run the latest deputy out of town, the sheriff being located too far away to prove a realistic deterrent. The last vestige of the law in town is Judge Holloway (Wallace Ford), who continually reminds everyone that he is not an official judge, but only "on acceptance." He criticizes the town for hiring Blaisedell, a "vigilante, gambler, gunman," as marshal: "You're using anarchy and murder to try to prevent anarchy and murder…. Law and order, that's the alternative." The historical precedents for such an arrangement, the attempt to impose order on a community by someone operating on the fringes of acceptability, reducing lawlessness but himself occupying a legal grey area, certainly existed in the Old West. Blaisedell has performed the same role in a succession of towns and informs a town meeting, "I come here as your salvation at a very high wage. I establish order. Ride roughshod over offenders. First you're pleased because it's a good deal less trouble. Then a very strange thing happens. You begin to feel I'm too powerful. You begin to fear me. Not me, but what I am. And when that happens, we will have had full satisfaction from one another. It'll be time for me to leave."

Warlock is one of many classic westerns depicting a moment of social shift that consigns the frontier era to history, and crystallizes its conflict in three characters: Johnny Gannon (Richard Widmark), the former delinquent cowboy who sees the error of his ways and becomes deputy; Blaisedell who ultimately realizes that his methods are those of the past; and Morgan who refuses to move with the times. The film effectively has two climaxes: one where Gannon must face down his former buddies in the cowboy gang, and the second one in which Gannon confronts Blaisedell after demanding the gunman leave town. Before the first, Blaisedell and Gannon are allies, with the gunman prepared to fight alongside the sheriff. At this moment, Blaisedell senses that the days of the gunslinger are slipping away. He tells Morgan, "The Law is taking over…. Let's see if Warlock is grown up enough to take care of itself…. Maybe it's time. Maybe we've run out of towns." Henry Fonda displays his immaculate technique in the scene in which Blaisedell passes the torch to Gannon: "Hold strictly to the rules. It's only the rules that matter. Hold onto them like you were walking on eggs." The rules, however, are not the Law, and though Blaisedell possesses a robust morality, his instincts stem from his military background. Lily Dollar (Dorothy Malone), who harbors an intense grudge against Blaisedell, tells of how he was a colonel in the army at the age of 21: "All he knows is killing." His protector Morgan prevents him from assisting Gannon against the San Pablo cowboys, but Gannon recognizes that "it's time this town stood on its own." Unlike the confrontation at the beginning of the film where the townsfolk look on impotently as the deputy is run out of town, this time they appreciate that their community has come of age and they rally to Gannon's defense.

By this point of the story, all the characters representing facets of the law have become physically impaired—the Judge has been on crutches throughout, Blaisedell has been shot in the arm, Gannon has been stabbed in the hand. The one person connected with keeping order who has a permanent impairment is Morgan. His deformed foot is treated cruelly by former lover Lily ("You cripple!") but scarcely referred to by anyone else. He later warns Lily, "I'll kill anybody that's dangerous to Clay. Even you, Lily. Because he's the only person, man or woman, who looked at me and didn't see a cripple." But Morgan is the one person who is unable to move with the times and notes ruefully that "civilisation is stalking Warlock." When Blaisedell informs him that he is settling down with Jessie Marlow (Dolores Michaels) and tells him to move onto the next town alone, Morgan provokes a gunfight ("I'm better than you!") in which his partner kills him. Fonda again magnificently rises to the challenge of portraying a man with the desire to settle but whose instinct to move on proves insuperable. Brimming with emotion at having shot his friend, he carries Morgan to the saloon they had set up together, makes a funeral pyre for him and, as a thunderstorm breaks, sets fire to the building and his life of the last decade.

The *Sturm und Drang* of this tumultuous climax gives way to the quietly tense encounter between Blaisedell and Gannon the next morning. The marshal recognizes the truth of what the Judge had told him: "Blaisedell, don't you understand that as long as you stay here there'll be killing? You're a target, a symbol, and they must come after you." Looking at the charred shell of the saloon and realizing he is among the last of a dying breed, Blaisedell rejects Jessie's offer to make a life with her: "Times are changing, sure. But there'll be enough towns to last my lifetime." The final minutes of the film unspool without dialogue. Walking past Lily, dressed against the morning chill in black clothing that resembles widow's weeds, Blaisedell confronts Gannon, who has discarded the bandage on his hand, symbolically whole again. They both draw guns but neither shoots. Blaisedell has given Gannon the chance to kill him and his outmoded ways. In response, he throws his gold-handled Colts into the newly dampened dust and rides out of town to an uncertain future, leaving a definitively discarded past.

Warlock is distinguished by a particularly complex quintet of protagonists, resistant to stereotype and subject to constantly shifting loyalties and allegiances. Both Blaisedell and Gannon reject the example of the two men closest to them. Filial loyalty is discarded when Johnny Gannon's brother Billy remains an outlaw, and Tom Morgan intends to continue profiteering on the grey fringes of the law regardless of Blaisedell. Both men die due to their intransigence. The relationship between Morgan and Blaisedell is fascinating and could be interpreted as unrequited love on Morgan's part. He lives for the excitement of moving to the next town with his partner, enjoys making their living quarters comfortable and erases anyone who threatens the partnership. His warning to Blaisedell that "thinking of weddings could lead to a funeral" goes unheeded, and when the final rejection comes, life is no longer worth living. Morgan had had a relationship with Lily many years previously, but it had been one that straddled the line between pimp and partner. The Production Code refused Morgan's line "You might have to work your trade from time to time if I run short of cash, though. The way we used to do, Lily." The alternative line for Lily used in the film still has clear overtones of prostitution: "For what? So that you could send me back to work whenever you run short of money?"

The two women also exhibit interesting character arcs and fail to conform to the virgin and whore stereotypes. Jessie is a strong-minded individual, unafraid to show her initial distaste of Blaisedell. She longs to escape the strictures of her position as an unmarried respectable citizen. A courtship scene between them is accurately awkward and spectacularly shot, the piercing blue eyes of both Fonda and Michaels set against the blazing azure of the sky. Blaisedell calls Jessie "the miners' angel," to which she responds, "I hate being an angel." The scene concludes with a kiss and the succeeding scene, after a brief insert of the cowboys, is Jessie cooking breakfast for him, with the clear implication that he has spent the night in her house. An angel no more. This cooking scene deliberately echoes an earlier one between Lily and Gannon that similarly followed an initial outdoor encounter. Lily is travelling in the opposite direction, seeking respectability after a life devoid of it while remarking sarcastically on the limitations of a woman's role: "No, there's very little I know. I'm a woman. I only feel things." What is refreshing about the film is that the very spikiness of its characterization makes clichéd conclusions unlikely. And indeed, by the end the good girl is tearfully watching her commitment-ready maverick ride off into the blue.

It is intriguing to consider the entirely different dynamic that would have resulted if casting agent Billy Gordon's initially proposed preferences for the three male roles had been cast—Kirk Douglas as Blaisedell, Montgomery Clift as Gannon and Rod Steiger as Morgan. The contrast between Douglas' fierce intensity and Fonda's cool command is particularly sharp. Dmytryk as producer is likely to have refused the suggestion of Douglas due to their bitter experience on *The Juggler*, and probably felt that a third successive film with the troubled Clift, as fond as he was of the actor, was more than he was prepared to shoulder. *Warlock* was filmed in October and November of 1958 and released the following April to generally very positive reviews. It is a film that has gained in stature over the decades, with the cinephilic French holding it in particular affection. *Warlock* is visually and thematically rich, providing complexity along with generic pleasures such as well-staged shootouts, and stands as testament to the skill of Edward Dmytryk when he was in control of circumstance.

The Blue Angel (1959)

Remaking *Der Blaue Engel* was a forlorn venture. Josef von Sternberg's 1930 classic crackles with a Weimar intensity and generates sparks when Marlene Dietrich's Lola Lola is onscreen. Its status as the film that launched Dietrich internationally should have acted as a warning to producers but the voracious generational cycle of the Hollywood machine meant that by the late 1950s films of the late silent/early talkie period were now ripe for remake. *Imitation of Life* and *Ben-Hur* had successful reappearances in 1959, less so *Cimarron* and *The Four Horsemen of the Apocalypse* galloping over the horizon in the early 1960s.

Marilyn Monroe had initially been proposed as the reincarnation of Lola in late 1956 after filming *The Prince and the Showgirl*, with Spencer Tracy to play Professor Immanuel Rath. After watching the original, Tracy was enthusiastic about the role of the schoolteacher seduced by the nightclub performer ("Fabulous pic[ture] & part. O.K. if right <u>director</u>"[188]). However the project being set up by producer Buddy

Adler stumbled when Tracy heard stories about Monroe's behavior and then foundered when she declined, her contract by this stage including story approval. Producer Jack Cummings, veteran of MGM productions such as *Kiss Me Kate* and *Seven Brides for Seven Brothers*, persisted in pursuing the project at Fox, where Dmytryk had one more film to make in order to complete his contract. Eager to get to Paramount to make *The Mountain is Young*, he accepted the first proposal that was made to him, and his assessment of his own *The Blue Angel* is hardly a ringing endorsement: "we eventually wound up with a film none of us had to be ashamed of."[189]

Curt Jürgens was cast as the victim of Lola's siren song, leading to his decline and fall. The team behind the film knew they had a problem in casting the central female role, especially having made the decision to film exteriors in Germany and have the English dialogue spoken by accented European actors. Eventually the role fell to May Britt, the 25-year-old Swedish actress whose first U.S. production had been *War and Peace*, shot in Italy, and whose Hollywood debut was in *The Young Lions*. Dmytryk's recollection of her casting as Lola is disturbingly blunt: "I'd brought her to the studio for *[The] Young Lions*, but I knew that she couldn't act. She was a very nice gal and a very attractive gal and a sexy gal, but she couldn't act, and I knew she couldn't carry this."[190]

Theodore Bikel, while judging himself to have done well in the role of Lola's manager Klepert and finding Jürgens "very good,"[191] was also critical of his female co-star: "The big problem was Mai Britt."[192] While Fox were clearly hoping that her looks would short-circuit any criticism of her acting abilities, class act Deborah Kerr was still employed to introduce Britt in a production trailer "in her familiar dulcet, soft-sell voice."[193] A 16-page section in the August 1959 edition of trade magazine *Film Bulletin* trumpets "the Most Ballyhooed New Star of the Generation": "This incandescent Swedish siren with the silken blonde hair, the curvaceous legs and the devastatingly attractive charms stands poised on the brink of a career that promises to make her the toast of moviegoers throughout the world."[194]

May Britt was not the first starlet unable to live up to the hype but the odds were stacked against her by evoking her iconic predecessor so strongly, as in her miming of *Falling in Love Again* in very Dietrich-like tones. Though Dmytryk noted that she "worked very, very hard,"[195] she didn't possess the skills to produce a shaded performance. Bikel felt that "the question in the end was not whether a Swede could be a German, but whether anybody could be Marlene."[196] With the doubts harbored about Britt by the production team, this is a question that should never even have been posed. Although the plot wheels of the remake turn in almost precisely the same manner as in von Sternberg's version, one notable difference is a softer Lola. The sardonic edge to Marlene's aura is replaced by May's well-intentioned gentleness, at least initially. In response to Rath's assertion that he is not a ladies' man, Lola says, "It's never too late to begin." When he declares his love and proposes to her, she sweetly accepts but with a warning that wasn't given in the previous version: "I fall in love of course all the time but it never lasts. Perhaps I'm even a little bit in love with you now, because you're different. But after a little while, I should want someone else, who's different again."

This forewarning of Rath's fate saps some energy from his downfall. The rollercoaster that von Sternberg constructs for Rath propels him in rapid succession from marriage proposal to wedding reception to honeymoon night, and mere minutes later, he is four years into his marriage and applying the clown makeup that signifies his abjection. By contrast, each of those stages are extended in Dmytryk's film, with no appreciable benefit. The May Britt Lola initially gives up the stage to be a good wife to Rath, who experiences rejection from prospective employers because of his unsuitable marriage. Lola has to be coaxed back to the stage by Klepert, and Rath only agrees due to the dire financial straits of the couple. At this point both Klepert and Lola's attitude towards Rath abruptly hardens. Klepert taunts, "At least I never let a woman keep me," while Lola's reaction is even harsher: "Well don't worry about it. I've kept better men than you. And worse." Rath's reaction to this humiliation is taken directly from the earlier film—he storms out, returns meekly and submissively puts her stockings on for her, while she flicks through a magazine contemptuously: "Poor Immanuel."

Despite being located "down by the docks" of the fictional port of Lenzburg, generally a sleazy part of any town, the production designers have made The Blue Angel nightclub a flashy joint. Here the wide CinemaScope format is a disadvantage. The stage is wide, the lighting un-atmospheric and the auditorium spacious and lacking in seedy intimacy. The aesthetic of the film is unexceptional, and any potential seediness is washed out in the high-key lighting from Leon Shamroy. Adele Balkan's costumes for Lola consciously reference those worn by Dietrich, in particular the dress which reveals underwear at the rear. Lola is surrounded onstage by performers oozing lethargy, and it is perplexing to employ the great choreographer Hermes Pan to stage the dances when the result is merely languid sashaying. Scriptwriter Nigel Balchin has made scant effort to inject individual personality into the troupe, so that while a chorus girl mourns the death of Tonno the clown, the viewer has scarcely been made aware of his existence.

Professor Rath is a botanist in this version of the story, which introduces fertility symbolism into his instruction on plants and provides the opportunity for his class to mock his stiffness in the guise of innocent questions. When the most rebellious of his pupils asks him, "What are stamens for?" Rath recognizes the taunt and makes the boy write out 100 times "The stamens are the pollen-producing organs." As in almost any film about schooldays, the actors are scarcely credible as the 17-year-old boys they are portraying, making the contrast between their sexual curiosity and Rath's virginity all the more marked. The location filming took place in Rothenburg ob der Tauber in Bavaria and while disbelief can be suspended for the combination of all signage being in German and all dialogue being in English, a certain sloppiness to the production permits a park sign forbidding the picking of flowers to be in English. It is indicative of a film which feels lazy, unwilling to strive towards its potential, an underachieving student in Rath's class.

The return of Klepert's troupe to Lenzburg, the location of The Blue Angel and Rath's school, provides the film with its climax. After three years of Rath hawking saucy postcards of his wife to members of her audience and being porter for her luggage, Klepert sees financial reward in making Rath part of the show in his hometown, replacing Tonno as clown sidekick in his magician act. Rath bristles and refuses, until a visit to his old school, during which the sympathetic Principal Harter (John Banner) calls his decision to marry Lola a mistake, emboldens him and he agrees to take to the stage. The scene in which he smears himself in clown make-up was foreshadowed during his initial encounter with Lola when she blew powder in his face. That playful flirtation is now replaced by a dismissive Lola telling him that her affections have moved on. Not only must he brave the stage in a demeaning routine in front of old colleagues and acquaintances, but he must endure the indignity of watching his wife cavort with an old flame in the wings.

The climactic moment when Rath loses control onstage and then attempts to strangle Lola is lacking in impact. Dmytryk's handling of the scenario of a formerly upright citizen provoking ridicule at his diminished circumstances is slack, and the performance of Jürgens, generally solid if overly deliberate up to this point, veers into overacting. It is a fumbled conclusion, pale in comparison to that of *Der Blaue Engel*. The pathos of the earlier film, in which Emil Jannings returns to his old classroom to clutch his desk in a death-grip, is replaced by Jürgens being led from the nightclub by Harter. As they walk away through the deserted streets, Lola singing *Falling in Love Again* to her new flame echoes over the soundtrack, and the spirit of Marlene Dietrich cannot help but echo through the mind of the viewer.

The May Britt explosion never happened. Despite the "Britt Big Build-Up"[197] including the cover of *Life* magazine, she never became the promised "household byword from coast-to-coast."[198] She made one more film, *Murder Inc.*, the following year before marrying Sammy Davis, Jr., and retiring from the cinema screen. Theodore Bikel managed to gauge the reaction of the iconic Lola to the remake: "I happened to run into Marlene Dietrich at a dinner later. 'I saw the picture,' she said to me. Not daring to ask what she thought of it, I waited. Then she said, 'Well, it certainly didn't do *you* any harm.'"[199] She wasn't wrong—Bikel gives the strongest performance in the film. Dmytryk wasn't completely dissatisfied with his *The Blue Angel* and recalled reviews comparing it favorably to the original, yet there was ruefulness in retrospect: "The rule still holds—never remake a classic, even a minor one."[200]

VI

Sustaining Stardom
(1961–1969)

Edward Dmytryk had been with the Famous Artists Agency since his success with *Hitler's Children* at RKO in 1943. His agents there, Charles Feldman and Jack Gordean, had helped him build his career and then resurrect it after his entanglement with HUAC. Feldman's side-line as a producer was distinguished with the triumph of *A Streetcar Named Desire* and, as well as Elia Kazan, he had produced the work of Billy Wilder, Mitchell Leisen and Frank Borzage. Feldman offered Dmytryk a new seven-year deal with the agency if he would direct his production of **Walk on the Wild Side** starring Feldman's French girlfriend Capucine. This inappropriate casting, combined with Feldman's heavy-handed approach to his role, led to a major confrontation between producer and director, a severing of ties and the loss to Dmytryk of more than $70,000 in deferment to extricate himself from the Famous Artists Agency. In 1962, the year of *Walk on the Wild Side*'s release, Feldman sold the Agency, failed to set up a film version of the life of Mary Magdalene starring Capucine and lost her romantically to William Holden on the set of *The Lion*.

Dmytryk's next choice was an unpredictable sidestep into the realm of religiosity, **The Reluctant Saint**, which his friend John Fante had co-written and which Dmytryk agreed to produce and direct for Columbia. After the trials of *Walk on the Wild Side*, a stroll on the mild side must have seemed attractive, as did being his own boss far away from studio interference on location in Italy. Regrettably, the film did nothing for his career artistically or with regard to his profile. The trip to Italy was a family affair. He employed his son Michael as assistant director and installed the pregnant Jean, Rick and Vicky in four blocked off rooms at the Caesar Augustus hotel overlooking the Via Francia in Rome. Concerns grew about the treatment Jean would receive at the hospital where she was scheduled to give birth and, after one disconcerting false alarm and with memories of her difficult labor in London in 1949, she decided to book a return flight for her and the children, employing truth economizing with TWA about the advanced stage of her pregnancy. Dinah Shore was on the same flight and provided welcome assistance. Three weeks later, in November 1961, Rebecca Dmytryk was born.

Edward Dmytryk effectively took 1962 off. The 53 year old had been a studio director for over two decades but the sands of the movie business were shifting: "Physically, I was in my prime, but, mentally, I was hamstrung. I decided to take it easy. Hollywood was in the doldrums, and I wallowed in the calms—but from choice,

The Dmytryk family in 1965: (left to right) Vicky, Jean, Rebecca, Eddie and Rick.

not from necessity."[1] The Hawaiian coffee farm he and Jean had bought five years previously proved to be more of a financial drain than boon and they sold it, as they did their plot at Agoura. This spot in Los Angeles county which they had bought in 1947 for $16,000 was intended for their dream dwelling and horse farm but the year 1947 had other plans for the Dmytryks. They sold the plot to a property developer for $400,000. With batteries recharged and bank account replenished, he welcomed the overtures from new Paramount production chief Martin Rackin. Despite the fact that his contract with Paramount stipulated that he produce, Dmytryk waived this clause since Joe Levine was determined to produce *The Carpetbaggers* himself. With the risqué subject-matter, there was nervousness at the first preview in Chicago but only a few walkouts. A worried Levine spoke to Dmytryk in the cinema foyer: "'They're laughing a lot,' he said. 'And in all the right places,' I said. 'I planned it that way.' He looked a little unsure, but the preview cards convinced him…. We had a hit."[2] And one of the biggest hits of Dmytryk's career. The follow-up was another collaboration with Levine, *Where Love Has Gone*, Dmytryk's last film at Paramount, the studio that had started him as a messenger boy.

Dmytryk's quest for bucolic bliss continued and eventually rested on a dairy ranch north of San Francisco, just off the highway between Petaluma and Bodega Bay. It had 500 acres of land, a two-acre lake, some barns and an 1848 house with seventeen rooms, four fireplaces and a carved staircase leading off the entrance hall. The couple fell for it instantly, though Jean had some qualms about the isolation, with no other house in sight from their property. They decided to buy the farm with Michael, who was to be in charge of the cattle, and Dmytryk's art director on *The Carpetbaggers*, Walter Tyler, helped Jean to redesign the house. In June 1964 they moved out of their Bel Air home of thirteen years and embraced their new life on the land at the Double D Ranch. After wrapping up *Where Love Has Gone*, Dmytryk enjoyed throwing himself into seeding of pasture land, baling of hay and calving, though for Jean, the contrast to Bel Air life was jarring. When Dmytryk got a call from his agent at the end of that summer that Universal wanted him to make **Mirage** with Gregory Peck, the initial plan of Jean holding the Double D fort while he directed the movie proved unworkable, and the family moved back to Bel Air, leaving the ranch in the care of Felix, the foreman.

In the mid–1960s, Edward Dmytryk found himself in a similar situation to the leading actors that he directed—Bette Davis, Susan Hayward, Gregory Peck, William Holden, Richard Widmark, Robert Mitchum. All were operating in a vastly different landscape to that which had nurtured and nourished them in the 1940s—the 1930s in the case of Davis—and were struggling to maintain relevance. Hits could still happen but the style of movie that stars and directors had finely honed in their heyday was rapidly going out of fashion and tended only to hit the jackpot when a producer like Joe Levine ladled over as much sex as he could get away with. Dmytryk's last three films of the sixties—**Alvarez Kelly**, **Anzio**, **Shalako**—were old-fashioned action-oriented filmmaking, all well executed, though the improbable presence of Brigitte Bardot was almost enough to capsize the last of the three.

Dmytryk spent a lot of time on his ranch—"a constant source of hard work and spiritual replenishment"[3]—and was not seeking work to the extent that he had at the beginning of the decade, but opportunities were diminishing, as they were for all directors of his vintage. Hollywood had lost interest in the old-timers and *Anzio* and *Shalako* were both European productions. Dmytryk felt that, in his case, there was something else in play, a "reverse blacklist" that encroached as HUAC receded. He had faced blacklisting in the 1940s and "the same thing is true now. There's nobody in town who will come and say, 'We don't like Dmytryk, because he betrayed his buddies,' and yet I know time and again that it's happened for that very reason. [Billy] Wilder is one…. He's been one of my worst enemies in this way…. [John] Houseman is another one…. They never signed anything. They were good liberals, who took no chances, but they're very free with their vitriolic tongues and goddamning anybody who went against what they think the principles are … there are a number of guys in that position in this town, who I know don't like what I did, who don't like my stand, who don't even know me, but who assume I'm some kind of a real son-of-a-bitch."[4]

The repercussions of his testimony were felt personally as well as professionally by the Dmytryks, with negative judgment stemming from both Left and Right. Back in 1952, Adlai Stevenson had been the Democratic Party nomination for President and the Dmytryks sent a check to attend a formal fundraising dinner for him. Jean received a phone call from a friend from her days at MGM, thanking her for the check but informing her that she was returning it and uninviting the couple, due to their controversial political past. In 1965, while Dmytryk was busy with *Alvarez Kelly*, his daughter Vicky was accepted at an exclusive school, once she had graduated from her preparatory school. The uniforms were bought, the open day was attended, introductions were made to the teachers. The day after the open day, Jean was phoned by the school and informed that Vicky would not be able to attend after all. When pressed, the entanglements of the past again proved to be the cause. While the professional rejections were subtle and disguised, the personal slights were direct and bruising.

Dmytryk accepted *Anzio* from Dino de Laurentiis after being told by his business manager, "You're short of cash ... and running into debt. You'd better get a job."[5] Jean, Vicky and Rebecca joined him while he was filming in Italy in the summer of 1967, and in order to ease tensions on what was becoming a tricky shoot in Taranto, Jean threw a party for the entire company. It was becoming clear to Dmytryk that work would be based in Europe from now on, so in 1968 he reluctantly sold his farm and cattle "and said good-bye to another dream."[6] Their Bel Air home yo-yoed in and out of their ownership. They sold it in 1967, rebought it in 1968 when Dmytryk was in Spain for *Shalako* and definitively sold it in 1971, after eighteen years: "much as we loved it, [it] was chewing up our meagre savings at a prodigious rate."[7]

In the summer of 1967, Dmytryk met Ennio De Concini, the Oscar-winning writer of *Divorce, Italian Style* and future scripter of *Bluebeard*, and discovered that both had an abiding fascination with Christopher Columbus. Dmytryk had researched the subject and had long harbored the desire to make a film that would puncture the many myths that had grown around the explorer. The director and writer met with Marcello Mastroianni over dinner, signed an agreement and "toasted our partnership with champagne, a very treacherous drink."[8] De Concini completed what the director described as a beautiful script and Dimitri de Grunwald, who had financed *Shalako*, set about finding the funding. The pre-production publicity caught the eye of Columbus scholar and justice of the Pennsylvania Supreme Court Michael Musmanno, who had written a book called *Columbus was First* and who was therefore very much in favor of the myths remaining intact. He objected vociferously to the press reports about a film that was nowhere near entering production and the controversy caused Mastroianni to withdraw from the project. Financing possibilities shriveled up as the industry retreated into its shell towards the end of a bruising decade, especially now that the package had lost its star actor, and at de Grunwald's final financing attempt, Paramount balked at the cost. Rival Christopher Columbus films would be made a quarter of a century later to celebrate the 500th anniversary of 1492, in a sideways echo of the rival anti–Semitism films that had sprung up in 1947. For Dmytryk, failing to get *Columbus* into production, after working on it salary-free for the best part of a year, was a crushing blow to his career and lamentably the shape of things to come. With bitter timing, Michael Musmanno, whose objections had torpedoed the project, died in October 1968, just after *Columbus* had sunk without trace.

Walk on the Wild Side (1962)

Walk on the Wild Side struts onscreen with a sleekly filmed title sequence from the peerless Saul Bass. A black cat prowls its turf to a sinuous Elmer Bernstein score. Bass explained his rationale behind the concept: "The film's setting is New Orleans in the early thirties, and deals with the disenfranchised, tough, seamy characters of a despairing time. Symbolic of this is the black cat and its movement though this environment. The title opens with him emerging from a culvert and looking around. We watch him prowl through the back alleys, roam through his territory, meet another cat, an outsider, a quick fight, the intruder scuttles off. The cat resumes his stealthy *Walk on the Wild Side*."[9] Dmytryk didn't collaborate with Bass since, by the time the credit sequence was shot, he was no longer involved with the production. "It's the best part of the picture," conceded Dmytryk. "I'm very frank about my work."[10]

Saul Bass's feline scrap echoes not only the brawl between prostitutes towards the climax of the film but also the catty behavior on display throughout the fraught shoot. Anne Baxter sets the scene: "The atmosphere on the set was ghastly, just ghastly. Indescribable. The royally spoiled [Laurence Harvey] had made some charming, scathing remarks about the lack of talent to do with [Capucine] and she was in tears most of the time. He fought with the director and stalked off the set and was never on time. One day he kept us waiting one hour and a half. Highly professional Barbara [Stanwyck] was furious. So was I. But I had lied rather boldly about an increasingly pregnant self and was keeping a rather low profile. Well, when he finally drifted back on the set, Barbara chewed him out with such icy grace that I wanted to cheer. He never did it again. Never."[11]

Laurence Harvey was notorious in the industry for his ill-mannered arrogance—"a rude man ... a horrible man,"[12] was the verdict of Sarah Miles, whom he directed in *The Ceremony*. He did indeed make ungallant comments about Capucine and reportedly chewed garlic in his scenes with her. He judged *Walk on the Wild Side* to be a "ghastly film ... made even more so by that ghastly woman. I suppose it's not her fault she can't act."[13] Not that he was any more obliging with his other co-stars— he would pull faces when they were given their close-up. Jane Fonda said, "It's like acting by yourself. No, it's *worse* than acting by yourself."[14] Harvey's verdict on her: "What a strange girl! She has a few things written about her and she comes to the conclusion she's the biggest star in the movie business. You can't tell her anything. Two hours on the set and she's playing director and running the outfit."[15]

Fonda had not enjoyed the experience of her only previous film, *Tall Story*, and had sworn off the "morons in the film business,"[16] but financial obligations led to her accepting the role of Kitty Twist. She hoped that such an unscrupulous, voracious character would provide a drastic change of image: "I knew that playing Kitty Twist would make me look very ugly. I thought my career might be ended because of it, but I went and did it anyway."[17] To help her deliver a truthful performance, she was determined to have ready assistance from Andreas Voutsinas, who had helped her prepare

Here, Kitty: Jane Fonda gets into character for her director on *Walk on the Wild Side* (1962).

the scene that had gotten her into the Actors Studio. Despite a ban on personal advisors on the production, she brought him to the set in the guise of her secretary, relying heavily on his advice. Though Anne Baxter was sympathetic ("For her he was a kind of electric security blanket.... She would do anything that Andreas asked her to do"),[18] his constant presence was a bone of contention. Harvey thought Voutsinas was a "creep"[19] and Dmytryk bridled at this "young Greek exquisite"[20] tactilely whispering with Fonda before takes and encouraging her to enlarge her acting at the same time as Dmytryk was attempting to restrain her performance. On a mission to create a more sexual persona for the young star, Voutsinas told Fonda to soak her already figure-hugging dress in water so that it clung to her hips and bottom. She was wearing no underwear, also on the suggestion of her coach, and refused Dmytryk's request to put some on, on the pretext that it would be inauthentic.

In her autobiography, Jane Fonda reflected on perceptions of divadom: "I'd pulled that once in *Walk on the Wild Side* when I was scared to go into a particular scene and kept having my makeup redone—as though different eyebrows and more rouge would somehow make things right. When I finally did show up on the set, I could feel people's anger and I froze. I learned then that if the on-set vibes toward me were negative, it was harder to do good work."[21] Voutsinas was ultimately barred from the set and relations between Fonda and Dmytryk improved. The part of Kitty Twist had been hewn back to bolster the prominence of Hallie, played by Capucine, but Fonda remembered that she and Dmytryk "waged a little secret fight to get Nelson Algren's book, which I knew so well, back into the picture. I think we did, too."[22]

Some fights were secret, others less so. Charles Feldman had been Dmytryk's agent, and already had the producing successes of *A Streetcar Named Desire* and *The Seven Year Itch* behind him. In order to gain studio interest in his latest project, a Nelson Algren novel with prostitution at its heart, Feldman was obliged to gain approval from the Production Code Administration. He employed Dmytryk as director of *Walk on the Wild Side* and set him the task of getting the script, which had been cobbled together from the work of a series of writers, past the ever-watchful eye of PCA head Geoffrey Shurlock. Initially, Shurlock's main objection was the suggestion of a lesbian relationship between Hallie and brothel madame Jo, an element that had originated with Feldman. Shurlock's solution was that Jo should be portrayed as having a maternal interest in all of the girls in her "establishment" and that with "regard to Hallie, this unusually accentuated possessiveness came from the fact that Hallie possessed a great artistic talent as a sculptress, and Jo saw in her a possibility of the fulfilment of a career to which she had been denied because of a physical deformity—possibly a deformed or amputated hand."[23] Portrayal of Jo's establishment was to be treated with the utmost care and "it would be helpful if you were to pursue the further idea of illegal gambling, and in this way all the more minimize the idea that this is a brothel."[24] Dmytryk must have complied with the required amputee lesbian, for two months later Shurlock was delighted with "the splendid way in which these several extremely troublesome elements have been corrected."[25] Having received script approval, Feldman got a deal with Columbia—and quickly set about reinstating the censored material, much to the annoyance of Dmytryk.

The annoyances started to accrue. Feldman insisted on the role of Hallie, object of desire for both Dove (Laurence Harvey) and Jo (Barbara Stanwyck), going to his French girlfriend Capucine, which obliged giving the character a resoundingly bogus background in Paris. Dmytryk tried to get out of making the film but had signed himself into a new seven-year agency contract when he accepted directing duties. He later lamented to an interviewer about how Feldman "was always getting Clifford Odets or somebody[26] to rewrite and sending me material and I'd look at it, and I'd tear it up and I'd throw it [away] … because it was completely wrong … it was just not the character [of Hallie]. It was quoting obscure Roman poets and French poets … making her some kind of lady, which was not what the story was about. It was a little girl from Texas. She was not an intellectual…. Oh, she's French, of course…. She obviously perhaps would have gotten some veneer of sophistication from two or three years in New Orleans, but not that much. She wouldn't have got a liberal education, for Christ's sake. So we had a big battle about it, and it was a much better picture before."[27]

Feldman had promised Dmytryk that he would head for Europe when production started and would not interfere with filming. After a comparatively smooth location shoot in New Orleans, the company returned to Hollywood, where Feldman had not only broken his promise to leave but was insistent on a hands-on producing role. While in New Orleans, Capucine had been dressed in 1930s-inflected designs but during the studio shoot Feldman insisted she wear the latest Pierre Cardin fashions.

The producer would keep sending rewrites that were so salacious, there was no way they would be passed. The director would show the rewritten scenes to his cast and, with their consent, bin the new material. Dmytryk said that Feldman "lied to me all the way through. I almost punched him one time. It got to that degree."[28]

Dmytryk had some sympathy with Capucine, feeling that she was inevitably under the influence of her boyfriend, but his patience ran out when it came to shoot Hallie's death scene. Prior to filming the next day, Dmytryk had rehearsed the scene with the cast, almost all the main characters being present at this climax, but overnight Capucine had devised some fresh concepts to spice it up. Dmytryk recalled: "It looked like something 'choreographed' for an amateur ballet. When she had finished, Harvey was seething. The other players looked embarrassed."[29] She tried to defend her artistic choices, only for Harvey to explode in rage at her. The set was cleared of all cast and crew, and Dmytryk decided to exert the authority that had been seeping from him. He barred Andreas Voutsinas and the art director Richard Sylbert, an ally of the Capucine/Feldman faction, from the lot for the duration of the shoot, and insisted the scene be played as rehearsed. The experience of *Walk on the Wild Side* became such an endurance for Dmytryk that he forewent final cut on the picture: "I gave [Feldman] a first cut and left, because I wanted to [break] my contract with him, and it cost me 75,000 bucks in deferred money and everything, that I had to give up to get out of the damn thing. And then he cut the first part of the picture, all of which had to do with establishing [Harvey's] part.[30] … Texas background and all that, which was very important…. Then he got Blake Edwards in to reshoot some scenes and to shoot some added scenes … that I had refused to shoot."[31]

This post-first-cut tinkering is visible onscreen. Edward Dmytryk was a skilled editor, with experience stretching back to the 1930s, and all of his films exhibit tight, fluent cutting. During several sections of *Walk on the Wild Side*, in particular the opening scenes between Dove and Kitty, the connective tissue between sequences is flabby and jarring. There will be a sudden fade to black or a poor re-dubbing or a frustrating termination. The lack of fluidity creates a choppy sense of narrative and an incomplete grasp of character. Observation, for instance, of the scene where Dove and Kitty hop a freight train indicates awkward re-editing and was presumably one of the scenes which illuminated Dove's character. The superb score by Elmer Bernstein provides supple accompaniment to the action but Feldman obviously decided to have Mack David put lyrics to two of the themes after shooting had wrapped. This leads to the jarring effect of Brook Benton singing on the soundtrack while we watch the Dollhouse in-house band play Bernstein's music, with vocalist nowhere to be seen.

The script, ultimately credited to John Fante and Edmund Norris, fails to get to the core of the story's personalities, who in many cases lie stranded between inappropriate casting and befogging censorship. Fante had written *Jeanne Eagels* and would write *The Reluctant Saint* for Dmytryk, neither film meticulously perceptive of character, while Norris' career was almost entirely in television. The risk of using relatively inexperienced writers doesn't pay off, and the uncredited contribution of seasoned talent Ben Hecht is only fitfully apparent. The film's greatest cinematic flair is displayed when the camera prowls around the multi-level brothel set, observing the prostitutes and pimps through shutters and shrubbery. Richard Sylbert's set design is

Laurence Harvey and Dmytryk (both seated) are observed by cinematographer Joe MacDonald (second right, flanked by two unidentified personnel) on the set of *Walk on the Wild Side* (1962).

stylish, evocative and accurate, judging from a New Orleans location used in another simmering melodrama released the following year, *Toys in the Attic*. While cinematographer Joe MacDonald's work here is not on the level of the other black-and-white films he made with Dmytryk, *The Young Lions* and *Mirage*, the brothel set provides opportunities for atmospherically shadowy camerawork.

Walk on the Wild Side's most enduring element is the performance of Jane Fonda. Her Kitty Twist is a mesmerizing creation, a manipulative creature who most resembles the alley cat of the credit sequence and whose motto is "A good time is right, everything else is wrong." In Kitty's early encounter with Dove, her eyes flick between seduction and petulance as he rebuffs her advances. Her wounded reaction "Who are you saving it for, Dove?" is a line that the PCA objected to but which sneaked into the final cut. Fonda gives Kitty a consistency, visible in the smallest gestures. As a penniless vagrant Kitty would lick her cheap tobacco into roll-up papers. In the Dollhouse she still licks more expensive pre-rolled cigarettes out of habit. Kitty's discovery of scruples late in the film, for once overcoming her instinctive self-interest, is a character shift that Fonda renders credible, and the insolence with which she instigates a fight with another of the girls (Sherry O'Neil) is delectable. Fonda pushed her method rather too far in this scene and O'Neil ended up with

Not so easy in the Big Easy: Capucine and Laurence Harvey (both seated, in front of an unidentified actress) receive direction from Dmytryk on *Walk on the Wild Side* (1962).

a bloody nose and bruises. Adding salaciousness to injury, the gossip columnist Sidney Skolsky reported that Fonda had "hurt other important parts of Miss O'Neil."[32]

Barbara Stanwyck took on the role of Jo after Jeanne Moreau turned it down because she refused to work with Edward Dmytryk. Stanwyck had been Henry Fonda's favorite co-star and someone Jane had known since childhood. One scene required Kitty to use salty language in a confrontation with Jo, which Fonda found so uncomfortable to perform, the scene was given an alternative blocking so she wouldn't have to look Stanwyck in the face. The redoubtable presence of Stanwyck, a performer of fierce range in the classical style, is a slightly uneasy mix with the acting approaches and abilities of those she must perform opposite. Her most important scenes are with Hallie, and Capucine's talent is regrettably only to be found in her graceful looks. Stanwyck over-compensates her own performance in response to the lassitude of her French co-star. The script injects a bitchiness into their exchanges. When Hallie sneers at Jo, "What do you think I'll mature into? You?" she receives an immediate slap. They brawl when Jo threatens to reveal Hallie's unsavory past to Dove and Hallie later snaps, "Take your claws off me!" But the possessiveness is merely an expression of Jo's desire for Hallie and she tenderly tries to persuade Hallie to abandon Dove: "You've been dreaming. You've had a brief dream of young love and candy kisses. And it's all so foolish, so unreal."

There is a sharp contrast between her affection for Hallie and her contempt for her husband (Karl Swenson), a double amputee who wheels himself around on a cart, his virility diminished figuratively and literally. When he speaks of love, Jo's attitude towards men becomes apparent: "Love. Can any man love a woman for herself without wanting her body for his own pleasure? Love is understanding and sharing, enjoying the beauty of life without the reek of lust. Don't talk to me about love! What do you know, what does that young fool know, what does any man know?" The casting of Stanwyck as this coded lesbian raised eyebrows since rumors had persisted about her own private life. When Louella Parsons had questioned her acceptance of the part, Stanwyck was defensive: "What do you want them to do, get a real madam and a real lesbian?"[33] That Jo was lesbian was not apparent to everyone, as a self-congratulatory letter to Geoffrey Shurlock proved: "I saw it at a private screening today. One or two there argued there was no such thing as lesbianism in the picture. One said: 'What are you talking about? Jo was protecting the girl because she was the friend, the private friend, of the lawyer who protected the joint.' This is a tribute to you, too. Let the audience argue. We can only win such arguments over the existence or non-existence of sexual aberrations."[34] Clearly many were of the opinion that lesbianism was invisible and therefore barely existed. *Walk on the Wild Side* was released practically simultaneously with William Wyler's *The Children's Hour*, where the nature of Lillian Hellman's play was finally allowed to speak its name. It is a shame that Dmytryk's film did not manage to be a little franker, like its contemporary. But then Jo would probably have had to die.

With its director having departed and its sexual content ramped up as high as Feldman could get away with, *Walk on the Wild Side* was released in February 1962, with Columbia not shying away from its controversial nature in the poster tagline: "A side of life you never expected to see on the screen!" Such selling generally proves successful and indeed the film ended up earning a sizeable $8.6 million. After all of the grief he had put Edward Dmytryk through, Charles Feldman was less than supportive of his final product. He wrote to Joe Mankiewicz, who was on location in Rome for *Cleopatra*: "I have forgotten all about *Walk on the Wild Side*—except that I continue to get wonderful reports as to business. It really looks like a hit. Certainly the best picture boxoffice-wise that Columbia has had in a very long time, with the possible exception of [*The Guns of*] *Navarone* and *Suddenly Last Summer*. If it should play in Rome, for Christ's sake miss it, though I do think Cap is quite good. She got wonderful reviews, as I heretofore told you, throughout the entire country—with the exception of *Time* Magazine."[35] Needless to say, Feldman's assessment of the film's critical reception is selective, to say the least. For Bosley Crowther of the *New York Times* it was "incredible that anything so foolish would be made in this day and age."[36]

The experience of filming *Walk on the Wild Side* was probably the least enjoyable of Edward Dmytryk's career, and since he did not deliver the final cut, it is something of a fatherless child regarding directorial credit. It is an uneven film, entertaining in bursts but piled high with might-have-beens and hampered by the affectless performances of Capucine and Laurence Harvey. With its bitchy exchanges and iconic casting, it has acquired something of a camp reputation, one that is not wholly undeserved. The choice of a cat as a publicity hook came solely from the creative genius of

Saul Bass and was applied to the film once it was in the can. One final regret persisted with Dmytryk. If he had known, he would have put cats in the film.

The Reluctant Saint (1962)

"The rapturous flights of St. Joseph of Copertino have hardly a parallel as to frequency and duration in the lives of the saints."[37] That such a banal statement of miraculous occurrence should have been written in a 1918 biography of a saint is perhaps unsurprising. They were simpler, less questioning times. Less expected is the scholarly volume that appeared in 2016 examining St. Joseph's life, historically verifying witness accounts to his levitation and seeking explanations for the phenomenon: "Joseph's story has implications for the mind-body problem, for the study of extraordinary mental and physical phenomena, for possible links to the new physics, and for new ways of approaching the old debate between science and religion."[38] Almost exactly between these publication dates came the mid-century telling of the tale in Edward Dmytryk's *The Reluctant Saint*. Who would have expected the "ex-Communist and self-professed agnostic"[39] to have produced such a blithe celebration of a Renaissance holy-man?

"The story you are about to see is true in its essential details" reads the text that prefaces the film. In Hollywood the words "true" and "essential" are relative terms— the Truth, the partial Truth and something like the Truth. Giuseppe Desa's parentage was more complex than depicted and his religious observation more fervid. He was a severe penitent, wearing a hair shirt and an iron chain with cutting spurs, and staying on his knees for hours on end until they became infected. However, the broad strokes have basis in record. He was not quick-witted and was a poor student, somewhat ironically given his current status as patron saint of students. He was thrown out of the Capuchin order where he was a lay brother, declared "absolutely not suited for Religion, thickheaded and neglectful, ignorant and unfit for society."[40] His acceptance into the priesthood under the Franciscans had something of the miraculous about it: in the first examination, he was tested on the one passage from the Gospels that he could quote; in the second, the bishop who was in charge of the process had to leave abruptly and the exam was waived for Giuseppe and some others. Though, as we shall see, the film's version of this event is somewhat cuter. And once ordained, the levitation occurrences commenced.

A script treatment of the story by John Fante and Joseph Petracca, based on their own book, found its way into Dmytryk's hands and charmed him. Mike Frankovich at Columbia also saw potential in the story and agreed to finance it, installing Dmytryk as producer/director. Laurence Harvey expressed interest in the role but was ultimately unavailable. This can be regarded as a blessing, for saintly simplicity is a quality that Harvey did not exude. The fact that Dmytryk considered Jerry Lewis as suitable for the role ("but nobody would have believed him"[41]) makes the final casting appear somewhat perverse. Maximilian Schell had made his first Hollywood film for Dmytryk, *The Young Lions*, and had just shot *Judgment at Nuremberg* for Dmytryk's savior from the early 1950s, Stanley Kramer. After this worthy, lengthy film, heavy of theme and treatment, the light-hearted tale of a levitating Franciscan must have seemed like a joyous change of direction. Dmytryk flew to Munich to offer him the part—"entranced,"[42] he accepted. By the time *The Reluctant Saint* was released in November 1962, Schell was the freshly minted Best Actor Oscar winner for Kramer's film.

Setting up the production in Italy proved a different beast to Dmytryk's experience as producer on *Warlock* and *The Mountain*. From his base in the Excelsior Hotel on the Via Veneto in Rome, he attempted to gather an able crew and was dismayed at what he was told: "Time meant nothing; cheating and stealing were rampant; contracts were worthless."[43] He employed a colleague from his English films, John Sloan, as production manager, co-producer and bulwark against incompetence. Cyril Pennington-Richards, his cinematographer on *Obsession* and *Give Us This Day*, had turned to directing by 1961, but returned to photography one last time as a favor to Dmytryk. His name arose at a dinner party involving Dmytryk and Laurence Harvey when the actor was still a consideration for the film. Pennington-Richards said, "Laurence Harvey's secretary was an ex-girlfriend of mine. And they got talking about me and Eddie said did she think that I would go back on the camera for him? And she said, 'Why don't you go over and see him and try?' Which he did, we had lunch together and I agreed to do it."[44]

Despite the support of these trusted collaborators, the process ground Dmytryk down. He ruefully recalled what he had been told at the outset: "'The three most apt Italian mottoes,' said one informant, 'are, *Non funzione* (It doesn't work), *Non e mea culpa* (It's not my fault), and *Non so niente* (I know nothing).' Like most scuttlebutt, it was just talk—the truth was much worse."[45] He had praise for Italian electricians and grips, disdain for the rest of the crew. Costumes failed to turn up, continuity was ignored. One scene involved Giuseppe cutting down a tree and accidentally demolishing a hut. Once it was discovered that the hut was being constructed of solid cement blocks that would remain impervious to earthquake, a hydraulic ram was constructed inside the hut and timed to implement the destruction when the tree was felled. This it noisily failed to do, and the scene was cut from the script. The 60-day shooting schedule, twice what it would have taken Dmytryk to make the film in Hollywood, became an endurance. Indeed, the pre-production had already sapped his energy. Pennington-Richard's recollection of the "ghastly film"[46] was that "at the end of day one Eddie had slipped so badly it was unbelievable, it was unbelievable. Max Schell was playing in it and he took the film over…. Eddie just … didn't put his imprint on it."[47]

While Pennington-Richard's assessment of the film appears overly harsh, there is an undeniable slippage in quality regarding Dmytryk's work in *The Reluctant Saint*, even compared to *Walk on the Wild Side*, an experience that he hated. There is scarce inventiveness in camera set-up, rarely visual distinction, a jarringly uneven tone. This last mentioned can be blamed on the script, which veers from slapstick comedy to sincere devotion. Maximilian Schell is unable to credibly bridge the gap between the saccharine and the sacred. Much of the film is in a light register, and those actors who are required to give merely comic performances come off best. Schell initially plays Giuseppe broadly, with wide-eyed innocence and gormless charm. When the film shifts gear into religiosity and the character lapses into ecstatic trance, the amiable idiot squirms uneasily under the weight of divine intervention. As accomplished an actor as Schell indisputably was, the tonal shifts defeat him.

Three members of the supporting cast fare better. The chaotic pre-production did touch serendipity once when Dmytryk encountered Ricardo Montalbán at a restaurant outside Rome. The actor was able to step from the Italian swashbuckler he was finishing into the sandals of Father Raspi, Giuseppe's nemesis. Raspi's perpetual look of incredulous disdain at Giuseppe's antics provides a dose of skepticism to the blind faith on display. Akim Tamiroff, so often cast in disreputable subsidiary roles, delivers a charming comic performance as the Vicar General, for whom treatises on dogma are tedious and the simplicity of Giuseppe's explanation of the Trinity is revelatory. He insists that Giuseppe be trained for the priesthood, despite the doubts of the Franciscans and the reluctance of the novice himself, and crucially, when it appears that Giuseppe will fail his final exam, appears as a *deus ex machina* to waive his requirement to be tested.

The most accomplished performance in the film comes from a former colleague of Dmytryk's, Lea Padovani, who had appeared in *Give Us This Day* as Geremio's Italian bride. Here she plays a variation on the formidable Italian mother archetype, one who consistently greets her son by slapping him on the face in frustration and who will march him back into a male-only monastery demanding to know why he has been ejected. When Giuseppe attains his Holy Orders, an ecstatic smile erupts on her face and she welcomes the locals to her home with irrepressible pride: "He slept in my bed last night. Imagine—a priest in my bed!" And from the woman for whom he could do little right: "There was always something special about Giuseppe. Maybe the others couldn't see it, but I knew all the time." It is a delightful, impeccably timed performance from Padovani, who milks the comic potential from an imperfect script. Raspi comments to Father Giovanni (Harold Goldblatt), "Your sister is a remarkable woman, Father. If she were a man, she'd be a bishop." Giovanni responds wryly, "She'd be the Pope."

What the lengthy shooting schedule enabled, and what Hollywood could never provide, was the ability to film in settings that appeared superficially unchanged in a millennium. Roberto Rossellini had utilized authentic locations a decade earlier in his meditation on another Italian saint, *Francesco, Giullare di Dio*, and Franco Zeffirelli's Shakespeare adaptations later in the 1960s, *The Taming of the Shrew* and *Romeo and Juliet*, benefited enormously from their rich Renaissance backdrops. *The Reluctant Saint* also gains from unfolding in villages, churches and farmhouses that bore the heft of centuries, though Pennington-Richards' photography only comes into its own in the interiors, where he is able to perform his habitual magic with shadow. The decision to shoot in black-and-white may have been financial or due to the cinematographer's skill in monochrome, but the austere result is more in keeping with the tone of Rossellini's film. The flippancy of *The Reluctant Saint* had more in common with Zeffirelli's works and would likely have suited a colorful palette.

Nino Rota provides a sprightly, playful score, counterpointing the action well, consistent with other religious work from the composer. According to Richard Dyer, Rota "produced a considerable quality of sacred works throughout his life. Some of these are touched by his characteristic impish humour, but in a spirit of joy, laughter as a gift from God."[48] There is notably no scoring of the ill-judged climactic scene, the attempted exorcism of Giuseppe by Raspi. This sequence is presented in deadly earnest and is over-extended, displaying none of Dmytryk's characteristic editing zip. It sits uneasily with the rest of the film and culminates with an offscreen miraculous light source which we observe only through Raspi's stunned expression. The comic coda amuses but fails to amend for the preceding misjudgments.

In his autobiography, Edward Dmytryk professed to be satisfied with the final film. He said the Columbia executives were "delighted—with the picture, but not with its prospects."[49]

A friend told him at one showing, "I didn't want to come tonight, Eddie. I expected to be completely bored. But I enjoyed it thoroughly. You have a great film here."[50] Ultimately, he claimed it was the only film of his that never came out of the red. *The Reluctant Saint* is a competent piece of work, lying somewhere between the great film his friend told him it was and the damning judgment of Cyril Pennington-Richards: "I thought it was a terrible film and I went to John Sloane after the first day and I said, 'John, this film will be unshowable.' Because I could see the way it was going. And he said, 'Oh come, come, come, first day, you don't know as much as Eddie does,' which is quite true, I'm sure I don't! But it was quite obvious what was happening. And that film was finished, it ran for a week in Dublin, it has never been released to my knowledge. I was driving through Hampton Court one night and there was a hand-written notice, crayon, on a board, 'By kind permission of Columbia Pictures for one night only, *The Reluctant Saint*' that's all. That presumably was 16mm you know. It was sad really, very sad, 'cause Eddie was a marvellous director at one time. Technically for me he was the top."[51]

The Carpetbaggers (1964)

"Don't miss *The Carpetbaggers* because, like The Beatles, it has to be seen to be believed."[52] Producer Joseph E. Levine would have been overjoyed to see this line appear in *Cosmopolitan* in 1964, but in retrospect it is jarring to think of this movie and the Fab Four being simultaneous sensations. The Beatles inaugurated a new era of loosened strictures but *The Carpetbaggers*, although sprinkled with new-fangled sex, was defiantly old-fashioned filmmaking. The surge of the Sixties had barely begun in 1964. So, while the bracing originality of *A Hard Day's Night* made it the ninth biggest hit at the American box-office that year ($16.2 million), the pulpy pleasures of *The Carpetbaggers* put it in number four position ($36.3 million).[53] It was Paramount's biggest hit since *The Ten Commandments* in 1956.

Enjoying a chummy cigar with Elizabeth Ashley and George Peppard on the set of *The Carpetbaggers* (1964).

The Carpetbaggers was another popped button in the Production Code girdle protecting onscreen modesty. Joseph Levine was shifting into major scale production after making cheap European product starring the likes of Steve Reeves. He had bought the rights to the Harold Robbins bestseller in September 1961, paying $300,000 against fierce competition. The book was reviled in literary and religious circles but devoured by a public suddenly exposed to sexually explicit literature. In 1960 the obscenity ban on *Lady Chatterley's Lover* had been overturned by the U.S. Supreme Court and 1961 saw the publication of another sexually explicit novel, Henry Miller's *The Tropic of Cancer*. The salacious content in the book of *The Carpetbaggers*, or what Dmytryk termed "Robbins' porno sequences,"[54] combined with an expansively racy plot featuring characters thinly rooted in real-life figures, were reasons for its millions-selling status as well as major obstacles to it being put on the American screen. The new production chief at Paramount, Martin Rackin, was advised that "adapting this material to the screen calls more for a careful, even shrewd, job of editing than for any creative effort…. [R]etain the *Peyton Place* feeling…. As for the erotic content, I believe all of this can be handled by shading and excision without destroying the exploitation value of the book."[55] John Michael Hayes, screenwriter of *Peyton Place*, was appropriately handed this job of editing and excision.

The tussling over permissible content began in 1963 when Levine signed a three-picture deal with Paramount and Hayes delivered his script. Levine's aim in making pictures was to make them as commercial as possible and that meant "sex, violence and action—just the things that sell."[56] He was an uncredited producer on Jean-Luc Godard's *Le Mépris* that year and insisted that extra nude scenes of Brigitte Bardot be inserted into the final cut. Although he knew he was doomed to failure, particularly since he was operating under the auspices of a major studio, he decided to bait the Production Code with a Carroll Baker nude scene in *The Carpetbaggers*. There was a firm rejection in a letter of 5 April 1963 from the MPAA to a scene of Baker's character Rina Marlowe in her dressing room "seated on a low, almost backless seat.... We see her from the back, and all she is wearing is a pair of high-heeled slippers.... She is relaxed, poised, and from the back flawlessly beautiful."[57] Nevertheless, the scene was shot. A screen was placed around Baker sitting at the dressing table in a robe. Non-essential crew members were then required to leave the set, the camera was started, the robe taken by the wardrobe mistress and the screen removed. The quick glimpse of Carroll Baker's back was committed to celluloid. Dmytryk recalled, "A few years later, I was driving into Rome from the airport, and passed a poster of Carroll's latest Italian film. It was titled *Orgasm* [*Orgasmo*]. I wondered what the hell I'd been such a gentleman about."[58]

In the months that followed, the MPAA made further objections regarding "Rina's tendency towards nymphomania"[59] and Jennie (Martha Hyer) exposing herself to Jonas (George Peppard). It was felt that the "suggestion of a love affair between Rina and Woolf [Tom Lowell] ... tends to overload the script, rather arbitrarily in our opinion, with illicit sex."[60] The scene in which Jennie no longer exposed herself to Jonas became problematic with its suggestive dialogue; various lines were rejected:

"Have you ever been made love to in a mink coat?"

"23 different ways."[61]

And: "Have you ever acted like a mink in a mink coat?"[62]

The scene as finally shot has the saxophone on Elmer Bernstein's score doing most of the suggestive work as Jennie, swathed only in a fur wrap, is asked by Jonas:

"Do you like the coat?"

"So much, I don't know what to say."

"Then don't say anything, just show me."

Having met further ultimata that all kissing scenes be shortened, and that ceiling shots and finger gestures be removed, *The Carpetbaggers* was granted its Production Code of America Seal on 22 October. The attritional process of script revision ultimately proved beneficial for both sides. Permitting saucier content than heretofore gave the impression that the MPAA was moving with the times, while giving Levine a tantalizing hook on which to hang his promotion. Despite the fact that Carroll Baker's bare back was only used in the European release of the film, its very existence was used as an exploitative tactic. *Newsweek* reported that "once the wraps were back on Carroll, they were off the press agents, who lost no time in getting the exposure exposed."[63] Levine knew that claiming the moral high ground would only whet the public's appetite for the low ground: "The book was filth. Filth and dirt. We don't have any of that in the picture, but the wonderful thing about the film is that you have the feeling that you are reading the book."[64] It was a hugely successful publicity tease.

The three main characters in the film are tycoon Jonas Cord (unmistakable echoes of Howard Hughes), Hollywood star Rina Marlowe (hints of Jean Harlow) and

Nevada Smith (a Western actor amalgam of Tom Mix and Ken Maynard). Edward Dmytryk was approached by Martin Rackin and signed to the film in March 1963. His contact with his producer was minimal: "I saw Levine on the first day of shooting, he came out to have some publicity pictures taken with the girls. I didn't see him again until we went to preview in Chicago. So, you know, I did everything."[65] Everyone was in agreement that the star was the title of the best-selling book so major marquee names were not necessary. George Peppard was best known at this point for his role in *Breakfast at Tiffany's*, as well as being one of the expansive cast-list of *How the West was Won*. On the latter film Carroll Baker, in reality two and a half years Peppard's junior, had played his mother. When they were cast together in *The Carpetbaggers*, she played his stepmother. Baker found him "a pretentious, egotistical brat,"[66] recalling his insincerity on *How the West was Won*: "Although I had met his wife and children, even in front of me he denied their existence. He claimed to be a bachelor, and he had conveniently dropped seven years off his age."[67] A few years later on Dmytryk's film, he had sunk even lower in her estimation: "He acquired delusions of being far more than just a talented young actor who was working his way up the ladder of success. I got the impression he felt he was God's gift to women and the cinema."[68] Acting as though he had never met her before or was aware of her marital status, he was insistent about getting to bed with her: "He showed up uninvited at my house late one night and gave me a stern warning: 'If you don't have a love affair with me, I'll make love to Elizabeth Ashley.'"[69] Dmytryk recorded no ego problems with his lead actor but judged him to have a "hard, poker-faced personality."[70]

Carroll Baker, on the other hand, was "very, very intelligent"[71] according to Dmytryk and she "worked extremely hard."[72] Finding an actress with physical youth and innate maturity for the role of Rina proved a challenge in 1963. The director believed that Jean Harlow and Loretta Young possessed a type of worldly wise juvenility that had existed in the 1920s but that hadn't outlasted the 1930s. Around ten girls were tested for the role, one of them was Katharine Ross, whom they liked but felt she lacked the necessary qualities for Rina—the test was passed on to Universal who gave Ross a contract on the back of it. Carroll Baker and Martha Hyer, who played Jennie Denton, one of Jonas Cord's conquests, were ultimately cast by Levine, the only time he exercised his producer's prerogative, according to Dmytryk. Baker had met Levine at a charity ball in New York: "He said, upon meeting me, 'You're just the girl I want for my next film. It's the best part you've had since *Baby Doll*, but you have to take my word for that. Without any question, you must accept the part and shake my hand to bind the deal.'"[73] Without knowing what she was accepting, Carroll Baker shook his hand. Dmytryk did cast the other major female role, that of Cord's wife Monica. He found Elizabeth Ashley to be an "exceptional actress."[74]

Twenty-three years after Dmytryk had given Alan Ladd an early break in *Her First Romance*, he was to direct him in his final film. Levine said that Ladd was "Edward Dmytryk's personal choice"[75] for the role of Nevada Smith, but Dmytryk himself wrote, "I had serious doubts about Ladd's ability to handle the part of Nevada Smith, but Rackin felt a strong obligation to Alan for past favors, and insisted we take a chance."[76] Although Ladd stayed sober for the duration of the shoot, his problems with alcohol had impacted on both his physical condition and his ability to perform. Carroll Baker wrote: "I remember how his hands used to shake. One day during a scene with me his drink spilled over the sides of his glass because of the trembling. Out of sheer frustration, he punched the door of the set with his hand still holding the glass and cut himself quite badly."[77] An assistant director was instructed by the studio to record the number of spoiled takes and to note in each case the person responsible for wasting time and money. Ladd reacted nervously to this culture of blame but Baker remembered his colleagues rallying around him: "Our director, Eddie Dmytryk, when he saw Alan begin to flounder, would jump in with, 'Cut! It's my fault. I'd like to go again.'"[78] The only one not to display this compassion was George Peppard, according to Baker.

The parallels between Jonas Cord and Howard Hughes are intentional and unmistakable, not least the acquisition of a Hollywood studio (Hughes bought RKO, Cord buys the studio of Bernard Norman, played by Martin Balsam) and a pioneering interest in aviation. Hughes famously developed the *Spruce Goose*, the largest flying boat ever built, which held the record for the airplane with the largest wing span for 70 years but which only flew once. There is something of the *Spruce Goose* about Levine and Dmytryk's *The Carpetbaggers*. This is a long film, bulky and loaded with character and incident, but it lumbers at a low altitude and never truly soars into flight. Dmytryk's renown for efficient filmmaking, bringing productions in on time and on budget, results in this case in efficiency without flair, a long succession of scenes unspooling without the imaginative glint of which he was capable. Partially this can be attributed to the budget—the film came in $127,000 under budget with a final cost of $3,249,000 which, for a two-and-a-half-hour movie, was not sufficient for a "wow" factor to appear onscreen. The shoot involved 51 days filming in the studio and only eight days on location. Thus, much of the film takes place in offices or hotel rooms, with a production design that tends towards the bland, and one senses that Dmytryk was adapting to the constraints imposed by Joseph Levine at the expense of his own signature. The Paramount production files contain a memo from March 1963 which detail ways in which to reduce the budget by $224,000, among them a more economical way to shoot a car crash involving Rina. That this dramatic moment has muted impact can likely be attributed to budgetary limitations.

There are other curious missed opportunities. One scene has Rina cavorting on a glass chandelier high above a party of dozens of costumed extras before the chandelier comes crashing down. The sequence has clearly involved some preparation and is related in Carroll Baker's autobiography as an incident that nearly caused her serious injury, but it lasts precisely 30 seconds onscreen and its effect is throwaway. The scenes that take place on Hollywood soundstages should have been a gift for vibrant visuals but Dmytryk takes his cue from the uninspiring set with unexciting direction. Dmytryk worked here with two former collaborators, cinematographer Joe MacDonald and composer Elmer Bernstein. Neither of them reaches the heights that they had achieved on earlier Dmytryk films, Bernstein's score being functional and unmemorable, MacDonald's photography disappointingly flat. There are occasional flashes of MacDonald's visual ability that distinguished *Broken Lance* and *Warlock*—such as Cord confronting his childhood demons, half of his face obscured in black shadow, lurid red wallpaper leering like a primal force behind him—but these moments are too few.

At one point, Cord's wife Monica berates him with "Would you stop talking like a damn footnote!"—a criticism that could be leveled at the script in general. The dialogue is so overloaded with overwritten epigrams that most lines carry the embossing of typewriter keys. Characters become repositories of witticisms defined by a single characteristic rather than fleshed-out complex beings. It is hard to credit John Michael Hayes as the screenwriter of four Hitchcock films, including *Rear Window*. Thus, Jonas Cord is irredeemably unpleasant to everyone he encounters, a trait that is explained away by his fear of having inherited the insanity that somehow killed his twin brother at the age of nine. His associate McAllister (Lew Ayres) delivers a poorly structured, pop-psychology speech about Cord's failings that concludes with "Who knows, you might even be the devil." Though the script lacks the satisfaction of rounded characterizations, it provides the pleasures of bitchy put-downs and winking *double entendres*. Monica is asked by Cord what she wants to see on her honeymoon, to which she replies, "Lots of lovely ceilings." Rina starts her seduction of a character called David with a Gershwin lyric: "Little David was small, but oh my!" Deprived of the promised nudity, the 1964 audience gobbled up such unaccustomed naughtiness.

Carroll Baker was underrated as an actress, but Rina's vicissitudes of character defeat even her talent. Rina flips wildly between utter detestation of Cord and uncontrollable desire for him, and is draped seductively in Edith Head creations at the beginning of almost all of her scenes. She possesses clear echoes of Jean Harlow—for one of the scripts she is assigned, the Africa-set *Blue Goddess*, read Harlow's *Red Dust*. *The Carpetbaggers* gives as accurate a telling of Jean Harlow's story as Levine's production of the following year, *Harlow*, also starring Carroll Baker—which is to say, hardly at all. Alongside Baker, Elizabeth Ashley also gives a good account of herself in tackling Hayes' dialogue, but Peppard is an uncharismatic lead. Edward Dmytryk's daughter, credited as Victoria Jean, made her film debut as Jo Ann, the daughter of Cord and Monica, in a single scene where Jo Ann and Monica are confronted with the fur-swathed naked form of Jennie. Vicky Dmytryk recalls her father's style of direction was to delegate: "Dad wasn't exactly an extrovert, so I don't remember him as being involved with much that happened on the set."[79]

The film is rapacious in its consumption of character actors—within the first five minutes, Dmytryk regulars Leif Erickson and Charles Lane are introduced and summarily dispatched.[80] One of the most engaging scenes is when movie mogul Norman (Martin Balsam, reliably excellent) and agent Dan Pierce (Bob Cummings, effectively sleazy) turn the tables on Cord and make him pay over the odds for Norman's studio. For Dmytryk, Cummings was "pure actor, pure ham…. But a bright ham. And a very good comedian."[81] Alan Ladd gave "one of the best performances of his life,"[82] according to Dmytryk, and his character was such a successful presence he was revived two years later in a prequel called *Nevada Smith* starring Steve McQueen. The concluding fight scene between Cord and Nevada is a blistering three minutes requiring genuine effort from Ladd, Peppard and their stunt doubles, with Ladd requiring a skull X-ray after a close shot resulted in him striking his head on a mantelpiece. By accident or design, Nevada Smith's final line in the film is more than reminiscent of Rhett Butler's in *Gone with the Wind*. Asked by Cord, "Nevada, what can I do?," he pauses at the door and responds, "Jonas, I haven't the faintest idea." They were Alan Ladd's last words onscreen. By the time the film was released, he was dead from an accidental drug and alcohol overdose.

The Carpetbaggers, which had begun shooting on 13 June 1963, wrapped on 28 August, five days ahead of schedule. The originally shot final scene, a particularly schmaltzy cocktail involving a fresh proposal of marriage from Cord to Monica with the cloying input of their daughter Jo Ann, was shelved and a new one between Cord and Monica shot on 30 October. The schmaltz was toned down but the blandness was resurgent, with Monica's final line—"You need me"—weak, and the location—a filing room at her office—insipid. This was of no consequence to Joseph Levine. The man who was reputed to have said "You can fool all of the people all of the time if the advertising is right and the budget is big enough"[83] had his publicity hooks and spent the nine months between the completion of the shoot and the Gala Premiere at Grauman's employing them. Carroll Baker was given an enormous publicity push, was engaged in person as much as she could tolerate and when that wasn't possible, as in a promotional tour of Australia, Levine sent along one of her dresses with instructions for holding lookalike contests. It was a triumphant campaign that succeeded beyond anyone's expectations, with the possible exception of Levine. In April 1965 the taboo of female nudity on the American screen would be broken by Sidney Lumet's *The Pawnbroker*, a dark and serious piece of work. *The Carpetbaggers* was the fluffy preamble to this milestone, a striptease of a film—promising much but coyly not delivering.

Where Love Has Gone (1964)

On Good Friday 1958 the fatal stabbing of her abusive lover Johnny Stompanato by her daughter Cheryl Crane had the potential to derail Lana Turner's career. Instead it boosted the takings of her current film *Peyton Place* and helped make a huge hit of the following year's *Imitation of Life*. In testimony, Crane recalled small-time gangster Stompanato threatening her mother: "You'll never get away from me. I'll cut you good, baby. You'll never work again. And don't think I won't also get your mother and your kid."[84] Despite Turner allegedly asking the Beverly Hills police chief to let her take the blame, Cheryl Crane confessed and was found to have committed justifiable homicide in order to protect her mother's life. The scandalous cocktail proved intoxicating to the public and it should come as no surprise that Harold Robbins seized on this dramatic moment and, much as he had done in *The Carpetbaggers*, lightly fictionalized it and constructed a whole trashy novel around it.

The comment made by Bette Davis that if there had been more credible interplay between her and her co-star Susan Hayward in the film adaptation of *Where Love Has Gone*, "it wouldn't have turned out so trashy"[85] is thus somewhat ironic. Silk purses have on occasion been made out of sows' ears, but not in this case. Everyone seemed to recognize that the script by John Michael Hayes was not up to the standard of his *Rear Window, The Children's Hour* or even *Peyton Place*, and, according to Dmytryk, "even Hayes admitted it lacked quality."[86] But for Paramount, the chance to reunite the producer, director and scriptwriter of *The Carpetbaggers* was an opportunity for lightning to strike twice. Dmytryk had one film left on his Paramount contract, having been paid for one project that hadn't got off the ground, but the production slate was thin: "[I]n a moment of overconfidence, and feeling I couldn't decently take money for another unrealized picture, I agreed to take on the assignment. I felt that, given a good cast, I could rewrite the material and wind up with a decent enough movie. I had done it a number of times and had usually succeeded."[87]

Susan Hayward was signed up first as the Lana Turner surrogate, although her character Valerie Hayden was a successful sculptor rather than actress. Despite a few decades of playing murderesses, alcoholics and assorted firebrands, Hayward apparently balked at playing a sexually promiscuous woman and demanded that the moral tone of the script be raised. She was not alone in this wish. The script that had been completed in February 1963 underwent a prolonged tussle between Paramount and the Production Code of America in the autumn of that year before the film went into production in December. The statues of male athletes in Valerie's studio were not to be completely nude; a sheer nightgown worn by Valerie was not to be transparent and care was to be taken in ripping it; the line "I'm only 14 years old" was to be deleted. Dani, Valerie's daughter played by Joey Heatherton, was aged a year to become 15.

Two sexually connoted lines became particular sources of contention: "You see darling, you're not the first today. I'm just getting warmed up!" and "That could have happened horseback riding. You know that Dave, that's the oldest excuse in the book." After two months of concerns being expressed about the acceptability of these lines, a story conference at Paramount agreed to shoot the scenes both with and without the "offensive" wording. Both lines made it into the release cut.

Bette Davis was cast as Hayward's mother, though she felt too young for such casting, given that she was her senior by only nine years. A white-haired wig was employed to create the illusion, and a $125,000 pay check (as against $300,000 for Hayward) was employed to soothe the ego. The wig was foisted on Davis against her wishes: "I felt Mrs. Hayden would have her hair dyed and never allow herself to look like a white-haired old lady. The studio felt the white hair necessary to establish a definite age difference between Miss Hayward and me."[88] Despite her role being clearly subsidiary, her contract stipulated that "Miss Davis is to receive the same treatment in all respects to Miss Hayward's billing."[89] By the mid–1960s, the two formidable actresses had been at the top of their profession for decades and neither was prepared to concede status to the other. Davis claimed that they could have been good friends "but she was aloof,"[90] and was not the first co-star to comment on the unapproachability of Susan Hayward.

Dmytryk found Hayward to be "not a very good actress, and she knew it"[91] and Davis to be "an extraordinary actress and an unusually hard worker."[92] "They were exact opposites."[93] His plans to rewrite the script were scuppered by a combination of Davis's lack of tact and Hayward's insecurity. He arrived on set one morning early in the shoot with some freshly reworked scenes and discussed them with Davis in her dressing room—"She was always ready before her call."[94] Davis was in agreement and, while Hayward was still being made up, Davis walked onto the set and greeted the crew: "Hold everything, boys. We've just made a few changes in the scene."[95] This behavior enflamed Hayward, who summoned her agent and pointed out that she was contractually obliged only to play the script that she had originally been offered. Fearful of her co-star's role being beefed up at the expense of her own, she would accept no rewrites.

The mood on the set thereafter remained frosty. Mike Connors, playing Valerie's ex-husband Luke, recalled, "I remember it, and so did Eddie Dmytryk, as an atmosphere of armed truce—and a mean, icy truce it was, too."[96] Bette Davis expressed frustration that a rapport with Hayward had failed to materialize: "I'd admired Hayward for years. Her *Smash Up: The Story of a Woman* was simply wonderful, but she wouldn't give me anything in our scenes. It was like playing to a blank wall. After weeks of this, keeping my temper and being polite to her on the set, I'd really had it. Everyone else on the picture was great. Anyway, after my last scene, just before I went into my dressing room, I took off the wig and threw it at her. 'Fuck you, Susie!' I said and that was the last time I ever saw her."[97]

However, the saga of the unsatisfactory script hadn't yet reached its climax. The film finished shooting in February but in March an additional climactic scene was written for Bette Davis in which Mrs. Hayden goes mad ("Valerie, please come down! I want to tell you I love you! I love you Valerie! I love you!"[98]) and slashes her own portrait. Davis refused to shoot the new scene, arguing that if she had known her character would end up insane, she would have played the matriarch differently throughout the picture. At the start of June while shooting *Hush … Hush Sweet Charlotte*, the 20th Century–Fox film that was suffering its own production difficulties with Joan Crawford, Davis received a court injunction forbidding her from appearing in any film until she had completed her scenes on *Where Love Has Gone*. In the District Court of Appeals she managed to stay the Paramount injunction and at a subsequent hearing on 29 June, the court found in her favor and ruled that for reasons of artistic integrity she was not required to film the new scene. That portrait wasn't going to slash itself though, and in the released film it was Susan Hayward who performed the honors.

The film wrapped on 10 February 1964, four days ahead of schedule, and $96,000 under its initial budget of $2,989,000. Dmytryk was respected in the business for his adherence to schedule but this degree of efficiency speaks of a man not wholly engaged with the project, completing a contractually obliged film. And when Edward Dmytryk was not enthused by his material, the result was generally visible onscreen. *Where Love Has Gone* exhibits a bland aesthetic, with few attempts to add visual spice to the mundane script. Much of this can be blamed on producer and budget. Scene after interior scene depicts upper-class rooms of suffocating opulence or airless municipal buildings, with rare sorties into the open. When the film does have the chance for some visual variety, it ducks the opportunity. Once Valerie decides to abandon her dull married existence and hit the town, she is greeted by the doorman of a nightclub (with "SEX-ATIONAL FLOOR SHOW" on the marquee) as a long-lost valued customer. She flounces through the door to the decadent delights inside, leaving the audience outside with her car.

There is a pleasing symmetry to the manner in which Dmytryk introduces his female stars. Susan Hayward is introduced in a hung-over haze, slumped face down on her bed, the camera dollying in on her as the phone rings. Lighting her first cigarette, Valerie learns it is her mother, the last voice she wants to hear. She terminates the call and gulps down some aspirin with her coffee. Cut to close-up on Bette Davis, regal of posture and refined of accent. The camera performs a reverse movement, pulling back from her and revealing the luxury of her home. It is a neat juxtaposition of these women—mother assured in her surroundings, daughter struggling to keep it together. This film is a woman's picture par excellence. Despite the contractually stipulated equal-sized credit that Michael Connors receives beneath Hayward and Davis, he is no acting equal to either and his character is reactive to the whims of the women. DeForest Kelley plays Sam Corwin, a lover of Valerie's, but he has ultimately no more agency than the succession of men Valerie hosts in her bedroom. Dani the daughter and the probation officer Miss Spicer, firmly played by Jane Greer, are the other characters that propel the story forward. The men are disposable.

Valerie is an artist whose muse appears to operate in tandem with her libido. Her art suffers when marriage to Luke domesticizes her, and, as he gets ground into a job for the Hayden family business that he didn't want and uses alcohol as a refuge from his self-loathing, she fumes in unfulfilled solitude. One night spent waiting hopefully in her negligee, only to be informed that her husband lies in a drunken stupor elsewhere, is the night she snaps. She smashes a photo of Luke and pulls a red dress from her wardrobe, as a prelude to recommencing her hedonistic lifestyle. Art critic Sam is satisfied with this outcome: "The old Valerie Hayden is back. Sculptor. Pagan. Alley cat." Edith Head regularly costumes her in red thereafter, an emblem of her status as a voracious woman, most strikingly in a scene with Miss Spicer, whose disapproval is fully on display. The censor, with the consent of Hayward, may have prevented full detailing of Valerie's sexual appetite but references to naked male models in her studio leave the viewer in little doubt that, as Sam tells her, "With you, art and sex go hand in hand." The makers have some fun by slipping in character judgments under the radar, such as a shot of Valerie performing a symbolic castration on a metal sculpture with her blowtorch.

The Hayden family is replete with emotionally dysfunctional females, stemming from the current matriarch. Davis plays her with crisp diction and an entitled froideur. Mrs. Hayden dominates and manipulates each character to her will, right from the moment we encounter her in a flashback to 1944, when she rapidly decides that homecoming hero Luke is the man that her daughter will marry. That plan succeeds and she buys them a house, complete with portrait of herself displayed prominently. Just like her less than benign influence, the eyes of the portrait "always seem to follow you, wherever you go." She names the couple's baby, arranges for Luke's independent business ventures to fail and decides when it is time for Valerie to seek a divorce. When she rebukes her daughter with "You have only one concept of love, a vile and sinful one," Valerie shoots back with "When you're dying of thirst, you'll drink from a mudhole!" The lack of maternal affection drives Valerie into the arms of men: "I don't have many women friends."

The sins of the mothers seep down to Dani, a sullenly overwrought performance from Heatherton. She loses her virginity, we must assume, to her mother's lover and festers in self-loathing after killing him: "I love all the wrong people and I hate all the right ones." Luke, who has been forcibly ejected from his daughter's life by the Hayden women, initially inspires our sympathy but his wife's philandering ways lead him to slap her and attempt marital rape: "What do you think you're going to do?" asks Valerie when he has thrown her on the bed. "What I've got a right to do!" is his response. She calls his bluff by encouraging him to have sex with her as lovelessly as with a prostitute, a taunt that has him heading for the door. Despite the wrangling with the MPAA, producer Levine has prevailed and the sexual content of the film is rather raw for 1964. Depictions are muted but references are blunt: "A rich hooker! You're not a woman, you're a disease!" What the script lacks in subtlety, it makes up for in salaciousness.

The climax is muffled. The courtroom revelation that Dani had been attempting to kill her mother when their mutual lover got in the way is delivered by Susan Hayward without the spirited flare that she could be capable of. A flashback would have boosted the scene but the filmmakers had presumably expected Hayward to provide the necessary fireworks. Valerie dashes from the courtroom and speeds off in her convertible. The film gulps in air as she drives past a picturesque succession of San Francisco landmarks on her way home. There, blinded by glycerin tears, she delivers the requisite slashing of the matriarchal portrait before stabbing herself with the same chisel that had killed her lover. Now a contrite mother, she has abandoned the red dresses and wears a more sober Edith Head design for her self-sacrifice.

Savvy producer Joseph Levine was well aware that exploitative material benefits from full "exploitation"[99] and demanded total merchandising including product placement: "United Airlines will receive excellent identification."[100] It proved to be another financial success but was poorly received by the critics, the *Newsweek* review being particularly sniffy: "One watches *Where Love Has Gone* in disbelief, wondering how, in a movie from a major studio, there could be such universal and serene ineptitude.... Joey Heatherton the world's least promising starlet.... And one must credit Miss Hayward at least for slashing a terrible portrait of Bette to shreds.... Still, Bette Davis is splendid."[101] The film is a choice credit of nobody involved but Dmytryk wryly recalled the reaction of the studio: "The New York executives, who hadn't broken into unrestrained cheering after the finish of *The Carpetbaggers*, which was to make them a fortune, called me after viewing *Where Love Has Gone*, to say they considered it one of the best films Paramount had turned out in a number of years."[102]

Mirage (1965)

By the time *Mirage* was released in May 1965, the fade-out had begun for the black-and-white Hollywood movie. The year of 1966 would be the final year that the Academy awarded separate Oscars for achievements in cinematography,

art direction and cos-
tume design in color and
black-and-white. The main
black-and-white contend-
ers that year were *Who's
Afraid of Virginia Woolf?*,
Seconds and *The Fortune
Cookie*, all of which have
matured into classics. The
first two were at the "arty"
end of the commercial
spectrum and the third
was the last monochrome
gasp of an old master. The
glossy, audience-chasing
pursuit thrillers of the era
had all migrated to color.
*Charade, Arabesque, Blind-
fold, The Prize* and their ilk
reveled in the colorful situations the perplexed hero
and heroine found them-
selves in.

Central Park is over there: Dmytryk with Gregory Peck on location for *Mirage* (1965).

So, to choose to shoot *Mirage* in black-and-white
was more an artistic decision than a commercial one. It was the last black-and-white
feature film[103] released by Universal in the 1960s, and thus before choosing not to
shoot in color had become a directorial statement. The choice in this case is entirely
appropriate and works wonderfully. From the opening scene, a skyscraper power
outage shot superbly by frequent Dmytryk collaborator Joe MacDonald, our amnesiac hero is stranded in a world that he is at a loss to understand. The sense of uneasy
artificiality evoked by the cinematography creates a much more threatening environment than the gloss of Technicolor would. The high contrast photography resembles
that of *Bunny Lake is Missing* from the following year, in which the heroine is similarly cast adrift in an alien-seeming city. For that film, director Otto Preminger "told
the lab technicians to make the blacks blacker and the whites whiter,"[104] and Dmytryk
and MacDonald's palette is similarly stark. These deep shadows were a clear artistic
decision: "I worked with that [*noir*] style whenever I feel it's necessary. For instance,
Mirage."[105]

After the false starts of *The Left Hand of God* and *The End of the Affair*, Dmytryk
finally got to work with Gregory Peck. Peck's production company was operating in
co-operation with Universal on the film and hired scriptwriter Peter Stone, who had
written the touchstone for this type of romantic thriller, *Charade*. At the first script
conference, Peck noted the humor in certain of the characters and expressed the
hope that his character David Stillwell would be given some funny leading-man lines.

However, Cary Grant's character in the earlier film was much in control of events while Stillwell is a victim of them. Dmytryk felt that "Peck has wit, but it is very dry. What's more, the character of a man seeking his lost persona has hardly the makings of a stand-up comic."[106]

After Peck had left the meeting, Dmytryk addressed Stone's reservations about scripting a witty amnesiac and told him to give Peck his desired wisecracks. He was confident that Peck was an honest enough actor to realize at the first rehearsal that the quips from him were inappropriate. This assessment was accurate, the funny lines were dropped and Stillwell remained doggedly confused. Peck's heavily annotated copy of the final screenplay of 12 October 1964 reflects his interpretation of a stiller Stillwell: "Keep it simple…. Not too much voice…. Don't be nonchalant"[107] His summation of the character occurs on the first page: "Watch being *vocal*. Makes it pompous. *Clear*—not too kind. Intel[ligent]."[108]

The humor in *Mirage* is mainly centered around Ted Caselle, the private detective perfectly incarnated by Walter Matthau. Peck had seen him onstage: "I think my main contribution to the film was that I hired Walter and virtually launched him on his screen career."[109] This is something of a revisionist viewpoint. Matthau had been an established supporting actor on screen since the mid–1950s and had made strong impressions in *Charade* and *Strangers When We Meet*, at the very least. It is true though that the trajectory of his career really began to soar at this point. Not everyone recognized the direction of the trajectory. Dmytryk recalled:

"One day I was congratulating Matthau on a particularly well-played scene. I was, perhaps, a little patronizing. 'You should have a great career in films,' I assured him. 'You can be one of our top character actors.' 'Character actor, hell!' said Matthau. 'I'm going to be one of the top leading men.'"[110] A press report indicated that Matthau was prepared to fight for the limelight: "Walter Matthau recently lost an argument with director Ed Dmytryk over cuts Mr. D had made in the movie *Mirage*—but it was a beauty of an argument that developed repercussions all the way to the Board of Directors!"[111]

The 44-day shoot began on Saturday 24 October 1964 in New York City on Broadway near Columbus Circle, and continued the following week with scenes on Central Park West and the Zoo. *Mirage* is a film that has a sinewy sense of Upper Manhattan, and 15 days were spent filming there. Over the credits, the camera pans across the familiar skyscraper skyline until one of the buildings is plunged into darkness. In this opening power-cut sequence, the deep shadows are as black as *noir*. We discover Gregory Peck's character David Stillwell as disorientated as we are by the pervasive blackout. The tone shifts from jokey—a female employee tells a colleague, "I just had to get out of there—their hands are grabby enough when the lights are on"—to the ominous appearance of Josephson (Kevin McCarthy) mentioning a character named Major to the perplexing encounter with Shelah (Diane Baker) on the stairwell, as they descend together by torchlight into the darkness in a sequence lit with striking accomplishment.

The fractured state of Stillwell's memory is conveyed by sharp jump-cuts to flashback, a rather novel technique in the commercial sphere. For this innovation, Dmytryk would "happily take the responsibility…. During our story conferences, we debated at length the method of identifying these shots. In the script, Stone had suggested oil dissolves ... but I felt the time factor in any dissolve would invalidate the instantaneous triggering that was so vital to our film.... I decided to try straight cuts—if they didn't work at the preview, other solutions could be sought. They worked—and have worked in many theatrical and TV films ever since. But at that time, it was a brand-new technique, never before used in a film, certainly not in Hollywood."[112] Dmytryk pushes his claim for ownership too far—jump-cuts were familiar in *Nouvelle Vague* cinema, for instance—but he is correct about their effectiveness in *Mirage*. The momentary stabs of illumination into Stillwell's consciousness, often just a line or an image, find perfect expression in the technique. Dmytryk was justified in not underestimating the ability of the public to process this fresh style of editing.

The music cues from Quincy Jones assist the audience in this respect. One flashback to two men talking together under a tree is accompanied by an orchestral moment that is strongly reminiscent of Bernard Herrmann's *Vertigo*, though Jones does not rely on Hitchcockian tropes for his score. Gregory Peck's revisionist streak appeared again with respect to Jones. In correspondence he wrote of *Mirage* being Jones' "first major motion picture score,"[113] whereas it was in fact his second American feature film after *The Pawnbroker*.

Jones uses a pleasing mix of styles in the film, from lushly romantic to jazzily syncopated. Intriguingly a jolt of recognition at the cause of amnesia is underlaid with a four-note riff that is almost identical to that which would introduce Michael Jackson's *Bad*, produced by Quincy Jones, over 20 years later.

The casting of Diane Baker is one of the weaker elements of the film. Though an able actress, her screen personality is not sufficiently vibrant to pierce through the murk of Stillwell's amnesia. She enjoyed working with Peck ("He was a sharing actor. He liked the joint effort of making the scene work."[114]), but there is a dull pallor to the romantic scenes between his befuddled male and her enigmatic female. She respected Dmytryk, even if his hands-off attitude to her performance was not her preferred way of working: "He was a really bright man and very talented, but he was very calm and quiet during the making of this. It was almost as if he was subdued."[115] Shelah is a duplicitous dame, whose motives are continually suspect and who is complicit with the head villain, Major Gilkuddy (Leif Erickson). It's a role in the mold of Eva Marie Saint's Eve in *North by Northwest*, another Herrmann theme that Quincy Jones consciously references. Two much more interesting prospects than Diane Baker for the role were Tippi Hedren and Leslie Caron. Hedren was unable to accept the offer because she was still under contract to Hitchcock ("I knew Hitchcock was doing everything in his power to keep his promise to ruin my career"[116]) and Caron turned it down because of her then partner: "Warren [Beatty] made me refuse it, to the chagrin of my agents. In retrospect, I'm sorry I declined the part, too."[117]

The wit of Stone's script and Dmytryk's deft handling of it is on display in Stillwell's encounter with Lester (Jack Weston). Stillwell's disorientation having left the blackout building makes him feel like he has lost two years of his life. So much has changed—Idlewild has changed its name to Kennedy Airport and elevator operators, the Fran Kubeliks of this world, have been made redundant by voice recordings. Lester joins Stillwell in the elevator of his apartment block and jokes about whether or not this is progress. "What are you doing for dinner tonight, honey?" he quips to the absent operator. "Watch your step please'" is the disembodied response. Lester is one of the Major's heavies and ambushes Stillwell as he enters his apartment. When he switches on the TV, his remarks about the onscreen wrestling bout is a sharp comment on Hollywood's mid–1960s identity crisis: "I know it's supposed to be fixed, but so is everything else. Now that all the westerns have gone psycho, this is the only place left where you can tell for sure who the bad guys are." When Stillwell jumps on Lester, Dmytryk slyly cuts to the television and, as we watch the wrestling, he lets the commentator describe the offscreen struggle: "Boy, the Arab never knew what hit him." And when the bad guy has been overcome: "Well, I guess that's it."

While Stillwell attempts to navigate his way of his mental mire, with the assistance of Caselle, the combative obstruction of Lester and Willard (George Kennedy) and the disingenuous friendliness of Shelah and Josephson, *Mirage* maintains its grip through the bewilderment. In a film such as this, which had effectively been trademarked by Hitchcock, the fingerprints of the Master have been deliberately dabbed on certain scenes. The shot of peace campaigner Calvin (Walter Abel) falling from a skyscraper cannot help but evoke the demise of Hitchcock's *Saboteur* in 1943. The reaction of bystanders to this death plunge, the key to Stillwell's amnesia, is realistically blasé. There is giggling at the comment, "Couldn't he wait for the elevator?" and someone recalls experimenting with dropping watermelons from an upper-story window. A shot of a watermelon smashing on a sidewalk is inserted into Stillwell's flashbacks on a few occasions, though Gregory Peck expressed reservations about the shot and wanted it cut altogether. There is in fact a notably visceral portrayal of violence in the film, an aspect the Production Code highlighted at the script stage: "beating is unacceptably brutal."[118] A fistfight between Stillwell and Willard pulls the viewer right into the brawl, with tight close-ups on Stillwell's face as he punches his assailant unconscious. When they encounter each other again at the climax, Willard declares, "I owe you some pain, Mr. Stillwell," which he duly delivers. The impact of blows is palpable. During another *noir*-tinged scene, in an apartment shrouded in inky shadows, Stillwell forces Shelah, her complicity in the conspiracy increasingly obvious, to look at the corpse of an innocent character. Similarly, Dmytryk forces us to the realization that punch-ups aren't pretty.

The generic pleasures of the film are plentiful. Stillwell darts into a crowd of schoolchildren to escape an assailant which leads to an exciting pursuit through Central Park and a well-photographed stand-off in a tunnel with Josephson at one end and Willard at the other. There is an encounter with a skeptical doctor who provides the genre requirement of some medical background information: "You've stubbed your conscious mind and you've put a bandage of forgetfulness on it until it recovers." Peck wrote of this scene in his script, "I owe the *audience* here an inner cry *for help* at this nightmare closing in." Matthau's performance as Caselle, the novice private detective so ill-suited to the tough guy role that he orders Dr. Pepper in a bar, is a masterclass in relaxed comic delivery. On the page, the line "I can't help it—I'm excessively happy-go-lucky" is unexceptional. Matthau finds the exceptional in it. A fizz escapes from the film with the premature death of Caselle.

Mirage unfortunately deflates during the climactic scene. All of the surviving characters gather in the office of the Major, and after Willard pulverizes Stillwell, he plays Russian Roulette against our hero's temple. Before the second chamber is emptied, Stillwell's life flashes before his eyes and he recalls the traumatic moment of realizing his mentor Calvin is a pawn of the military. Calvin's lines as he looks out of his office window to the streets far below is strongly reminiscent of Harry Lime's Ferris-Wheel speech in *The Third Man*: "Look at them. Do they look like human beings? Or ants? You're quite right, David. They are statistics." Watching Calvin accidentally plunge to his death has caused the rupture in Stillwell's memory. Gregory Peck's character note in the script at this point indicates the change in his character from victim to manipulator of the situation: "NOW I KNOW I DIDN'T KILL HIM I'M MYSELF AGAIN." The lengthy flashback combined with a surfeit of exposition become an obstacle to momentum and the film rather fizzles out. The rapprochement between Stillwell and the highly complicit Shelah signally fails to convince. Not long before their romantic coda, Stillwell had skewered her culpability: "Do you really think that keeping me alive will help buy back your soul?"

Mirage nevertheless emerges as one of the best of the mystery caper sub-genre that flourished in the 1960s. It was generally well-received—"prime-quality suspense"[119]; "veteran Edward Dmytryk has directed with a quick hand … and some of his sequences … are little masterpieces of cinema"[120]; "Take *Mirage* as a popular appeal feature and it might be a failure. Put it into a film festival where the stress is on the serious film and it becomes a masterpiece."[121] Gregory Peck, presumably taking it as a popular appeal feature that failed to be a smash hit, expressed some disappointment at the outcome: "It needed a much more modern kind of photographic approach and less literalness."[122] At the remove of half a century, it feels that Peck's judgment was flawed and that the solid pleasures of *Mirage* outweigh those of *Arabesque*, also starring Peck in the same sub-genre, flashily shot and modishly directed by Stanley Donen.

Alvarez Kelly (1966)

According to Abraham Lincoln, and the script, it was "the slickest piece of cattle stealing I ever heard of." The true story of a Confederate cattle rustling raid on the Union during the Civil War was the basis for *Alvarez Kelly*, a project that was roped together by Jack Gordean, friend of producer Sol Siegel and agent of both Edward Dmytryk and William Holden. Dmytryk had been director on Holden's first film (*Million Dollar Legs*, where Holden had been an extra) but their contact during the intervening three decades had been merely casual. Holden had misgivings about Dmytryk's political background, Dmytryk was concerned about Holden's drinking and neither was enthusiastic about the script. "The script was pretty sick and needed a lot of help, but so did Sol,"[123] wrote Dmytryk. Daniel Taradash was hired as script doctor and went on location to Louisiana to perform his surgery.

On location for *Alvarez Kelly*, Rebecca, Jean and Edward Dmytryk (left to right) chat with Arthur Franz, the director's most frequently cast actor. Franz appeared in eight films for Dmytryk (1966).

The issue with Holden's alcohol intake was less easily resolved. When they met in Hollywood to discuss the project, Holden assured Dmytryk that his drinking was under control, since he had been to France on a cure. His description of the regime there was not however completely reassuring: "The French have an intelligent way of doing it: they let you drink some wine."[124] Initially Holden's behavior on location alleviated these concerns but some days into the shoot Dmytryk was approached by co-star Richard Widmark to tell him they had a problem: "Holden is out. I don't think you'll get anything out of him today. He's gone!"[125] Having worked with Widmark twice before, Dmytryk knew that he had zero tolerance for lack of professionalism. In this instance, Widmark reacted against type: "He drenched Holden with black coffee, walked him around a bit, and in about 45 minutes Bill was sitting on his horse and ready to get on with the scene—a bit surly, but serviceable."[126]

Holden behaved himself during filming hours and didn't show up drunk again but after heavy sessions the night before, he would arrive with bloodshot eyes and have difficulty maintaining focus on his lines. Dmytryk had to reduce some of his scenes to short takes, infuriating Taradash, who was performing rewrites at night: "What is the sense of my sweating out this dialogue if you're gonna let Bill Holden ad lib whatever he wants to say?"[127] An additional issue according to the director was that his lead actor didn't really believe in the role, and indeed it is a stretch for the viewer to accept him as an Irish-Mexican. But even rewritten, Holden still wasn't satisfied with the material he was working with. Hung over one morning and dealing with an uncooperative horse, he rolled up the script and pretended to shove it in the horse's rear: "*That's* where it belongs!"[128]

Once the cameras had stopped rolling, Holden was unleashed. When behind the wheel to some drinking spot or other, he drove so erratically that Taradash would close his eyes, and his speeding would terrify Widmark. On one weekend trip to New Orleans with Widmark and Harry Carey, Jr., another co-star, he attempted the trick of pulling the tablecloth from underneath a tableful of crockery and glassware—unsuccessfully. Despite their different attitudes to the party lifestyle and their divergent politics—Widmark a liberal Democrat, Holden appreciably more conservative—the two actors bonded well, and Widmark may have been a moderating influence on some of their carousing outings.

One story offers up an interesting perspective on Holden's attitude to the new generation of star that was supplanting him. He and Widmark were eating in Fat Jack's in Baton Rouge one evening when Steve McQueen and a group from the set of *Nevada Smith* (also filming locally) entered. "McQueen sent a waiter with an invitation for Holden and Widmark to join his table. 'Fuck him,' Bill replied, indignant at the presumption of a Johnny-come-lately. 'Let *him* join *us* if he wants to.' He fumed through the dinner, then passed McQueen's table on the way out of the restaurant. 'Would you like a drink?' McQueen asked. 'Sure!' said Bill, sitting down at the table. That was the last Widmark saw of Bill for the rest of the evening."[129]

Third lead Patrick O'Neal, "a Southerner from Ocala, Florida,"[130] caused enough of a stir one evening on location for the keen ears of gossip columnist Hedda Hopper to prick up and demand elaboration, which O'Neal duly provided in a note. Word had it that he had been beaten up in a restaurant in Baton Rouge but he dismissed these reports as "grossly exaggerated."[131] He had been approached in the restaurant by five men and was initially engaged in polite conversation, "and then one of them started talking bigot nonsense, expecting me to agree. I did not, and asked them to leave my table. They countered with such stupid racist venom that I had to laugh."[132] The men asked him to step outside, he refused and then "one of them hit me full across the side of the head, and knocked me off the chair. Two drivers from the movie company rescued me. NO one else in the crowded restaurant had moved during all of this."[133] The altercation left him angry and bruised: "At the moment of the blow, my actor's ego took over—and all I could think was: don't damage the face, I've got a scene tomorrow—(the bump on the temple we covered with hair, and the black eye with makeup—NO problem)."[134]

The shoot also weathered Widmark getting the flu but when Holden contracted salmonella, filming had to be suspended for six weeks and was completed in Hollywood. The studio work is regrettably visible on screen. Interiors were naturally shot on sound-stage but a great deal of the film is handsomely filmed in its Louisiana locations, so the horseback back-projection shots are somewhat jarring in a film from the mid–1960s. The actual events of the story had taken place in Virginia (the original title was *The Richmond Story*), which was scouted for locations but proved over-developed. Dmytryk and team also dismissed Oregon after exploration, due to the large number of electricity pylons. So, the production headed to the under-developed South and found a large plantation near Baton Rouge for its main location work.

For the two prominent female roles, stars such as Janet Leigh, Vera Miles and Eva Marie Saint were considered but, for what one can only assume were budgetary reasons, the rather less stellar Janice Rule and Victoria Shaw were employed. The two male stars took a huge chunk of the acting budget—Holden was paid $250,000 for 10 weeks' work and Widmark $200,000 for 14 weeks, while O'Neal got $18,500 for 10 weeks and Shaw $12,500 for 5 weeks. Daniel Taradash chose not to publicize his reworking of Franklin Coen's script, writing to the Writers Guild of America, "I do not wish to be given screen credit on this project."[135] However, good reviews such as the following in the *New York Times* must have stung enough for him to keep the clipping in his papers: "And let's not forget Franklin Coen, the writer, for blueprinting a fresh idea and salting it with some tingling, unstereotyped behavior and gristly dialogue."[136]

The *Alvarez Kelly* that emerged is a shifting stand-off between two intriguing characters—a Mexican (Holden) and a Confederate (Widmark). At the start of the film, Kelly has spent three months driving 2,500 cattle from Mexico to a Union camp commanded by Major Stedman (O'Neal). He makes clear his lack of allegiance to either side in the conflict by relating the story of how his father was killed by U.S. soldiers while defending his land during the Mexican War: "So I say, Alvarez Kelly, take what you can from either side. Small return for your birth-right." He is a free agent whose politics are irrelevant and whose motives are mercenary. "You'd do business with the Confederates?" asks Stedman. "No," replies Kelly. "Their money's no good." When asked by Southern belle Charity Warwick (Shaw) whether he has no sympathy for her and her cause, he replies "I have no sympathies. Only instincts. And they shy away from losers."

War widow Warwick's attempted seduction of Kelly causes him to drop his guard sufficiently for Colonel Rossiter (Widmark) to perform an ambush. William Holden affects his best sardonic tone in chiding Charity, "So there was someone under the bed all the time. Just how far would you have gone?" Her hesitant response is all he needs to know and he wryly asks Rossiter's men, "You bastards couldn't have waited a while longer?" Rossiter's Confederate group steal the money that Kelly had been paid by Stedman and kidnap him to help steal the cattle back from the Union.

While Holden coasts on his charm and makes of Kelly an affable rogue unburdened by scruples, Widmark's characterization is altogether darker. Having lost an eye, Rossiter refuses to marry his fiancée Liz Pickering (Rule) for the duration of the war, fearful of returning to her even less of a man than he already feels. This sensitivity to mutilation does not prevent him from shooting a finger from Kelly's hand in order to make him sign up to the rustling scheme, with the promise to continue removing digits for the next ten days and beyond until he agrees to help. Widmark projects an intensity that nicely counterbalances the dash of the leading man, burning Kelly's cash in front of him with a cruel glint in the eye. This is slightly undone by the appearance in one scene of the Widmark giggle. The high-pitched laughter that had made him such a memorable villain in his debut *Kiss of Death*, a star-making factor, is incongruous here and undermines the tone of his performance.

The film's sympathies lie firmly with its titular figure. The pomposity of the Union side and the deviousness of the Southerners, in particular the women, leaves the film's stance as apolitical as Kelly's. The slaves mostly stand around in mute support of their owners, and in a climactic sequence one female slave hides an apple core to disguise the fact that Rossiter's men are hiding in Warwick's fruit cellar. Stedman is incredulous of their passivity: "We're down here fighting for you. Fighting to free you! Ruth, how can you be so loyal to someone who wants to keep you a slave?" Yet moments later Ruth's self-appointed liberator will be using her as a human shield to protect himself from gunfire. At this point in the film, because Kelly has committed to the Confederate cattle raid, so has the viewer, and Ruth's action to protect her oppressors is depicted sympathetically. The film doesn't probe the causes and moralities of the Civil War and adheres to its genre as an action movie, but in assessing where sympathies lie, action speaks louder than words.

Liz Pickering is the other scheming Southern female to feign sexual interest in Kelly for her own ends, in this case to escape the South. Kelly responds to her advances chiefly to get back at her fiancé Rossiter but retains an affection after spending the night with her. She is grateful for his lack of chivalry: "Thank God you're not one of those honourable men." Their farewell conversation after he has arranged her passage from Richmond is shot and performed touchingly, back to back at adjacent tables in a restaurant in order to avoid observation. In the cases of both Charity and Liz, an insincere seduction initiated by the female is transformed by the irresistibility of Holden's Kelly into genuine longing.

The final third of the film depicts the cattle raid and escape via swampland and over a wooden bridge which Kelly had the foresight to reinforce when initially crossed. Rossiter's discovery that he has been cuckolded solidifies his enmity towards Kelly and his judgment grows increasingly impaired. When he realizes the bridge is defended by Union cavalrymen with Howitzers, he proposes killing the cattle by driving them into a swamp. Kelly is scathing: "3,000 miles to drown in a stinking swamp. Rossiter, you're long on gallantry but short on sense." The cattleman provides the voice of reason, a role he has fulfilled to both sides of what to him is a senseless conflict, and perceives with clarity the solution that the military man is blind to. There are 300 Union soldiers, 100 Confederate soldiers—and 2,500 head of cattle. "That makes 2,600 for our side."

Dmytryk recognized that this long climactic sequence was where the success of the film lay, whatever its other shortcomings: "It always amazes me how well such pictures do abroad, where nuances of language mean little, and action is everything."[137] Being sprung from the soundstage and released on location puts breath in the film's nostrils. The stampede across the bridge is thrillingly shot and edited, a bravura sequence. There is a genuine sense of jeopardy as cattle hurtle past actors, including the expensive star Widmark, with apparently inches to spare. Dmytryk's editing knowhow, honed over decades, effectively intercuts the mayhem of the stampede with the ongoing personal conflicts. Unfortunately, when the bridge is dynamited, Kelly's jump for survival is rather too obviously a pickup shot in the studio and proves climactically limp.

In the year that *Who's Afraid of Virginia Woolf* helped hammer the final nails into the coffin of the Production Code, *Alvarez Kelly* evoked feeble protests from the censors over its use of "God damn it," "bastards" and the line "If you'd been rather more intent on pleasing her than *spilling your seed* on the Majestic Lost Cause." The increasingly toothless PCA granted its approval on 27 May 1966. The film's box-office haul was mediocre in the USA ($3.5 million) but more impressive overseas. The critics were mostly lukewarm, with *Newsweek* damning it with the faintest of praise: "When a cowboy picture is denied a major opening and begins its run in the neighborhood theaters, it is usually either a sleeper or a loser. Two new studio stepchildren *Alvarez Kelly* and *Texas Across the River* are not sleepers. *Alvarez Kelly* is the more interesting of the two because at least it is—sort of—non-commercial."[138] Nobody would blame William Holden for the comparative disappointment of the film's reception, but one can't help feel he was miscast as Mexican-Irish. There is no record of anyone having considered casting the one star who actually had both Mexican and Irish roots—frequent Dmytryk collaborator Anthony Quinn.

Anzio (1968)

When Edward Dmytryk finally accepted an offer from producer Dino De Laurentiis, it was 1967 and the old guard were on the way out. "'Eddie,' my agent told me, 'it's much easier for me to sell some clown who's never directed a film, than it is to sell George Cukor.'"[139] Their first encounter had been when De Laurentiis brought Dmytryk to Rome to discuss a proposed film on Simon Bolivar which enthused the director. He was less enthusiastic when it became clear that the Bolivar project was nowhere near ready and the producer began to push a script about a quintet of Yugoslav women, cast out of their town for consorting with Nazi occupiers, who join a band of partisans. Dmytryk passed on this and it was eventually directed by Martin Ritt as *Five Branded Woman*. Dmytryk's verdict—"It wasn't very good"[140]—is accurate. Despite four fabulous faces (Jeanne Moreau, Vera Miles, Silvana Mangano and Barbara Bel Geddes) the film is unconvincing and the direction from Ritt flat-footed. Dmytryk's second encounter with De Laurentiis was when the Italian turned down the opportunity to co-produce *The Reluctant Saint* with Columbia. "He liked the story, he said, but it wouldn't make a lira. He was so right."[141]

Third time was lucky due to the lack of alternative offers. De Laurentiis had the rights to *Anzio*, a book by Wynford Vaughn-Thomas about the disastrous 1944 landing by U.S. troops on the coastline south of Rome. Dmytryk dismissed the producer's concept of incorporating an utterly ahistorical massive German cannon, suspiciously like the one in *The Guns of Navarone*, but worse was to come from the writer assigned to the project. Harry Craig, son of a clergyman from County Cork ("I am unreasonably immune to 'Irish charm,' suspicious even when it's on the level"[142]), had written radio plays for the BBC but this was his first film. John Huston had told De

Robert Mitchum and Dmytryk on location for *Anzio* (1968).

Laurentiis, whose English was very much a secondary tongue, that Craig was one of the most brilliant playwrights in the English language. John Huston was also an inveterate practical joker.

On his first visit to Los Angeles for script meetings, Craig evaded Dmytryk for a couple of weeks before revealing, just before returning to Rome, that he had committed almost nothing to paper. When Dmytryk was finally able to view the script, in Rome prior to shooting, he considered it unusable: "At one point he had Bob Mitchum escaping from his Nazi jailer by confusing him with a series of perfectly executed bird calls."[143] He was not alone in his reservations. When the actors started to arrive, having signed up script unseen, De Laurentiis almost had a mutiny. Robert Mitchum declared it to be "violently anti–American"[144] while Peter Falk wanted to fly straight back to the U.S. Mitchum's issue was that the reputation of the generals would suffer in the depiction of the botched campaign, whereas this aspect of the script was accurate. By delaying after landing on Anzio beach, the American forces gave the Germans the opportunity to mass forces and stage a devastating attack. Major General Lucas was relieved of his command after a month of sustained fighting. The final script renames this character as Major General Lesley, played in the film by Arthur Kennedy.

Unlike Dmytryk, Falk had been won over by the Irishness of Craig: "We met at the Beverly Hills Hotel, where I found myself charmed immediately by the writer's foreign accent. I'm a sucker for foreign accents."[145] Falk initially turned the role down because he found it silly, but was persuaded to sign up when he was promised shared above-the-title billing with Robert Mitchum. Arriving in Rome, he fell asleep reading the script: "The characters were all clichés ... my part was lousy."[146] Dmytryk greeted him the next day with a bear hug and was immediately informed that Falk was abandoning the production and was booked on a 1 p.m. flight to New York. When De Laurentiis was informed of Falk's decision, he insisted on driving him to the airport. He sat in the front with his chauffeur, joshing via translator with Falk in the rear seat, believing that the actor was merely seeking a better deal. As they passed a sign for the airport, "'Stop the car,' Dino ordered. He turned around in his seat, his eyes leveling with mine. 'WHAT DO YOU WANT?' he bellowed."[147] Taken aback, Falk said he merely wanted a better part. With a shake of the hand in the back of Dino De Laurentiis' limousine, Falk became the writer of his own character, Corporal Rabinoff.

Dmytryk persuaded De Laurentiis to employ Frank De Felitta, a writer who had served in the U.S. Italian campaign, under the pretext of making the dialogue more authentic. The script was substantially rewritten just before filming started, a process that continued throughout the shoot. According to Dmytryk, most of Craig's contributions "ended up in the wastepaper basket."[148] There is a blotchy sense to the dialogue, occasionally insightful, frequently banal. The haphazard pattern of multiple contributors and last-minute rewrites is apparent. One scene that has the patina of truth about it has Rabinoff bidding farewell to a trio of Italian prostitutes in the back of a truck, a surprisingly tender scene. The conception of this scene was entirely Peter Falk's.

Now in his fourth decade of directing films, *Anzio* provided a reunion with some of the actors Dmytryk knew well. In minor roles of Major and General were two actors that he had worked with multiple times: four times previously with Robert Ryan and six times previously with Arthur Franz. Franz was to make one final appearance in a Dmytryk film, *The Human Factor* in 1975. Earl Holliman, who had made an impact as Spencer Tracy's dumbest son in *Broken Lance*, was cast in the pivotal role of Sgt. Stimmler. And top of the casting food chain was Robert Mitchum,

Robert Ryan and Dmytryk (both seated) at the Colosseum on location for *Anzio* (1968).

with whom he had already worked twice, but not since *Crossfire*. In an interview, Dmytryk recalled the reunion: "He was still the same relaxed guy, good actor. There were changes, sure. He was a drunk now. But listen, I like to say that I directed all the great drunks of Hollywood ... many of the great stars were drunks—Bogart, Gable, others I can name.[149] And they were the best. And Mitchum would say, 'Don't use me

Edward the Lionheart: Dmytryk on the set of *Anzio* (1968).

after six o'clock.' But no matter how much he drank at night, or drugged, or whatever he was doing, in the morning he was there, perfect."[150]

Mitchum believed in the value of play as much as that of work, and Bob certainly wasn't a dull boy. Reni Santoni, who played Pte. Movie and was then 28 years old, remembered how the star preferred after-hour adventures with the younger cast members over those of his own vintage. Having already spent jail time for marijuana possession in 1948, it was no surprise that Mitchum was partial to recreational smoking. Santoni recalled, "The Goose loved to get high. The first night Mitchum sent for me he says, 'Uh, I have some stuff that you might find … interesting.' And he had gotten some spectacular Afghanistan hashish…. He was very, very generous. And he was a connoisseur, like a wine expert with this stuff."[151] Mitchum and Santoni spent one evening in a hotel room, dressed in their military fatigues, stoned from grass that had been sent from the U.S. concealed in a doll and listening to one of the first copies of *Sgt. Pepper's Lonely Hearts Club Band*: "He was incredibly cool."[152] On another occasion they ran into Ava Gardner in a smoky, down-market bar, where the two stars renewed their old friendship in a booth. Yet, mere hours after these nights of carousing, Dmytryk was in awe of Mitchum's professionalism: "at 8:00 am, he will glance very briefly at five pages of dialogue, walk into the scene and never miss a beat."[153]

Quite apart from the script issues, there was a certain chaos to the shoot that Dmytryk believed was inherent to any production filmed in Italy. Promised equipment, military hardware and extras failed to appear. When shooting the landing sequence with his actors tightly packed onto a boat, Dmytryk noticed a bend in one of the weapons and discovered that the guns were all made of rubber. He learnt that De Laurentiis refused to pay the gun supplier what he demanded and had furtively resorted to this cheap solution. Dmytryk refused to continue shooting without the necessary hardware, which duly arrived after lunch. Santoni recalled "Fast Eddie" saying, "I've had better production value on pictures that cost ten thousand dollars!"[154] One scene of some scale shut down the picture. The embarkation for the operation was filmed at a naval base in Taranto with an impressive number of extras. Unfortunately the mass of troops on the dockside caused a delay to the car of the admiral, who ordered an immediate cessation of filming. Appeals from naval command brought a resignation threat from the admiral but after a few days' stoppage De Laurentiis struck some pacifying deal to enable shooting to recommence.

The structure of the film is uneven and its two halves unequally compelling. The preparation for and actual landing on Anzio beach is rather routinely portrayed, although Dmytryk does manage to wring some spectacle from the military resources that had underwhelmed him. The water splashes on Giuseppe Rotunno's camera instill immediacy to the troops making their unopposed landing. With comparisons constantly being drawn to the landings at Salerno, General Lesley (Arthur Kennedy) urges restraint and orders the fatal policy of digging in: "The first duty of a general is to secure his position." Official war correspondent Dick Ennis (Mitchum) deflates the top brass with cynicism: "They used to say that the first duty of a general was to succeed." The British command are also shown to disagree with this tactic, Patrick Magee's General Starkey shooting Lesley a particularly withering glance. By the end of the film, all blame for the failure of the operation has been placed on Lesley's shoulders and he is relieved of his post. The habitual twisting of lawsuit-threatening reality into film-friendly fiction is reflected in Lesley quoting Winston Churchill's denunciation of the Anzio landing—"I had hoped we were hurling a wildcat onto the shore, but all we got was a beached whale"—words that had actually condemned Lesley's non-fictional counterpart, Maj. Gen. Lucas.

Dmytryk organizing military maneuvers on *Anzio* (1968).

Once the Allied troops have been decimated by the German counter-attack, the film's shift in focus becomes much more persuasive. Whether coincidental or not, the concentration on the eight survivors of an ambush echoes Dmytryk's 1952 film about the Italian campaign, *Eight Iron Men*. The characters in *Anzio* are not as sharply drawn as in the earlier, more successful film, but the narrowing of perspective is much to its benefit. There is a succession of tense, well-executed set-pieces which cohere the diverse group around the survival instinct—evasion of a tank, navigation of a minefield, escape from a barbed wire labyrinth. One striking image occurs after one of the group is captured and then shot when he tries to retrieve the family photo that his captor has casually tossed away. The photo of the smiling child floats down a shallow stream and comes to rest underneath the boots of its lifeless father.

The most effective sequence in the film comes when the seven remaining soldiers take refuge in a farmhouse, occupied by a mother and her two daughters. It also directs a well-written and excellently acted spotlight onto Rabinoff, the film's most intriguing character. Rabinoff is a womanizer capable of great tenderness, and a loose cannon, constantly spoiling for a fight among his comrades and ready to slice the throat of his enemies. It emerges that he was severely injured by a Japanese grenade and suffers crippling stomach pain when tense, but instead of going to hospital when he was sent home, he went to Canada and re-enlisted. "How'd you get past the doctors?" asks Ennis. "I lied about my age" is his typically wise-cracking response. Ennis probes further and wants to know why he keeps coming back for more. Rabinoff responds, "A guy sells shoes for 40 years. I live more in one day. I see more and I feel more. I taste more. I think more. I'm more, understand? I'm more. You know, there's more to living than just breathing." Falk utterly breathes life into this role. Rabinoff and Ennis emerge as the only rounded characters in the film, more due to the skill of Falk and Mitchum than to any insight of the script.

The end of Rabinoff is brutally sudden. After the peaceful interlude with the Italian farming woman, the men are disturbed by German troops and end up dispersed in ditches under fire from snipers. In a bid for a better position, Rabinoff decides to go over the top. He pauses and says to war correspondent Ennis, "Just in case—I hope it's a good story." A sniper's bullet curtails his story instantaneously. The loss of this vibrant character is an affecting moment. It also motivates Ennis to pick up a gun, something the journalist has pointedly refused to do thus far. Ennis had explained that his reason for persisting with his dangerous occupation was to discover why men kill each other. After he manages to shoot the sniper, Mitchum underplays perfectly the look of resigned regret that flickers over his face. Pte. Movie's line "Welcome to the club, Mr. Ennis" is a sardonic underscoring of the threshold he has crossed.

Dmytryk had intended *Anzio* to be a strong anti-war statement, in tune with the disillusionment of the era. Ultimately its message is blunted. Ennis calls war "the ultimate game" and concludes that "Men kill each other because they like to." After watching the Allied troops led by General Carson (Ryan) parade triumphantly into Rome, Ennis says to Stimmler, "Well, we've seen the conquering hero. Let's go." It's an ineffectual conclusion, but Dmytryk had to fight for even this degree of muted cynicism. Months after editing the film, he learned that Columbia had re-cut it: "Sure enough, every line in the film which suggested that war was not exactly a glorious pastime had been deleted."[155] He confronted the studio front office in London and was told that they feared a negative reception from the American public currently embroiled in Vietnam. Dmytryk insisted that his vision be respected and ultimately concessions to that vision were made, though he lamented that it "wasn't quite the film I thought I'd made."[156] He blamed Columbia for this timidity and remained respectful of his producer. "I would just as soon make a picture for Dino De Laurentiis as any other producer I know,"[157] he wrote in 1978, when further collaboration was still a possibility.

Shalako (1968)

Edward Dmytryk returned to the Western with *Shalako*, his third action-based film in a row and his eighth and final of the 1960s. Euan Lloyd had begun his career as a trainee manager in Birmingham for Associated British Cinemas, rising through the ranks of publicity manager and personal assistant to Irving Allen and Albert Broccoli, to reach the point of making his first venture as independent producer. He approached Dmytryk while the director was preparing *Anzio* with a script based on a novel by the extravagantly named Louis L'Amour. As well as *Shalako*, the writings of the man born Louis LaMoore were the inspiration for the films *Hondo* and *Catlow*. Dmytryk was not remotely impressed with the script that Lloyd was hawking but the producer, desperate to get his only property made, was tenacious. Dmytryk suggested a friend of his, Jim Griffith, to rework *Shalako* and proposed that if an important enough cast could be assembled on the resulting script, he would direct the film. The script that Griffith and collaborator Hal Hopper produced "wasn't exactly *Shane*, or even *Warlock*, but it wasn't bad."[158]

The original casting was Henry Fonda opposite Senta Berger, but when Fonda dropped out, Dmytryk was astonished to discover that Lloyd had secured Sean Connery for the title role as the star's first vehicle after quitting the James Bond juggernaut (for the first time). Dmytryk met with Connery at the Grand Hotel in Rome and together they watched Scotland play an international football match. Having cheered his team to victory, Connery was happy to continue the winning streak and signed an extremely lucrative deal—a reported $1.2 million alongside 30 percent of the producer's profits and 100 percent of the Spanish profits. Euan Lloyd was full of casting surprises and next chose Brigitte Bardot to star opposite Connery. The actor's initial reaction of "Bloody marvellous!"[159] was tempered when he discovered that Bardot wanted to meet with him before she would sign, "to test the vibrations."[160] Connery's response was brusque: "If she thinks I am going over to France to be given the once-over, she can forget it."[161] He was persuaded to relent and the stars met in Deauville in the company of Bardot's husband Gunter Sachs. The summit was successful though the chemistry was weak, Connery judging her to be "all girl, but if I must say so, all on the outside."[162]

Lloyd managed to assemble an impressive roster of stars for the supporting roles, among them Jack Hawkins, Stephen Boyd, Honor Blackman and Alexander Knox. The Canadian Knox had been nominated for an Oscar in 1944 for playing the President in *Wilson*, but his career seriously stalled after he too became entangled with HUAC. In August 1952, his agent informed him that 20th Century–Fox, the only studio that was then interested in employing him, "submitted your name to an industry organization and the report came back that, because of some question concerning your past political affiliations, you were not acceptable."[163] Despite support from the likes of writer-producer Philip Dunne at Fox, he found himself unemployable. Dunne wrote to him that "the Motto for 1952 is not *Death Before Dishonor* but *Sauve Qui Peut*."[164] In Italy Knox made one film for Roberto Rossellini, *Europa '51* with Ingrid Bergman, but decided not to put himself up for roles in films financed by U.S. companies, preferring to seem "unavailable": "My reason for being 'unavailable' is simply that it does me no good in England to be associated too much with 'refugees.' English companies are, naturally, anxious to avoid trouble and when there is a choice, they tend to give employment to innocuous people. This applies especially to the Rank organisation."[165]

In April 1954 Knox was informed by his business manager that "as far as I could find out you had been removed from the so-called 'grey list.'"[166] Having received this unofficial green light, he put himself forward for a part in Edward Dmytryk's *The End of the Affair*. The frustrations involved in his pursuing the role of Sarah Miles' husband typify the purgatorial limbo in which blacklisted and grey-listed artists found themselves. It was initially indicated that he had the role, then he heard from John Mills that he had turned the part down. He was then given a "firm offer," only to be informed the next day that it was all off. Attempting to navigate through the motivations of the various parties, he learned that "Columbia (West Coast) was pleased that I was playing the part and that there was no ban"[167] but that Leo Jaffe, a Columbia official in New York, was the source of the objection to him. Knox wrote, "I took the trouble to contact Dmytryk privately to ask his opinion and he was quite definite that he had no doubt whatever that the ban was still political."[168] Peter Cushing got the part of Henry Miles and played it extremely well. Alexander Knox continued to languish on the Hollywood grey list and played almost exclusively in British productions in the decade and a half between missing out on working with Edward Dmytryk on the Graham Greene adaptation and managing to work with him on the Louis L'Amour.

Shalako was originally slated to be shot in Mexico but production shifted to Spain due to the threat of a Mexican labor strike. The desert area near Almeria had become the popular location for shooting spaghetti westerns, and while *Shalako* was filming, it was also hosting the World War II action movie *Play Dirty*, directed by André de Toth and starring Michael Caine. Caine recalls a near collision between tanks from Rommel's Afrika Korps and a stagecoach pursued by Native Americans: "As soon as they saw the tanks, the horses reared up and threw their riders and we had to hang about while they were picked up and dusted off and all the horseshit and hoofmarks were eliminated."[169] Accounts vary as to the offscreen antics of Brigitte Bardot but she certainly arrived in style, somewhat belatedly, in a white Rolls-Royce driven by a black chauffeur, tailed by a phalanx of press and personal attendants. Connery complained, "Someone has to tell this lady this is going to be a serious film, not a bloody circus."[170] Whether or not Stephen Boyd was a former lover from the set of *The Night Heaven Fell* in 1957; whether she had screaming rows with him or he became a "kind of hugging buddy"[171]; whether she departed for St Moritz in a tantrum to be consoled by her husband or he had asked her to take a few days off to meet him; whether she threatened to walk off the set halfway through the shoot—all depends on which account is followed.

The publicity circus that swirled around Bardot at the time lives on in the maelstrom of conflicting gossip in reminiscences about her. She certainly seemed to party hard when the cameras were absent. Euan Lloyd remembered that she "had no fixed rules about whom she befriended. If a shoeshine boy had something she liked, he was her friend."[172] For publicity manager Kenneth Green, "She seemed obsessed with the idea that she was ageless. A perennial teenager who wanted to show that she could go on dancing, singing, and whooping it up all night."[173] Honor Blackman was not impressed with Bardot's antics and sympathized with her former *Goldfinger* co-star Connery: "Once Sean was over that bad start, he kept out of it. He took a rented villa nearby, where he stayed with his family and made a point of concentrating on doing as good a job as possible under the circumstances."[174] She concluded that "Eddie Dmytryk's patience was truly remarkable. Then, with Brigitte, I guess we all deserved credit."[175] And yet, Dmytryk, not shy about expressing a critical opinion about the actors with whom he had worked, wrote in his autobiography that Bardot was "a pleasant surprise ... a most conscientious worker."[176]

In counterbalance, Dmytryk also wrote that Bardot "had no feel for acting and seemed to take no particular interest in it."[177] Unfortunately it is this characteristic that is detrimental to the quality of *Shalako*. The film carries strong echoes of the previous year's *Hombre*, which was based on an Elmore Leonard novel and starred Connery's wife Diane Cilento: an outside character, respected by Native Americans to some degree and with superior knowledge of the environment, helps a group of travellers survive a hostile attack. Connery is "Shalako" Carlin, an ex–Army wild west wanderer, and Bardot is Countess Irina Lazaar, an aristocrat of indeterminate nationality on a game expedition to New Mexico with other members of the European nobility. Bardot mangles the English language, her line-readings leaving no doubt that these were words on a page that she was obliged to learn, and she utterly fails to convince as someone from the nineteenth century, let alone a woman of noble birth. Throughout the dusty escapades of her party, her blonde tresses remain carefully crafted and her eyes heavily and immaculately kohled. One romantic scene between Irina and Shalako after a day-long trek has Connery's sweating sun-burnished face signally failing to find chemistry with the perfect maquillage of Bardot. The semi-naked bathing scene she is gifted towards the end finds her in familiar Vadimesque territory, deploying the coquettish looks and teasing reveals that were part of her repertoire more than a decade earlier. Bardot's is a spot of stunt casting that undermines the enterprise.

Its sex kitten notwithstanding, *Shalako* is a brisk, entertaining western, well-staged by Dmytryk and delivering the requisite thrills from the unusual perspective of European nobility. A written prologue to the film by Louis L'Amour points out that wild west big game attracted a succession of wealthy hunting parties in the nineteenth century. The film depicts the Old World rubbing abrasively against the New, its clash of class occurring not just between aristocracy and hired hand but within the pan-European hunting group itself. A marital alliance is being sought between Countess Irina and Baron Frederick (a smartly supercilious performance from Peter van Eyck) in order to enrich and bolster the position of Sir Charles and Lady Julia Daggett (Jack Hawkins and Honor Blackman). There is no sense of unity among the aristocracy, which is riven by jealousies, infidelities and greed. The threat of attack by Apaches only momentarily unifies the males of the party in the blindness of entitled bravado, while their wives plead restraint, but this meeting of minds is soon fractured as they realize the degree to which their Old World ranks are meaningless on this frontier.

The most interesting character is Julia, played with feline cunning by Honor Blackman. Julia is sexually voracious, a string of infidelities behind her ("I've always taken what was available") and openly flirting with their shifty guide Fulton (Stephen Boyd), their interplay strongly edged with dominance and submission. She has her eye on a diamond necklace of the financially more secure Irina and, when she decides to abandon her party to escape with the nefarious Fulton, she is immediately rewarded for being a traitor to her tribe when Fulton gives her the necklace. Severe punishment for her class disloyalty soon follows. She is blooded twice when two men die on top of her and, after capture by the Apaches, she is made to eat dirt and is finally choked to death on the necklace she coveted. Native Americans are depicted in the film as much savage as noble. Julia's long-suffering husband Charles is a portrayal made under the most trying circumstances. *Shalako* was the first film release for Jack Hawkins after cancer of the throat obliged him to have his larynx removed in February 1966. He had to learn the technique of speaking via the esophageal voice, and would drink Black Velvet, the Guinness and champagne cocktail, to provide the belch that could start him talking. Charles Gray post-dubbed Hawkins' voice for the first of many times in *Shalako*, though this initial experience proved tricky: "Part of the trouble was that Jack had been saying the lines in his own voice and therefore gulping. So we came to a sort of arrangement. I said, 'In future, could you possibly try not to vocalise but just to mime the words?' which is an awful thing to say to an actor…. But afterwards it was much easier because there weren't those unnatural lulls between words."[178]

Though Shalako is clearly master of his environment and doesn't hesitate to take command of the group, his leadership eschews machismo. He avoids confrontation rather than pursuing it as the Baron and Fulton do, and he is unafraid to cede ground and share responsibility. The Baron initially displays only arrogance towards his social inferiors and ignorance of how to react in dangerous situations, but his pomposity is wholly punctured by Shalako's superior nous. Unexpectedly, the Baron then gains some character, to some degree admitting his errors. When the group are confronted by a rock face, the Baron is able to prove himself by organizing an ascent, thanks to his skill at mountain climbing. "A dilettante sport," he remarks ironically. Reaching the summit just after the Baron, Shalako wheezes, "You do this for pleasure, eh?" Connery is at his best in these moments of self-effacement, his years in Bondage having honed his sardonic edge.

Dmytryk shoots this rock-climbing sequence with unshowy assurance, making deft use of the Franscope screen. His experience in filming *The Mountain* undoubtedly came in useful, though this time no sequences were performed back in the studio and the precipitous drops are genuine. *Shalako* is distinguished by several impressively mounted action sequences, including a stagecoach pursuit and a final shootout that echoes the climactic battle in *Anzio* that same year. Particularly sharply filmed is the initial Apache assault on the hunting party's camp which Dmytryk shoots and edits with textbook precision, sometimes cutting rapidly to ramp up the momentum. His ability as an action director is evident in these late works, which makes it all the more regrettable that his career was rapidly running out of steam and he was no longer considered bankable. *Shalako* received its world premiere in Munich in September 1968 with a charity London premiere at the Coliseum Cinerama Theatre on 12 December. With a complicated pre-financing scheme behind its production, involving advance guarantees of release from dozens of countries, the ultimate profitability of the film is obscured by accountancy mists, and it appears that neither Connery nor Bardot received any of their contracted profit share. Whether due to *Shalako*'s mixed reviews or to a "reverse blacklist" or to a sense that he was yesterday's man, the calls stopped coming and Edward Dmytryk did not make another film for four years.

VII

Out of Time
(1970–1975)

"It was 1971. I had been idle for nearly three years. Nothing worthwhile was coming my way, and I was getting scared. I was too young to die. And if I didn't die of boredom, we would all die of starvation."[1] One after another, hopeful projects continued to peter out. A script titled *That Woman* by Robert Alan Aurthur was earmarked for Elizabeth Taylor but came to nothing. Bart Spicer's novel *Act of Anger* was optioned by Dmytryk and adapted by television writer Peter Allan Fields into a screenplay. Stephen Boyd, a friend of Dmytryk's since *Shalako*, was to play the lead and the project was set up at Warner Bros.–Seven Arts. Despite the enthusiasm the studio had shown the script, Seven Arts was suddenly sold to another company and all projects not already filming were abruptly cancelled. The relationship between the two men survived the disappointment and they eventually set up their own company, Dmytryk-Boyd Productions, Inc.

In June of 1971, Edward, Jean and Rebecca Dmytryk left their Bel Air home for the last time and caught a flight to London. England, where he had made his films in exile, as well as his artistic successes *The End of the Affair* and *So Well Remembered*, was to be their new home. It was a move that had been seriously contemplated while he was in prison but Jean's love for London was only puddle deep and the lure of Californian skies always won out. They had a good network there after many visits over the decades and this time were able to flat-sit in Westminster for their friends since the 1950s, James and April Clavell, while they were spending the summer in Canada. The Dmytryks spent an enjoyable summer in London, Rebecca delighting in the bird life in St James's Park, but realized while house hunting that desirable properties had risen out of their price range. Jean had a fascination for the character of Rasputin and, with the intention of writing a script, made a short research trip to Leningrad in August. When Dmytryk met with Alexander Salkind, in an encounter brokered by Boyd for a project that would develop into **Bluebeard**, Jean had doubts about settling in London while her husband would be shuffling between Rome, Paris, Montreux and Budapest, constructing another film project after several fruitless years. It was finally decided for Jean and Rebecca—"Southern Californians in every conceivable way"[2]—to return to Los Angeles at the end of the summer, the Californian skies proving victorious one more time.

The *Bluebeard* affair in Budapest was eventful and a colorful immersion in the lives of the superstars, with Elizabeth Taylor's 40th birthday party a weekend to remember. Jean wrote her *Rasputin* script and Dmytryk-Boyd productions attempted to get it made. Discovering that a version of the same story was being mooted in the USSR, they nevertheless wrote to Sovinfilm in Moscow, "I do hope that it is enough unlike *Agony* and has sufficient merit in its own right to warrant your interest in it as a co-production."[3] *Agony* was released by Mosfilm in 1981. Jean Porter Dmytryk's *Rasputin* was never made. In desperation, Dmytryk accepted an offer from producer James Polakof to make **He Is My Brother**, the nadir of his film career, before reuniting with one of his favorite actors, John Mills, on his final production, **The "Human" Factor**. In 1975, the clapperboard sounded on an Edward Dmytryk film for the last time.

Few filmmakers perform a conscious swansong and the next few years witnessed fresh attempts and dashed hopes. The realization that it was time to start plowing a different furrow came in 1977 when Stephen Boyd died at the age of 45 and Dmytryk was offered a teaching post at the University of Texas in Austin. It was an invigorating change of direction at the age of 69 and he relished the challenges of his new role as lecturer on film and directing. The initial year-long contract was extended and he stayed in Austin until 1981. In 1979, he directed a short film about date rape called *Not Only Strangers*, with cast and crew comprised of students. It is a well-intentioned appeal for the reporting of sexual assaults and is noteworthy as the screen debut of Oscar-winning actress Marcia Gay Harden, then Marcia Harden, who was studying Theater at the University of Texas.

In 1981, Dmytryk took up a new teaching post at the University of South California and he and Jean moved to Laurel Canyon. They had weathered a marital rough patch during his time in Austin but now he was loving his teaching career and she was dabbling in real estate. After a gruesome murder involving drugs and

Edward Dmytryk (circa 1972).

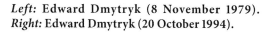
Left: **Edward Dmytryk (8 November 1979).**
Right: **Edward Dmytryk (20 October 1994).**

pornography took place near them, Jean placed an eye-catching advertisement in *The Hollywood Reporter* in her professional capacity: "Live in Laurel Canyon, where murders are colorful, drug busts are frequent, and helicopters circle overhead at odd hours. Rub elbows with political giants and social outcasts. Live in wonder and experience the unknown. 2 BR and 1 BA legit, with some hidden rooms rented. How can you lose at $155,000? Even has a garage. Call Jean Dmytryk...."[4] The advertisement caused ripples nationwide and Kenneth Anger reprinted it as a coda page in *Hollywood Babylon II*. Her husband's reaction is unrecorded. Tangential to his teaching career, Dmytryk wrote a series of successful text books—*Cinema: Concept & Practice, On Screen Directing, On Screen Acting, On Screen Writing, On Film Editing*—as well as an autobiography and a memoir of his experience with the Hollywood Ten.

Though still a side-lined figure due to the political controversy that clung onto his name, Dmytryk occasionally benefited from the nostalgic revival of interest in Hollywood's Golden Age that had begun in the 1970s. He was invited to give a film workshop at the University of Television and Film in Munich in May 1981 and was one of the celebrity attractions on a Caribbean cruise called "The RKO Years," along with Dorothy McGuire, Virginia Mayo, Sam Jaffe and Pandro S. Berman. In October 1990, he was invited to attend what this author believes to be the only major retrospective of his work, in the German city of Essen. There he gave a seminar on direction and a monograph on his films was published with translated sections from his autobiography as commentary.

Much more often the attention focused on him was negative. Between April and June 1977, Laemmle Theatres in Los Angeles put on "A Retrospective on the Blacklist Period" showing films such as *Force of Evil, Mission to Moscow, The Brave One* and *The Front*, with guest speakers including Abraham Polansky, Albert Maltz and Ben and Norma Barzman, and the children of Dalton Trumbo, Herbert Biberman and Alvah Bessie. Edward Dmytryk's *Crossfire* was shown on 8 May. The panel invited to discuss this film included its screenwriter John Paxton, who was not a Communist and never blacklisted, Alfred Levitt, screenwriter of *The Boy with Green Hair*, and his wife Helen, both of them blacklisted, and Dorothy Healey of the Communist Party of America. The choice of *Crossfire* as the film to discuss is perverse since the director of the film was not invited.

When Dmytryk was invited, however, the outcome was ugly. In July 1988, the Barcelona Film Festival invited him to join a panel to discuss the HUAC era. The other members of the panel were directors John Berry and Jules Dassin, writer Walter Bernstein, actress Rosaura Revueltas and Daniel Taradash, the non-blacklisted writer/director of *Storm Center*, an anti–McCarthyite drama starring Bette Davis. As *Daily Variety* reported, "Dmytryk had been asked to remove himself from the panel and was seated in the audience. Dassin and Berry had informed a festival official that they would not sit on a panel with Dmytryk."[5] It is interesting to compare the different accounts of that evening. Bernstein, the blacklisted writer of *The Front*, told an interviewer, "They showed *The Front*, and then we all went to a dais at this hall, and there sitting in the front row facing us was Dmytryk. Before the panel could start, Dmytryk grabbed the mike, giving his apologia for what he did, and actually attacking John Berry, for example, totally gratuitously. We were furious. I had to restrain Berry from going down and throttling him. Dassin got up with great dignity and said, 'This is not why we came here.' We all just got off the stage and left."[6]

The press account is somewhat different. Thomas Pryor wrote: "[Bernstein, Berry and Dassin] turned the Barcelona 'homage' into a 'vengeance is mine' session, hurling such epithets as 'scum,' 'Judas' and 'informer' at Dmytryk. Their vituperative comments did not shed light on the greatest crisis Hollywood has ever experienced. It amounted to an outpouring of pus from a Hollywood wound which apparently will never be healed…. This is not meant to imply that Dmytryk sat silently by; he responded to his tormentors without apology and with a dignity they did not accord him…. Instead of an intelligent, unemotional examination of a witch-hunt that adversely affected many careers, including some innocents, this 'homage' turned out to be nothing more than a vendetta."[7] Dmytryk for his part wrote: "I was conscious of Jean's anger and pent-up tears as she sat rigidly at my side. Some of their lies about our pre–1951 association included Jean, especially the distortions of Dassin."[8] Dmytryk was relieved to be "surrounded by a crowd of sympathizers"[9] when they left the room and especially heartened to receive the vocal support of the Russian screenwriter Valery Fried. Dmytryk noted in his book *Odd Man Out* that the Soviet Union collapsed the following year and wondered if the display of hatred toward him that night might not have been intensified by the imminent collapse of Communism, of which the panelists were aware "at least subliminally."[10]

In December 1992, the Dmytryks suffered the awful tragedy of their son Rick dying at the age of 43. Rick had struggled with health issues all his life and was finally diagnosed with inoperable lung cancer. They buried their son the day after Christmas. Eddie and Jean spent their last years together on Westfall Drive in the Encino Hills overlooking the San Fernando Valley. On 1 July 1999, Edward Dmytryk died at home of congestive heart failure at the age of 90. He is buried at Forest Lawn Memorial Park in the Hollywood Hills. Contemplating his legacy in 1974, he concluded,

"That's all I was, a storyteller. I might have made a little personal statement here and there, but primarily I tried to tell a story."[11]

Bluebeard (1972)

On Tuesday 23 November 1971 Richard Burton wrote in his diary about a meeting in Paris: "Am supposed to have lunch at Fouquet's with the director—one called Dmytryk who—I've only just discovered this morning—I've been confusing for years with a man called Siodmak. Both have their similarities in that they started off well and then tapered off into the usual mediocrity."[12] Perhaps Burton failed to recognize the irony of this last sentence with reference to his own career, or perhaps he was only too aware that, despite being half of the most high profile and highly paid celebrity couple in the world, his output since *Who's Afraid of Virginia Woolf?* was unlikely to trouble the canon compilers. His diary confession during filming that "there is but no question that I am the laziest actor in the world with the possible exception of Marlon,"[13] may indeed indicate the requisite degree of self-awareness.

The seed of *Bluebeard* grew from the friendship between Edward Dmytryk and Belfast boy Stephen Boyd. They had enjoyed a good working relationship on *Shalako* and planned to set up a company together to make the adaptation of a novel called *Act of Anger*, a project which fell through. Boyd had just made a film in Spain for the producer Alexander Salkind with the immortal American title of *Kill! Kill! Kill! Kill!* and informed Dmytryk that Salkind was seeking a director for one of a number of possible projects. Dmytryk had not worked for nearly three years and enthusiastically agreed to meet Salkind's son Ilya in London, where he was currently based with Jean and Rebecca. The plan was hatched to produce a film about Gilles de Rais, a companion-of-arms of Joan of Arc and confessed killer of many dozens of children. A later meeting in Geneva saw the demise of this project when Salkind revealed that his distributor network, upon which his funding mechanism was dependent, balked at the hard sell of such a gruesome tale. It is believed that de Rais was the inspiration for French folktale *Barbe bleue*, the serial wife-murderer who made the crossing into Anglo-Saxon legend as Bluebeard. The Geneva meeting between Salkind, Dmytryk and two Italian scriptwriters decided that murders of attractive females would be a more palatable prospect than murders of young boys, and *Bluebeard*, Dmytryk's induction into the more sexually permissive European market, was born.

The Salkinds had anticipated producing a horror movie and were initially dismayed when Dmytryk, Ennio De Concini and Maria Pia Fusco delivered the screenplay of a black comedy. They were eventually persuaded of the merits of the concept, but everyone recognized that good casting was essential to raise sufficient money for *Bluebeard* to rise above the level of exploitation. The meeting at Fouquet's with Richard Burton was brokered by Dmytryk's agent, Kurt Frings, and led to the actor being given a generous deal: "a sizeable amount for expenses … and a hefty percentage

Dmytryk and Richard Burton on the set of *Bluebeard* (1972).

of the distributor's gross. For him there were no box-office failures."[14] Burton was sniffy about accepting the role: "It's rubbish but it's something I've never done which is a 'horror film' and which the kids have been anxious for one or the other of us to do for many years."[15] With a star of the magnitude of Burton[16] in place, filling the roles of the eight disposable wives was a less daunting prospect, though the international distribution arrangement which was financing the film necessitated actresses from the United States, France, Germany and Italy. In December, Burton wrote in his diary: "And they told me they had Virna Lisi and almost had [Ursula] Andress and Ann-Margret."[17] "Almost" is an essential word in any film producer's vocabulary.

The American actresses signed were at different stages of the typical career trajectory: Raquel Welch's star was still shining brightly; Joey Heatherton's was waning. Burton confided blunt judgments to his diary—Welch was "very pretty though a trifle hard faced"[18] while he found Heatherton "unbelievably ordinary which might be good for the part. She has one of those one-on-every-street-corner blonde rather common and at the drop of an insult I'm sure vicious bitchy faces."[19] Other wives were to be played by Italian Virna Lisi, German Karin Schubert, French Nathalie Delon and Austrian Sybil Danning. Rounding up this cast required visiting casting directors in Paris and Munich, and the final months of 1971 also involved visiting prospective locations in Yugoslavia, Bulgaria and Hungary, before the last of these was chosen as the setting for the estate of Baron Kurt von Sepper, Bluebeard himself. Dmytryk was initially disappointed that Budapest was more faded than grand but grew to appreciate the Hungarians: "a bit subdued, perhaps, but still in love with the good and gay life—at least as good and as gay as they could get it."[20] For Welch, the surveillance was hard to bear: "Budapest was great, but it's a occupied country, and we had this Comrade Julie with us the whole time."[21]

Burton's shoot began on 10 February 1972 and his mind was more focused on a prospective film adaptation of Malcolm Lowry's *Under the Volcano* with Elizabeth Taylor than on his scene with Joey Heatherton. He had been warned that Raquel Welch was "an arch fiend…. They expect me to awe her and frighten her into good behaviour. I have no intention of doing anything of the kind unless she really does behave boringly in which case I will turn all my ice-cold intellectual guns on her."[22] Dmytryk had received the same warnings about Welch's attitude but found her to be "a doll."[23] Burton felt Heatherton possessed "a natural hardness"[24] but though his relations with her were cordial ("She seems perfectly innocuous to me but everybody else seems to loathe her"[25]), he was withering about her talent: "I must confess that she is about as stimulating an actress as the worst I've known but I keep on telling myself that it doesn't really matter. We can slide around her with cunning and girls in horror movies are always props after all. All they have to do is be pretty and dumb."[26] Burton's acidity was not confined to his leading ladies: "Dmytryk is very little and very brisk and light-voiced and intelligent and pretends to knowledge that he doesn't really have or has forgotten."[27] Burton gave some credence to rumors that Heatherton was "having a ding-dong, as the vernacular goes, with Dmytryk. I wouldn't be at all surprised as however else did she get the part?"[28]

Elizabeth Taylor had accompanied Burton to Budapest, but their marriage was in difficulty. He was not drinking at this point, but she wouldn't let his sobriety interfere with her own enjoyment of alcohol. Knowing that he was going to be surrounded by a bevy of international beauties was an additional inducement to make the trip with him and her jealousy did erupt on one occasion. Taylor recalled, "There was someone who put too much passion in certain scenes. And moreover, she was naked. I smacked her face for her pains. And Richard, I don't know how many plates I broke over his head."[29] Dmytryk also remembered this incident with the frustratingly unnamed actress: "Richard and the actress were enjoying it, and Elizabeth saw what was happening. Well, she landed one on the girl…. It was terrible to see. Richard was behaving very oddly. It was like he was trying to goad Elizabeth. Or maybe he had just lost interest in her."[30]

During the shoot, Taylor turned 40 years old and, starting on Saturday 26 February, threw a lavish quadruple-party birthday celebration—"the cocktail party when we arrived, the cellar party, the brunch party the next day and the posh party at night."[31] Around 80 guests flew in, including Princess Grace, Michael Caine, Ringo Starr, David Niven and many of Taylor and Burton's family members. By all accounts, the weekend was a roaring success, with Princess Grace particularly loving the opportunity to let her hair down, literally and figuratively. Burton, who remained sober, recalled sitting in a booth with Frankie Howerd and Susannah York and watching the rest of the party sweep past doing the conga: "Led by the family the whole thing passed before our eyes with Grace in the middle of it all. Unbelievable."[32]

Edward Dmytryk, an avowed party-hater, had to concede that it "was the most wonderful party I have ever been to."[33]

Taylor had originally invited the cast of *Bluebeard* but thought better of it and uninvited the glamorous female performers, although Raquel Welch re-invited herself. According to Welch's secretary at the time, the actress's fling with Burton was "[o]ne of the biggest affairs of Raquel's life, although it lasted only three days."[34] Taylor was relying on the indiscretion of the entourage that she was employing and they duly provided her with the damning information. Burton was phoned from Rome at five o'clock one morning with the command to "Get that woman out of my bed!"[35] Burton also had an affair with Nathalie Delon and possibly other members of the cast, with the exception of Virna Lisi who remained immune to his charms.

On 23 March, Burton and Taylor flew to London to attend the funeral in Wales of his beloved brother Ivor. When he returned to Budapest, he was "a different man. He looked older. As he carried on with the filming, he seemed agitated, frustrated, desperate."[36] He had resumed drinking. Initially he was able to control his consumption but after one evening as guests of the British Ambassador, the wheels really came off Burton's wagon. At this official dinner, he drank all evening while eating nothing and, by his own admission, insulted two ambassadors and their wives, said something obscene to the British ambassador and walked out, leaving Taylor on her own. Around midnight the following evening, as the last set-up of a night shoot was being prepared, Burton disappeared without warning with Natalie Delon, leaving Dmytryk and the whole crew incredulous and abandoned on a Budapest street. Dmytryk cancelled the next day's shooting and refused to answer the phone, until Burton sent a note in the afternoon, apologizing profusely. But the behavior worsened as sober moments became a rarity. He was often drunk when he arrived at the studio in the morning and always drunk by the end of the afternoon's filming. Dmytryk watched the quality of his performance deteriorate in the three to four hours' work that he managed to squeeze out of him each day. "Burton was a very bad drunk"[37] who would turn mean and made the rest of the shoot an endurance. He did not abandon self-awareness however and admitted to Dmytryk, "I used to think I could act just as well when I was drunk as when I was sober. I've found out I can't."[38]

Contemporary reviews of *Bluebeard* classed it as an allegory on fascism, due to its setting in Europe in the 1930s and a swastika-type emblem that is prominent on uniforms and on flags. What was barely identified at the time and is still unclear to modern viewers since it is not highlighted in onscreen dialogue, is that the film is set in Austria prior to 1938. The emblem was the symbol representing the *Vaterländische Front* (Fatherland Front), slightly modified to more closely resemble the Nazi swastika. The VF was a far-right nationalist group, organized along the lines of Italian fascism with strong alignment to the Catholic Church, which was banned upon the Austrian *Anschluss* to Nazi Germany in March 1938. Baron Kurt von Sepper (Richard Burton) is a fictional Austrian nobleman and aviator who, in order to hide scar tissue from a plane crash, has grown a beard that has turned blue through some chemical reaction. He is a leading member of the VF who has taken part in massacres and the expulsion of Jewish citizens from their homes.

Bluebeard is the last of a quartet of films through Edward Dmytryk's career that addressed anti–Semitism, the others being *Crossfire*, *The Juggler* and *The Young Lions*. The attitudes espoused by von Sepper and his cronies are more closely aligned with Nazi ideology than the historical VF. Modern art is to be found in a "decadent Jewish exhibition" and to solve society's ills "order is what we need, order!" One of von Sepper's wives comes from Linz—"That's Hitler's city; that was the only good thing about her"—and to another he says, "You're even more beautiful when you're pale, so Aryan." Aligning von Sepper's racial attitudes and political stance with the fascists of the time is clear but what is intriguing from Dmytryk in his only on-screen writing credit (though he contributed to many other of his screenplays) is the red-baiting in the dialogue. By the early 1970s, Dmytryk's status as *bête noire* of the Left was decades-old and refusing to fade. His decision to put in the script lines such as "The trouble is, my dear Baron, that some Bolshevik ideas have managed to get through, even to the farmers" and "Men … who have faced machine guns, bombs, even Communists!" can only have been taken with his tongue in his cheek and with a somewhat defiant gesture to his former Comrades.

This political element sits rather uneasily with the stylistic excesses and farcical content of *Bluebeard*. The film veers from horror to absurd comedy to soft core nudity without pausing for breath, a generic waywardness that is reflected in the instability of its color palette. The stately home of von Sepper boasts a lurid color scheme in each room, a kaleidoscope of purple, red and mustard—a Baronial bordello. On the walls he hangs Rorschach-type pictures which are in reality impenetrable portraits of his succession of wives and a taunt to the curious to peer into his psyche. The one who succeeds in unpicking him is wife number seven, Anne (Joey Heatherton). After she discovers the other dead wives stored in a freezer, von Sepper admits to his crimes ("They forced me to it—I didn't want to kill them") and before killing her out of necessity, he relates the stories of her predecessors.

These vignettes are played as black comic interludes, with their success dependent on the skill of the actress involved. Perhaps the funniest involves wife number two (Virna Lisi) who refuses to stop singing and at the moment of sexual consummation on a guillotine suffers a premature decapitation. Raquel Welch is wife number four, whom von Sepper first encounters as a statuesque, white-swathed nun and whose hair becomes looser and whose décolletage becomes more pronounced as she reveals just how many lovers she has had since losing her virginity. These two sequences are the most enjoyable due to their utter absurdity and the fact that they are the least problematic regarding the representation of women. Tellingly, Lisi and Welch are the only two of the wives not to go topless.

Certain of the other vignettes are harder to accept from a modern perspective and bear the producer's imprint. Dmytryk recalled how, after the first cut of the film was produced, Alexander Salkind told him, "The Germans insist on getting more sex and more violence, or they won't distribute the film."[39] The director had "played the sex and murder scenes obliquely, with only a slight bit of nudity to appease the distributors," but now agreed to film more exploitative material to maintain some control over the final product. Thus, we have wife number three, Erika (Nathalie Delon), who insists on infantile talk and whose inexperience leads von Sepper to hire a prostitute (Sybil Danning) to educate her. After some lesbian writhing between the two, they are both impaled by an elephant tusk. Wife number six, Caroline (Agostina Belli), is constantly naked until von Sepper has his hawk attack and kill her gruesomely. Most problematic is wife number five, Brigitt (Marilu Tolo), who "didn't seem interested in a sexual relationship at all. She hated men. It was like a challenge to a duel." When he responds to her kicking him in the groin by slapping her, she becomes sexually aroused and demands ever more extreme physical violence, until she is drowned in a vat of red wine. Such content is unthinkable in modern mainstream cinema and demonstrates how far removed we are from the 1970s, as does another scene of a hunting party early in the film where we witness the genuine slaughter of a succession of wild animals.

Richard Burton's performance wavers due to the rigors of his drinking, the degree of talent of his opposite numbers and the variability of his dialogue. In his diaries, he cited Vincent Price as an inspiration on how to play the role, commenting that "it has to be done with immense tongue in cheek."[40] Unfortunately even this strategy is defeated when the actress he spends most screen time with is the sullenly inexpressive Joey Heatherton. Her character Anne unlocks the secret of his murderous misogyny—a fear of sex: "You killed them at the very moment when they tried to give themselves to you." *Bluebeard* is a lurid, sometimes unpalatable but rarely dull, time capsule from the time when the directors of Hollywood's Golden Age felt obliged to up the salacious content of their films to remain relevant. Hitchcock's *Frenzy*, containing another uncomfortable scene involving sex and violence, was released in the UK four months prior to *Bluebeard*. The most compelling element of Dmytryk's film is probably the haunting theme music from Ennio Morricone, played on cimbalom. The remainder is best summed up by von Sepper's final words as he is assassinated by the Jewish violinist whose parents he had murdered: "It's absurd. It's ridiculous."

He Is My Brother (1975)

When Edward Dmytryk wrote his autobiography *It's a Hell of a Life but Not a Bad Living* in 1978, he listed the films he had made in a Filmography, giving *Bluebeard* (1972) and *The "Human" Factor* (1975) as his final two films. Ever the expert editor, Dmytryk is here performing some creative cutting, for between these two he also directed *He Is My Brother*. The opportunities to work had withered away by the mid–1970s. In an interview with Mitch Tuchman in 1976, Dmytryk discusses the reasons for this and whether he was the victim of a reverse blacklist or was simply perceived as "old hat": "My whole background, the pictures I've made, all that means nothing, you know. They look at the two or three pictures I've made lately that I don't think are particularly good as real pictures—the technique is fine—but they're the only ones I could take and I had to make a living. That's the situation. [Tuchman: What pictures were those?] Pictures like.... I'm not.... *Human Factor, Bluebeard*. There were some interesting things about *Bluebeard*, but it wasn't a good picture.

It wasn't a picture I'm proud of. I needed money. I had to live."[41] *He Is My Brother* certainly isn't a good picture, and Dmytryk omitting it in the apparent hope that it would fade into obscurity and not darken his distinguished name in years to come is a desire that is perfectly understandable, if forlorn.

The film was entirely shot on the Hawaiian island of Kauai and concerns the colony for those suffering from leprosy that was set up in the 1860s on the Kalau-papa Peninsula of Molokai, also in Hawaii. A prologue relates the history of the colony under the care of Father Damien, a Belgian priest who died in 1889, and discloses that the film's fictional story is of his successor Brother Dalton, played by Keenan Wynn. Into this forsaken shore of the 1890s crashes the vessel carrying brothers Jeff and Randy Remington (Bobby Sherman and Robbie Rist), shipwrecking the boys with their perfect 1970s haircuts and their crisply laundered white t-shirts and shorts. During their enforced sojourn among the afflicted natives, the boys encounter the dark magic of the local spiritual leader, the Kahuna (Joaquin Martinez), and discover compassion, romance and hang-gliding.

He Is My Brother is a lamentable post-script to Dmytryk's career. None of the ingredients provide distinction—from the script that is replete with anachronistic dialogue ("You're all nuts"; "You're the biggest pain the ass I ever met"; "Okie-dokie") and narrative dead-ends to the glutinous score that is ladled over proceedings. Dmytryk is operating with the lowest of budgets, most clearly discernible in the awkward sound editing, and since the film has no credit for cinematographer, Dmytryk was presumably directing the camera operator himself. His son Michael acted as assistant director. Though Dmytryk attempts to provoke interest in a sequence cross-cutting between a Catholic Mass and a ceremony performed by the Kahuna, more representative of the film's flaccidness are a slow-motion scene of young lovers frolicking in the water and an over-extended sequence of nineteenth century hang-gliding. Keenan Wynn does his best with an ineffectual role, but we are never convinced other than that Sherman and Rist are merely Californian boys enjoying a working vacation in Hawaii. Fortunately, Dmytryk had one more feature film in him, for *He Is My Brother* would have made a wretched swan song.

The "Human" Factor (1975)

What are the odds that two old Hollywood veterans, born within three years of each other in the first decade of the century, should have bowed out of their careers in the 1970s with identically titled films? Yet the parallels between the careers of Otto Preminger and Edward Dmytryk do not end there. Naturally there are huge differences—Preminger was a formidable producer, originating projects and taking huge risks to put controversial topics on screen. He was also a notoriously difficult martinet of a director, whereas hardly a single one of Dmytryk's colleagues had a bad word to say about his working practices. But both directors made their names in the mid–1940s, were inconsistent in quality, veered from hit to flop and suffered a marked decline in their final films. Both made seminal *noirs* (*Laura, Fallen Angel* / *Crossfire, Murder, My Sweet*), films with censor-baiting material (*The Moon is Blue, The Man with the Golden Arm* / *The Sniper, The Carpetbaggers*), respectable literary adaptations (*Bonjour Tristesse* / *The End of the Affair*), racy literary adaptations (*Forever Amber* / *Walk on the Wild Side*), sprawling wartime dramas (*In Harm's Way* / *The Young Lions*) and 1960s black-and-white what-the-hell-is-going-on thrillers (*Bunny Lake is Missing* / *Mirage*). Their films featured Catholic clergymen (*The Cardinal* / *The Left Hand of God*), saints (*Saint Joan* / *The Reluctant Saint*), courts-martial (*The Court-Martial of Billy Mitchell* / *The Caine Mutiny*) and trail-blazing depiction of the new state of Israel (*Exodus* / *The Juggler*). They both stepped out of their comfort zones with late misfires (*Skidoo* / *Bluebeard*) and their final films were both titled *The Human Factor*. And at the end, the political outcast bettered the Austrian autocrat.

Dmytryk's *The "Human" Factor*[42] combines two of the most common thriller tropes of the 1970s—terrorism and vigilantes. George Kennedy plays John Kinsdale, a computer engineer at the NATO base in Naples pursuing a personal vendetta to kill the terrorists who slaughtered his family in their home. In an interview from 2006, Kennedy was refreshingly self-deprecating about getting the role: "They had budget problems and what have you. Sure, they would've rather had Burt Lancaster or somebody.... I said, 'I'll try. I'm not the kid I used to be, but I'll try.'"[43] Indeed, Kennedy had lost some of his physical condition since he had played a villain in Dmytryk's *Mirage*, and hauling his 6'4" frame up flights of stairs and across Neopolitan roofs in chases involves obvious effort. It must also be conceded that, although Kennedy is a credible and likable presence as expatriate family man and father of the barely teenage Danny Huston, some of the more emotionally distraught scenes stretch his abilities.

It is worth quoting Kennedy at length on his experience of Dmytryk's working processes at the very end of his career, after 40 years as a director:

> "Eddie was a good guy—a careful, caring director.... [He] was very precise. He, as any good director will, was very well-prepared for the next day's shooting. There was none of this 'Let's wing it' from him. He knew at the beginning of the day, like Hitchcock, he knew not only what he was going to do but what order he was going to do it and what cuts he was going to make.... Most directors are the same way.... But the great ones know, without it going to the cutting room, where the cuts are going to be. They've already seen the movie. Eddie ... listened to everybody. He would show displeasure mostly on the physical things.... Although he never yelled or anything, he would show impatience. It's five o'clock or six o'clock in the evening, and I'm so damned exhausted ... he'd say, 'Come on!' I understood it but it didn't make it any easier to do."[44]

Urban violence and fear of home invasion was a common concern in the 1970s, as capitalized on by Michael Winner in *Death Wish*, which Kennedy misremembers as succeeding *The "Human" Factor*. That the culprits in the Dmytryk film are a band of anarcho-terrorists attacking American citizens is lent an uncanny resonance in the twenty-first century by the name of the computer system that simulates war games at NATO and which is used to identify certain of the terrorists: 9/11. John Mills plays a computer boffin who assists Kinsale in his increasingly obsessive quest to apprehend the terrorists, and here is an actor utterly at ease with the material he has been given. Both Dmytryk and Kennedy were full of praise for Mills—"I will never work with a finer actor or a better man"[45] and "Oh, what a delightful man!"[46] The film's trust in the white heat of 1970s computer technology is endearing, with psychological profiles run through 9/11 before the "human" may be factored in to the calculation.

The mean New York streets of *Death Wish* are replaced by the labyrinthine courtyards and alleyways of Naples, the location shoot delivering a sure sense of place. Dmytryk's camera tails Kennedy's breathless pursuit with sharp editing and maintains a propulsive pace. One car chase benefits from the city's traffic chaos and was barely faked. Kennedy recalled, "Naples in those days was unbelievable. You put lines on the street, you know three lanes. I don't know why they wasted the paint. Nobody ever goes in line…. And Naples people drive like maniacs anyway. So, I fit right in."[47] He recalls the director telling him, "Floor it. If the cops chase you, we'll pay the ticket."[48] It is an effective sequence and Dmytryk, who had despaired of Italian working practices while making *The Reluctant Saint* and *Anzio*, was now using that brand of managed mayhem to his advantage. At one point the action moves to Rome, and Dmytryk's camera adopts possibly the exact same vantage point at the Colosseum as it had taken in *Anzio*.

Arthur Franz, who made more films with Dmytryk than any other actor, completed his octet in this final film. The World War II airman had risen through the ranks since appearing as an infantryman in *Eight Iron Men*—Lieutenant (*The Caine Mutiny*, *The Young Lions*), Captain (*Alvarez Kelly*), Major General (*Anzio*)—and was now accorded the rank of General in Edward Dmytryk's swansong. Kennedy claimed that the money behind the film had its roots in the Mafia and one scene has Kinsdale arrive at the home of an American family, only to discover that they have their own armed bodyguard and appear to be in hiding from organized crime. Here, as in every other scene, the focus is strongly on the male. Females in this macho vigilante world are there to be threatened or to provide concerned support, as with Rita Tushingham's thankless role as Kinsdale's colleague. The sole woman with agency in the film, apart from the female terrorist who lulls victims into dropping their guard, is the woman in the climactic supermarket shootout who grabs a gun and dispatches one of the bad guys, much to the seemingly genuine horror of the young child beside her.

This final sequence is well-staged and blood-soaked according to mid–1970s norms. The setting is the commissary at the NATO headquarters where the terrorists launch their campaign of private home executions into the public sphere. Under a sign reading "Remember you are guests in this country. Do not abuse your privileges," the American housewives rush through the doors to purchase, only to be held hostages to consumerism. The film itself mounts a defiant protest to the anti-capitalist renegades, with prominent product placement for Pepsi-Cola through the whole of its running time. The tall pyramid of Heinz Tomato Soup may be an obvious candidate to be toppled during the melee, spilling some of its blood-colored contents, but the product will endure. When Kinsdale arrives by car, rather than insinuating his way into the hostage situation, he drives straight through the doors of the supermarket, a narrative jolt but totally in keeping with his unrestrainable mental state. The terrorist bloodbath is his vengeance and his catharsis. The final moments, when he pursues one of the terrorists (played by the film's producer Frank Avianca) outside, shoots him beside a trash can and unloads every bullet in his gun into the prone body, came under criticism at the time for being gratuitous and eroding sympathy for Kinsdale. Kennedy claims credit for this choice: "It wasn't written. I said, 'Let me just keep firing the blanks'…. There was nothing else in his life. And Dmytryk said, 'That's a nice bit of business. I'm glad you added that.' Some critics didn't like it but I never understood. It wasn't vicious. I'm not a critics' darling anyway."[49]

The "Human" Factor is not one of the top rank in Edward Dmytryk's filmography. Its low budget is evident and its edges aren't smooth. It is, however, an effective genre piece, efficiently delivered, with a script that hits the maverick vigilante notes more successfully than the emotive ones. It is a full-blooded conclusion to the director's career, its grungy aesthetic and visceral violence nicely offset by Ennio Morricone's lushly elegiac theme. The script also features one reference with an air of sweet serendipity. The war games overseen by Arthur Franz's General have the code-name Operation Hawk. The first film directed by Dmytryk exactly 40 years previously was titled *The Hawk*. The convoluted path that his career had taken between that film and this one, through acclaimed peaks and reviled troughs, was Edward Dmytryk's own Operation Hawk. Mission accomplished.

Filmography

Title

Date of American release
Studio
Producer—Screenwriter—Photographer—Music
Actors
Running Time

The Hawk

13 May 1935
Independent
H.A. Wohl—James Oliver Curwood, Griffin Jay—Roland Price—Hal Chasnoff
Bruce Lane, Betty Jordan, Dickie Jones, Lafe McKee, Rollo Dix, Don Orlando
55 mins

Million Dollar Legs

14 July 1939
Paramount (Co-director Nick Grindé)
William C. Thomas—Lewis R. Foster, Richard English—Harry Fischbeck—John Leipold
Betty Grable, John Hartley, Donald O'Connor, Jackie Coogan, Buster Crabbe, Thurston Hall,
Peter Lind Hayes, Dorothea Kent, Richard Denning
65 mins

Television Spy

20 October 1939
Paramount
William LeBaron, Edward T. Lowe Jr.—Lillie Hayward, Horace McCoy, Endre Bohem,
William R. Lipman—Harry Fischbeck—Boris Morros
William Henry, Judith Barrett, William Collier, Sr., Richard Denning, John Eldredge,
Dorothy Tree, Anthony Quinn, Minor Watson, Morgan Conway, Byron Foulger
58 mins

Emergency Squad

5 January 1940
Paramount
William LeBaron—Stuart Palmer, Robert Musil, Garnett Weston, Michael Raymond—
Stuart Thompson—John Leipold, Leo Shuken

William Henry, Louise Campbell, Richard Denning, Robert Paige, Anthony Quinn,
John Miljan, John Marston
58 mins

Golden Gloves

2 August 1940
Paramount
William LeBaron, Carl Krueger—Lewis R. Foster, Maxwell Shane, Joe Ansen—Henry Sharp—
Friedrich Holländer, Paul Marquardt
Richard Denning, Jeanne Cagney, J. Carrol Naish, Robert Paige, William Frawley, Robert Ryan,
Edward Brophy, Leona Roberts
66 mins

Mystery Sea Raider

9 August 1940
Paramount
Eugene J. Zukor—Edward E. Paramore Jr., Robert Grant—Dewey Wrigley, Harry Fischbeck—
Victor Young, Albert Hay Malotte
Carole Landis, Henry Wilcoxon, Onslow Stevens, Kathleen Howard, Wally Rairden,
Sven Hugo Borg
80 mins

Her First Romance

7 July 1941
Monogram
I. E. Chadwick—Adele Comandini, Gene Stratton-Porter—John Mescall—Gregory Stone
Edith Fellows, Wilbur Evans, Julie Bishop, Alan Ladd, Judith Linden, Roger Daniel,
Marian Kerby, Marlo Dwyer
73 mins

The Devil Commands

3 February 1941
Columbia
Wallace MacDonald—Robert Hardy Andrews, Milton Gunzburg, William Sloane—
Allen G. Siegler—Morris Stoloff
Boris Karloff, Richard Fiske, Amanda Duff, Anne Revere, Dorothy Adams, Walter Baldwin,
Kenneth MacDonald, Shirley Warde, Cy Schindell
65 mins

Under Age

24 April 1941
Columbia
Ralph Cohn—Stanley Roberts, Robert Hardy Andrews—John Stumar—Morris Stoloff
Nan Grey, Alan Baxter, Mary Anderson, Tom Neal, Leona Maricle, Don Beddoe
60 mins

Sweetheart of the Campus

26 June 1941
Columbia
Jack Fier—Edmund L. Hartmann, Robert Hardy Andrews—Franz Planer—Morris Stoloff
Ruby Keeler, Ozzie Nelson, Harriet Nelson, Gordon Oliver, Don Beddoe, Charles Judels,
Kathleen Howard, Byron Foulger, George Lessey, Zoot Watson, Four Spirits of Rhythm
70 mins

The Blonde from Singapore

16 October 1941
Columbia
Jack Fier—George Bricker, Houston Branch—L. William O'Connell—Morris Stoloff
Florence Rice, Leif Erickson, Gordon Jones, Don Beddoe, Alexander D'Arcy, Adele Rowland,
Lumsden Hare, Richard Terry, Emory Parnell
69 mins

Secrets of the Lone Wolf

13 November 1941
Columbia
Jack Fier—Stuart Palmer—Philip Tannura—Morris Stoloff
Warren William, Ruth Ford, Roger Clark, Victor Jory, Eric Blore, Thurston Hall, Fred Kelsey,
Victor Kilian, Marlo Dwyer, Lester Sharpe
66 mins

Confessions of Boston Blackie

9 January 1942
Columbia
William Berke—Jay Dratler, Paul Yawitz—Philip Tannura—Morris Stoloff
Chester Morris, Harriet Nelson, Richard Lane, George E. Stone, Lloyd Corrigan, Joan Woodbury,
Walter Sande, Ralph Theodore
65 mins

Counter-Espionage

3 September 1942
Columbia
Wallace MacDonald—Aubrey Wisberg—Philip Tannura—Morris Stoloff
Warren William, Eric Blore, Hillary Brooke, Thurston Hall, Kurt Katch, Forrest Tucker,
Lloyd Bridges
73 mins

Seven Miles from Alcatraz

8 January 1943
RKO
Herman Schlom—Joseph Krumgold, John D. Klorer—Robert De Grasse—Roy Webb
James Craig, Bonita Granville, Frank Jenks, Cliff Edwards, George Cleveland, Erford Gage,
Tala Birell, John Banner, Otto Reichow
62 mins

Hitler's Children

6 January 1943
RKO
Edward A. Golden—Emmet Lavery—Russell Metty—Roy Webb
*Tim Holt, Bonita Granville, Kent Smith, Otto Kruger, Hans Conried, H.B. Warner,
Lloyd Corrigan, Erford Gage, Nancy Gates, Gavin Muir*
82 mins

The Falcon Strikes Back

7 May 1943
RKO
Maurice Geraghty—Edward Dein, Stuart Palmer, Gerald Geraghty—Jack MacKenzie—
Roy Webb
*Tom Conway, Harriet Nelson, Jane Randolph, Edgar Kennedy, Cliff Edwards, Rita Corday,
Erford Gage, Wynne Gibson, André Charlot, Richard Loo, Cliff Clark, Edward Gargan,
Frank Faylen, Byron Foulger*
66 mins

Captive Wild Woman

4 June 1943
Universal
Ben Pivar—Ted Fithian, Neil P. Varnick, Griffin Jay, Henry Sucher—George Robinson—
Hans J. Salter
*Acquanetta, John Carradine, Evelyn Ankers, Milburn Stone, Lloyd Corrigan, Fay Helm,
Martha Vickers, Vince Barnett, Paul Fix, Ray Corrigan, Fred Aldrich, Clyde Beatty*
61 mins

Behind the Rising Sun

1 August 1943
RKO
Edward Dmytryk, Howard Hughes—Emmet Lavery—Russell Metty—Roy Webb
*Margo, Tom Neal, J. Carrol Naish, Robert Ryan, Gloria Holden, Donald Douglas, George Givot,
Adeline De Walt Reynolds, Leonard Strong, Mike Mazurki*
88 mins

Tender Comrade

1 June 1944
RKO
David Hempstead—Dalton Trumbo—Russell Metty—Leigh Harline
*Ginger Rogers, Robert Ryan, Ruth Hussey, Patricia Collinge, Mady Christians, Kim Hunter,
Jane Darwell, Richard Martin*
102 mins

Murder, My Sweet

22 February 1945
RKO
Adrian Scott, Sid Rogell—John Paxton—Harry J. Wild—Roy Webb
*Dick Powell, Claire Trevor, Anne Shirley, Mike Mazurki, Miles Mander, Otto Kruger,
Douglas Walton, Donald Douglas, Esther Howard, Ralf Harolde, Paul Phillips*
95 mins

Back to Bataan

31 May 1945
Robert Fellows—Richard H. Landau, Ben Barzman—Nicholas Musuraca—Roy Webb
John Wayne, Beulah Bondi, Anthony Quinn, Fely Franquelli, Richard Loo, Philip Ahn,
Alex Havier, Ducky Louie, Lawrence Tierney, Leonard Strong, Paul Fix
95 mins

Cornered

23 November 1945
RKO
Adrian Scott—Ben Hecht, John Wexley, John Paxton—Harry J. Wild—Roy Webb
Dick Powell, Walter Slezak, Micheline Cheirel, Nina Vale, Morris Carnovsky, Edgar Barrier,
Steven Geray, Jack La Rue, Gregory Gaye, Luther Adler, Ellen Corby, Byron Foulger
102 mins

Till the End of Time

23 July 1946
RKO
Dore Schary—Allen Rivken—Harry J. Wild—Leigh Harline
Dorothy McGuire, Guy Madison, Robert Mitchum, Bill Williams, Tom Tully, William Gargan,
Jean Porter, Johnny Sands, Ruth Nelson, Selena Royle, Richard Tyler, Loren Tindall,
Harry von Zell, Richard Benedict
105 mins

So Well Remembered

4 November 1947
RKO-Rank
Adrian Scott—John Paxton—Freddie Young—Hanns Eisler
John Mills, Martha Scott, Patricia Roc, Trevor Howard, Richard Carlson, Reginald Tate,
Beatrice Varley, Frederick Leister, Ivor Barnard, Julian D'Albie, Juliet Mills
114 mins

Crossfire

22 July 1947
RKO
Adrian Scott—John Paxton—J. Roy Hunt—Roy Webb
Robert Young, Robert Mitchum, Robert Ryan, Gloria Grahame, Paul Kelly, Sam Levene,
Jacqueline White, Steve Brodie, George Cooper, Richard Benedict, Tom Keene,
William Phipps, Lex Barker, Marlo Dwyer
86 mins

Obsession

8 January 1950
Sovereign Films
Nat Bronstein—Alec Coppel—C. M. Pennington-Richards—Nino Rota

Robert Newton, Phil Brown, Sally Gray, Naunton Wayne, James Harcourt, Betty Cooper,
Michael Balfour, Ronald Adam, Roddy Hughes, Allan Jeayes, Olga Lindo, Russell Waters, Lionel
Watts, Sam Kydd
96 mins

Give Us This Day

20 December 1949
Plantagenet
Rod Geiger, Roland Reed—Ben Barzman–C. M. Pennington-Richards—Benjamin Frankel
Sam Wanamaker, Lea Padovani, Kathleen Ryan, Charles Goldner, Bonar Colleano,
William Sylvester, George Pastell, Philo Hauser, Sid James, Rosalie Crutchley
120 mins

Mutiny

5 March 1952
King Brothers
Frank King, Maurice King—Philip Yordan, Sidney Harmon—Ernest Laszlo—Dimitri Tiomkin
Mark Stevens, Angela Lansbury, Patric Knowles, Gene Evans, Rhys Williams, Robert Osterloh,
Peter Brocco, Emerson Treacy, Morris Ankrum, Norman Leavitt, Todd Karns
77 mins

The Sniper

9 May 1952
Columbia
Stanley Kramer—Harry Brown, Edna Anhalt, Edward Anhalt—Burnett Guffey—
George Antheil
Adolphe Menjou, Arthur Franz, Gerald Mohr, Marie Windsor, Frank Faylen, Richard Kiley,
Mabel Paige, Marlo Dwyer, Geraldine Carr, Carl Benton Reid, Harry Cheshire, Charles Lane,
Byron Foulger
88 mins

Eight Iron Men

1 January 1953
Columbia
Stanley Kramer—Harry Brown—J. Roy Hunt—Leith Stevens
Bonar Colleano, Lee Marvin, Arthur Franz, Richard Kiley, Nick Dennis, James Griffith,
Dickie Moore, Mary Castle, George Cooper, Barney Phillips, Robert Nichols,
Richard Grayson, Douglas Henderson
80 mins

The Juggler

5 May 1953
Columbia
Stanley Kramer—Michael Blankfort—J. Roy Hunt—George Antheil
Kirk Douglas, Paul Stewart, Milly Vitale, Joseph Walsh, Alf Kjellin, Charles Lane,
Beverly Washburn, John Banner, Oskar Karlweis
84 mins

The Caine Mutiny

24 June 1954
Columbia
Stanley Kramer—Stanley Roberts—Franz Planer—Max Steiner
Humphrey Bogart, Van Johnson, Fred MacMurray, José Ferrer, Robert Francis, E.G. Marshall,
Tom Tully, May Wynn, Katherine Warren, Lee Marvin, Claude Akins, Arthur Franz,
Warner Anderson, Jerry Paris, Steve Brodie
124 mins

Broken Lance

25 September 1954
20th Century-Fox
Sol C. Siegel—Richard Murphy, Philip Yordan—Joe MacDonald—Leigh Harline
Spencer Tracy, Robert Wagner, Jean Peters, Richard Widmark, Katy Jurado, Hugh O'Brian,
Eduard Franz, Earl Holliman, E.G. Marshall, Carl Benton Reid, Philip Ober, Robert Burton
96 mins

The End of the Affair

24 February 1955 (UK release date)
Columbia
David Lewis, David Rose—Lenore Coffee—Wilkie Cooper—Benjamin Frankel
Deborah Kerr, Van Johnson, John Mills, Peter Cushing, Michael Goodliffe, Stephen Murray,
Charles Goldner, Nora Swinburne, Frederick Leister, Elsie Wagstaff, Joyce Carey
105 mins

Soldier of Fortune

25 May 1955
20th Century-Fox
Buddy Adler—Ernest Gann—Leo Tover—Hugo Friedhofer
Clark Gable, Susan Hayward, Michael Rennie, Gene Barry, Tom Tully, Alexander D'Arcy,
Anna Sten, Leo Gordon, Jack Kruschen, Richard Loo, Soo Yong, Mel Welles
96 mins

The Left Hand of God

2 September 1955
20th Century-Fox
Buddy Adler—Alfred Hayes—Franz Planer—Victor Young
Humphrey Bogart, Gene Tierney, Lee J. Cobb, Agnes Moorehead, E.G. Marshall, Jean Porter,
Carl Benton Reid, Victor Sen Yung, Philip Ahn, Benson Fong, Robert Burton
87 mins

The Mountain

14 November 1956
Paramount
Edward Dmytryk—Ranald MacDougall—Franz Planer—Daniele Amfitheatrof
Spencer Tracy, Robert Wagner, Claire Trevor, William Demarest, Barbara Darrow, Richard Arlen,
E.G. Marshall, Anna Kashfi, Richard Garrick, Harry Townes, Stacy Harris
105 mins

Raintree County

20 December 1957
Metro-Goldwyn-Mayer
David Lewis—Millard Kaufman—Robert Surtees—Johnny Green
Montgomery Clift, Elizabeth Taylor, Eva Marie Saint, Nigel Patrick, Lee Marvin, Rod Taylor, Agnes Moorehead, Walter Abel, Jarma Lewis, Tom Drake, Rhys Williams, Russell Collins, DeForest Kelley, Eileen Stevens
168 mins

The Young Lions

2 April 1958
20th Century–Fox
Al Lichtman—Edward Anhalt—Joe MacDonald—Hugo Friedhofer
Marlon Brando, Montgomery Clift, Dean Martin, Hope Lange, Barbara Rush, May Britt, Maximilian Schell, Dora Doll, Lee Van Cleef, Liliane Montevecchi, Parley Baer, Arthur Franz, Hal Baylor, Richard Gardner, Herbert Rudley, Michael Smith
167 mins

Warlock

30 April 1959
20th Century–Fox
Edward Dmytryk—Robert Alan Aurthur—Joe MacDonald—Leigh Harline
Henry Fonda, Richard Widmark, Anthony Quinn, Dorothy Malone, Dolores Michaels, Wallace Ford, Tom Drake, Richard Arlen, DeForest Kelley, Frank Gorshin, Regis Toomey, Vaughn Taylor, Don Beddoe, Whit Bissell, Bartlett Robinson
122 mins

The Blue Angel

4 September 1959
20th Century–Fox
Jack Cummings—Nigel Balchin—Leon Shamroy—Hugo Friedhofer
Curd Jürgens, May Britt, Theodore Bikel, John Banner, Fabrizio Mioni, Ludwig Stössel, Wolfe Barzell, Ina Anders, Brian Avery, Richard Tyler, Edit Angold, Stella Stevens
107 mins

Walk on the Wild Side

21 February 1962
Columbia
Charles Feldman—John Fante, Edmund Morris—Joe MacDonald—Elmer Bernstein
Laurence Harvey, Capucine, Jane Fonda, Anne Baxter, Barbara Stanwyck, Joanna Moore, Richard Rust, Karl Swenson, Don Barry, Juanita Moore, John Anderson, Ken Lynch, Todd Armstrong, Sherry O'Neil
114 mins

The Reluctant Saint

3 December 1962
Columbia

Edward Dmytryk—John Fante—C. M. Pennington-Richards—Nino Rota
Maximilian Schell, Ricardo Montalbán, Lea Padovani, Akim Tamiroff, Harold Goldblatt,
Arnoldo Foa, Carlo Croccolo, Giulio Bosetti, Armand Mestral, Elisa Cegani
105 mins

The Carpetbaggers

1 July 1964
Paramount
Joseph E. Levine—John Michael Hayes—Joe MacDonald—Elmer Bernstein
George Peppard, Alan Ladd, Carroll Baker, Robert Cummings, Martha Hyer, Elizabeth Ashley,
Lew Ayres, Martin Balsam, Ralph Taeger, Archie Moore, Leif Erickson, Arthur Franz,
Tom Tully, Audrey Totter, Anthony Warde, Charles Lane, Tom Lowell, Victoria Jean
150 mins

Where Love Has Gone

2 November 1964
Paramount
Joseph E. Levine—John Michael Hayes—Joe MacDonald—Walter Scharf
Susan Hayward, Bette Davis, Mike Connors, Joey Heatherton, Jane Greer, DeForest Kelley,
George Macready, Anne Seymour, Willis Bouchey, Walter Reed, Whit Bissell
111 mins

Mirage

26 May 1965
Universal
Harry Keller—Peter Stone—Joe MacDonald—Quincy Jones
Gregory Peck, Diane Baker, Walter Matthau, Kevin McCarthy, Jack Weston, Leif Erickson,
Walter Abel, George Kennedy, Robert H. Harris, Anne Seymour, House Jameson,
Hari Rhodes, Syl Lamont, Eileen Baral, Neil Fitzgerald, Franklin Cover
108 mins

Alvarez Kelly

6 October 1966
Columbia
Sol C. Siegel—Franklin Coen—Joe MacDonald—Johnny Green
William Holden, Richard Widmark, Janice Rule, Patrick O'Neal, Victoria Shaw, Roger C. Carmel,
Richard Rust, Arthur Franz, Don Barry, Harry Carey, Jr., Duke Hobbie, Howard Caine
106 mins

Anzio

24 July 1968
Columbia
Dino De Laurentiis—Harry Craig—Giuseppe Rotunno—Riz Ortolani
Robert Mitchum, Peter Falk, Robert Ryan, Earl Holliman, Mark Damon, Arthur Kennedy,
Reni Santoni, Joseph Walsh, Thomas Hunter, Giancarlo Giannini, Anthony Steel,
Patrick Magee, Arthur Franz, Tonio Selwart, Elsa Albani, Annabella Andreoili,

Wolfgang Preiss
117 mins

Shalako

7 October 1968
Cinerama
Dimitri De Grunwald, Euan Lloyd—J. J. Griffith, Hal Hopper, Scott Finch—Ted Moore—
Robert Farnon
*Sean Connery, Brigitte Bardot, Jack Hawkins, Stephen Boyd, Peter Van Eyck, Honor Blackman,
Woody Strode, Alexander Knox, Eric Sykes, Valerie French, Julian Mateos, Don Barry,
Rodd Redwing, Chief Tug Smith, Hans de Vries*
113 mins

Bluebeard

18 August 1972
Cinerama
Alexander Salkind—Edward Dmytryk, Ennio De Concini, Maria Pia Fusco—Gabor Pogany—
Ennio Morricone
*Richard Burton, Raquel Welch, Virna Lisi, Nathalie Delon, Karin Schubert, Agostina Belli,
Sybil Danning, Joey Heatherton, Edward Meeks, Jean Lefebvre, Erica Schramm,
Doka Bukova, Mathieu Carriere, Karl-Otto Alberty, Marilu Tolo, Mag-Avril*
125 mins

He Is My Brother

29 January 1975
Atlantic Releasing Corporation
James Polakof—David Pritchard—No credit for Photographer—Ed Bogas
Bobby Sherman, Kathy Paulo, Keenan Wynn, Robbie Rist, Joaquin Martinez, Benson Fong
90 mins

The "Human" Factor

19 November 1975
Bryanston
Frank Avianca—Peter Powell, Thomas Hunter—Ousama Rawi—Ennio Morricone
*George Kennedy, John Mills, Raf Vallone, Rita Tushingham, Barry Sullivan, Shane Rimmer,
Thomas Hunter, Frank Avianca, Haydée Politoff, Arthur Franz, Fiamma Verges,
Danny Huston*
95 mins

Chapter Notes

Introduction

1. Dmytryk, *It's a Hell of a Life*, 207.
2. Schary, *Heyday*, 158.
3. Edward Anhalt Oral Testimony, 335.
4. Pennington-Richards Interview with Lawson & Moffat.
5. McGilligan and Buhle, *Tender Comrades*, 54.
6. *Ibid.*, 73.
7. Barzman, *Red and the Blacklist*, 47.
8. Letter from Paxton to Clay Steinman, 1977.
9. Interview with Glen Lovell, *Los Angeles Times*, 28 January 1996, 65.
10. Interview with author, 2 April 2019.
11. Navasky, *Naming Names*, 375.
12. *Los Angeles Times*, 30 October 1947.
13. Ronald Davis interview, 76.
14. Interview with author, 28 March 2019.
15. Interview with author, 10 October 2019.
16. *Ibid.*
17. *Ibid.*
18. Interview with Glen Lovell, *Los Angeles Times*, 28 January 1996, 65.

Chapter I

1. Mordden, *Hollywood Studios*, 24.
2. Ronald L. Davis interview, 12.
3. Dmytryk, *It's a Hell of a Life*, 4.
4. *Ibid.*, 15.
5. *Ibid.*, 18.
6. *Ibid.*, 20.
7. *Ibid.*, 21.
8. *Ibid.*, 31.
9. *Ibid.*, 28.
10. Dmytryk was clear about his preference for the word "cutter" over "editor," in what he disapproved of as the intellectualization of the movies.
11. Barzman, *Red and the Blacklist*, 282.
12. Dmytryk, *It's a Hell of a Life*, 40.
13. *Ibid.*, 31–32.
14. "Socially he was a doll, really great guy, sweetheart. On the set, he was the nastiest man that ever lived, the crews wanted to kill him." Ronald L. Davis interview, 35.
15. *Ibid.*, 42.
16. *Ibid.*, 37.
17. Callow, *Charles Laughton*, 92.
18. Dmytryk, *It's a Hell of a Life*, 25.
19. Callow, *Charles Laughton*, 89.
20. Dmytryk, *It's a Hell of a Life*, 38.
21. *Ibid.*
22. Jewell, *A Titan is Born*, 175.
23. Dmytryk, *It's a Hell of a Life*, 41.
24. *Ibid.*, 52.
25. Ronald L. Davis interview, 14.
26. Dmytryk, *It's a Hell of a Life*, 42.
27. Vermilye, *Buster Crabbe*, 113.
28. Dmytryk, *It's a Hell of a Life*, 44.
29. *Ibid.*, 44.
30. *Showmen's Trade Review*, 10 June 1939.
31. Dmytryk, *It's a Hell of a Life*, 45.
32. *Ibid.*, 46.
33. Quinn, *One Man Tango*, 150.
34. Quinn, *One Man Tango*, 148.
35. Dmytryk, *It's a Hell of a Life*, 47.
36. *Ibid.*, 47.
37. Marrill, *Films of Anthony Quinn*, 68.
38. Dmytryk, *It's a Hell of a Life*, 48.
39. Ronald L. Davis interview, 49–50.
40. *Ibid.*
41. Dmytryk, *It's a Hell of a Life*, 48.
42. *Ibid.*
43. Rainey, *Serial Film Stars*, 552.
44. Dmytryk, *It's a Hell of a Life*, 48.
45. *Ibid.*, 49.
46. *Ibid.*
47. Dmytryk, *It's a Hell of a Life*, 49.
48. Gans, *Carole Landis*, 45.
49. *Ibid.*, 53.
50. Dmytryk, *It's a Hell of a Life*, 49.
51. *Ibid.*, 50.
52. *Motion Picture Herald*, 3 August 1940.
53. *Motion Picture Herald*, 28 December 1940.
54. *Ibid.*
55. Linet, *Ladd*, 43.
56. Dmytryk, *It's a Hell of a Life*, 52.
57. *Ibid.*, 53.
58. "They were two long scenes. It took me five hours to see the rushes of them. There was one head-on shot both Stevens and I were particularly proud of which showed the essence of this woman. This was removed, too. Stevens fought for me, but his hands were tied, contractually. Before the cutting, my part in *A Place in the Sun* was the best work I'd ever done in Hollywood." Anne Revere interviewed for McClelland, *Unkindest Cuts*, 40.

59. Barranger, *Unfriendly Witnesses*, 58.
60. *Ibid.*, 60.
61. *Ibid.*, 63.
62. Revere terminated her "rather loose association" with the Party in 1945 or 1946, "as soon as the war was over." See Barranger, *Unfriendly Witnesses*, 63. Dmytryk was a member of the Party in 1945.
63. Weaver, *Flashbacks*, 103.
64. Jacobs, *Boris Karloff*, 264.
65. Dmytryk, *It's a Hell of a Life*, 53.
66. Weaver, *Flashbacks*, 103.
67. *Ibid.*, 104.
68. *Ibid.*, 105.
69. Cook, *Trumbo*, 314.
70. Barranger, *Unfriendly Witnesses*, 61.
71. *Ibid.*, 61.
72. Bubbeo, *Women of Warner Brothers*, 111.
73. Dmytryk, *It's a Hell of a Life*, 53.
74. Nelson, *Ozzie*, 157.
75. *Ibid.*, 161.
76. Ronald L. Davis interview, 14.
77. *Ibid.*, 58.
78. *Picturegoer's Who's Who*, 388.
79. Brideson, *Also Starring*, 74.
80. *Ibid.*
81. Greene, *The Pleasure-Dome*, 239.

Chapter II

1. Jewell, *Slow Fade to Black*, 1.
2. Ronald Davis interview, 60.
3. Jewell, *Slow Fade to Black*, 9.
4. When Welles learned he had been fired, he wired his associates, "Don't get excited. We're just passing a rough Koerner on our way to immortality." RKO's response—"All's well that ends Welles." Jewell, *Slow Fade to Black*, 7.
5. Dmytryk, *It's a Hell of a Life*, 58.
6. Letter from Paxton to Clay Steinman, 1977.
7. Ronald Davis interview, 38.
8. *Motion Picture Daily*, 5 October 1943, 4.
9. Dmytryk, *Odd Man Out*, 3.
10. *Ibid.*, 6.
11. *Ibid.*, 7.
12. *Ibid.*
13. *Ibid.*, 8.
14. *Ibid.*
15. *Ibid.*, 8–9.
16. Jewell, *Slow Fade to Black*, 35–36.
17. Dmytryk, *It's a Hell of a Life*, 72.
18. *Ibid.*, 79.
19. Jewell, *Slow Fade to Black*, 16.
20. Dmytryk, *It's a Hell of a Life*, 82.
21. *Ibid.*, 84.
22. Jewell, *Slow Fade to Black*, 49.
23. Dmytryk, *It's a Hell of a Life*, 88.
24. *Film Bulletin*, 24 December 1945.
25. *Film Bulletin*, 19 August 1946.
26. Dmytryk, *It's a Hell of a Life*, 46.
27. Jewell, *The RKO Story*, 181.
28. Ziemer, quoted in *Life* 1 February 1943, 40.
29. Production Code files.
30. Dmytryk, *It's a Hard Life*, 55.
31. *Ibid.*, 55.
32. *Life*, 1 February 43.
33. Dmytryk, *It's a Hard Life*, 55.
34. Jewell, *The RKO Story*, 181.
35. *Ibid.*
36. Dmytryk, *It's a Hard Life*, 55.
37. *Life*, 1 February 1943, 37.
38. *Ibid.*, 40.
39. Production Code files.
40. Tuchman interview with Dmytryk.
41. *Ibid.*
42. *The Falcon Takes Over* was directed by Irving Reis, the original director on *Hitler's Children* before being replaced by Dmytryk.
43. Sanders, *Memoirs of a Professional Cad*, 202.
44. Production Code files.
45. *Ibid.*
46. The final cost of $116,665 was $30,000 less than Jacques Tourneur's *The Leopard Man*, also on the RKO B-production slate of that year.
47. Mank, *Women in Horror Films*, 207.
48. *Ibid.*, 210.
49. Interview with Ronald L. Davis, 63.
50. Mank, *Women in Horror Films*, 209.
51. *Fangoria* #94, 16.
52. *Ibid.*
53. Mank, *Women in Horror Films*, 209.
54. Koppes & Black, *Hollywood Goes to War*, 249.
55. *Ibid.*, 249.
56. *Ibid.*, 248.
57. *Ibid.*, 271.
58. *Ibid.*
59. *Ibid.*
60. Dmytryk, *It's a Hell of a Life*, 56.
61. Introduction to *Behind the Rising Sun* booklet from RKO Studios, 1943.
62. Koppes & Black, *Hollywood Goes to War*, 274.
63. Jewell, *Slow Fade to Black*, 17.
64. Rogers, *Ginger*, 257.
65. *Motion Picture Daily*, 29 December 1943, 7.
66. *Motion Picture Daily*, 29 April 1943, 2.
67. *Motion Picture Herald*, 3 July 1943, 31.
68. Val Lewton did produce this film, retitled once again as *Youth Runs Wild*. It was directed by Mark Robson and released in 1944.
69. Ronald L. Davis interview, 66.
70. *Ibid.*, 65.
71. Barranger, *Unfriendly Witnesses*, 113.
72. Letter from ARI, Ginger Rogers at RKO Collection, 8 October 1943.
73. ARI report, 4 October 1943.
74. *Ibid.*
75. *Ibid.*
76. An RKO film of this title was produced by David Hempstead, with Clifford Odets as director and Cary Grant as star, and was released in October 1944.
77. Message from Ulric Bell of OWI to RKO, 30 December 1943.
78. Preview card at Glendale, 16 December 1943.
79. Preview card at Pasadena, 14 December 1943.

80. Hannsberry, *Bad Boys*, 524.
81. Letter to Keith Kelly, undated, likely 1976–77.
82. Letter to Stephen Pendo, 1973.
83. *Ibid.*
84. *Ibid.*
85. *Ibid.*
86. *Ibid.*
87. *Ibid.*
88. Parrish, *RKO Gals*, 290.
89. Barzman, *Red and the Blacklist*, 178.
90. Letter to Stephen Pendo, 1973.
91. *Saturday Evening Post*, 12 October 1946.
92. Hannsberry, *Bad Boys*, 525.
93. Dmytryk, *It's a Hell of a Life*, 59.
94. Hannsberry, *Bad Boys*, 525.
95. Jewell, *Slow Fade to Black*, 30.
96. Letter to Stephen Pendo, 1973.
97. *Ibid.*
98. *Ibid.*
99. *Ibid.*
100. *Ibid.*
101. Hannsberry, *Bad Boys*, 524.
102. *Saturday Evening Post*, 12 October 1946.
103. Interview with Robert Porfirio in Porfirio et al., eds., *Film Noir Reader 3*, 35.
104. Hannsberry, *Bad Boys*, 526.
105. Letter to Stephen Pendo, 1973.
106. Riggin, *John Wayne: A Bio-Bibliography*, 58.
107. *Ibid.*
108. Dmytryk, *It's a Hell of a Life*, 65.
109. *Ibid.*, 67.
110. *Ibid.*, 68.
111. *Ibid.*, 66.
112. *Screenland*, May 1945, 90.
113. Barzman, *Red and the Blacklist*, 45.
114. Wills, *John Wayne's America*, 198.
115. Barzman, *Red and the Blacklist*, 53.
116. *Ibid.*, 56.
117. Roberts & Olson, *John Wayne: American*, 259.
118. Koppes & Black, *Hollywood Goes to War*, 253.
119. Dmytryk, *It's a Hell of a Life*, 66.
120. Interview with Robert Porfirio in Porfirio et al., eds., *Film Noir Reader 3*, 32.
121. Dmytryk, *It's a Hell of a Life*, 70.
122. Langdon-Teclaw in Krutnik et al., eds., *Un-American Hollywood*, 158.
123. *Ibid.*
124. Dmytryk, *It's a Hell of a Life*, 70.
125. Langdon-Teclaw in Krutnik et al., eds., *Un-American Hollywood*, 159.
126. McGilligan and Buhle, *Tender Comrades*, 716.
127. *Ibid.*
128. Dmytryk, *It's a Hell of a Life*, 71.
129. McGilligan and Buhle, *Tender Comrades*, 716.
130. Dmytryk, *Odd Man Out*, 21.
131. Andersen in Krutnik et al., eds., *Un-American Hollywood*, 256.
132. Dmytryk, *It's a Hell of a Life*, 71.
133. Production Code files, 14 June 1945.
134. *Ibid.*
135. Dmytryk, *It's a Hell of a Life*, 77.
136. Hofler, *Man Who Invented Rock Hudson*, 123.
137. Dmytryk, *It's a Hell of a Life*, 77.
138. Ronald L. Davis interview, 85.
139. *Ibid.*, 83.
140. Server, *Robert Mitchum*, 115.
141. *Ibid.*, 116.
142. Dmytryk, *It's a Hell of a Life*, 73.
143. Obituary, Tom Vallance, *Independent*, 17 September 2001.
144. Dmytryk, *It's a Hell of a Life*, 78.
145. Server, *Robert Mitchum*, 120.
146. *Ibid.*
147. Interview with Robert Porfirio in Porfirio et al., eds., *Film Noir Reader 3*, 34.
148. Dmytryk, *It's a Hell of a Life*, 80–81.
149. *Ibid.*, 84.
150. Pickford, *Macclesfield*, 96.
151. *Ibid.*
152. Dmytryk, *It's a Hell of a Life*, 85.
153. *Ibid.*
154. Letter from PCA, 16 July 1946.
155. Dmytryk, *It's a Hell of a Life*, 85.
156. Jewell, *Slow Fade to Black*, 79.
157. Brooks, *Brick Foxhole*, 88.
158. *Ibid.*, 92.
159. *Ibid.*, 43.
160. *Ibid.*, 36, 32.
161. *Ibid.*, 120.
162. *Ibid.*, 131.
163. *Ibid.*, 224.
164. *Ibid.*, 155.
165. *Ibid.*, 31.
166. Letter from Breen to William Gordon, 17 July 1945.
167. Screenplay, 19 February 1947.
168. Draft Continuity, 25 January 1947.
169. Jewell, *Slow Fade to Black*, 68.
170. *Ibid.*
171. Samuel Goldwyn had bought the rights to *Earth and High Heaven*, a novel from 1944 that addressed anti–Semitism, and had treatments made by screenwriters Ring Lardner, Jr., Howard Koch and Elmer Rice. None were accepted by the producer and with the release of *Gentleman's Agreement*, Goldwyn gradually lost interest.
172. Letter from Paxton to Clay Steinman, 1977.
173. *Ibid.*
174. *Ibid.*
175. Letter from Breen to RKO, 27 February 1947.
176. *Ibid.*
177. *Ibid.*
178. Letter from Paxton to Clay Steinman, 1977.
179. Dmytryk, *It's a Hell of a Life*, 90.
180. By way of comparison, Dudley Nichols was simultaneously shooting *Mourning Becomes Electra* with Rosalind Russell and Michael Redgrave at RKO. It was budgeted at $800,000 for "talent," ended up costing $2,342,000 and brought the studio a colossal loss of $2,310,000.

181. Letter from Paxton to Clay Steinman, 1977.
182. Dmytryk, *It's a Hell of a Life*, 90.
183. Screenplay, 25 January 1947.
184. Screenplay, 19 February 1947.
185. Letter from Paxton to Clay Steinman, 1977.
186. Quoted in letter from Clay Steinman to John Paxton, 1 July 1977.
187. *Ibid.*
188. *Ibid.*
189. Letter from Paxton to Clay Steinman, 1977.
190. *Life*, 1 December 1947.
191. Letter from Dmytryk to *New York Times*, 10 August 1947.
192. *P.M. Daily*, 23 July 1947.
193. Jewell, *Slow Fade to Black*, 69.

Chapter III

1. Freedland, *Hollywood on Trial*, 27.
2. *Ibid.*, 104.
3. *Ibid.*, 107.
4. *Ibid.*
5. *Ibid.*, 22.
6. *Ibid.*, 23.
7. Navasky, *Naming Names*, 78.
8. Freedland, *Hollywood on Trial*, 21.
9. McGilligan and Buhle, *Tender Comrades*, 454.
10. Dmytryk, *It's a Hell of a Life*, 94.
11. Interview with Mitch Tuchman.
12. Dmytryk, *It's a Hell of a Life*, 95.
13. HUAC hearings, 21 October 1947.
14. HUAC hearings, 23 October 1947.
15. HUAC hearings, 29 October 1947.
16. *Ibid.*
17. Huston, *An Open Book*, 133.
18. Dmytryk, *Odd Man Out*, 73–74.
19. HUAC hearings, 30 October 1947.
20. Dmytryk, *Odd Man Out*, 90.
21. Freedland, *Hollywood on Trial*, 211.
22. Eyman, *Print the Legend*, 385.
23. Freedland, *Hollywood on Trial*, 104.
24. *Ibid.*, 70.
25. Dmytryk, *It's a Hell of a Life*, 105.
26. Dmytryk, *Odd Man Out*, 104.
27. Interview with Mitch Tuchman.
28. Rossen was one of the "Unfriendly Nineteen" in 1947, refused to testify when brought back before HUAC in 1951, was blacklisted and ultimately named names in his testimony before the Committee in May 1953.
29. Freedland, *Hollywood on Trial*, 229.
30. McGilligan and Buhle, *Tender Comrades*, 105–106.
31. Dmytryk, *It's a Hell of a Life*, 127.
32. Biberman served his prison time with Alvah Bessie in Texarkana, Texas.
33. Interview with Mitch Tuchman.
34. Freedland, *Hollywood on Trial*, 93.
35. Letter to Jean Porter Dmytryk, 30 July 1950.
36. Interview with Mitch Tuchman.
37. Dmytryk, *Odd Man Out*, 144.
38. Letter to Jean Porter Dmytryk, 13 September 1950.
39. Letter to Jean Porter Dmytryk, 3 November 1950.
40. Dmytryk, *It's a Hell of a Life*, 145.
41. Freedland, *Hollywood on Trial*, 163.
42. Dmytryk, *It's a Hell of a Life*, 146.
43. Freedland, *Hollywood on Trial*, 227.
44. HUAC hearings, 25 April 1951.
45. *Ibid.*
46. *Ibid.*
47. Maltz interview with Mitch Tuchman.
48. Dmytryk interview with Mitch Tuchman.
49. McGilligan and Buhle, *Tender Comrades*, 678.
50. Freedland, *Hollywood on Trial*, 228.
51. McGilligan and Buhle, *Tender Comrades*, 73.
52. Barzman, *Red and the Blacklist*, 48.
53. *Ibid.*, 591.
54. Freedland, *Hollywood on Trial*, 228.
55. *Ibid.*, 228.
56. McGilligan and Buhle, *Tender Comrades*, 718.
57. Freedland, *Hollywood on Trial*, 228.
58. Interview with author, 2019.
59. Cook, *Trumbo*, 313–314.
60. Freedland, *Hollywood on Trial*, 2.
61. *Ibid.*, 232.
62. *Variety*, 24 November 1948, 2.
63. Dmytryk's preferred mode of working, post-*Crossfire*, was to finish shooting at 4:30 p.m. and then take up to half an hour to rehearse the next day's work. The cameramen and crew would take the 60–90 minutes thereafter to begin lighting the first set-up of the next morning.
64. Dmytryk, *It's a Hell of a Life*, 112.
65. *Ibid.*, 113.
66. Penrose, *Apologise Later*, xiii.
67. Dmytryk, *It's a Hell of a Life*, 113.
68. Navasky, *Naming Names*, 348.
69. Dmytryk, *Odd Man Out*, 187.
70. Location work was filmed in Mayfair and the devastated Church Row in Hampstead.
71. Dmytryk, *It's a Hell of a Life*, 113.
72. *Ibid.*, 114.
73. Dmytryk, *It's a Hell of a Life*, 122.
74. Barzman, *Red and the Blacklist*, 129.
75. Dmytryk, *Odd Man Out*, 107.
76. Dmytryk, *It's a Hell of a Life*, 119.
77. Barzman, *Red and the Blacklist*, 140.
78. Dmytryk, *It's a Hell of a Life*, 120.
79. Barzman, *Red and the Blacklist*, 156.
80. *Ibid.*, 155.
81. Dmytryk, *It's a Hell of a Life*, 117.
82. *Ibid.*, 123.
83. *Film Illustrated Monthly*, Vol. 4, No. 7, 8.
84. *Ibid.*, 8.
85. *Ibid.*, 7.
86. *Ibid.*, 8.
87. Dmytryk, *It's a Hell of a Life*, 121.
88. Interview with Lawson & Moffat, 1990.
89. Dmytryk, *It's a Hell of a Life*, 124.
90. *San Francisco Chronicle*, 12 October 1950, 13.

91. Letter from Irving Levin to Dmytryk, 13 October 1950.

Chapter IV

1. King Brothers Production Files.
2. The deal had been arranged by George Willner, who was Dalton Trumbo's agent. Willner was named before HUAC by a friendly witness in April 1951. He appeared before the Committee eleven days later, invoked the Fifth Amendment and was blacklisted.
3. *The Hollywood Reporter*, 7 June 1951.
4. Dmytryk, *It's a Hell of a Life*, 148.
5. Kramer interview with Tuchman, 11 October 1976.
6. Ronald Davis interview, 121.
7. Kramer interview with Tuchman, 11 October 1976.
8. Dmytryk interview with Tuchman.
9. Maltz interview with Tuchman.
10. *Ibid.*
11. Jean Porter Dmytryk, Unpublished memoir.
12. *Ibid.*
13. Kramer, *Mad, Mad World*, 120.
14. Hanson, *Dalton Trumbo*, 96.
15. *Ibid.*
16. Edelman and Kupferberg, *Angela Lansbury*, 93.
17. McGilligan and Buhle, *Tender Comrades*, 270–271.
18. Interview on Arrow Blu-Ray of *Horror Express*.
19. Dmytryk, *It's a Hell of a Life*, 148.
20. Production Code Administration files, 26 July 1951.
21. *Variety*, 29 May 1951.
22. Edward Anhalt Oral Testimony, 198.
23. *Ibid.*, 203.
24. *Ibid.*, 291.
25. PCA files, 14 August 1951.
26. *Ibid.*
27. *Ibid.*
28. *Ibid.*
29. PCA files, 4 September 1951.
30. Freedland, *Hollywood on Trial*, 62.
31. Krutnik et al., *Un-American Hollywood*, 280.
32. Freedland, *Hollywood on Trial*, 62.
33. Interview with Mitch Tuchman, 11 October 1976.
34. Kramer, *Mad Mad World*, 92–93.
35. Dmytryk, *It's a Hell of a Life*, 166.
36. *Ibid.*
37. Edward Anhalt Oral Testimony, 445.
38. *Ibid.*, 323.
39. Dmytryk, *It's a Hell of a Life*, 166.
40. Kramer, *Mad Mad World*, 93.
41. Edward Anhalt Oral Testimony, 444.
42. *Ibid.*
43. Quoted in Edward Anhalt Oral Testimony, 201–202.
44. Dmytryk, *It's a Hell of a Life*, 167.
45. *Ibid.*, 168.
46. Kramer, *Mad, Mad World*, 97.
47. Dmytryk, *It's a Hell of a Life*, 168.
48. Epstein, *Lee Marvin*, 81.
49. *Ibid.*, 81.
50. *Ibid.*, 82.
51. Kramer Production Files.
52. *Ibid.*
53. Douglas, *Ragman's Son*, 205.
54. *Ibid.*
55. Ronald Davis interview.
56. Dmytryk, *It's a Hell of a Life*, 90.
57. *Ibid.*, 169.
58. *Ibid.*
59. *Ibid.*, 170.
60. Douglas, *Ragman's Son*, 208.
61. *Ibid.*
62. *Ibid.*, 205.
63. Kramer, *Mad World*, 102.
64. Navasky, *Naming Names*, 378.
65. Michael Blankfort Papers, 21 April 1953.
66. *Ibid.*, 15 December 1953.
67. Douglas, *Ragman's Son*, 202.
68. Kramer, *Mad World*, 105.
69. Michael Blankfort Papers, 1979.
70. Erens, *Jew in American Cinema*, 217.
71. Kramer, *Mad World*, 105.
72. Wouk, *Caine Mutiny*, 129.
73. Sperber & Lax, *Bogart*, 479.
74. *Ibid.*, 478.
75. *Ibid.*, 480.
76. *Ibid.*
77. Kramer, *Mad World*, 119.
78. Kramer, *Mad World*, 111.
79. Callow, *Charles Laughton*, 232.
80. Dmytryk, *It's a Hell of a Life*, 172.
81. Sperber & Lax, *Bogart*, 484.
82. Robert Francis didn't get the chance to develop as an actor after this debut, his career tragically cut short when he died in a plane crash in July 1955.
83. Kramer, *Mad World*, 115.
84. Tranberg, *Fred MacMurray*, 147.
85. Davis, *Van Johnson*, 159.
86. Shipman, *Great Movie Stars*, 281.
87. Davis, *Van Johnson*, 159.
88. Somewhat perversely, Tully earned an Oscar nomination for Best Supporting Actor. Any of MacMurray, Johnson and Ferrer would have been a much more appropriate choice. None were nominated.
89. Tranberg, *Fred MacMurray*, 147.
90. Kramer, *Mad World*, 118.
91. Dmytryk, *It's a Hell of a Life*, 178.
92. Sperber & Lax, *Bogart*, 484–5.
93. Kramer, *Mad World*, 118.
94. *Ibid.*, 120.
95. Kazan, *A Life*, 500.

Chapter V

1. Dmytryk, *It's a Hell of a Life*, 187.
2. *Ibid.*

3. *Ibid.*, 190.

4. *Ibid.*, 191.

5. *Ibid.*, 195.

6. *Ibid.*, 219.

7. *Ibid.*, 223.

8. *Ibid.*, 239.

9. The film finally emerged in 1962 as *Escape from Zahrain*, directed by Ronald Neame and starring Yul Brynner.

10. *Hollywood Reporter*, 23 July 1954.

11. Dmytryk, *It's a Hell of a Life*, 181.

12. Curtis, *Spencer Tracy*, 654.

13. Holston, *Richard Widmark Bio-Bib*, 123.

14. Curtis, *Spencer Tracy*, 659.

15. Dmytryk, *It's a Hell of a Life*, 180.

16. *Ibid.*, 179–180.

17. Fisher, *Spencer Tracy Bio-Bib*, 231.

18. Curtis, *Spencer Tracy*, 658.

19. *Ibid.*, 661.

20. Swindell, *Spencer Tracy*, 229.

21. Dmytryk, *It's a Hell of a Life*, 185.

22. *Ibid.*

23. Undated letter from E. G. Marshall to Katharine Hepburn.

24. *Hollywood Reporter*, 23 July 1954.

25. Dmytryk, *It's a Hell of a Life*, 180.

26. Wiley & Bona, *Inside Oscar*, 250.

27. Greene, *The End of the Affair*, 1.

28. Gregory Peck Papers, Letter of 3 February 1952.

29. Letter of 24 February 1952. After the release of *The Sound Barrier* in July 1952, Lean's next completed project was *Hobson's Choice*, released in April 1954.

30. Letter of 1 March 1952.

31. Falk, *Travels in Greeneland*, 109.

32. William Wyler Papers, Letter from David Lewis, 20 August 1952.

33. Wyler Papers, Cable from David Lewis, 5 September 1952.

34. Wyler Papers, Letter from Ray Stark, 21 November 1952.

35. Wyler Papers, Letter from Herman Citron, 4 December 1952.

36. Wyler Papers, Letter from Ray Stark, 11 December 1952.

37. MPAA Files, Letter to Joseph Breen, 6 February 1952.

38. MPAA Files, Memo of 10 March 1952.

39. *Ibid.*

40. MPAA Files, Memo of 17 November 1952.

41. Wyler Papers, Cable from David Lewis, December 1952.

42. Wyler Papers, Letter from Herman Citron, 4 February 1953.

43. Wyler papers, Cable from Herman Citron, 24 February 1953.

44. Coffee, *Storyline*, 106.

45. McGilligan, *Backstory*, 148.

46. *Ibid.*

47. Braun, *Deborah Kerr*, 148.

48. *Ibid.*, 151.

49. McGilligan, *Backstory*, 148.

50. Falk, *Travels in Greeneland*, 109.

51. Greene in Parkinson, ed., *Greene Film Reader*, 555.

52. Davis, *Van Johnson*, 171.

53. *Ibid.*, 169.

54. Dmytryk, *It's a Hell of a Life*, 188.

55. Coffee, *Storyline*, 106.

56. Dmytryk, *It's a Hell of a Life*, 188.

57. Coffee, *Storyline*, 106.

58. Greene in Parkinson, ed., *Greene Film Reader*, 555.

59. Greene, *The End of the Affair*, 32.

60. Essoe, *Films of Clark Gable*, 56.

61. Dmytryk, *It's a Hell of a Life*, 190.

62. LaGuardia and Arceri, *Red*, 3.

63. *Ibid.*, 57.

64. Linet, *Susan Hayward*, 180.

65. Holston, *Susan Hayward*, 106.

66. Dale Logue acted as Hayward's body double, a role she also fulfilled in Dmytryk's *Where Love Has Gone*.

67. Production Code of America files, 11 October 1954.

68. *Ibid.*, 19 October 1954.

69. *Ibid.*, 9 November 1954.

70. *Ibid.*

71. Ronald Davis interview, 36.

72. Production Code of America files, 3 November 1954.

73. The word "communist" is notable by its absence in the script.

74. Dmytryk, *It's a Hell of a Life*, 192–3.

75. *Ibid.*, 193.

76. *Variety*, 25 May 1955.

77. Grant, *Clark Gable*, 57.

78. MPAA files, Paramount Inter-office communication, 21 July 1950.

79. Memo of 25 July 1950.

80. Warner Bros. letter of 31 July 1950.

81. Warner Bros. letter of 3 August 1950.

82. Warner Bros. letter of 31 July 1950.

83. Breen letter of 16 November 1950.

84. *Ibid.*

85. *Ibid.*

86. Breen letter of 5 January 1951.

87. Breen letter of 18 January 1951.

88. Memo of 28 April 1954.

89. *Ibid.*

90. Peck letter of 18 September 1954.

91. *Ibid.*

92. Leff and Simmons, *Dame in the Kimono*, 63.

93. *Ibid.*

94. Dmytryk, *It's a Hell of a Life*, 197.

95. Nissen, *Films of Agnes Moorehead*, 214.

96. Dewey, *Lee J. Cobb*, 155.

97. *Ibid.*, 157.

98. Dmytryk, *It's a Hell of a Life*, 197.

99. *Ibid.*

100. Curtis, *Spencer Tracy*, 687.

101. *Ibid.*, 689.

102. *Ibid.*, 694.

103. Maychick & Borgo, *Heart to Heart*, 27.

104. Curtis, *Spencer Tracy*, 694.

105. Dmytryk, *It's a Hell of a Life*, 207.

106. *Ibid.*, 201.

107. *Ibid.*

108. Later the press would claim that Kashfi was not genuinely Indian since she travelled by British passport under the name of Joanna O'Callaghan. She explained that she used her stepfather's name to ease immigration entry into the United States, on the advice of Spencer Tracy.

109. Kashfi, *Brando for Breakfast*, 18.

110. *Ibid.*, 19.

111. *Ibid.*, 14.

112. Dmytryk claimed that, when they first interviewed her in Paris, the assistant producer A. C. Lyles had promised to introduce Kashfi to Brando in Hollywood.

113. Maychick & Borgo, *Heart to Heart*, 28.

114. Curtis, *Spencer Tracy*, 696.

115. *Ibid.*, 696.

116. Paramount Production Files, communication from Harry Caplan to Frank Caffrey.

117. Curtis, *Spencer Tracy*, 698.

118. *Ibid.*, 702.

119. *Ibid.*, 704.

120. *Ibid.*, 707.

121. *Ibid.*, 707–8.

122. Paramount Production Files, communication from Harry Caplan to Frank Caffrey, 22 November 1955.

123. *Ibid.*

124. Dmytryk, *It's a Hell of a Life*, 206.

125. *Ibid.*, 205.

126. Paramount Production Files.

127. LaGuardia, *Monty*, 142.

128. *Ibid.*, 143.

129. Taylor, *Elizabeth Taylor*, 57–58.

130. LaGuardia, *Monty*, 165.

131. Dmytryk, *It's a Hell of a Life*, 212.

132. Ronald Davis interview, 142.

133. *MGM Camera 65* publicity booklet

134. Dmytryk, *It's a Hell of a Life*, 209.

135. Dmytryk, Unpublished *Raintree County* manuscript, 16.

136. Dmytryk, *It's a Hell of a Life*, 210.

137. Dmytryk, Unpublished *Raintree County* manuscript, 65.

138. *Ibid.*, 69–70.

139. *Ibid.*, 73.

140. *Ibid.*, 84.

141. Ronald Davis interview, 143.

142. Dmytryk wrote about the location shoot, "Our chief problem was finding lodging for a couple of black players we had with us. In our travels through the South, they usually wound up staying with a local black minister, one of the few places where Christian charity was practiced." *It's a Hell of a Life*, 213.

143. Dmytryk, Unpublished *Raintree County* manuscript, 102.

144. *Ibid.*

145. Ronald Davis interview, 143.

146. *Ibid.*

147. *Ibid.*, 144.

148. Dmytryk, Unpublished *Raintree County* manuscript, 145.

149. *Los Angeles Times*, 9 October 1957.

150. *Ibid.*

151. Letter from Irwin Shaw to Fred Zinnemann, 31 October 1951.

152. Letter from Fred Zinnemann to Irwin Shaw, 15 February 1952.

153. *Ibid.*

154. Letter from Al Hine to Fred Zinnemann, 26 March 1952.

155. Bosworth, *Marlon Brando*, 127.

156. *Ibid.*, 127.

157. *Ibid.*, 128.

158. *Ibid.*, 127.

159. *Ibid.*

160. Dmytryk, *It's a Hell of a Life*, 220.

161. *Ibid.*, 101.

162. *Ibid.*, 102.

163. *Ibid.*

164. Author's translation of Schell, *Ich Fliege über Dunkle Täler*, 86.

165. Schell, *Ich Fliege über Dunkle Täler*, 77.

166. Bosworth, *Marlon Brando*, 128.

167. Dmytryk, Unpublished *Raintree County* manuscript, 113.

168. Dmytryk, *It's a Hell of a Life*, 221.

169. Bosworth, *Marlon Brando*, 127.

170. Ronald Davis interview, 141.

171. Dmytryk, *It's a Hell of a Life*, 226.

172. *Ibid.*, 225.

173. Schoell, *Martini Man*, 119.

174. Dmytryk, *It's a Hell of a Life*, 231.

175. Hardy, *The Western*, 271.

176. Interview with Ronald Davis, 149.

177. Dmytryk, *It's a Hell of a Life*, 232.

178. *Ibid.*, 233.

179. Quinn, *One Man Tango*, 4–5.

180. *Ibid.*, 5.

181. Interview with Ronald Davis, 148.

182. *Ibid.*, 149.

183. Dmytryk, *It's a Hell of a Life*, 235.

184. *Ibid.*

185. *Ibid.*

186. *Ibid.*, 235–236.

187. *Ibid.*, 236.

188. Curtis, *Spencer Tracy*, 738.

189. Dmytryk, *It's a Hell of a Life*, 243.

190. Interview with Mich Tuchman, 62.

191. Bikel, *Theo*, 200.

192. *Ibid.*, 201.

193. *Film Bulletin*, August 1959, 20.

194. *Ibid.*, 16.

195. Dmytryk, *It's a Hell of a Life*, 243.

196. Bikel, *Theo*, 201.

197. *Film Bulletin*, August 1959, 24.

198. *Ibid.*, 25.

199. Bikel, *Theo*, 201.

200. Dmytryk, *It's a Hell of a Life*, 243.

Chapter VI

1. Dmytryk, *It's a Hell of a Life*, 256.

2. *Ibid.*, 262.

3. *Ibid.*, 270.
4. Interview with Tuchman.
5. Dmytryk, *It's a Hell of a Life*, 274.
6. *Ibid.*, 281.
7. *Ibid.*, 286.
8. *Ibid.*, 282.
9. Bass & Kirkham, *Saul Bass*, 205.
10. Mitch Tuchman interview, 1976
11. Di Orio, *Barbara Stanwyck*, 194.
12. *The Movie* magazine, volume 5, 1132.
13. Sinai, *Reach for the Top*, 266.
14. Andersen, *Citizen Jane*, 84.
15. *Ibid.*, 84.
16. *Ibid.*, 83.
17. *Ibid.*, 85.
18. Guiles, *Jane Fonda*, 78.
19. Bosworth, *Jane Fonda*, 160.
20. Dmytryk, *It's a Hell of a Life*, 246.
21. Fonda, *My Life So Far*, 254.
22. Kiernan, *Jane*, 135.
23. Letter from Shurlock to Dmytryk, 12 December 1960.
24. *Ibid.*
25. Letter from Shurlock to Dmytryk, 3 February 1961.
26. Ben Hecht performed uncredited work on the screenplay, although Feldman felt it was insufficiently sexy.
27. Tuchman interview.
28. *Ibid.*
29. Dmytryk, *It's a Hell of a Life*, 247.
30. Feldman called Harvey back for an additional four weeks after Dmytryk had departed, informing him that his was the only weak performance in the picture.
31. Tuchman interview.
32. Kiernan, *Jane*, 135.
33. Callahan, *Barbara Stanwyck*, 207.
34. Letter to Shurlock, 3 January 1962.
35. Letter from Feldman to Mankiewicz, 14 March 1962.
36. Andersen, *Citizen Jane*, 85.
37. Pastrovicchi, *St. Joseph*, iii.
38. Grosso, *Man Who Could Fly*, 1.
39. Dmytryk, *It's a Hell of a Life*, 255.
40. Grosso, *Man Who Could Fly*, 19.
41. Dmytryk, *It's a Hell of a Life*, 249.
42. *Ibid.*, 249.
43. *Ibid.*
44. Interview with Lawson & Moffat.
45. Dmytryk, *It's a Hell of a Life*, 249.
46. Interview with Lawson & Moffat.
47. *Ibid.*
48. Dyer, *Nino Rota*, 177.
49. Dmytryk, *It's a Hell of a Life*, 254.
50. *Ibid.*, 255.
51. Interview with Lawson & Moffat.
52. McKenna, *Showman of the Screen*, 99.
53. The top three U.S. money-makers released in 1964 were *Mary Poppins* ($75.6 million), *Goldfinger* ($62.3 million) and *My Fair Lady* ($56.6 million).
54. Dmytryk, *It's a Hell of a Life*, 260.
55. Letter from Curtis Kenyon, former president of Writers Guild of America West, to Martin Rackin, 4 October 1962.
56. McKenna, *Showman of the Screen*, 102.
57. Script dated 11 April 1963.
58. Dmytryk, *It's a Hell of a Life*, 262.
59. Production Code of America files, letter of 19 April 1963.
60. *Ibid.*, 19 April 1963.
61. *Ibid.*, 5 April 1963.
62. *Ibid.*, 19 April 1963.
63. McKenna, *Showman of the Screen*, 107.
64. *Ibid.*
65. Ronald Davis interview, 152.
66. Baker, *Baby Doll*, 235.
67. *Ibid.*
68. *Ibid.*
69. *Ibid.*
70. Dmytryk, *It's a Hell of a Life*, 261.
71. Ronald Davis interview, 157.
72. Dmytryk, *It's a Hell of a Life*, 262.
73. Baker, *Baby Doll*, 237.
74. Dmytryk, *It's a Hell of a Life*, 261.
75. Linet, *Ladd*, 253.
76. Dmytryk, *It's a Hell of a Life*, 261.
77. Baker, *Baby Doll*, 236.
78. *Ibid.*, 236.
79. Interview with author.
80. Clint Eastwood was turned down for a role, just prior to making *A Fistful of Dollars* for Sergio Leone.
81. Ronald Davis interview, 158.
82. Dmytryk, *It's a Hell of a Life*, 261.
83. McKenna, *Showman of the Screen*, 14.
84. Staggs, *Born to be Hurt*, 64.
85. Stine, *I'd Love to Kiss You*, 227.
86. Dmytryk, *It's a Hell of a Life*, 265.
87. *Ibid.*, 264.
88. Stine, *Mother Goddam*, 278.
89. Paramount Studios Production Files, 11 November 1963.
90. Stine, *I'd Love to Kiss You*, 227.
91. Ronald L. Davis interview with Dmytryk
92. Dmytryk, *It's a Hell of a Life*, 264.
93. Spada, *More Than a Woman*, 375.
94. Dmytryk, *It's a Hell of a Life*, 264.
95. *Ibid.*, 264.
96. Spada, *More Than a Woman*, 376.
97. Stine, *I'd Love to Kiss You*, 227.
98. Paramount Studios Production Files, 13 March 1964.
99. *Ibid.*, 13 August 1964.
100. *Ibid.*, 27 November 1963.
101. *Newsweek*, 16 November 1964.
102. Dmytryk, *It's a Hell of a Life*, 265.
103. *Dark Intruder* was released two months after *Mirage* but was an hour-long supporting feature.
104. Fujiwara, *World and its Double*, 334.
105. Tuchman interview with Dmytryk.
106. Dmytryk, *It's a Hell of a Life*, 267.
107. Gregory Peck papers.
108. *Ibid.*
109. Haney, *Gregory Peck*, 326.

110. Dmytryk, *It's a Hell of a Life*, 268.
111. McClelland, *Unkindest Cuts*, 194.
112. Dmytryk, *It's a Hell of a Life*, 269.
113. Gregory Peck papers.
114. Fishgall, *Gregory Peck*, 248.
115. *Ibid.*, 248.
116. Hedren, *Tippi*, 74.
117. Caron, *Thank Heaven*, 171.
118. MPAA files, 5 August 1963.
119. *Time*, 28 May 1965.
120. Richard Schickel, *Life*, 18 June 1965.
121. *Cork Examiner*, 17 September 1965. *Mirage* was the U.S. entry at the Cork International Film Festival.
122. Fishgall, *Gregory Peck*, 248.
123. Dmytryk, *It's a Hell of a Life*, 270.
124. Thomas, *Golden Boy*, 158.
125. Dmytryk, *It's a Hell of a Life*, 272.
126. *Ibid.*, 273.
127. Capua, *William Holden*, 129.
128. Thomas, *Golden Boy*, 159.
129. *Ibid.*, 159.
130. Letter to Hedda Hopper, 8 September 1965.
131. *Ibid.*
132. *Ibid.*
133. *Ibid.*
134. *Ibid.*
135. Letter of 3 February 1966.
136. Howard Thompson, *New York Times*, 17 November 1966.
137. Dmytryk, *It's a Hell of a Life*, 273.
138. *Newsweek*, October 1966.
139. Dmytryk, *It's a Hell of a Life*, 274.
140. *Ibid.*, 275.
141. *Ibid.*
142. *Ibid.*, 276.
143. *Ibid.*, 276–277.
144. Server, *Robert Mitchum*, 500.
145. Falk, *Just One More Thing*, 129.
146. *Ibid.*, 130.
147. *Ibid.*, 131.
148. Dmytryk, *It's a Hell of a Life*, 277.
149. Tracy, Clift, Holden go unspoken.
150. Server, *Robert Mitchum*, 500–501.
151. *Ibid.*, 503.
152. *Ibid.*, 504.
153. Dmytryk, *It's a Hell of a Life*, 279.
154. Server, *Robert Mitchum*, 502.
155. Dmytryk, *It's a Hell of a Life*, 279.
156. *Ibid.*
157. *Ibid.*, 276.
158. Dmytryk, *It's a Hell of a Life*, 280.
159. Roberts, *Bardot*, 220.
160. Feeney Callan, *Sean Connery*, 165.
161. Roberts, *Bardot*, 220.
162. Yule, *Sean Connery*, 100.
163. Letter from MCA Artists Agency to Alexander Knox, 18 August 1952.
164. Letter from Philip Dunne to Knox, 19 September 1952.
165. Letter from Knox to Philip Dunne, 1954.
166. Letter from Lewis Deak to Knox, 14 April 1954.

167. Letter from Knox to Philip Dunne, 1954.
168. *Ibid.*
169. Caine, *The Elephant to Hollywood*, 142.
170. Roberts, *Bardot*, 221.
171. Singer, *Brigitte Bardot*, 93.
172. Roberts, *Bardot*, 220.
173. *Ibid.*
174. Feeney Callan, *Sean Connery*, 166.
175. *Ibid.*, 171.
176. Dmytryk, *It's a Hell of a Life*, 284.
177. *Ibid.*
178. Norman, *The Movie Greats*, 134.

Chapter VII

1. Dmytryk, *It's a Hell of a Life*, 286.
2. *Ibid.*, 287.
3. Letter from Dmytryk to U. Xodzhaev of Sovinfilm, 9 October 1973.
4. Anger, *Hollywood Babylon II*, 321.
5. *Daily Variety*, 20 July 1988.
6. McGilligan and Buhle, *Tender Comrades*, 53.
7. *Daily Variety*, 20 July 1988.
8. Dmytryk, *Odd Man Out*, 198.
9. *Ibid.*, 199.
10. *Ibid.*
11. Interview with Porfirio in Porfirio et al., Eds., *Film Noir Reader 3*, 35.
12. Burton, *Diaries*, 534–5.
13. *Ibid.*, 578.
14. Dmytryk, *It's a Hell of a Life*, 289.
15. Burton, *Diaries*, 534.
16. The *Motion Picture Herald*'s annual ratings published in February 1972 had Burton as the number one box office draw in Europe.
17. Burton, *Diaries*, 554.
18. *Ibid.*, 587.
19. *Ibid.*, 578.
20. Dmytryk, *It's a Hell of a Life*, 291.
21. Haining, *Raquel Welch*, 129.
22. Burton, *Diaries*, 577.
23. Dmytryk, *It's a Hell of a Life*, 291.
24. Burton, *Diaries*, 580.
25. *Ibid.*, 582.
26. *Ibid.*
27. *Ibid.*, 579.
28. *Ibid.*
29. Steverson, *Richard Burton*, 189.
30. Munn, *Richard Burton*, 196.
31. Burton, *Diaries*, 587.
32. *Ibid.*, 588.
33. Munn, *Richard Burton*, 195.
34. Haining, *Raquel Welch*, 130.
35. Dmytryk, *It's a Hell of a Life*, 295.
36. Munn, *Richard Burton*, 196.
37. Dmytryk, *It's a Hell of a Life*, 294.
38. *Ibid.*
39. *Ibid.*, 295.
40. Burton, *Diaries*, 579.
41. Tuchman interview, 54.
42. The quotation marks around the word Human are the only distinction from the title of

Preminger's film, which is based on the novel by
Graham Greene.

    43. Interview on *The 'Human' Factor* DVD

    44. *Ibid.*

    45. Dmytryk, *It's a Hell of a Life*, 85.

    46. Interview on *The "Human" Factor* DVD

    47. *Ibid.*

    48. *Ibid.*

    49. *Ibid.*

Bibliography

Andersen, Christopher. *Citizen Jane: The Turbulent Life of Jane Fonda*. New York: Henry Holt and Company, 1990.

Arranger, Milly S. *Unfriendly Witnesses: Gender, Theater, and Film in the McCarthy Era*. Carbondale, Illinois: Southern Illinois University Press, 2008.

Baker, Carroll. *Baby Doll: An Autobiography*. London: W. H. Allen, 1984.

Ball, Gregor. *Curd Jürgens: Seine Filme—Sein Leben*. Munich: Wilhelm Heyne Verlag, 1982.

Bandsman, Fred. *The John Wayne Filmography*. Jefferson, North Carolina: McFarland, 2004.

Bass, Jennifer and Kirkham, Pat. *Saul Bass: A Life in Film & Design*. London: Laurence King Publishing, 2011.

Baxter, Anne. *Intermission: A True Story*. New York: G P Putnam's Sons, 1976.

Barzman, Norma. *The Red and the Blacklist: The Intimate Memoir of a Hollywood Expatriate*. New York: Nation Books, 2003.

Bikel, Theodore. *Theo: The Autobiography of Theodore Bikel*. New York: HarperCollins, 1994.

Bojarski, Richard and Beale, Kenneth. *The Films of Boris Karloff*. Secaucus, New Jersey: The Citadel Press, 1974.

Bosworth, Patricia. *Jane Fonda: The Private Life of a Public Woman*. New York: Houghton Mifflin Harcourt, 2011.

Bosworth, Patricia. *Marlon Brando*. London: Weidenfeld & Nicholson, 2001.

Braun, Eric. *Deborah Kerr*. London: W. H. Allen, 1977.

Brideson, Cynthia and Sara. *Also Starring... Forty Biographical Essays on the Greatest Character Actors of Hollywood's Golden Era*. Duncan, Oklahoma: BearManor Media, 2015.

Bubbeo, Daniel. *The Women of Warner Brothers: The Lives and Careers of 15 Leading Ladies*. Jefferson, North Carolina: McFarland, 2002.

Buehrer, Beverley Bare. *Boris Karloff: A Bio-Bibliography*. Westport, Connecticut: Greenwood Press, 1993.

Caine, Michael. *The Elephant to Hollywood: The Autobiography*. London: Hodder & Stoughton, 2010.

Callahan, Dan. *Barbara Stanwyck: The Miracle Woman*. Jackson, Mississippi: University Press of Mississippi, 2012.

Callow, Simon. *Charles Laughton: A Difficult Actor*. London: Vintage, 1995.

Capua, Michelangelo. *Deborah Kerr: A Biography*. Jefferson, North Carolina: McFarland, 2010.

Capua, Michelangelo. *William Holden: A Biography*. Jefferson, North Carolina: McFarland, 2010.

Caron, Leslie. *Thank Heaven: My Autobiography*. London: JR Books, 2009.

Ceplair, Larry and Trumbo, Christopher. *Dalton Trumbo: Blacklisted Hollywood Radical*. Lexington, Kentucky: University Press of Kentucky, 2015.

Coffee, Lenore. *Storyline: Recollections of a Hollywood Screenwriter*. London: Cassell, 1973.

Collier, Peter. *The Fondas: A Hollywood Dynasty*. New York: G P Putnam's Sons, 1991.

Cook, Bruce. *Dalton Trumbo*. New York: Charles Scribner's Sons, 1977.

Davis, Ronald L. *Van Johnson: MGM's Golden Boy*. Jackson, Mississippi: University Press of Mississippi, 2001.

Dewey, Donald. *Lee J. Cobb: Characters of an Actor*. Lanham, Maryland: Rowman & Littlefield, 2014.

Dick, Bernard F. *The Merchant Prince of Poverty Row: Harry Cohn of Columbia Pictures*. Lexington, Kentucky: The University Press of Kentucky, 1993.

DiOrio, Al. *Barbara Stanwyck*: A Biography. New York: Coward-McCann, 1983.

Dmytryk, Edward. *It's a Hell of a Life but not a Bad Living*. New York: Times Books, 1978.

Dmytryk, Edward. *Odd Man Out: A Memoir of the Hollywood Ten*. Carbondale, Illinois: Southern Illinois University Press, 1996.

Douglas, Kirk. *The Ragman's Son: An Autobiography*. London: Simon & Schuster, 1988.

Dyer, Richard. *Nino Rota: Music, Film and Feeling*. London: Palgrave Macmillan, 2010.

Edelman, Rob and Kupferberg, Audrey E. *Angela Lansbury: A Life on Stage and Screen*. New York: Birch Lane Press, 1996.

Epstein, Dwayne. *Lee Marvin: Point Blank*. Tucson, Arizona: Schaffner Press, 2013.

Erens, Patricia. *The Jew in American Cinema*. Bloomington, Indiana: Indiana University Press, 1984.

Essoe, Gabe. *The Films of Clark Gable*. Secaucus, New Jersey: The Citadel Press, 1973.

Eyman, Scott. *Print the Legend: The Life and Times of John Ford.* New York: Simon & Schuster, 1999.

Falk, Peter. *Just One More Thing: Stories from My Life.* London: Arrow, 2008.

Feeney Callan, Michael. *Sean Connery: His Life and Films.* London: W H Allen, 1983.

Finler, Joel W. *The Hollywood Story.* London: Wallflower Press, 2003.

Fisher, James. *Spencer Tracy: A Bio-Bibliography.* Westport, Connecticut: Greenwood Press, 1994.

Fishgall, Gary. *Gregory Peck: A Biography.* New York: Scribner's, 2002.

Fleming, E.J. *Carole Landis: A Tragic Life in Hollywood.* Jefferson, North Carolina: McFarland, 2005.

Fonda, Jane. *My Life So Far.* New York: Random House, 2005.

Freedland, Michael. *Hollywood on Trial: McCarthyism's War Against the Movies.* London: Robson, 2007.

Freedland, Michael. *Jane Fonda: A Biography.* New York: St Martin's Press, 1988.

Fujiwara, Chris. *The World and its Double: The Life and Work of Otto Preminger.* London: Faber & Faber, 2008.

Gans, Eric. *Carole Landis: A Most Beautiful Girl.* Jackson, Mississippi: University Press of Mississippi, 2008.

Goldrup, Tom and Goldrup, Jim. *Growing Up on the Set: Interviews with 39 former child actors of classic film and television.* Jefferson, North Carolina: McFarland, 2002.

Grant, Neil. *Clark Gable in His Own Words.* London: Hamlyn, 1992.

Greene, Graham. *The Pleasure-Dome.* London: Secker and Warburg, 1972.

Grosso, Michael. *The Man Who Could Fly: St. Joseph of Copertino and the Mystery of Levitation.* Lanham, Maryland: Rowman & Littlefield, 2016.

Guiles, Fred Lawrence. *Jane Fonda: The Actress in Her Time.* Garden City, New York: Doubleday and Company, 1982.

Haining, Peter. *Raquel Welch: Sex Symbol to Superstar.* New York: St Martin's Press, 1984.

Hammond, John R. *A James Hilton Companion: A Guide to the Novels, Short Stories, Nonfiction Writings and Films.* Jefferson, North Carolina: McFarland, 2010.

Haney, Lynn. *Gregory Peck: A Charmed Life.* New York: Carroll & Graf, 2003.

Hannsberry, Karen Burroughs. *Bad Boys: The Actors of Film Noir.* Jefferson, North Carolina: McFarland, 2003.

Hanson, Peter. *Dalton Trumbo, Hollywood Rebel: A Critical Survey and Filmography.* Jefferson, North Carolina: McFarland, 2001.

Hardy, Phil. *The Aurum Film Encyclopedia: The Western.* London: Aurum Press, 1995.

Hedren, Tippi. *Tippi: A Memoir.* New York: HarperCollins, 2016.

Henry, Marilyn and DeSourdis, Ron. *The Films of Alan Ladd.* Secaucus, New Jersey: The Citadel Press, 1981.

Hickey, Des and Smith, Gus. *The Prince: The Public and Private Life of Laurence Harvey.* London: Leslie Frewin, 1975.

Hirsch, Foster. *Elizabeth Taylor.* New York: Pyramid Publications, 1973.

Hodgson, Michael. *Patricia Roc: The Goddess of the Odeons.* Bloomington, Indiana: AuthorHouse, 2013.

Hofler, Robert. *The Man Who Invented Rock Hudson: The Pretty Boys and Dirty Deals of Henry Willson.* New York: Carroll & Graf, 2005.

Holston, Kim. *Richard Widmark: A Bio-Bibliography.* New York: Greenwood Press, 1990.

Holston, Kim R. *Susan Hayward.* Jefferson, North Carolina: McFarland, 2002.

Hulse, Ed. *The Films of Betty Grable.* Burbank, California: Riverwood Press, 1996.

Huston, John. *An Open Book.* London: Macmillan, 1981.

Jacobs, Stephen. *Boris Karloff: More than a Monster.* Sheffield: Tomahawk Press, 2011.

Jensen, Paul M. *Boris Karloff and His Films.* South Brunswick and New York: A. S. Barnes, 1974.

Jewell, Richard B. *RKO Radio Pictures: A Titan is Born.* Berkeley: University of California Press, 2012.

Jewell, Richard B. *Slow Fade to Black: The Decline of RKO Radio Pictures.* Oakland: University of California Press, 2016.

Jones, Ken D. and McClure, Arthur F. *Hollywood at War: The American Motion Picture and World War II.* South Brunswick and New York: A. S. Barnes, 1973.

Kashfi Brando, Anna and Stein, E. P. *Brando for Breakfast.* New York: Crown Publishers, 1979.

Kazan, Elia. *A Life.* London: André Deutsch, 1988.

Kiernan, Thomas. *Jane: An Intimate Biography of Jane Fonda.* New York: G P Putnam's Sons, 1973.

Knight, Vivienne. *Trevor Howard: A Gentleman and a Player.* London: Muller, Blond & White, 1986.

Koper, Richard. *Fifties Blondes: Sexbombs, Sirens, Bad Girls and Teen Queens.* Duncan, Oklahoma: BearManor Media, 2010.

Koppes, Clayton R. and Black, Gregory D. *Hollywood Goes to War: Patriotism, Movies and the Second World War from Ninotchka to Mrs Miniver.* London: Tauris Parke, 2000.

Krutnik, Frank; Neale, Steve; Neve, Brian and Stanfield, Peter. *"Un-American" Hollywood: Politics and Film in the Blacklist Era.* New Brunswick, New Jersey: Rutgers University Press, 2007.

LaGuardia, Robert. *Monty: A Biography of Montgomery Clift.* New York: Primus, 1988.

LaGuardia, Robert and Arceri, Gene. *Red: The Tempestuous Life of Susan Hayward.* London: Robson Books, 1986.

LaSalle, Mick. *Dangerous Men: Pre-Code Hollywood and the Birth of the Modern Man.* New York: Thomas Dunne Books, 2002.

Lentz, Robert J. *Gloria Grahame, Bad Girl of Film Noir.* Jefferson, North Carolina: McFarland, 2011.

Lentz, Robert J. *Lee Marvin: His Films and Career.* Jefferson, North Carolina: McFarland, 2000.

Linet, Beverly. *Ladd: The Life, The Legend, The Legacy of Alan Ladd.* New York: Arbor House, 1979.

Linet, Beverly. *Susan Hayward: Portrait of a Survivor.* New York: Atheneum, 1980.

Madsen, Axel. *Stanwyck.* New York: HarperCollins, 1994.

Mank, Gregory William. *Women in Horror Films, 1940s.* Jefferson, North Carolina: McFarland, 1999.

Marlow-Trump, Nancy. *Ruby Keeler: A Photographic Biography.* Jefferson, North Carolina: McFarland, 1998.

Marrill, Alvin H. *The Films of Anthony Quinn.* Secaucus, New Jersey: The Citadel Press, 1975.

Maychick, Diana and Borgo, L. Avon. *Heart to Heart with Robert Wagner.* New York: St Martin's Press, 1986.

McClelland, Doug. *The Unkindest Cuts: The Scissors and the Cinema.* New York: A. S. Barnes and Company, 1972.

McGilligan, Pat. *Backstory: Interviews with Screenwriters of Hollywood's Golden Age.* Berkeley: University of California Press, 1986.

McGilligan, Patrick and Buhle, Paul. *Tender Comrades: A Backstory of the Hollywood Blacklist.* New York: St Martin's Griffin, 1997.

McKenna, A. T. *Showman of the Screen: Joseph E. Levine and His Revolutions in Film Promotion.* Lexington: University Press of Kentucky, 2016.

Mordden, Ethan. *The Hollywood Studios: House Style in the Golden Age of the Movies.* New York: Fireside, 1989.

Munn, Michael. *Richard Burton: Prince of Players.* London: JR Books, 2008.

Munn, Michael. *Trevor Howard: The Man and His Films.* London: Robson, 1989.

Navasky, Victor S. *Naming Names.* New York: Hill and Wang, 2003.

Nelson, Ozzie. *Ozzie.* Englewood Cliffs, New Jersey: Prentice-Hall, 1973.

Nissen, Axel. *Actresses of a Certain Character: Forty Familiar Hollywood Faces from the Thirties to the Fifties.* Jefferson, North Carolina: McFarland, 2007.

Nissen, Axel. *The Films of Agnes Moorehead.* Lanham, Maryland: Scarecrow Press, 2013.

Norman, Barry. *The Movie Greats.* London: Hodder and Stoughton, 1981.

Parish, James Robert. *The RKO Gals.* New Rochelle, New York: Arlington House, 1974.

Pastrovicchi, Angelo. *St. Joseph of Copertino.* St. Louis, Missouri: B. Herder Book Company, 1918.

Penrose, Mark. *Apologise Later: The Biography of Robert Newton.* London: The Olchon Press, 2013.

Pettigrew, Terence. *Trevor Howard: A Personal Biography.* London: Peter Owen, 2001.

Pickford, Doug. *Macclesfield—So Well Remembered.* Wilmslow: Sigma Press, 1993.

Picturegoer Weekly. *The Picturegoer's Who's Who and Encyclopaedia of the Screen To-Day.* London: Odhams Press, 1933.

Porfirio, Robert; Silver, Alain and Ursini, James (Eds.) *Film Noir Reader 3: Interviews with Film-makers of the Classic Noir Period.* New York: Limelight Editions, 2002.

Quinn, Anthony and Paisner, Daniel. *One Man Tango.* New York: HarperCollins, 1995.

Quirk, Lawrence J. *Fasten Your Seat Belts: The Passionate Life of Bette Davis.* New York: William Morrow, 1990.

Quirk, Lawrence J. *The Films of William Holden.* Secaucus, New Jersey: Citadel, 1973.

Rainey, Buck. *Serial Film Stars: A Biographical Dictionary, 1912–1956.* Jefferson, North Carolina: McFarland, 2005.

Riese, Randall. *All About Bette: Her Life from A to Z.* Chicago: Contemporary Books, 1993.

Rigid, Judith M. *John Wayne: A Bio-Bibliography.* Westport, Connecticut: Greenwood Press, 1992.

Roberts, Glenys. *Bardot.* New York: St Martin's Press, 1984.

Roberts, Randy and Olson, James S. *John Wayne: American.* New York: The Free Press, 1995.

Rogers, Ginger. *Ginger: My Story.* New York: HarperCollins, 1991.

Sanders, George and Thomas, Tony. *Memoirs of a Professional Cad.* Metuchen, New Jersey: Scarecrow Press, 1992.

Schary, Dore. *Heyday: An Autobiography.* Boston: Little, Brown and Company, 1979.

Schell, Maximilian. *Ich Fliege über Dunkle Täler: Erinnerungen.* Hamburg: Hoffman und Campe, 2014.

Schoell, William. *Martini Man: The Life of Dean Martin.* Dallas, Texas: Taylor Publishing, 1999.

Server, Lee. *Robert Mitchum: "Baby, I Don't Care."* London: Faber & Faber, 2002.

Shipman, David. *Brando.* London: Macmillan, 1974.

Shipman, David. *The Great Movie Stars: 2 The International Years.* London: Macdonald & Co, 1989.

Shull, Michael S. and Wilt, David Edward. *Hollywood War Films, 1937–1945.* Jefferson, North Carolina: McFarland, 1996.

Sinai, Anne. *Reach for the Top: The Turbulent Life of Laurence Harvey.* Lanham, Maryland: The Scarecrow Press, 2003.

Singer, Barnett. *Brigitte Bardot: A Biography.* Jefferson, North Carolina: McFarland, 2006.

Smith, Steven C. *A Heart at Fire's Center: The Life and Music of Bernard Herrmann.* Berkeley: University of California Press, 1991.

Spada, James. *More Than a Woman: An Intimate Biography of Bette Davis.* New York: Bantam Books, 1993.

Sperber, A. M. & Lax, Eric. *Bogart.* New York: William Morrow, 1997.

Steverson, Tyrone. *Richard Burton: A Bio-Bibliography.* Westport, Connecticut: Greenwood Press, 1992.

Stine, Whitney. *"I'd Love to Kiss You…" Conversations with Bette Davis.* New York: Pocket Books, 1990.

Strangeland, John. *Warren William: Magnificent Scoundrel of Pre-Code Hollywood.* Jefferson, North Carolina: McFarland, 2011.

Svehla, Gary J. & Svehla, Susan (ed.). *Boris Karloff.* Bristol: Hemlock Books, 2014.

Swindell, Larry. *Spencer Tracy.* New York: New American Library, 1969.

Tanitch, Robert. *John Mills.* London: Collins & Brown, 1993.

Taylor, Elizabeth. *Elizabeth Taylor.* New York: Harper & Row, 1965.

Thomas, Bob. *Golden Boy: The Untold Story of William Holden.* New York: St. Martin's Press, 1983.

Tillman, Larry. *Betty Grable: A Bio-Bibliography.* Westport, Connecticut: Greenwood Press, 1993.

Tosches, Nick. *Dino: Living High in the Dirty Business of Dreams.* New York: Doubleday, 1992.

Tranberg, Charles. *Fred MacMurray: A Biography.* Albany, Georgia: BearManor Media, 2007.

Vogel, Michelle. *Gene Tierney: A Biography.* Jefferson, North Carolina: McFarland, 2005.

Weaver, Tom. *Science Fiction and Fantasy Film Flashbacks: Conversations with 24 Actors, Writers, Producers and Directors from the Golden Age.* Jefferson, North Carolina: McFarland, 1998.

Wiley, Mason and Bona, Damien. *Inside Oscar: The Unofficial History of the Academy Awards.* New York: Ballantine Books, 1988.

Williams, Chris (ed.). *The Richard Burton Diaries.* New Haven, Connecticut: Yale University Press, 2012.

Wills, Garry. *John Wayne's America: The Politics of Celebrity.* New York: Simon & Schuster, 1997.

Young, Freddie and Busby, Peter. *Seventy Light Years.* London: Faber & Faber, 1999.

Yule, Andrew. *Sean Connery: From 007 to Hollywood Icon.* New York: Donald I Fine, 1992.

Zolotow, Maurice. *Shooting Star: A Biography of John Wayne.* New York: Simon & Schuster, 1974.

Other References

An Oral History with Edward Anhalt, interviewed by Douglas Bell, Academy Oral History Program, AMPAS (Academy Foundation, 2013), Margaret Herrick Library, Beverly Hills.

Interview with Edward Dmytryk by Ronald L. Davis (2 December 1979). DeGolyer Library, Southern Methodist University, Ronald L. Davis Oral History Collection.

Interview with Edward Dmytryk by Mitch Tuchman (5 October 1976). Mitch Tuchman interview transcripts, Margaret Herrick Library, Academy of Motion Picture Arts and Sciences.

Interview with Stanley Kramer by Mitch Tuchman (11 October 1976). Mitch Tuchman interview transcripts, Margaret Herrick Library, Academy of Motion Picture Arts and Sciences.

Interview with Albert Maltz by Mitch Tuchman (12 October 1976). Mitch Tuchman interview transcripts, Margaret Herrick Library, Academy of Motion Picture Arts and Sciences.

Interview with Ben Margolis by Mitch Tuchman (13 October 1976). Mitch Tuchman interview transcripts, Margaret Herrick Library, Academy of Motion Picture Arts and Sciences.

Interview with Cyril Pennington-Richards by Alan Lawson and Colin Moffat (9 January 1990), BECTU History Project—Interview No. 122. © British Entertainment History Project, www.historyproject.org.uk.

Interview with Bernard Vorhaus by Sid Cole and Alan Lawson (23 October 1991), BECTU History Project—Interview No. 219. © British Entertainment History Project, www.historyproject.org.uk.

Interview with L. P. (Bill) Williams by Rodney Giesler (12 August and 10 November 1993), BECTU History Project—Interview No. 295. © British Entertainment History Project, www.historyproject.org.uk.

Interviews with Vicky Dmytryk by author (28 March and 2 April 2019).

Interview with Rebecca Dmytryk by author (10 October 2019).

Index

Numbers in **bold italics** indicate pages with illustrations